THE WORLD OF MYTHS
& MYTHOLOGY

THE WORLD OF
MYTHS
&
MYTHOLOGY

A SOURCE BOOK

Sarah Bartlett

BLANDFORD

A BLANDFORD BOOK

First published in the UK 1998
by Blandford, a Cassell imprint

Cassell plc
Wellington House
125 Strand
London WC2R 0BB

Distributed in the United States by
Sterling Publishing Co. Inc.
387 Park Avenue South
New York
NY 10016–8810

A Cataloguing-in-Publication Data entry for this title is available from the
British Library

ISBN 0–7137–2673–3

Designed by Chris Bell
Printed and bound in Great Britain by MPG Books Ltd, Bodmin, Cornwall

CONTENTS

Introduction 8

Time Chart 10

1 THE GREAT MYTHS OF CREATION 11

Eurynome 13
Neith 13
Atum and Ra 14
Marduk and Tiamat 15
Bomong and Bong 17
Purusha 18
Woyengi 19
Gaia and Ouranos 20
Ameta and Hainuwele 21
Ymir 23
Hurakan 25
Bumba 26
Nyambi and Kamonu 27
P'an Ku and the Cosmic Egg 28
Izanami and Izanagi 29
Rangi and Papa 32
Qat 33
Ta'aroa and the Egg 34
Earth-initiate and Coyote 36
Taiowa, Sotuknang and Spider
  Woman 38

Raven 42
Puana, Kuma and Itciai 43
Amana 44
Water-beetle and the Great Buzzard 45
Djanggawul 46
Mulungu and the Chameleon 47

2 SUN, MOON, HEAVEN AND EARTH 49

Ra 51
Indra, the Rain Bringer 52
Agni, Bringer of the Vital Spark 54
Ushas, Ratri and the Aswins 55
Soma, the Moon-god 55
Helios and Apollo 56
Chiron – The Constellation
  Centaurus 58
Poseidon 59
The Quest for the Sun 61
Yi and the Ten Suns 64
Mani and Sol 67
Idun and the Golden Apples 68
Thunder and the Elephant 70
Amaterasu and Susano 71
Pele, the Goddess of Volcanoes 74
The Sun Tamer 76
The Cold Weather Lord 77

Raven and the Sun 79
Glooskap and the Summer 81
The Children of the Sun 83
Nantu and Etsa 85
Ag-Ag and Klang 86
The Fine Weather Woman 88
The Moon 89

3 DEATH, RE-BIRTH AND
   THE UNDERWORLD 91

Inanna and Ereshkigal 93
Ka and Ba 95
Anubis 95
Osiris 96
Yama 99
Hades and the Underworld 102
Demeter and Persephone 104
Valhalla and the Valkyries 106
Ragnarok and the Death of Balder 107
Xibalba – The Place of Phantoms 108
The Land of Ghosts 110
The Snow Spirit 113
Yomi 115
Po 116
Pare and Hutu 117
Sayadio 119
Sedna 120
The Resurrection of Papan 122
The Journey to the Land of the
   Grandfather 125
Dubiaku 126

4 HEROES, WARRIORS
   AND THEIR QUESTS 129

Gilgamesh 131
Sekhmet 135
Rama 136
Perseus 140
The Earth-born Giants 143
Odysseus 144
Gassire and the Singing Lute 149
The Great Yu 151
Cú Chulainn 154
Conaire Mór 159
Sigmund and Sigurd 161
Vainomoinen 165
The Adventures of Rata 169
Ahaiyuta 173
Beowulf 176
Huitzilopochtli, God of War 179
Chacopee – White Feather 180
Simpang Impang 183

5 LEGENDARY LOVERS
   AND DIVINE DESIRES 187

Ishtar 189
Krishna and the Cowgirls 190
Bitiou 192
Aphrodite 195
The Loves of Zeus 197
Kama and Rati 202
Orpheus and Eurydice 204
Pomona and Vertumnus 206

Etain and Midir 208
Freya, the Goddess of Sexual Desire
212
Frey 214
The Herdsman and the Weaver Girl
215
Tristan and Iseult 218
The Convolvulus Fan 221
Scar-face 224
Rakian and the Bees 226

6 TRICKSTERS 229

Isis 231
Enki 232
Hanuman 233
Circe, the Witch-goddess 235
Hermes 237
Heimdall 239
Loki 241
Merlin and Nimuë 244
Huveane and Hlakanyana 246
Taliesin 249
Glooskap 251
Blue Jay 255
Tezcatlipoca 258
Ictinike and the Rabbit 259
Coniraya 261
Maui 263
Olifat 267
Tjinimin 268

7 BEASTS AND MONSTERS 271

The Eagle 273
Ganesa 274
Garuda, the Bird King 276
The Nagas 278
The Rakshasas and the Demon-king
Ravana 278
Greek Beasts and Monsters 280
Chinese Beasts and Monsters 286
Hymir the Giant 290
Fenrir the Wolf 292
The Great Macaw 293
The Death-stone 295
The Kindly Skeleton 297
The Pursuing Head 301
The Snake-men 303
The Ogre-killers 304
Bat-light 306
Kinie Ger 308

Further Reading 311

Index 313

INTRODUCTION

*T*HROUGHOUT the history of the world, mythology's powerful and inspiring imagery has reflected the human quest for a meaning in life and a deeper understanding of the mystery of being. *The World of Myths & Mythology* is a unique guide to the myths, gods and goddesses that are evocative of mankind's great visions. It is an anthology of world myths that reveal an extraordinary universal affinity, even though they appear in a myriad of guises in civilizations separated not only by geography but also by time.

Most cultures have a myth that explains the origin or creation of the universe. There are usually also a trickster myth and a 'heroic journey' myth. There are generally myths explaining celestial phenomena – where the stars come from, why the sun sets in the west or why the moon has a cycle of its own. Mystical beasts abound, often representing the projections of our fears, the monsters of our own imagination and the dark shadows of our subconscious. And, of course, there are divine lovers – gods and goddesses who symbolize our sexual urges and our capacity to love or desire other beings, whether human or not.

These stories are often the 'carriers' of our universal affinity to know who we are and where we have come from. An old Zen koan asks: 'Who were you before you were born?' We can never answer this question, but it is one that somehow awakens the feeling of a distant connection to the past by way of the darkness of our unconscious. It is this reservoir of common feeling that we project so powerfully into our myths. Jung called mythical archetypes 'great dreams of humanity'. He also believed that 'we have recollected ourselves from the universe' and that our projections happen to us rather than that we 'make them happen'. In a sense, it is the myth dreaming us, rather than us dreaming the myth.

Myths are a reflection of the whole, of the place from which we have arrived and the place to which we may return. Through the symbols of myth we can perhaps obtain an insight that will help us in our understanding of that place.

The word myth derives from the Greek *muthos*, which means simply 'word', 'narration', 'tale' or 'speech'. Over thousands of years the word has suffered an etymological metamorphosis, and it is now commonly used to describe a lie or a stupid belief.

Myths are very different from fables or legends, which are more to do with aspects of morality and social patterns within a society. These stories are generally concerned with laws or with the values that are intrinsic to a particular culture, ethos, civilization or era. They are also often connected to historical fact. Myths, on the other hand, are stories that concern the gods, and our inner relationship with the divine or that which cannot be made manifest. Myths retell our experiences with our own inner gods and goddesses.

Many scholars have tried to give rational explanations for myths. One theory is that myth-makers were primitive scientists who were trying to explain the beginnings and origins of everything, according to the limits of the society of the time. Another idea was that myths explained natural laws in terms of the actions of the gods. For example, the elements such as thunder and lightning were Zeus's responsibility, and earthquakes and tidal waves were Poseidon's, simply because the consciousness of mankind could not comprehend them to be anything other than divinely ordered events. Myths were also used to explain the rituals and ceremonies concerned with the cycles of nature. These were widespread among ancient peoples. Another view was that society created law and order through the oral tradition of myths, and one hypothesis is that myths were created so that man could ascend to the level of the gods themselves.

However, it is probably Jung's breakthrough in thinking that has reawakened our connection of what myths mean to us. Myths are the voices of our ancestors and the collective, and they are, therefore, also our own inner voice. Through myths we can reconnect to nature because we are a part of that universal nature. No matter how existential (in the sense that we create our own sets of values separate from objective, universal ones) we may want and seem to be, we are still connected to that underlying thread that weaves us into a tapestry of wholeness through the world of myths.

THE TIME CHART

The time chart on page 10 gives an added dimension to this book. Throughout the text dates indicate the approximate period in which the myth first appeared or was recorded. Obviously, with over four thousand years of history, the times and dates when myths first emerged into a culture are loose and sometimes ambiguous.

However, feeling our way back through the dark and discovering that time is merely the invention of humankind provide a sense of our own connection to the immutability of these myths and the beings that people them. These concepts, gods and shadows are as much a part of today's consciousness as they were four or five millennia ago.

TIME CHART

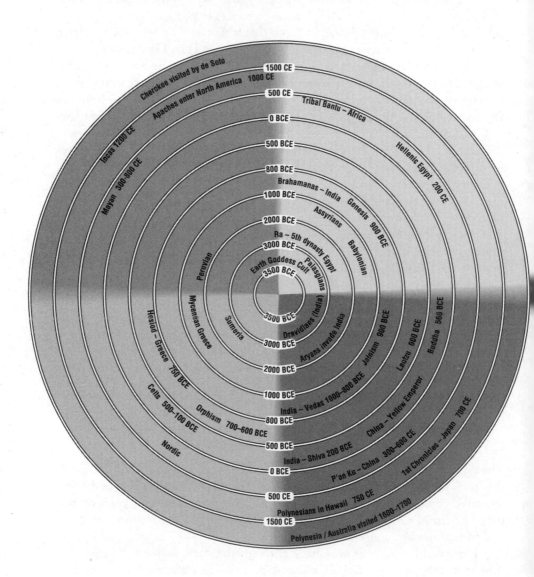

ONE

THE GREAT MYTHS
OF CREATION

*T*HE COMMON DENOMINATOR in this section is the similarity throughout different civilizations and cultures of themes about *how* humankind and the universe came into being. For many cultures, the *why* does not often enter into the myth, perhaps because myth-tellers usually assumed that creation does not need to be questioned.

These myths focus on either primary or secondary creation. Primary creation was when gods or beings acted on their own; secondary creation occurred when different gods got together or had offspring they could put to work towards bringing humanity into fruition. Either way, the vast range of creation myths is probably the simplest way of demonstrating how our common spiritual quest has many disguises. These stories also reveal the same compelling search for the truth about *how* it all began.

As these creation myths were often among the first to be told within any society, they are often poignant in their simplicity yet understandably stark in their content. Where religion has underpinned power in any culture, with the exception of India, creation myths have been generally picked over by those in the highest positions of religious power as if they were searching for tiny specks of gold. If the gold added glamour or force to their doctrines, it was inevitable that the myths became distorted.

EURYNOME

GREECE, 3500BCE

THIS version of a Greek creation myth favours the ancient cult of the mother-goddess, which appeared on the Greek peninsula around 3500BCE, when the Pelasgians arrived from Asia Minor. The main theme of chaos as the beginning of all things is repeated here as in many other Near Eastern myths, with the essential addition of chaos evolving into the mother-goddess, Eurynome.

All was chaos in the beginning. The wild emptiness tossing and turning forever, rolling into spirals and spiralling into waves of eternal ecstasy, until it formed into a wide-wandering dance of energy.

This was Eurynome, who, finding that she could neither stop at any moment in time nor place her feet down to dance, divided chaos into the sea and the sky. As she danced across the lashing waves of the seas, she caused a wind to blow up behind her. The north wind seemed something separate from herself and something she could use to begin her masterpiece of creation. She clutched the north wind between her hands and danced madly with it until it changed into a giant, fertile snake, Ophion. The wilder her dance, the more excited grew Ophion, until he could resist her no longer. Once she had coupled with him, she changed into a dove so that she could lay the first egg on the ocean. Ophion was ordered to coil around the egg seven times to incubate it. As the egg hatched, out fell all the things that exist – the earth, the stars, the sun and moon, and everything that lives.

Eurynome and Ophion ruled Olympus, but Ophion quarrelled endlessly with her, assuming that he had created the universe. She fought with him and banished him to the underworld, where he swore to be her enemy forever. Next, Eurynome created the Titans to rule the seven planets, and finally she created the first man, Pelasgus, the ancestor of the Pelasgian race, who taught humans how to lead civilized lives.

NEITH

EGYPT, 3000BCE

NEITH is a creator-goddess who was already considered ancient in Egypt by the time of the first dynasty (c.3100–2890BCE). The tomb of Tutankhamun (c.1325BCE) has a wonderful golden statue of Neith in her aspect as a golden cobra wearing the shuttle on her breast as a sign of a goddess who rules destiny. As the early goddess of weaving and the loom, she was also a creator-goddess, and no mortal could look at her face. On one of her statues is an inscription that Plutarch has transcribed: 'I am all that is or has been or that will be and no mortal has yet raised my veil.'

Originally Neith was one of the aspects of the great goddess of the Nile Delta region. From the primeval waters of nothingness, she arose spontaneously and created childbirth by bringing forth the great god Ra. But Neith was not satisfied with only the great primordial ocean and only a god as her creation, so she took up her shuttle and, by stringing the sky across her loom, she wove the world.

With her great net she dipped down into the great primordial waters and gathered all the living creatures to place them on the land. In some versions of this myth, Neith was the mother of crocodiles and created the great snake of darkness, Aapep, by spitting at the male god Nun, who also arose from the great primeval ocean. Aapep, the snake of darkness, was the nothingness that swallowed light and lay in wait every day for Ra the sun-god as he made his journey across the skies.

When the gods Seth and Horus were battling for supremacy, the gods asked Neith which should be allowed to win. She told them that both had the right to live because Seth had protected Ra the sun-god from the snake of darkness and Horus had the gift to journey between mortals and the gods. She warned them, however, that if they did not follow her advice she would unpick her tapestry of the universe and destroy all that she had created by doing so.

ATUM AND RA

EGYPT, 2500BCE

IN Egyptian mythology, Ra was the supreme power of the universe, and his cult took over from that of the creator-god, Atum, who was worshipped in Heliopolis as a deity long before Ra. Atum was the originator, the primordial ocean from which Ra created himself, but eventually Atum became one aspect of the god Ra, as Atum-Ra, the god of the evening sun. There are many versions of these intertwining myths, but they are still pre-dated by those of Neith and her fragile threads of creation.

Atum, as the primordial ocean, created himself and gathered together his own shapeless self into the form of a man. Some say that he spat into the void, others that he masturbated into it, to make Shu and Tefnut, the air and the moisture. Some Egyptian priests changed this story so that Atum used his male part (penis) and his female part (hand) to mate together. The 'Hand of

Atum' was, in fact, worshipped as a separate deity. But as the cult of Atum declined, Ra began to be regarded as the creator of Shu and Tefnut, who in turn became the parents of Geb, the earth, and Nut, the sky.

Geb and Nut mated to create the universe and the other gods, Osiris, Seth, Isis and Nephthys. Ra created himself out of the primordial darkness to be light. Aapep, the snake of darkness, had only the desire to engulf Ra and all his creations.

Ra would sail across the sky every day in his golden boat, travelling along the pathway of the Milky Way, which some say was the arched body of Nut. Every day he brought warmth to the world, and at night he would travel through the underworld, always avoiding the jaws of the great Aapep. Another version of this myth says that Ra lived in a golden age, when everything he had created was perfection. Because everything he saw was so perfect, it dazzled his eyes and the first tears that formed dropped on to the world below and created living creatures, including humans, wherever they fell. But because even Ra's tears would dry up in the light of his own scorching heat, these creatures made from tears also dried up and eventually died.

While they were on earth, these creatures began to realize that they could do as they liked, and some began to have no respect for their creator Ra, who at the end of each day seemed to grow older and disappear and leave them to the powers of the night-time snake of darkness. Ra was angered by their lack of worship, and he tore out his eye and from it created the goddess Sekhmet to bring destruction to the world. As the eye of Ra, Sekhmet was a fierce and warlike goddess. At the last minute, Ra changed his mind and could prevent Sekhmet from destroying the universe only by intoxicating her with a mixture of pomegranates and beer, which he spilled across the land. When she swooped down to lap up what she thought was blood, she fell asleep like a cat, and Ra saved the world from its destruction.

MARDUK AND TIAMAT

BABYLON, 2000BCE

MARDUK was an important national deity during the first Babylonian dynasty (c.2057–1758BCE). This myth was re-enacted as a new year ritual before his statue to ensure the continuity and connection between the gods and humankind and the assurance of fertility as Marduk conquers the forces of evil for another year.

Although the major source of this myth was found among the ruins of King Ashurbanipal's library at Nineveh, which dates from c.650BCE, fragments of earlier texts suggest that the end of the story is based on earlier beliefs that the gods created humans to be their slaves. The epic text on which this myth is based was probably a piece of propaganda to uphold Marduk's power as chief deity and the high-ranking status of Babylon itself. The rather loose story of creation may well be merely a backdrop for the more divine message of the epic struggle between two deities and the fact that if the gods created humans to be their slaves, why did they then make them capable of turning against them?

The ocean and the primeval waters lay together at the beginning of time when all was chaos. The ocean was Apsu, and the waters were Tiamat. Together they produced many young gods, Lakhmu and Lakhamu (silt and slime), Anshar and Kishar (the horizons of the earth and sky), Anu (heaven) and Ea (the waters of the earth). But as they grew older, these young gods became rebellious and decided to create order in the universe. Apsu and Tiamat called on Mummu (the mist of the clouds), and together they joined in a conspiracy to destroy the young gods. Tiamat, however, for all her fierce, dragon-like power, withdrew from the plan, guilt-ridden at the thought of slaying her own offspring. Ea destroyed Apsu and locked the mist of the clouds away forever. Tiamat then created the most terrifying monsters to destroy the young gods and spitefully married the monsters' chief, Kingu.

Marduk was Ea's son. Tall, energetic, fierce and proud, he offered to be the gods' champion and to slay the sea-dragon, Tiamat, and her partner, Kingu, if he was rewarded with the post of supreme god. Armed with a bow, the force of lightning and a net held up by the four winds, Marduk rode off on a hurricane to battle with Tiamat.

The young god caught Tiamat easily in his net, but she opened her great dragon-mouth wide as if to swallow him, and he sent the four winds rushing down into her throat. With her body distended by so much wind and before she could belch it all up again, Marduk shot a hundred arrows straight into her mouth. They whizzed down her gullet. When they pierced her heart she died instantly, and gave out one great final burp of air that sent Marduk flying backwards.

Stealing the Tablets of Destiny from Kingu to make sure he would become the most powerful of all beings, Marduk began his quest to create order in the universe. He first sliced Tiamat in two and raised half of her to form the heavens and placed the other half opposite Ea's great watery face to form the earth. He created the constellations, the stars and the planets. The rebellious Kingu was executed, and under Marduk's direction Ea took the blood that drained from his body and created humankind to be the slaves of the gods. In return, the grateful gods kept their promise and built a city for Marduk called Babylon. As the supreme god of the Babylonian pantheon, Marduk could assume the role of any god. He was an extremely popular sun-god, and also became god of the planet Jupiter, equivalent in power to that of the moon-god, Sin.

BOMONG AND BONG

NEARLY one-third of India's population are not touched by Hinduism or the other religious systems. This ancient myth tells of the overthrow of the originators of the universe by their offspring and the subsequent need to restore the balance between darkness and light.

To begin with all was darkness, and there was Sedi (the earth), who was a woman, and Melo (the sky), who was a man. The Wiyus were the people and animals who were created when Sedi and Melo came together. But because the Wiyus were cramped and crushed between Sedi and Melo, one of the greatest Wiyus, Sedi-Diyor, grabbed hold of the sky, his father, and kicked him until he fled up into the heavens alone.

At the time of the sky's escape, Sedi gave birth to two daughters, but because Melo had left her, she could not bear to look at them. So Sedi-Diyor found them a nurse. As the two children grew older, light began to shine from them, and by the time they could walk the light grew brighter and brighter. Eventually the old nurse died, and Sedi-Diyor buried her. The children were grief-stricken and wept so much for her that they also died, and the light that had shone from them died too.

All was in darkness again, and the Wiyus were so afraid that they thought that the nurse had perhaps stolen something from the children. So they dug up her body to find out what it was. But her body had begun to rot away, and only her eyes were left. As they gazed into the bright shining eyes in the darkness, they caught a glimpse of their own reflections and thought these were the dead children. They took the eyes to a river and washed them for five days and nights, and they shone even more brightly. But they could not remove the eyes that looked back at them from within the eyes, and still believed that these were the dead children.

A carpenter carefully cut open the eyes and removed the reflections, which turned into real children. They called one Bomong and the other Bong. But Bomong and Bong were so bright and shone so much that when they came out of the house there was too much light and too much heat. The rocks began to crumble, the trees began to wither, and the rivers began to dry up. The heat was intense, and there was no darkness. Bomong, dressed in beautiful clothes and exquisite ornaments, went off to wander through the world and disappeared across the hills. The Wiyus agreed that they must kill one of the children of light so that there would be times of darkness in the world, but they were afraid to do so. In the end it was a frog who had the terrible task of killing Bong. As she walked past him, dazzling him and drying him up in her radiant heat, he shot an arrow into her eyes and she died. Immediately it

17

was not so hot, and the trees grew again and the people began to work, but although it was not as bright there was still no darkness.

Kirte, a Wiyu rat, dragged the body of Bong on his back as far as the river, knowing that soon Bomong would come by. As he dragged her, she was so heavy that he kept falling over, and that is why rats have crooked legs. Bomong was so unhappy when she saw her dead sister and so afraid that the Wiyus would kill her too, that she ran away down a path that no one knew. She stopped in a clearing and placed a huge stone on her head, and with the shadow of the stone over her the world became dark.

The Wiyus were disturbed because the world was in darkness. They needed the light badly, because otherwise nothing would grow and they would not be able to live. They went to search for light, but they found nothing that gave out any light.

One of the Wiyus caught a rat, a wild bird and a cockerel. He told them to go and find Bomong in the hope that she would bring them back light. The cockerel travelled for many miles and eventually found the girl under her shadow of stone. He begged her to return, but she replied: 'How can I? You killed my sister and you might kill me. I'll only return if you bring my sister back to life.'

The cockerel told the Wiyus, and they agreed to bring Bong back to life. They found the carpenter, and he made Bong's body out of wood and put life into it. When Bomong heard that her sister was alive, she took the great stone off her head and the light radiated from her once again. The day returned, and the warmth of her light made the trees grow and the birds sing. The cock cried 'Cock-a-doodle-doo', the wild bird sang and the rat squeaked. And the Wiyus were happy in the light of the day.

PURUSHA

INDIA, 2000–1000BCE

THERE are many versions of this Indian myth from one of the first Hindu sacred books, which dates from 2000–1000BCE. This book is a collection of over a thousand 'hymns' composed by the Aryans who invaded India. It is known as the *Rig-Veda* ('Royal Knowledge'). In this particular version of the myth, sacrifice is seen as the means to creation. Purusha, primal man, is dismembered and given up to different principles of the material world. His story is reminiscent of Ymir's (see page 23), in that the essence of the world was made sacred from the greatest kind of sacrifice, self-sacrifice.

In the primordial ocean, in the swirl of dark nothingness fused with fire, there floated a golden egg. This egg had floated for one thousand god years or 1,576,800,000,000 mortal years in the great churning sea of chaos. Alone

18

inside this dark golden egg was Purusha, who needed to end his loneliness. As the fire heated the dark waters and churned the ocean into a whirling mass of fire and water, the egg cracked open.

Purusha was the universe, and he arose from the egg with a thousand heads, a thousand hands and a thousand eyes. Because he was lonely, he split himself in two parts. A quarter of him created earth and Viraj (female universal power), who was to join with him to create humankind, and the other three-quarters of Purusha remained the bigger universe and the gods. The gods needed to be respected and honoured, and to achieve this, humans had to learn to sacrifice to their gods and make the world and themselves holy.

The act of creation was itself a sacrifice, so Purusha dismembered all his remaining parts to bring about the rest of creation. His mouth became Brahman, the power of the universe, his eye became the sun, and his mind became the moon. From his breath the wind was born, and from his navel the air. From his feet came the earth, and from his ear the points of the compass. Nothing was wasted of Purusha's dismemberment, and he became part of everything that is in existence.

Purusha is in everything and is everything, and the myth reveals that the continuity of the universe can be assured only if Purusha continues to allow himself to be so disassembled and to be a sacrificial model for the world. If Purusha ever changes his mind and creates himself back out of the whole into his first manifestation as the sole being, the universe will end.

WOYENGI

IJAW, NIGERIA, AFRICA, probably 2700BCE (recorded c.1700CE)

THIS is a very ancient Nigerian creation myth, which is found in many versions. It is similar to creation myths from other continents in the assumption of an initial creator, but this is one of those rare myths that affirms the role of a woman as initiator.

In the vast eternity of nothingness something sparked and time was created. In that split second heaven and earth came into being, and a lightning storm channelled energy from the eternal space down to the earth. With the lightning came Woyengi, the creator, who stepped out of the lightning on to the earth. There was nothing on the earth – it was empty, nothing lived, no sound, no movement, no wind, no light. But there was a chair, a table and a flat stone, called the Stone of Creation.

Woyengi, the creator woman, knelt down on the earth and gathered large handfuls of thick, sticky mud. The chair was obviously to sit upon, so she sat on the chair. The table was obviously to put the mud upon, so she scooped the mud into a large mound on the table. The Stone of Creation was obviously for her feet to rest upon, so she put them on the stone while she worked. With the mud she shaped many dolls. Some were large, some small, some had two legs, some had four, but mostly they were humans. As she finished modelling each one, she placed it between her feet on the Stone of Creation. Then she leaned forwards, and as she gently opened each doll's eyes, she blew her breath across the doll's face to give it the kiss of life. As the doll awoke to life, she asked it, 'Would you like to be a man or a woman?' Whatever the answer, she would give the doll the right sexual organs.

Once the dolls were given life, she put them back in neat rows on the huge table. The dolls spread across the table until they covered the entire surface and all the mud was gone. Woyengi sat up straight and spoke carefully to them: 'As your first gift you were given life, then your second gift was to chose which sex you are. Now I give you your third gift, Chose the work you would like to do throughout your life.'

So the thousand dolls chose every kind of work there could be, from gardener to warrior, from cook to fisherman. When they had finished choosing, Woyengi took handfuls of them and set them down on the earth. She pointed to two streams that led away from the Stone of Creation and said: 'Now you must follow the right stream so that it can carry you to where you must be in the world.'

The people who had chosen a life that made them powerful or important or elitist had to go down the first stream, which was full of rapids and rocks and dangerous currents. The people who had chosen sedentary jobs, with no responsibility, had to follow the second stream. This was clear and calm, but with shallow stagnant pools in some places. People from each stream called back to tell the others what the stream was like, and some stopped and hesitated now they knew the kind of stream they would have to travel down and wanted to stay with Woyengi or change their minds. But she shook her head and pushed them on towards the stream of their choice. There was no turning back from the life they had chosen for themselves. Handfuls and handfuls of dolls stepped into the two streams and the waters carried them away to where they would fill the world with the first people.

GAIA AND OURANOS

GREECE, 750BCE

A T the end of the eighth century BCE the Greek poet Hesiod recorded in a wonderful work called the *Theogony* the myths of the universal Olympian order and the evolution of the gods. This is an epic myth of divine struggles, of passion and violence, of destruction and treachery. The creation of the gods and their extraordinary 'soap-opera' behaviour not only reflect the antics of mankind but also focus the force of creation itself into a distinctive philosophy, which is known as the Gaia hypothesis – that is, all things must be in balance to ensure the survival of the whole. This is similar to the main element of thinking behind the Taoist philosophy of ancient China.

Out of chaos appeared spontaneously Gaia (the earth), Tartarus (the underworld) and Eros (love). Eros, one of the most beautiful of the gods, came to be one of the most powerful in the minds and hearts of humans. Night and Erebos also spontaneously arose out of chaos and gave birth to day and space. Gaia then gave birth to her equal, Ouranos (the heavens), whom she allowed to cover her like a cloak as a resting place for all the gods. Gaia gave birth to the mountains and the sea alone, but then embraced Ouranus, and his life-giving rain filled Gaia's river-beds and streams, until all living things came into being.

Gaia and Ouranus created many children of other kinds: the Cyclopes, whom they blended with rock and fire; the hundred-handed giants, whom they made from trees and gods; and, most important of all, the Titans, great, shapeless monsters, at whom Ouranus could not bear to look. As each one was born, he hid them down in the darkness of the earth so that they could never see the light again. Gaia realized that the only way she could end the cruel tyranny of Ouranos was with an equally wicked plan.

With her ugly son Kronos, she lay in wait for Ouranus to come to her for love one night. Kronos leapt from his hiding place, and, as Ouranus made love to Gaia, he took the long, jagged sickle Gaia had given him and castrated Ouranos. He threw Ouranus's genitals away. The blood that fell into Gaia's womb became the Furies, and as the genitals fell into the ocean, they caused the sea to foam and out of this foam arose Aphrodite. Ouranus, now castrated, sought vengeance on and punishment for his sons the Titans. His ally, night, gave birth to blame and distress, famine, deceit, killings, lawlessness and ruin in an attempt to create balance as well as retribution for the Titans.

Gaia and Ouranos took little part in organizing the universe after this except when the whole balance and future of the world was threatened.

AMETA AND HAINUWELE

WEST CERAM, INDONESIA, 100CE

THIS simple but powerful myth originates from the many stories that surround one of the three goddesses who have been part of the rich tapestry of myths and religion throughout eastern Indonesia.

In the beginning there were only bunches of wild bananas, and the only place they could be found was on Mount Nunusaka. From these clusters of bananas were created the nine families of humankind, who went to live in the jungle at a place called Nine Dance Grounds.

Among these nine families was a man called Ameta. His only companion was a dog, for he had no wife. One day he went out hunting with his dog, which chased after a wild pig. The dog would not follow the wild pig into the pond but barked from the shore. The wild pig was quickly tired and soon drowned. Ameta swam across the pond and pulled the dead pig out of the water. On the end of the pig's tusk was a coconut, even though there were no coconut palms in the world.

Ameta took the coconut back to his hut and wrapped it in a cloth. During the night a strange man appeared in his dream and told him to plant the nut in the ground, otherwise it would not grow. The next morning Ameta planted the coconut, and three days later the palm was as tall as a hut. After another three days the palm was covered in blossom. Ameta wanted to make a special potion to drink from the beautiful blossom, but as he climbed the tree he slipped and gashed his hand on his knife, and his blood fell on one of the leaves.

Three days later he returned and found a mysterious face had appeared where his blood had dripped on to the leaf. Within a week the face had turned into a little girl. That night the strange man returned to Ameta in his dreams and told him to wrap the girl in his snake-cloth and take her home. So Ameta took the snake-cloth to the tree and carefully wrapped up the little girl and took her home. He called her Hainuwele (frond of the coco palm). Hainuwele grew very quickly into a beautiful woman, but the strangest thing about her was that whenever she defecated, her excrement consisted of the most beautiful objects and valuable goods. This made Ameta very wealthy.

At the great Maro dance celebrations, Hainuwele was placed in the centre of the dance to give out betel nuts to the dancers. Instead, however, she began to give away beautiful objects. First, she offered pieces of coral, then porcelain dishes, then great bush knives, then boxes made of copper, then golden earrings and glorious gongs. From night to night the value of the goods increased, until people became very suspicious and jealous of Hainuwele's power. They decided to kill Hainuwele, and at the last night of the Maro dance the men dug a deep hole. As she danced, they pushed her into the pit. They covered her quickly with earth, and the dancers trampled down on the earth with their feet.

Ameta was distressed when Hainuwele did not return from the Maro dance. Sensing that she was dead and using his special divining rods, he was able to locate Hainuwele's body at the dancing ground. Ameta dug up her corpse and cut it into many pieces, which, apart from the arms, he buried around the whole area of the dancing ground. All the pieces of Hainuwele

22

that he buried grew into different kinds of plants, which came to be the main source of food for the people.

Ameta gave the two arms to Satene, the great goddess of West Ceram. Satene had been created from an unripe banana. Everyone else had been created from ripe bananas, and for this reason she was the ruler of them all. Satene was angered by the killing of her sister-goddess, Hainuwele, and vowed that she would not stay on earth any more. She built a great gate, which swirled in nine spirals towards heaven, and stood in the centre, holding out the two arms of Hainuwele. She spoke sternly to the people: 'You have killed and done wrong. So I cannot stay here with you any more. You must all try to come with me through the gate, and only those who succeed can remain as people.'

So the people pushed and shoved and ran towards the great spiral gate to make sure that they could remain who they were, and those who were pushed out of the way became spirits or animals. Those who were strongest walked towards Satene, and as each one passed she would strike them with Hainuwele's arm. Some had to jump over five bamboo sticks and others over nine bamboo sticks. This was the beginning of the two tribes known as the Fivers and Niners. Before Satene departed she said: 'Only when you die will you be able to see me again, but even then you will have to suffer a terrible journey first.'

Satene went to live on the Mountain of the Dead, in the most inaccessible part of West Ceram, across nine great mountain ranges. Whoever tried to reach her would have to pass the most rigorous and dangerous journey of all, including death.

YMIR

NORTHERN EUROPE, 200CE

THE Norse myth of the beginning of the world and its one creator has many similarities to the Indian myth of Purusha (see page 18) in that both beings were dismembered in order for the world to be created and if ever they were to be joined together again the world would be destroyed. Some scholars believe that there may be a common source between these two widely different geographical and chronological cultures and their myths.

In the beginning was a yawning emptiness, an abyss called Ginnungagap, with frothing, boiling air and liquid streams, which ran between the endless realms of fire and ice. Long before the world was created there came to exist the great universal tree, Yggdrasil. This ash tree linked the nine other worlds. Under its roots to the south was a hot kingdom called Muspel. To the north, under another of Yggdrasil's roots, was the kingdom of Niflheim, a land of ice and darkness. Beneath another root was Hvergelmir, a cauldron of bubbling waters that was the source of twelve huge rivers. A terrible dragon, with its accomplices, monster worms, lived in the cauldron and continually gnawed at the roots of Yggdrasil. It was said that once the tree was killed the universe would come to an end.

All the water that streamed from Hvergelmir fell into Ginnungagap and became great blocks of ice and glaciers. Mist rose up into nothingness from Ginnungagap. The glaciers of the ice kingdom melted when the warm air of the south rose to meet them, and they spread wider and wider across the emptiness. Then, engulfed by the flames of the fire kingdom, Muspel, they quickly turned to water.

From the drops of misty air that rose from this melting furnace of flames and water a being came into creation. This was Ymir, which means 'two-in-one'. At this time was created from the same mist the primeval cow, Audhumla, who licked the cliffs of ice for nourishment. As she licked, her warm tongue melted two frozen gods who had been trapped within the icy wall. These were Buri and Bor. Unknowingly, as Audhumla licked the ice, Ymir drank from the cow's udders and grew into a terrible frost-giant. Ymir had the power to create life spontaneously, and while he slept even more ugly frost-giants were produced from the sweat from his armpits and all the other crevices where he sweated. From his left armpit he created both male and female frost-giants, and they began to mate with one another, creating a terrible race of giants.

Odin, Vili and Ve, the three sons of Buri, agreed that Ymir was too powerful and too dangerous and had to be destroyed. As the great Ymir slept, the three gods attacked him. Odin pierced the giant's heart with a spear made from Yggdrasil. Blood flowed from Ymir's wound like a torrent of ice water, like the great glaciers from which he had self-created. In this river of blood all the other frost-giants drowned or were washed away to another world called Jötunheim, except for Bergelmir and his wife, who managed to escape by jumping on to a hollow tree trunk.

Odin, Vili and Ve threw Ymir's corpse into the great void of the icy ocean of Ginnungagap where it broke apart and made the world. His flesh became the earth, his bones were mountains and his blood the rivers and the seas. His skull made the skies, his teeth made boulders and his hair the trees. With some of his blood the brothers gathered together the swirling ocean of Ginnungagap, and they called this creation, Midgard or Middle Land. This was where they built Asgard, their huge citadel, which they surrounded with a fortress made from Ymir's eyebrows. With the maggots that were left crawling about the giant corpse they made dwarfs to hold up the corners of the sky.

To make light in the world, the three brothers used embers from Muspel to create the stars, and the sparks made the sun and the moon. The giants that had survived the flood were blinded by the light of the sun and the moon and released great hungry wolves into the sky to devour them. One wolf still takes a bite out of the moon when he gets near, but the moon always escapes and grows whole again. The other wolf cannot get near the sun because it is too hot, but one day the wolves may devour the lights of the heaven forever.

HURAKAN

ONE of the most powerful peoples of the Mayan civilization were the Quiche. In the *Popol Vuh* ('The Collection of Written Leaves'), a sacred history of the Quiche peoples and probably one of the most important sources for pre-Columbian history and mythology, Hurakan, the heart of heaven and god of hurricanes, is the main creator.

Once there was only water, all calm and all in suspense. There was only the tranquil primeval ocean where nothing existed. There were only Tepeu and Gucumatz, the two sun-fire deities who lived in the depths of the water. They began to speak together, and it became clear to them that when dawn came, humans must appear. So they planned the creation of the earth and of humankind, and it was arranged by Hurakan, who was the heart of heaven.

Through the mists and the clouds above the dark water, Hurakan called out 'Earth! Let the emptiness be filled!' and the earth was created. The earth rose out of the void, and the gods agreed that now animals and trees and plants should be made. But the animals could not speak to worship their gods, so Hurakan set to work to make people. The first attempt was a disaster. The people were made from earth and mud, but they melted away in the sun and could not move without falling down. Their sight was blurred so they could not look behind or see where they were going. At first they spoke, but the people had no minds because they soaked away in the mud. They could not stand up but collapsed into muddy heaps and puddles. So Hurakan tried again to make people who could worship the gods properly.

The second race of people were created from wood. They looked like the first people, and they talked, and they produced more wooden figures themselves. But they did not have souls or minds, and they walked on all fours and quickly forgot Hurakan. These people had no blood and no substance, and their cheeks were dry, their flesh was cold, and they had no hearts. They were cruel to the animals and irreverent to the gods, so Hurakan at once set forth to destroy them all. He brought a great rainstorm to earth, a deluge that turned the wooden people into sodden statues that could not move because their legs were so heavy. And all the creatures and the monsters they had offended in the world turned on them, and their faces and heads were mangled. The only ones to survive ran into the forests and evolved into monkeys.

So Hurakan tried again. He used two kinds of corn, white and yellow, which he crushed into a paste. This corn meal dough made the first real people. The first four men were called Iqui-Balam (black sorcerer), Mahacutah (not brushed), Balam-Quitze (sorcerer of fatal laughter) and Balam-Acab (sorcerer of the night). Hurakan gave them great knowledge and the power to make fire. These men were grateful for their creation and worshipped Hurakan. But Hurakan was worried because the men were more like sorcerers and wizards than simple men. They seemed to have too much power, and too much wisdom would mean they could be more like gods than men. So he breathed a cloud of mist across their eyes so that they could no longer see as much or understand as much. While the men were asleep, he made four women called Caha-Paluna (falling water), Caquixaha (brilliant water), Tzununiha (water of humming-birds) and Chomiha (beautiful water), who became their wives.

From these four couples were descended the Quiche and all the other Central American tribes. After many generations they stood on the mountain top and watched the sun rise, and its heat solidified the earth and turned all the terrible monsters into stone.

BUMBA

ZAIRE, 500CE

THIS story comes from the Bantu people of the River Congo region. The Bushongo kingdom was one of the oldest and most civilized of the Bantu cultures, and its oral history goes back to the fifth century CE. The myth is similar to other African myths of self-fertile creatures emerging out of chaos.

There was a man called Bumba, who was all alone in the dark waters of the beginning of time. There was nothing around him except water and darkness, and he was very lonely. He wanted some company, but he did not know where to find it or how to look for it, as there was no light.

One day he began to feel a terrible pain in his belly. As the pains grew worse, he suddenly felt something rise to his throat and he vomited up the sun. Suddenly there was light everywhere. Bumba began to see everything, and as the sun got hotter it began to dry up the edges of the eternal water until there was some land, and the dark edges of the world began to show along the horizon as sandbanks and ridges of rocks above the water. Yet there were still no living things.

Bumba had another pain, and this time vomited up the stars and the moon so that the night also had flickering light and gentle shadows. The pains came back the following day, and this time he vomited nine different creatures, including the tortoise, the leopard, the eagle, the crocodile and a fish called Yo. He also created the lightning, which was deadly and cruel, but beautiful, too. Lastly, he vomited many men. The creatures all began to re-create themselves. The heron made all the birds in the air; the crocodile made serpents and iguanas and anything that had cold skin; the goat produced every other animal that had horns; Yo created all the fish in the sea; the beetle created every insect. Bumba's sons created the ants, the plants, trees and flowers. The third son wanted to create something special, but he was only allowed to make a bird called the kite because the heron had forgotten to make this himself.

Bumba was worried about the lightning, which was a trouble-maker, and he had to chase her back to the sky, although she still found chances to visit the earth when he wasn't expecting her.

Now creation was finished, and Bumba disguised himself as a man and travelled through the villages, telling all those he met how he had created everything in the universe except himself.

NYAMBI AND KAMONU

BAROTSE, UPPER ZAMBESI, 500CE

THIS myth comes from Zambia. Barotseland was first visited by the explorer David Livingstone in 1851, and it became a province of Northern Rhodesia (now Zambia) in 1911. This myth has a gentle, harmonious beginning, with a creator, Nyambi, who lived happily on earth but had to escape from the world, thus changing the whole balance of the earth. One version of this myth ends with the belief that only when Nyambi returns to the earth will peace and harmony be restored.

Nyambi was the creator-god of all things, and he lived very peacefully on earth with his wife, Nasilele. But one of Nyambi's creations was very different from the rest. He was called Kamonu, and he mimicked Nyambi and copied him all the time. He copied the way he worked, the way he ate, the way he gardened and even the way he defecated, farted and peed. Kamonu was not a very peaceful neighbour, and while Nyambi made scythes and ploughs to farm the earth, Kamonu made spears to kill the animals. Nyambi was very angry and sent Kamonu away to another land, but Kamonu returned to plague and irritate him again. Nyambi was at his wit's end but determined to escape the evil influence of Kamonu.

He decided it was time to leave the less peaceful lands of the world, and he and Nasilele sailed far away to an island in the middle of a huge lake. But Kamonu was clever and constructed a raft and followed them there. So

Nyambi made a huge mountain and ran away to live on the summit, sure that Kamonu would never get to the top. Nyambi was wrong, and a few years later Kumonu arrived at the top, breathless and panting: 'Hey, you cannot escape me, I will irritate you forever.'

In desperation Nyambi met with a magician to find out how he could escape the terrible influence of Kamonu. The magician said, 'You can only escape with the help of the spider.' So Nyambi found the spider, which spun him a silken thread up to the sky. Nyambi and Nasilele climbed up the dew-laden web after the spider to their new home in the sky. Before they left the earth, the magician warned Nyambi that the only way he could escape from Kamonu forever was to remove the spider's eyes, so that the spider could never find its way back to the sky again. Regretfully, Nyambi blinded the spider with his spear, the only cruel thing he had ever done since the beginning of creation.

Kamuno tried to build a huge tower to reach to the sky, but it only ever got higher and higher until each time it collapsed because it was too heavy. Kamuno never found his way up to the sky. So every day when the sun rose he thought it was Nyambi and worshipped the sun, thinking he must greet his hero, and every new moon he would worship the moon thinking it was Nasilele. And when all the other people saw Kamuno doing this, they mimicked him and worshipped the sun and the moon, too.

P'AN KU AND THE COSMIC EGG

CHINA, 500CE

THIS was a highly popular myth in southern China from the third to the sixth centuries CE. In one version, the god P'an Ku apparently arose out of 'nothing' as a child of a highly fertile chaos. The more popular version centres around the great cosmic egg, a symbol of fertility and wholeness, of duality and of the coming together of chaos and matter. Chaos is again the essential beginning of creation, which manifests as the yolk of the raw egg in which P'an Ku develops and hatches.

To begin with there was nothing. But as time passed nothing became something, and the forces of nothing and something became the cosmic egg. Inside the egg was chaos, and P'an Ku floated inside chaos for 18,000 years. He started off as a dwarf, but he grew so big that he eventually split the shell and burst out of the egg four times larger than any man.

In his hand he carried a hammer and chisel, and from his head grew two great horns, a symbol of supernatural power in China. Two great tusks grew from his jaw, and he was covered in thick black hair. For another 18,000 years P'an Ku set to work on chiselling apart the earth and the sky. He dug valleys and piled up mountains, he made river-beds, and in one version of the story, when he cried his tears became the great Yellow River of China. The world could never be finished unless P'an Ku died, for only his death could perfect the universe.

In a different version of the myth the sky was shaped from his skull, the fields from his flesh, the rocks from his bones, the rivers and seas from his blood, and the thunder from his voice. His left eye was the sun, his right eye was the moon. And from the lice and fleas that lived on his body and in his hair came humankind.

The other version suggests that P'an Ku formed the five sacred mountains of China. The east mountain rose from his head, the central mountain, Sung, from his body, the north mountain, Heng, from his right arm, and the mountain of the south from his left arm. The Hua Mountain of the west grew out of his feet.

P'an Ku made people out of clay and left them to dry out in the sun. As the rain fell he had to rush them under cover and in the process broke some of the models and that is why there are disabled people on earth.

IZANAMI AND IZANAGI

JAPAN, 700CE

WHETHER this myth originates from the *Kojiki* ('Records of Ancient Matters'), which dates from 712CE and is the oldest chronicle in Japanese, or from the *Nihongi* ('Chronicles of Japan'), which is slightly later, 720CE, sometimes causes confusion among scholars. But the myth is nevertheless based on original Chinese cosmology, which assumes an initial chaos. This is a beautiful myth that gives a powerful account of the process of creation through twin deities.

Izanami means 'she who invites', and Izanagi means 'he who invites'. Izanami became a feared goddess of death, but Izanagi became known only as the ancestor of the imperial dynasty.

All at first was chaos. The principles of masculine and feminine were not yet distinguished, and they formed an egg-like mass that contained only undefined limits and merged like a great porridge at some places and a thin brine at others. But what was pure and light floated upwards to form heaven, and what was heavy and thick settled downwards to become the principal of earth in the form of a semolina-like mass. Heaven and earth then created eight deities on a reed-shoot that grew between them, and the twin deities, Izanami and Izanagi, were invited to be the creators of the world by the great reed-shoot, which itself had been transformed into a god.

Up on the Floating Bridge of Heaven, in the swirling mist and cloud above the primordial waters, Izanami and Izanagi wondered if there was a land beneath them. All below the bridge seemed like nothingness. Izanagi dipped a beautiful jewelled spear down into the nothingness and began gently to stir the primordial ocean that moved like a great mass of pea soup. Izanagi pulled out the jewelled spear and from it fell drops of fatty soup, which congealed and formed an island.

Izanami and Izanagi stepped from the Floating Bridge of Heaven on to this island and built a tall pillar, which rose to the sky above and the ocean below. This was to prevent the island from floating away. But they did not know how to create anything else, so they began to dance in opposite directions around their great pillar. As they danced, each began to notice the difference in their physical forms.

Izanagi caught hold of Izanami each time they met at the other side of the pillar. They whirled round and around each other, until eventually Izanagi grabbed hold of Izanami who spoke first.

'How wonderful, I've met a lovely youth!'

Izanagi nodded, and breathlessly said, 'I have met a beautiful young maiden, and in my body is a source place of masculinity. Do you have a source place of femininity so that we can unite?'

Izanami nodded, so they had sex and their first creation was born. But it was an ugly, blood-sucking, water-leech child, and it was so horrible that they put it in the boat of heaven and left it to drift around the ocean forever.

Izanami and Izanagi were worried about why they had created such a monster, and the celestial council told them that because Izanami had spoken first everything she created would be corrupt. They went back to the pillar and circled it again and again, and each time from now on it was Izanagi who spoke first.

Their next creations were more successful. First, came the eight islands of Japan, the sea, the earth, the seasons, trees, animals and mountains. Next they decided to create someone to be the ruler of the universe, so together they produced the sun-goddess, who was so beautiful that they believed she was too good to stay on earth. So they sent her to heaven to look after the skies. The next child that came was the moon-god, and because he was as radiant and wonderful as the sun they sent him up to the heavens to join the sun.

But the last creation was the spirit of fire, Kagutsuchi, who scorched Izanami as he made his way out of her womb. She suffered such terrible internal burns that she died and descended to Yomi, the underworld. Izanagi was heart-broken and buried her body and then cut off the fire-god's head. But from its blood thousands of wild creatures were created, and from the dismembered body grew other gruesome monsters and five volcanoes.

So Izanagi went down to the underworld to find Izanami and beg her to return with him. In the darkness he could only hear her voice in the distance.

At the door of the Palace of Darkness he shouted to her: 'Izanami, the lands which we've made are still to be finished, please come back with me!'

But Izanami's only hope was to ask the spirits of the underworld to free her as she had already eaten the fruits of Yomi and could now never leave. Izanami warned Izanagi to stay where he was at the doorway, and not to dare to look in or try to speak with her until she had made her bargain with the spirits. But Izanagi was impatient. The silence was unbearable and he could not bear to wait any longer, fearing she had gone forever. He broke a tooth from his hair-comb and with his spirit-breath turned it into a magic torch. In the sudden blaze of the light he gasped and shuddered, for it was then he saw Izanami. His beautiful sister and lover was now no more than a corpse of rotting flesh crawling with maggots that ate her. Thunder-snakes coiled around her bones and emerged from between her ribs and loins. Izanami was so ashamed that she rose from the coffin and chased Izanagi towards the upper world. In fear for his life, all Izanagi could do was to throw his hair-comb behind him, and it turned into a bunch of grapes, which Izanami stopped briefly to devour. But she carried on after him and turned the thunder-snakes into eight spirits to chase him too. He threw down his other hair-comb, which turned into a hundred bamboo shoots, which Izanami again stopped to devour.

But near the pass between the underworld and the upper world, which is full of both strange delights and tempting treats for those who might pass downwards, there grew a peach tree. Izanagi picked as many peaches as he could from the tree. These were the fruits of life, and he hurled them at Izanami and her spirits. Then, before she could reach him, he rolled a huge stone in front of the entrance to the pass so that none could follow.

When Izanami arrived at the blocked entrance to Yomi, Izanagi formally divorced her. She screamed at him that she would devour a thousand people every day if he did so, and he replied that if she did he would simply create fifteen hundred more.

The creation of the living and the dead was now finished. Izanagi returned to the world and went to the ocean to wash himself of the corruption, filth and degeneration of the underworld. As he washed and swam in the great ocean, he created many other beings and deities. But his divine task was now accomplished and there was nothing left for him to do, so he built himself a gloomy house on the island of Ahaji and lived there forever as a hermit, in silence and solitude so that no one would ever find him.

The interesting twist to this tale is that the island Ahaji was created from the placenta of Izanami's first child, the blood-sucking water-leech. The gods thought the placenta so ghastly that they called the island Ahaji, 'the unpleasant land'.

RANGI AND PAPA

THIS is probably the best known of the Maori myths of creation. The initial separation of the primordial oneness of heaven and earth becomes an epic struggle between parents and children and the eternal struggle facing humankind once duality has been established in the world.

For over a million years Rangi and Papa had lain together, locked in an inseparable embrace. Rangi was father sky and Papa was mother-earth. From their unceasing mating and from the darkness between their two cosmic forms everything was created. But after thousands of years some of Rangi and Papa's child-gods became uncomfortable in the cramped space and could not stand the continuous darkness. The more beings Rangi and Papa created between them, the less room was there to move.

Six of these gods met in a secret council to find a solution to their predicament. The first to make a suggestion was Tu, the father of human beings, who proposed that they should kill Rangi and Papa. But this terrible suggestion was overruled by a better suggestion from the father of the forests, Tane-mahuta. 'If we push our parents apart and separate them, Papa will be the earth to nurture us and for us to live on, and Rangi will be the sky who looks down upon us and cares for us from a distance.'

So all the other gods apart from Tawhiri, the father of the winds and storms, agreed to this plan. Tawhiri was heartbroken that his parents were to be torn apart and that his own kingdom would, in turn, be redundant.

So the gods took turns to see if they could separate Rangi and Papa. First of all Rongo-ma-tane, the father of farming, tried to push against the great diaphragm of Rangi, but could not shift him at all. Next it was Tangaroa, the father of the ocean, who was just as unsuccessful. Tu, the father of human beings, failed just like the others, as did Haumiatikitiki the father of wild plants. But Tane-mahuta, the father of the forests, pushed his branching head of leaves and twigs on to the belly of Papa, and with his roots planted firmly on Rangi's stomach he began to grow upwards slowly until mother-earth and the sky parted and light filled the great space between them. The millions of creatures that Papa had created fell out all over Rangi's body and began to mate and create new animals, creatures and people.

In a great rage that she and Rangi should be separated, Papa cried out, 'How could you do this to us? How dare you commit such a crime on us, your parents?'

So Tawhiri, the god of winds, who had initially refused to agree to the splitting of his parents, sought revenge on his brothers. He escaped quickly to the safety of Rangi's domain in the sky and spent hours consulting both parents about how he could ensure that his brothers would never be spared any peace for their treachery. But it was against Tu, the father of human beings, that Tawhiri fought most strongly, while the others cowered on the earth, hiding from Tawhiri's wrath. For thousands of years he blew hurricanes and storms across mother-earth, causing destruction. Tu grew resentful towards his wimpish brothers and scorned them for their cowardice and for their fear of the god of wind. But Tu could not rid the earth of Tawhiri's anger, and so the last-born child of Rangi and Papa was left as a natural enemy of man, as he always blows hurricanes and storms on land and across the sea.

QAT

MELANESIA, 750CE

ONE of the main ways in which this myth differs from many others is that light was already vast and infinite and it was darkness that had no existence. It was the creation of darkness that was the problem for the creator, Qat, rather than finding the light. The Banks Islands are in the north part of Vanuatu (the New Hebrides), and early western settlers may well have reshaped the ending of this myth so that Qat paddles away into the sunset, to return one day. The first white man to appear in Melanesia was Captain Cook, whom the people of the Banks Islands believed was their god, Qat, finally come home.

The very centre of the world was Vanna Lava, and that was where Qat was born. Before this no one knows what happened for there was nothing to tell. Qat's mother was a great stone, which split in two and Qat came forth from the stone and named himself.

Qat had eleven brothers and no father, and as soon as he was born he immediately began to create things. At this time it was light in the world and there was no darkness. Qat made up all sorts of things he could create – fish and pigs and plants and trees and stones. Then he thought about humankind and decided to make people from the wood of the dracaena tree. He carved the arms and legs and the fingers and toes and the heads and the bodies in separate pieces then carefully fitted them together. He made six carved figures out of these pieces and, pleased with the way they looked, set about bringing them to life.

He placed the figures in a row and danced and sang in front of them. They began to move very slowly, very stiffly, and when Qat saw the life beginning to run through them he began to beat his drum. The magical rhythms of the drum made their feet move and their fingers tap at the air, and with each drum beat they began to dance the dance of life. The drum beat faster and faster until they could walk and run and do everything on their own. Qat divided the six people into three men and three women so that each man could have a wife and each wife a husband.

One of Qat's brothers, Marawa, was stupid and thought he could create people too. He cut down a tree and carved six figures just as Qat had done, but it was the wrong kind of tree. He danced and beat his drum, but when the figures began to move he threw them into a pit and buried them because he was bored and didn't want to waste any more time bringing them to life. A week later he went back to the pit and dug them up, but they were all rotten and stank. So Marawa had to leave the people buried in the earth and that was why death came to the world.

But Qat was worried about his pigs because he had made them with only two legs, and his brothers just laughed at them. So Qat, who was very sensitive and didn't like the pigs to be laughed at, shortened their arms and made them walk on all fours. So Qat went on making pigs and men, and food plants, and canoes and animals.

The endless light meant that no one could rest or sleep, and Qat knew he had to make darkness somehow even though he had no idea how to do it. One day he heard that there was something called night on another island. So he put a pig into his canoe and sailed across to Vava. In exchange for his pig he bought a piece of night from Qong who lived there. So Qat brought night back to Vanna Lava as well as some birds who would know how to let everyone know when night was over and it was time for day.

Qat showed everyone how to sleep by laying mats on the floor and closing their eyes when they lay down. As the sun moved into the west, he spread the darkness across the sky like a huge cloak of black feathers and told all his brothers and the people he had created that this was now a time to sleep, even though they feared it might be death.

At the end of the first night Qat made the birds sing and the cocks crow. He took a knife and cut a hole through the black feathers of the night and soon the dawn broke out and the sun shone. From then on there was night and day.

TA'AROA AND THE EGG

TAHITI, 750CE

THE creator-god Ta'aroa was the initial concept of the kernel of life, which is an eggshell within a shell. Ta'aroa was sometimes known in four aspects. He was god of the sky, of earth, of foundation and of the underworld. In some stories Ta'aroa also created himself into Tangaroa, the god of the sea.

Ta'aroa existed alone in timeless space. He lived in a cosmic egg that revolved endlessly in darkness and chaos. He was quite alone in his shell, which was called Rumia (upset). When he first hatched from this egg, he found that he was alone, and as much as he shouted and cursed for company or for land or for water, nothing came into being with him. As there was nothing except himself, he angrily retreated back into a new shell and spent thousands and millions of years in contemplation trying to work out what to do. Finally, he decided that the new shell he had created should be the foundation of all creations, the very world itself, and the old shell the dome of the sky.

To finish off his masterpiece of creation Ta'aroa used his own body. He used his arms and legs for the solidity of the earth, his bones for mountains, his organs for clouds, his intestines for fish and eels and his blood for the rainbows. So when creation was complete, he was at the same time everywhere and part of everything that ever had come into being. But Ta'aroa kept his head for himself. He decided, however, that he must have other gods as companions. And so Tu, who was an artisan of great skill and helped Ta'aroa to fashion humankind, became his famous co-creator.

Ti'i was the first man, and Hina was the first woman. Hina was a demigoddess, and she had a face on both the front and the back of her head. But her heart was full of goodness, and she guarded the creations of the universe and the fruits of the earth. Unfortunately, Ti'i was evil and wanted to corrupt people, and he used his evil powers to kill them.

For thousands of years there was harmony, but then wars began among gods and among different peoples, so Ta'aroa and Tu cursed everything they had created to punish the world for their treachery. The stars blinked every time they were cursed, and the moon waned and disappeared from view. But Hina used some of her goodness, and the stars carried on twinkling and the moon returned every time it hid a while from the curse.

The two creators put a curse on the sea so it would always be low tide, but Hina spoke her gentle words to the sea and it came up high to please her each time. They put a curse on the trees so that they lost their leaves, but Hina breathed her soft breath on them so that new growth appeared after the old had died and so that the leaves and the plants returned with the seasons. But there was nothing Hina could do for mankind.

She begged with Ti'i to stop making humankind corrupt. 'I can bring them back to life from the curse of the gods. Look what I have done for the stars and the trees.' But Ti'i ignored her plea and went on killing people. So it was that man and not woman took away eternal life. Not long after, Ti'i himself died but could not return to life because of the curse of the gods.

EARTH-INITIATE AND COYOTE

THIS is an example of an 'earth-initiate' myth, which assumes that after the initial nothingness several self-creating beings make a world of peace and harmony – until things began to go wrong. This is when a companion or an ambivalent being decides to take the law into his own hands and causes the world to be a mixture of good and evil. In this case, the villain of the piece is Coyote. Coyote is a trickster-god, who in some myths was also a shape-shifter who took on any form or role he wanted.

In this version the trickster-god chooses to take on the form of Coyote. He has limited power, and although he can shape people and create their form, he cannot put life into them. The myth ends with a theme common to many Native American myths: that when the great earth-initiate returns the world will be in harmony again.

Darkness was the beginning. There were no sun, no stars and no moon. In the darkness was only water.

From the north a raft came floating by, and on it were two beings, the turtle and father-of-the-secret-society. A rope of feathers was let down from the sky and earth-initiate climbed down it and jumped on to the raft. His body shone like a gleaming sun, but his face was always covered and could never be seen beneath his great black cowl. For a long time nobody spoke, but then the turtle asked, 'Where are you from?' and earth-initiate said, 'I've come from the above.'

The turtle then asked earth-initiate if he could make land so that sometimes he could get out of the water. But earth-initiate shrugged and said he couldn't make land if he had no earth to make it with. The turtle offered to fetch it for him if earth-initiate would tie a rock around the turtle's leg. Then he would dive down for some mud in the great dark water. From out of nowhere earth-initiate found some rope and did as the turtle said. With his leg tied to the rock, the turtle waved good-bye and jumped into the deep darkness of the water.

For many years earth-initiate and father-of-the-secret-society waited for the turtle. Six years later the turtle returned. He had been gone so long that he was covered in green slime and the only earth he had found was stuck under his nails, for on his journey up through the water the clumps of mud he had carried had been washed away.

After scraping out the earth from under the turtle's nails, earth-initiate rolled it together in the palm of his hands and made it into a ball of sticky dough-like mud. He left it on the stern of the boat and waited for it to grow.

After a long time the ball of mud grew so big that the raft ran aground on it. Everywhere they looked were mountains and islands with high cliffs or volcanoes. The raft bumped up against the land, which they called Ta'doiko. The turtle complained that it was too dark to do anything, so perhaps the earth-initiate could make some light, too.

Earth-initiate told his sister, the sun, to rise every day in the east and leave every night in the west and his brother, the moon, to rise at night, and he made a great tree, which grew twelve different kinds of acorns. So the turtle and earth-initiate and father-of-the-secret-society travelled around the world that earth-initiate had made.

While they were gone, Coyote and his dog, Rattlesnake, arose from beneath the water. Coyote was clever and could see earth-initiate's face beneath his black cowl.

One day earth-initiate decided he would make people, and with the red earth he moulded a man and a woman and lay them either side of him as he slept. In the night the woman figure tickled him in the ribs, but he did not dare laugh. The first man was called Ku'ksu, and the first woman was called Morning Star Woman.

Coyote was impressed with the people that earth-initiate had made, but he thought he could make better people himself. He did exactly as earth-initiate had done and moulded two figures out of clay. But when the woman poked him in his side during the night when he slept, he laughed, and so the people that he made were imperfect. Earth-initiate was furious and said, 'I told you not to laugh!' But Coyote shook his head and denied that he had laughed. It was the first lie.

Coyote wanted to have power like earth-initiate, and he had also got bored with the world being so perfect and harmonious. He decided that everyone should take part in a race that included his son, for the competition would make people start to fear loss. But Rattlesnake was fed up with Coyote's authority and decided to change things. He hid along the edge of the race-track where the runners of the world would pass, and as Coyote's son ran into the lead, Rattlesnake raised his head from his hiding place and bit the boy in the ankle. The boy died quickly, and Coyote realized he was dead. This was the first death.

The next year Coyote searched for his dead son and found Ku'ksu, the first man, and the boy at the spirit house. The boy was eating spirit food, and Coyote wanted to join in because he was hungry.

Ku'ksu put his hand across the food and said: 'But you have brought death and suffering to the world and now every man has to work for his food, then die and be buried until earth-initiate returns.'

Coyote wouldn't listen to Ku'ksu, for he was interested in his own hunger. 'No, you cannot have this food,' went on Ku'ksu. 'You must go back to the world and tell everyone this, and if you want spirit food, then the only way you can eat it is if you are a spirit, too.'

Coyote decided to kill himself, but when he returned to the spirit house there was no food left and his son and Ku'ksu had gone to heaven. It was too late for Coyote to go to heaven, and he was never seen again, except wandering the lands in search of spirit food.

TAIOWA, SOTUKNANG AND SPIDER WOMAN

HOPI, NORTH AMERICA, 1000CE

O F all the Native North American peoples the Hopi are probably one of the least influenced by European and Christian missionaries, and their remote location in northeastern Arizona probably had something to do with their isolation from major colonial influences. Hopi means 'peaceful one', and this almost epic myth reflects the Hopi philosophy of living a peaceful and happy life through honouring the initial harmony of creation, even though, as in many other myths, this turns sour once humans become aware of their inner creative wisdom and power.

To begin with there was only the creator, Taiowa. There were no form, no structure, no shape, no life and no time. These things were only part of the infinite mind of Taiowa, who decided to conceive form. The first thing that Taiowa created was Sotuknang, whom he called his nephew. 'I am your uncle, so you must be my nephew. Go out and create the universes in the correct way so that they can all work with one another.'

So Sotuknang did as he was told, and from the infinity of space he gathered anything that was solid and moulded it into form and arranged these into the nine universes. One was for Taiowa, one for himself and the others for the worlds that were to come.

He returned to Taiowa and asked if he had done his work well. Taiowa nodded and said, 'You have worked the universes beautifully, but now you must make the waters, and divide these equally among all the universes.'

Sotuknang gathered all the waters from the emptiness of space and placed them equally on each universe so that half would be solid and half would be water. Next, Sotuknang had to gather the forces of air to make peaceful energy all around the universes. Taiowa was so delighted with the winds that blew across the universes that he told Sotuknang that the last thing Sotuknang need do was to create life.

Sotuknang was sent to the universe that was called Tokpela, the first world, and from its core he created Kokyangwuti, Spider Woman, who was to remain on that world with him and be his helper. Sotuknang gave her life, and

38

as Spider Woman awoke into her life she said, 'Why am I here?'

Sotuknang explained that there was a beginning and an end, a time and space, shape and form, but no life, and no joy, no movement and no sound. 'You are here because you have the power to create life. You have knowledge and love, you have wisdom and the power to give all those you create that wisdom. too.'

So Spider Woman gathered earth and mixed it with some saliva from her own mouth. From this mixture of clay and spit she formed two beings and covered them with her veil of creative wisdom. To bring sound into their hearts she sang them the song of creation. When she took away the white veil, two beings sat up and asked, 'Who are we, what are we doing here?'

They were twins, and to the first twin, Poqanghoya, Spider Woman said: 'You must keep this world safe when there is life upon it. Go around the world and make it firm and secure, make it like a mother, nurturing and solid.' To the second twin, Palongawhoya, she said: 'You are here to make sure there is order in the world. You must send sound out into the world so that it can be heard everywhere. You will be the echo of the creator, for every sound will become the echo of the creator's sound.'

So Poqanghoya travelled far and wide around the earth and made the land firm for those who would live on it and the wild heights of formlessness into great mountain peaks and ranges. He made some land lush and undulating, soft enough to be worked upon by those people who would know the earth as their mother.

Palongawhoya made the whole earth into a great vibration of sound. As he travelled down valleys and as he rode up caverns and across deserts, he sounded out his music. The deepest centre of the earth vibrated to his song, and the universe shook in waves of tremors as the music stirred the farthest corners of time and space. He made the world his instrument of sound that would carry the love and harmony of the creator everywhere and to everyone. Taiowa was very pleased with his own song now that everything was in tune and vibrated in harmony.

So Spider Woman sent the twins one to each pole of the world's axis to make sure they kept the earth rotating at the right speed and at the right time. Poqanghoya, who lived at the North Pole, was given the power to keep the world in shape and form, while Palongawhoya, who lived at the South Pole, had power to govern the winds and the weather and to sound out a warning if harmony was disrupted.

After Spider Woman had created the plants and the trees and the birds and the animals and had covered them with her veil of creative wisdom, Taiowa was pleased with the work Sotuknang and Spider Woman had done, and he said: 'Now everything is ready for human life, now you must create people.'

This time Spider Woman used four different colours from the earth – yellow, red, white and black – and she clothed the eight mud shapes with her white veil of wisdom and sang her song of creation. Four were in the form of Sotuknang and four in her own form. It was at the dawn of creation in the dark purple light that these first beings came to life. Then, at the yellow light, they began to move and the breath of life entered their bodies. Soon the sun appeared at the time of the red light, the third phase of creation. Spider Woman told her creations that they were meeting their father, the sun. 'This is your creator, and you must not forget these three phases of creation. Purple is the mystery of creation, yellow is the breath of life, and red is the harmony of love.'

But the first people on earth could not speak, so Spider Woman found Palongawhoya and asked him to call for his uncle who had given Spider Woman all her powers. The echo twin sent his music through the centre of the world and across the oceans, and as it vibrated across the universe like a great hurricane, Sotuknang whirled towards them.

'What is it you need from me?' he asked.

'All the people I have created are properly formed with shape and colour and movement, but they cannot talk. Please can you give them speech so that they can enjoy their life and reproduce themselves and thank the creator for their life?'

Sotuknang nodded and gave them the power of speech and the wisdom of creativity. But before he returned to the universe, he sternly reminded Spider Woman and the first people that they must always respect and honour the creator and live in peace and harmony and use their wisdom for the good of the world.

The first peoples of the world knew that the earth was their mother, and when they found corn that grew on the earth to feed themselves, they believed that the corn was another aspect of their mother. The first people who lived on Tokpela, the first world, were very happy. But things began to change because people began to forget the wisdom and guidance of Spider Woman, Sotuknang and the plan of the creator.

The talker came along in the form of a bird, and he talked and talked and talked about the differences between everything. So the animals drew away from the people, and people began to draw away from each other, some refusing to believe the wisdom and peace of the creator now that they knew they could be different.

When Sotuknang heard of this he told the people who still believed in the creator's plan for the world that a new world must be made and the old one destroyed so that they could be happy again. Sotuknang led them to the great ant hills and told them that they must live with the ants while he destroyed everything that was the world. 'You'll be safe here, but you must learn from these ants. They live happily and peacefully with each other, and they obey the creator's plan.'

So the people went down into the ant chambers, and Sotuknang destroyed the world according to Taiowa's command. There were fire and volcanoes, hurricanes and tidal waves. Fire, air and water became one, and the outer world burned up in a vortex of energy. All that was left was the ant city with the people safely inside the deepest part of the earth.

Their emergence to the second world was fraught with similar problems, for now they were separated from the animals and they built their own homes and made their own food. They began to want more things for themselves and to trade and to forget to sing and enjoy their life and praise their creator. Instead they got greedy and were only happy when they gained at the market or stored more goods than their neighbour. The people began to irritate each other and to want more than their friends or be better at things than the next village, so they began to have wars and to fight.

There were still a few people who sang to their creator, and the wicked people laughed at them so they had to stop singing out loud and only do it in their hearts. But Sotuknang heard it still through the vibrations of the great threads of the earth and realized how selfish the people had become apart from these few. Again, he told the few people to stay safely in the ant's world while he destroyed the second world. When the few chosen people were safely underground, he told the twins, Palongawhoya and Poqanghoya, to leave the North and South Poles. Almost as soon as they departed, the world spun out of control. Mountains and seas churned and the world began to spin further and further away into space away from the great sun.

The third world was as difficult to live in as the last. When the people emerged from the underground world of the ant people the twins had put the earth back onto its orbit and it was spinning at the right speed, but on the third world, people spread out too quickly, and civilizations moved forwards too quickly. There were big cities and countries, and people preferred to make boundaries around them. Most people forgot the plan of the creator and the wisdom they had been given. They thought only about themselves and became influenced by the powers of wicked individuals who taught them how to use their creative wisdom to create weapons and have wars, just like in the second world.

For the fourth time Sotuknang realized he must destroy this world. With the help of Spider Woman, he saved those who still used the wisdom of the creator in the way that they had been told, and this time the world was destroyed by a great tidal wave. The oceans rose and the ice melted at the Poles, until all was water and the continents sank beneath the seas. The rains came and did not stop. The good people had hidden in a huge reed with Spider Woman. This giant reed floated on the water and after many years the people were happy when they saw land, and they danced and sang and believed that this was going to be the fourth world.

Spider Woman told them this time they would have to struggle to find the fourth world, and she said, 'Keep your spirits open to the place of emergence. I can do no more for you. But if you truly seek this place you will find it.' She wished them luck, and they continued on their journey crossing oceans and seas finding lands but knowing these were not the places of emergence.

Then they came to a place where the water made a gentle current and guided them on to a sandy beach. Sotuknang appeared in front of them and told them they had reached the place of emergence. 'You have arrived. This is the world complete. But it has both beauty and pain, suffering and love, happiness and despair. This time it has everything for you to choose from. But you must separate and follow your own star until it guides you to a place. There you will settle and determine whether the plan of creation will work.' This was the fourth world, the present world. It is called 'world complete', and this is our world as it is now.

RAVEN

CHUCKCHI INUIT, NORTH AMERICA, 1000CE

IN many Inuit (Eskimo) creation myths Raven is the primary creator, but in this particular version, Raven is a rather useless side-kick for the creator himself. Although Raven is entirely dispensable in this version, he did become known here as the first 'creature' of creation and therefore closest in spirit and form to the creator himself. This myth, like many other Inuit myths, assumes that the land is already in existence, and it is the duality of light and dark rather than of form and space that establishes creation.

Before time began there was only darkness and two lands, called Lu'ren and Qe'nievin. One day, the creator became bored with the darkness and began to work out how he could make sunshine. He decided to create Raven and told him to go and peck around in the east and set free the morning light. Raven flew to the east and pecked and pecked, but the sun did not rise. He returned to the creator and said, 'I pecked and pecked but I could not make any light.' The creator was angry and sent Raven away. So now Raven would have to search for his own food.

Next the creator made the wagtail, who was beautiful and bold. The wagtail also went to the east and pecked and pecked and began to wear out his beak with all his pecking. Finally, he made a tiny hole in the east and rushed back to tell the creator what he had done. But the creator ordered him back to the east.

'You must peck some more – this tiny hole is not big enough.' Wagtail went on pecking until he made a large hole in the mantle of the sky. Suddenly the dawn burst through the hole and light began. But the poor wagtail was exhausted from so much pecking. His feathers had fallen out, and he was thin and starved with hunger. His wings dropped off, and so he returned to the creator on his bird's feet. His claws were ragged and his beak withered. The creator anxiously asked if he had completed the job. 'Yes, yes. I pecked and pecked, and now there is light all over the earth.'

The creator was so pleased that he gave the wagtail new feathers and made his beak beautiful again. He even gave him a house under a grass hummock so that the worms that lived under the earth would became his food. Order was gradually being established now that light was feeding the earth.

The creator then proceeded to make people out of seal bones and scattered them across the earth. But he needed more messengers to travel between heaven and earth to keep him up to date with what was happening in the world. First, he tried sending other birds. The ptarmigan and the polar owl were unsuccessful. Birds seemed to have no sense of the importance of their mission, he thought, so he decided to create the arctic fox and the wolf. These creatures would be brave predators among the cold wastes of the Arctic, but both were terrified of mankind and would not go near them or bring back any news, so the creator sent them away to scavenge forever on earth.

Finally, the creator realized that he would have to go to earth himself and find out what was happening. When he arrived on earth and saw that men and women did not dare to look at one another nor even to sit down together, he brought them to a cold place and took the man and placed him on top of the woman so that they might enjoy each other's warmth. This was the beginning of humankind.

PUANA, KUMA AND ITCIAI

YARURO, VENEZUELA, 1200CE

THE valley of the Rio Capanaparo in Venezuela is home to the Yaruro people and their worship of a great goddess, Kuma. Only the shamans are able to get in touch with Kuma and can travel the same route as the soul's journey to where she lives in the land of the giants to the west. There are many versions of this myth; this is perhaps the simplest.

In the beginning there was nothing. But Puana, Kuma and Itciai came into being first. Puana, the snake, created water. Itciai, the jaguar, made the earth, and Kuma created all the people on the land. She wanted to be impregnated in her thumb, but Puana told her that was not the way to produce children, so she was made pregnant the right way, and the first child was born. He was called Hatchawa.

Puana made a bow and arrow for the boy and taught him how to hunt and fish. Hatchawa taught the people everything he learned. Kiberoh was also created at the same time as Kuma, and she carried fire in her breast. At Kuma's request she gave it to Hatchawa, but when Hatchawa wanted to give fire to the people, Kuma refused to let him, so the boy threw live fish into the heart of the fire so the hot coals spread across the land far and wide. The people grabbed at the burning coals and ran away so that they could start their own fires.

Horses were given to the Yaruros, but they were big and fast and the Yuroros did not dare to ride them. Kuma taught the women everything they know. She married the sun, and he taught the men everything that they know.

The sun travels in a boat from east to west. At night the sun visits Kuma's land. The stars are Kuma's children and they travel only at night. The moon is the sun's sister, who travels in a canoe across the sky.

AMANA

CALINA, SOUTH AMERICA, 1500ce

THE origins of this myth are obscure, and as with many South American myths they have been retold many times. The historical significance of European influences on most of the ancient cultures of South America has undoubtedly distorted many of these myths from their original form. This is an example of how the sun and moon became such powerful creative forces in the earlier ancient belief systems of South America.

To begin with there was only darkness and the emptiness of space. This was the floor of Amana's kingdom. Amana was the first being in the universe and her kingdom in the primeval waters was the Milky Way. She would dance through the great ocean of the Milky Way with other creatures from the watery emptiness – fish, otters and whales. The turtle was her ally and she would sit astride his back and travel across the Milky Way with her mermaid's tail streaming out behind her. In the void of the vast reaches of her ocean, volcanoes sent out great streams of lava, and rock floated around in space to become planets and stars. Amana made some of these planets beautiful lands and covered them with seas and mountains, trees and plants.

But her first creation, the sun, was also her rival and her greatest enemy. Everywhere she tried to create life, the sun burned the earth and killed the creatures and plants she had put there. The fire-serpents that destroyed the moon left only ashes behind. But the earth itself she saved from the sun's fire-serpents by plunging their fiery tongues into the ocean as they came blazing down to the earth. These fire-serpents still sizzle and boil under the surface of the earth and come to the surface sometimes as volcanoes and whirlpools.

To make sure that the sun could never have such power and destruction again, Amana created Tamusi (light), and Tamulu (darkness). Tamusi and Tamulu hated one another, but because they could never escape from each other as light cannot exist without dark and dark cannot exist without light, they agreed that while Tamusi ruled the day, Tamulu would sleep, and when Tamulu rose for the night Tamusi would take his turn to sleep.

In the daytime Tamusi attacked the fire-serpents as they rose out of the earth's crust. He would take his sword of lightning from its sheath and slash the serpents into fragments that scattered in the sky to become comets and shooting stars.

In the darkness Tamulu smothered the fire-serpents with his black cloak. Amana then ordered Tamusi and Tamulu to people the world now it was safe from the sun. Tamusi created children of the day – animals, insects and humans; and Tamulu created the children of the night – dreams, monsters, demons and beasts.

WATER-BEETLE AND THE GREAT BUZZARD

CHEROKEE, NORTH AMERICA, 1500CE

HERNANDO de Soto visited the southeastern area of the United States in 1540 and discovered a highly civilized and settled agricultural society. Some of these people's early rituals seemed to be connected with those of the Aztec empire, and even the rather unusual vision of a universe made of three different layers like a cake and held together by five strings is out of character with the usual myths of the Native American peoples. The Cherokee were the largest tribe in this part of the United States, until gold was found and they were expelled from their lands.

Once all was water. The animals who lived above the water had very little room to live, so they wondered what was beneath the water. The little water-beetle offered to go and see if he could find out. He swam all over the top of the water but he could not find anywhere solid to stop to sleep. So he dived to the bottom and brought to the surface some gluey mud, which began to spread all around until it became the island called the earth. Someone quite clever remembered to fasten this island to the sky with four cords, but no one knows who this was.

To begin with the earth was flat and very wet and sticky. So the animals sent down the buzzard to make the earth ready for them. As he flew down near the still soggy, wet surface of the earth he began to grow tired and his wings flapped too close to the ground. When he reached Cherokee country he became exhausted. Wherever his wings touched the ground he made valleys and where his wings lifted up to the sky he made mountains out of the mud that was dredged up with his dragging wings. The animals were worried that the whole of the earth would be mountains and there would be no flat land nor lush green valleys, so they shouted at him to return. He turned around just in time, but the Cherokee country is still mostly mountainous.

The animals had done a good job with the surface of the earth, but their one mistake was that they didn't place the sun far enough away from the earth in the sky. It was so hot that it scorched the crawfish on his back when he swam in the water and crawled onto the rocks. For ever after he has always had a red back, which reminds all the creatures to keep out of the sun or they will get burned, too. So the conjurers played a trick on the sun when it wasn't shining and raised it up seven hands high until it was just beneath the arch of the sky. Now every day the sun wanders across under this arch and returns at night to the other side of the arch to start his journey again.

No one knows who created the animals and plants. They were just there. The animals were told to keep awake for seven nights at the beginning of creation. Most of them fell asleep because they were too tired. Only the panther, the owl and several others were still awake after seven nights, so these were the creatures who were allowed to see in the dark and to prey on the animals who had fallen asleep.

Men came after the animals and plants, and at first there were only a sister and brother, until the brother hit the girl with a fish and told her to create children. In seven days a child was born and every seven days after that another and another child was born. But the world could not accommodate so many children, and so women were only allowed to have one child in each year rather than every week.

According to this particular myth, the earth will one day grow old and die. The cords will snap away from the sky, and the world will sink into the sea. All will be water again.

DJANGGAWUL

ABORIGINE, AUSTRALIA, 1600ce

DREAM Time and the beginnings of the world are the focus of the cultural mythology of the early Aboriginal peoples. For the Walumba people on the northernmost tip of Australia, the wonders of Djanggawul, the brother and his sisters, are vividly celebrated by the entire people on a regular basis. The myth recounts how the sisters originally played the most active role in creation, with their endless ability to produce people, animals or plants via their own incredibly large penis-like genitalia. The removal of their genitalia by their brother meant that man was now the superior creator. From then on, for the Walumba peoples, women played second fiddle in the evolution of humans.

There was sea, land and sky in the beginning. And on the land were animals and plants and trees. But man was not there. Far out to sea there was an island called Bralgu, the Island of the Eternal Beings, which later became the Island of the Dead. It was here at Bralgu that the Djanggawul lived. They had many sacred objects, drawings and emblems that they called 'dreamings' and they left many of their 'dreamings' on the island as sacred paintings, and rituals for the people who were to come.

The Djanggawul were three children of the sun. The two sisters, Bildjiwuaroju and Miralaldu, had enormous genitals, both male and female combined, so they carried these around in their arms or let them drag along the ground, when they left trails across the sand. But Djanggawul-brother had only one gigantic penis, which he hauled along after him.

One day they loaded their bark canoe with 'dreamings' and sailed across the ocean from Bralgu to arrive at the shore of the new earth that was still uninhabited by people. The sun's children began their journey inland, and as they travelled, creatures and plants were constantly being created. They made many sacred places and left their 'dreamings' everywhere. At all these places they established their own cult in readiness for the peoples who were to be created from their own offspring.

When night came the sun-children made a camp, and the two sisters fell asleep by the fire. Djanggawul-brother went hunting, but when he returned he cut off the enormous genitals of the two sleeping sisters leaving only vagina-shaped wounds. The next morning they carried on creating beings for their world by copulating with Djanggawul-brother. The two sisters had to follow him everywhere and could produce children only when Djanggawul-brother decided. The boys they created were put into the grass so that when they grew up they would have whiskers and hair. The girls they created were hidden under a mat so that they would not grow any hair and would have smooth bodies because girls were sacred.

The two sisters remained eternally pregnant as they travelled, following Djanggawul wherever he chose to go. And so it is for all women with their men.

MULUNGU AND THE CHAMELEON

AFRICA, recorded c.1700CE

THIS myth comes from the Yao peoples, who live on the edge of Lake Nyasa in Mozambique. The Yao are very different from other neighbouring peoples who have a more 'skywards' beginning for their creation stories. The Yao's vision of emergence in this particular myth is that humans came from the water to disturb the tranquillity and harmony of eternity.

The only existence in the world to begin with was Mulungu and the harmonious animals of the world. There were no people. Mulungu had created the world and everything in it, but because he had no form nor shape he was unable to have any physical contact with the worldly harmony that he had created and thus had so far not created mankind.

But one day the chameleon set a trap and put it in the great river. The next day he returned and found the trap was full of fish, which he duly took home and gorged upon.

The second day he set the trap, but this time there were no fish for his supper. 'Oh well,' he shrugged.

On the third day when he pulled the trap from the river there were two small people in it – a man and a woman. The chameleon didn't recognize these particular creatures so he thought he had better take them to Mulungu to find out what they were. Mulungu peered into the trap and nodded wisely. 'Take them out. If you let them loose on the earth they will grow.'

So the chameleon shook the two small people out of the net on to the ground, and the man and woman grew tall. Mulungu and the chameleon watched the people to see what they did in the world. First of all they made fire by rubbing two sticks together. But the fire turned into a ball of flames and set light to the bush. As it swept across the forest, the animals had to escape. So the people caught some of the animals and killed them, and roasted the animals over the fire. The next thing they did was to eat the dead bodies, which were all burned and charred. But the people must have liked burned things, because now they wanted to kill more and more animals and burn them in their fires and eat them, too.

Mulungu was horrified. 'They keep burning all the animals, they are killing all my creatures!' So the beasts and animals ran away to the jungles and forests and across the wide open plains where people could not follow. The chameleon went to live in the highest trees.

Mulungu was disappointed with the way the world was going. He said to the spider, 'I'm off. Show me how you climb up so high'.

The spider said, 'It's easy. Here's how.' So the spider spun Mulungu a beautiful silk thread that led to the heavens, and Mulungu climbed up and went to live in the safety of the sky. Man's cruelty had sent the earth's creator to live as far away as he possibly could.

TWO

SUN, MOON, HEAVEN AND EARTH

FOR ANCIENT CIVILIZATIONS the problem of explaining the weather, the rhythms of the sun and moon and the changing forces of nature and the stars was easily solved through mythology. Myth was either a way of reasoning with these elemental forces or a projection of belief systems and rituals that revolved around the cycles of nature. The myth-makers' imagination was as powerful as the very mysteries they were attempting to resolve. The sun and moon were the most potent and obvious forces apparent to many of the early civilizations, and because they held the magic of life and the ebb and flow of nature revolved around their movements in the heavens, both luminaries reflect more than just light in the myths across the continents. Whatever the weather, the constant comforters in early humans' existence were the heavenly bodies and as much a part of their daily lives as the food they ate. Strangely, these are the very things from which we now seem completely to separate ourselves.

RA

SIRIUS, the dog-star, and the sun were the most important heavenly bodies for the ancient Egyptians because together their placement in the sky marked the start of the year. In most Egyptian mythology Ra is responsible for the creation of the universe in his first manifestation as Atum (see page 14). However, the sun itself was originally known as Ra, and only later did Ra become the name of the god. Ra had many different names and forms, but the journey he took every day across the sky in his boat is perhaps the most evocative of the search for a meaning behind the sun's presence.

Another version of the myth suggests that Ra was born to die at sunset. Each morning he was merely a child, at noon he was a youth full of life, and as the afternoon wore on he would grow older, until at sunset he was an old man, ready to die as darkness fell upon him.

The dog-star, Sirius, was known as Sothis to the ancient Egyptians. Plutarch used the name Sirius for the Nile, and the star was an important celestial marker in the heavens for the time when the Nile was liable to flood. This usually coincided with the time when the star was lying above the horizon in the east just before sunrise. The Egyptians believed that it was the combined strength of the sun and Sirius that led to the very hot weather that followed. (This period is still known as the dog-days after the dog-star.)

The universal goddess, Isis, was linked with Sirius, and she was also known as the 'lady of the star' and Sothis. But Sirius is not a single star – it has a dark, foreboding partner called Sirius B. Osiris was originally associated with this dark partner for Isis, and one of his titles was 'the black god'. The new year alignment of the sun and Sirius was a highly important omen for the ancient Egyptians. It was then that both Isis and Osiris would appear in the sky to restore eternal life for the gods and to welcome the regeneration of the waters of the Nile.

When Ra existed the world was a very different place. Both men and gods lived side by side and the universe was known as the First Time. Ra ruled the earth with his daughter Ma'at, who was the arbiter of justice and honour. Ra would rise every morning after breakfast and board his sacred boat, which scudded across his kingdoms. With his scribes, he would travel across the twelve segments of his realm, and spend one twelfth of the daylight time in each one. But Ra became tired and worn out from his life on earth and longed to go back to the skies and let someone else rule the earth. His granddaughter, Nut, took on the form of a great cow, and he climbed on her back and reached up into the heavens where he has stayed ever since. Once he was gone, Thoth, the moon-god, took over and ruled the earth.

Each morning Ra would now set sail in his *manjet* boat (the barque of millions of years) and would appear in the east above the horizon. In addition to Ra, the *manjet* boat carried all the gods of creation, of wisdom and of the supernatural. Thoth stood at the bow to ward off all Ra's enemies, and Horus would guide the boat from the helm.

But Aapep the serpent lived in the deep waters of Nun and would not let Ra pass across the skies with ease. Each time the god passed by he rose up from the great waters to destroy the sun. This conflict between Aapep and the gods was never-ending, except for times when darkness fell across the lands when the fire of Ra should have been shining. This was when the serpent eclipsed the light and dragged Ra down to earth to be devoured. Yet Ra seemed always to escape and return to his journey across the heavens.

Throughout the night Ra had a ram's head and his name was Auf (corpse), and then he travelled on the *meseket* boat (the night barge). This night barge was made up of a crew of stars who were seen only for a short period each night. These stars were never weary, and left one by one to visit the west to be one of the night crew. The day barge was made up of those stars that never seem to set, but because of the fierce light of the sun they cannot be seen during the day, even though they are there.

Throughout the twelve hours of darkness Ra would visit his twelve kingdoms, but these were inhabited by evil demons and monstrous snakes, which sought only to capture the boat to prevent Ra from bringing light to the world.

INDRA,
THE RAIN BRINGER

VEDIC, INDIA, 1000BCE

THE Aryans were a warrior people who invaded India from previous migrations that had spread from the west into the steppes of central Asia. They had an easy conquest over the agricultural and peace-loving pastoral Dravidians and brought with them their own beliefs and mythology, which merged with the earliest surviving myths of around 4000BCE. But the Aryans had never been settlers, and their gods and mythology were connected not with the earth but with the universe itself. The Veda were a collection of hymns or poems that appear to have been completed by 1000BCE, and they are the main source for most of the Vedic mythology that grew to prominence until the emergence of Hinduism.

Indra was the storm-god and also the bringer of rain to the arid Indian countryside. He was the most respected and best known of Vedic gods and held his powerful position at centre-stage of Indian mythology for over a thousand years. As the Thunderer he carried a thunder-stone called Vajra in his right hand. Indra was like an Aryan warrior king, fair complexioned and golden haired, and he charged around on his horse, boasting, drinking and hurling himself around the universe. He was known to be a womanizer, and because he was so potent and so full of irascible energy, even from the moment he was born, he was destined to be a key god in the saving of the mortal world. For all his self-importance, he was highly regarded as the god who gave the breath of life to mankind.

When Indra was born, the demon Vritra had imprisoned the cloud-cattle so there was no rain. Drought and famine were spreading across the country, and the people were imploring the gods to help them destroy Vritra. Indra was an impulsive and energetic warrior from the moment that he was born. One day, as he stormed around the universe, he heard the mortals in their quest for someone to save them from the evil Vritra. Now Indra was rather fond of *soma*, the wonderful drink that ensured the immortality of the gods, but it also gave him enormous virility and power and filled him with such energy that he was totally addicted to it. Tvashtri was the magician who crafted the magic bowl that constantly replenished itself with *soma* as soon as a god had drunk from it. Tvashtri had also made the thunder-stone that Indra would flash around his head and brandish in front of him when he was feeling particularly full of himself.

Indra knew that he would have a mighty battle against the demon, so he snatched the whole bowl of *soma* from Tvashtri and drank gallons and gallons of the immortal brew, until he filled up two worlds' space with his power and mightiness. He grabbed the thunder-stone and set off to fight the demon. The heavens shook, and many of the other gods retreated as Indra drew closer to the demon in the sky. But Indra was so intoxicated and energized by the *soma* that he stormed on towards the fortress. With his thunder-stone he destroyed the ninety-nine palaces, found the evil demon and quickly finished him off with one mighty blow of the stone.

He released the cloud-cattle from their prison and torrents of water flowed down to earth, filling the river-beds and flooding the valleys. Each year the battle is repeated. When the drought comes, it is Vritra who steals the clouds and Indra who releases them so that it might rain again at the end of the summer.

AGNI, BRINGER OF THE VITAL SPARK

VEDIC, INDIA, 1000BCE

AGNI was the fire-god of Vedic mythology, and, like Indra, he arrived with the warring Aryans and was an equally powerful deity. For a while he rivalled Indra's might, but he developed his own mythology, symbolizing the vital spark that enflames life, whether it is in humankind, in creatures or in the trees. Agni was the brother of Indra, and there are many versions of how he came into being. As Indra's brother he was born from Privithi and Dyaus and, like his brother, was born fully grown and insatiably hungry. Fully mature, he at once set out to feed himself, and the first thing he ate were his parents. Still ravenous, he grew seven tongues to lap up the offerings of clarified butter that had been poured on the sacrificial fire.

Agni was the god of all kinds of fire, from the fire of anger to the spark of inspiration. He was also the originator of sacrificial rites, and he mediated between the gods and mortals by sending up columns of smoke to guide the gods to the sacrificial places. He was also re-born each time he was kindled, and when any mortal dared to poke a fire he was disturbed and enflamed into either a rage or billowing smoke.

His fire consumed as well as enflamed, but he was allowed to eat whatever he wanted because he earned a special dispensation so that whatever he ate, he remained pure. In turn, he also purified everything he consumed. This dispensation was given by the great sage, Brighu. Brighu had stolen a beautiful girl called Puloma from an *asura* (demon) and found himself the centre of some fiery attention. Agni's greatest gift was that of seeing and knowing everything in the universe – quite a common characteristic of sun- or fire-gods. After Puloma's disappearance, the furious demon asked Agni to tell him where his consort was. Agni was always truthful, whether to demons, gods or mortals, and he told the demon that the sage, Brighu, had stolen his bride-to-be.

When Brighu found out that Agni had ratted on him, he instantly put a curse on Agni. For the whole of eternity he would eat everything in the universe, pure and impure, but he would never be satisfied, no matter how much he ate and for how long. Agni quite shrewdly persuaded the jealous sage that as he was the god of fire, he had only spoken the truth. Would Brighu prefer it if the gods told lies rather than the truth? Brighu relented, and although Agni was still to suffer the torment of consuming everything that was put before him, whatever he ate would become pure as soon as it touched his mouth.

When the world ends, Agni will eat up all creation and there will be no more lies, no more darkness; there will be only truth.

USHAS, RATRI AND THE ASWINS

IN Vedic mythology, Ushas and Ratri were sisters of Agni. Ushas was the dawn, and Ratri was the night. The Aswins were the harbingers of Ushas and preceded her each morning in their golden chariot drawn by two horses. The Aswins were young, virile and handsome, and they had the power to give youth and virility to men.

Ushas was beautiful and inspired many poems and hymns. She was dressed in crimson or carmine-pink robes and each day would open the doors to heaven and bring light to the world. She wore a golden veil and was forever young, waking sleepers and bringing songs to the birds in their nests. Ushas also brought wealth and happiness to those who were good, yet left the wicked to sleep for eternity. Her other gift to mankind was time, its downside being that it brought with it age and mortality.

Her sister Ratri, the night, wore dark robes covered with twinkling stars, and she was never afraid when she came to the world, because with night, humans could sleep and cattle rest. Ratri was invoked for protection against robbers and wolves, and people would use her cloak of the night and pray to it so that they could be taken safely across her shadow. Once her shadow is cast, she wakes her sister Ushas and tells her to return.

SOMA, THE MOON-GOD

SOMA was also known as Chandra in Hindu myth and was the god of both the waxing and the waning moon.

Surya (the sun) nourishes Soma with water from the ocean, which he brings him when he is exhausted by the many beings who feed on his light. This is when he is waxing. During the other half of the month 36,300 deities feed upon Soma to assure themselves of their immortality. Creatures – animals, insects and mankind – also make use of the watery light when he begins to wane again.

Soma was married to the twenty-seven daughters of Daksha. But Soma preferred one daughter above all the others, Rohini. The other wives became madly jealous and went to Daksha to complain about their rejection by Soma. Daksha tried to reason with Soma, but it was no use. Like many lesser gods, Soma received a curse for his arrogance. However, thanks to the pleading of the other twenty-six wives, this lasted for only a cycle of fifteen days.

But Soma freed himself from Daksha's curse and made a sacrifice of a great horse, which protected him from further affliction. Soma felt invincible and was convinced of his potency and importance as a high-ranking deity. So sure was he that he could do more or less anything he like, he abducted Tara, the beautiful wife of the great sage Brihaspati. Brihaspati pleaded with Soma to let Tara return, but Soma was by now enmeshed in his own egotistic passions and felt sure that his universal powers would never be threatened.

Hearing of Soma's crazy abduction of Tara, Indra knew the only way to get her back would be by force. A lengthy battle took place between most of the other gods under the leadership of Brihaspati, and Soma and another sage, Usanas. There were many deadly battles and conflicts throughout the universe, which eventually ended in Shiva's trident slicing Soma into two pieces.

Next there was a stalemate in the heavens, and so Brahma made another appeal to Soma to return the beautiful Tara. Without hesitation he sent her back, mostly because he had grown bored with her but also because she was now pregnant. Brihaspati refused to have her back until the child was born. When he saw the beautiful infant she had created, Brihaspati claimed that it was his. There was nothing for it but for Brahma to clarify the matter and insist that Tara reveal the identity of the true father.

When Tara said that Soma was the true father, Brahma persuaded Brihaspati to take back Tara and forgive her. The child that was born became the father of all the lunar race.

Soma's behaviour led inevitably to disgrace. At first he was punished by Varuna and disinherited from his place in the heavens. Shiva came to his aid, and to honour Soma he wore a crescent moon on his forehead. But Soma was still sent to the outer atmosphere and forbidden to return to heaven. He remained in the cold, nocturnal realms of night, a red flag trailing behind his milky coloured chariot, which was drawn by ten ghostly white horses.

HELIOS AND APOLLO

GREECE, 750BCE

HELIOS was the Greek sun-god, but he was not as important nor as potent as Apollo. Helios was the actual form of the sun that could be tracked in the sky but not the bringer of light. The source of life's energy was deemed to be Apollo's realm, and Apollo was always considered more powerful than Helios.

Helios was the son of Hyperion, a Titan and brother of Eos (dawn) and Selene (the moon). He was the sun-god who symbolized the sun as a star, as it

rose and set in the sky. He galloped across the sky every day in his golden chariot, and every night he sailed around the earth in a golden bowl, on the encir-
cling waters of the ocean. Arriving back in the east just before dawn, Eos
would remind him it was time to rise into the sky and jump into his chariot
again.

His supernatural cattle were a form of the sun's energy, and he gave them
to Geryon, the giant, to protect them against thieves who might want to use
the powerful energy for their own use. His son, Phaethon, was an impetuous
boy who tried one day to ride and steer the golden chariot in the sky. But he
wasn't strong or wise like his father, and he could neither hold the reins nor
steer the chariot, so he lost control. Zeus saw what had happened and quickly grabbed hold of the runaway horses to prevent the earth from being
engulfed with the fire. Phaethon then proceeded to fall out of the chariot and
drowned in the ocean.

Because Helios was such a rather crazed and manic charioteer, his powers
were limited, and the main work of the sun to bring light and life to the earth
was given to Apollo, who shone brightly and beautifully and stirred the world
into growth. Apollo was the light of the sun made manifest, and he had great
powers that could either burn and scorch people to death or illuminate and
guide them. He was both a bringer of destruction and also a healer and a
prophet, best known for his oracular vision of past, present and mostly the
future. Apollo was the son of Zeus and Leto, and his twin sister was Artemis.
Hera was jealous of the birth of the twins to Zeus, and she sent a great serpent to hunt Leto and destroy her.

On the beautiful island of Delos, where the sun shone and the whole
island seemed to be made of gold, the young Apollo borrowed a bow and
arrow from Hephaestus and shot a serpent in the sacred caves at Delphi. In
other accounts he had a fight with the serpent, Python, who was one of Gaia's
offspring. This serpent sent revelations and prophecies through holes in the
rock so that the Pythia, or priestesses, could answer anyone who consulted
the oracle. After killing the great Python, Apollo took its place, and his ora-
cles although always ambiguous, were always true.

Apollo was a fierce and sometimes dangerous sun-god. He was unforgiv-
ing and lived a wild and often cruel life. But Zeus made Apollo pay for his
crimes by employing him as a servant of a mere mortal, and afterwards he
became one of the most dignified and serious of all the gods. In addition to
giving advice at the oracle at Delphi, he played music and healed gods and
mortals. He led the Muses in their dancing, singing and playing, and when he
played the lyre himself, the whole of creation stopped to listen to his voice.
This was the only time that the language of the gods could be heard on earth
to resonate with the divine in man's soul.

CHIRON – THE CONSTELLATION CENTAURUS

THERE are many versions of why Chiron was associated with the centaurs. Sometimes he is renowned as their ancestor and sometimes just as their companion, but more commonly he is said to have ruled over their kingdom in northern Greece.

Chiron was the son of Philyra, a nymph, and Kronos, the first Titan. Philyra had never wanted the attentions of Kronos, and she changed her form into that of a mare to try to escape from him. However, Kronos wasn't above deceit either, and he succeeded in mating with her by changing himself into a stallion. So Chiron was born, half-horse, half-human. Philyra was so disgusted by the child that she urged the gods to change her into anything other than a mortal, and so she was transformed into a linden tree.

The abandoned Chiron was brought up in Olympus by Apollo, who became his foster-father and taught him many arts and skills, including hunting, medicine, music and prophecy. Chiron became wise with this knowledge, and Zeus sent him to rule the unruly centaurs who had a small kingdom in northern Greece. Chiron became the mentor for many other famous Greek heroes, such as Heracles, Achilles and Asclepius.

One night Heracles was passing through Chiron's kingdom on his hunt for the Erymanthian boar. The centaurs invited Heracles to dinner and a centaur called Pholus opened a jug of wine to entertain the assembled party. But the smell of alcohol attracted a group of dissident centaurs who gate-crashed the party and caused a row. Heracles naturally began to fight, and the centaurs fled in different directions. As Heracles chased after the centaurs with his bow and arrows, one of the arrows accidentally hit Chiron in the leg. These arrows had been dipped in the poisonous blood of the Hydra. Chiron was immortal, so he couldn't die from the wound, but it would not heal, and Chiron suffered unceasingly from it. He could not die from it, and he could not cure it. Yet eventually Chiron was released from his torment by a strange twist of fate.

Zeus had been punishing Prometheus for stealing fire from the gods and giving it to mankind. Prometheus' terrible torment was to be bound to a rock, where every day a great eagle would visit him and eat his liver. His liver grew again each night and so each day the torture repeated itself. Zeus announced that the only way Prometheus could be freed was if an immortal agreed to take his place, and on condition that Prometheus wear a crown of willow leaves and a ring on his finger for ever.

Heracles told Zeus that Chiron needed to be released from his own torment and that he should take Prometheus's place. Zeus agreed, and when Chiron died Zeus honoured him and immortalized him by setting him up in the sky as the constellation Centaurus.

POSEIDON

GREECE, 750BCE

THROUGHOUT the history of European art, Poseidon has been depicted as a splendid king, brandishing his triton on a chariot pulled by dolphins. His hair, beard and clothes are the wild untamed areas of the sea itself, and his terrifying and yet romantic image is as ambiguous as the vast ocean.

Poseidon means 'drink-giver', and his Roman equivalent was Neptune. In Greek mythology he was the son of Kronos and Rhea and brother to Zeus and Hades. After the overthrow of their father, Kronos, the three sons joined the other gods in the battle against the Titans for universal power. After the gods won the war, Poseidon was given the sea to rule over, while Zeus ruled the sky and Hades the underworld, although they shared the rulership of the land. In some versions of this myth, however, Poseidon was the original ruler of the universe and was subsequently overthrown by Zeus, who banished him to his underwater kingdom. Here he caused great tidal waves to swallow up the sky and the land. He never succeeded and only eroded the coastlines and failed to drown the high cliffs that mother-earth had built to stop him taking away her land.

For the Battle of the Titans the Cyclopes crafted him a trident, a three-pronged fork, with which he could dig up whole islands and fork earth around from his position in the ocean. The trident was such a powerful weapon that he made new lands from the sea-bed or drowned existing lands. He was angered by the evil of mankind and would furiously hurl his trident at the mountains, causing earthquakes and thunderbolts, shattering rocks and shaking the very bowels of the earth. He was the ocean gardener, forever raking up the rocks and sea and causing tidal waves and great storms. But his fiery nature, so attuned to turmoil and disruption, would at times revert to complete passivity and gentleness.

He could calm the seas with one look across the horizon, and mortals made many sacrifices to him to encourage him to do this more often. Humans generally thought of him as a tempestuous god, and every rough or violent sea was attributed to his anger. Even Hades was terrified that his underworld kingdom might collapse under the virulent antics of Poseidon on his ocean bed.

He mated with mortals as well as sea-nymphs, including the feared Medusa from whose severed head sprang the great Pegasus. When Poseidon came ashore he, too, came in the form of a white stallion riding across the tops of the waves, both graceful and wild. It was said that he gave horses the power to find water where they stamped their hooves on the ground.

But the time came when Poseidon grew bored alone in his tumultuous sea kingdom beneath the waves and longed for a companion. Zeus had chosen Hera to live with him in the sky, and Poseidon needed to find a consort to provide him with the kind of status that his brother enjoyed. But Poseidon was rough and ready in his wooing. He first chose the sea-nymph Thetis to be his partner. But learning of her secret fate – that she would bear a son greater than his father – he abandoned her to a mortal and settled for her sister, Amphitrite, instead.

Amphitrite wasn't interested in the wild and passionate arms of Poseidon, and she escaped on an enormous tidal wave to the Atlas Mountains and in doing so drowned the whole continent of Atlantis. Poseidon, quite sensibly, sent one of his ambassadors to woo her. This was Delphinus, king of the dolphins.

Delphinus was charming, as dolphins are, and he played in the waves and jumped out of the sea, performed somersaults and made gentle noises in the water to convey the message that Poseidon wanted her as his wife. Amphitrite was so enchanted by the dolphin that she really believed that Poseidon would be kind and gentle and behave himself, and she returned with Delphinus to Poseidon's sea kingdom and his bed.

The marriage was an underwater delight. Any mortals out at sea would have glimpsed a moonlit procession of every kind of sea-creature dressed in shining silver and mermen and mermaids dressed in golden water, which fell like silk across their backs. Sea-nymphs rode on porpoises and whales, and it was the one night that the ocean was as calm as a dew-pond.

But after their marriage Poseidon reverted to his old gruff and arrogant ways and still hurled weapons at the cliffs in his fury. He forked up great rocks and shook the earth and lashed the world with storms and sea. Amphitrite became angry, and her unhappiness turned to vengeance, which she took out on mortals. Fishermen and sailors now had to contend with the rage of Amphitrite as well. She could be stopped only by Poseidon, who threatened her with his trident, and her father, who managed to lull her to sleep on the warm west winds.

Poseidon and Amphitrite lived near the island of Evia and had thousands of merchildren, half-human, half-fish, called tritons. And when he could keep Amphitrite contented, for she had as insatiable an appetite for sex as he did, he would go out and guide ships through safe passages and fill the fishermen's nets with endless food.

THE QUEST FOR THE SUN

SOUTH of Shanghai is an area called West Lake, one of the most beautiful, ancient and magical of areas of China. This wonderful myth, which comes from the West Lake region, encompasses both the simple human desire to establish order in the world as well as the ultimate human sacrifice and courage that is needed to guarantee any kind of universal harmony.

Lui Chun was a farmer who lived on the shore of West Lake beneath the purple canopy of Precious Stone Mountain. In the small village beside the great gentle waves of the lake, Lui Chun and his wife, Hui Niang, worked hard and were respected and honoured by the other villagers for their industrious lifestyle. The sun usually rose in the east across the lake, throwing glowing, red, jagged sparks across the water. But one morning a storm blew up just after sunrise. Black clouds gathered across the lake, bringing with them torrential rain, and the sun dropped back below the horizon. Eventually the clouds lifted, but the sky was empty for the sun had refused to rise again.

The plants began to wither and die, the crops turned brown, and the fields of seed failed to ripen. The world grew colder and darker. The wickedness of the night ventured out into this dark world to corrupt and destroy the daylight life.

The people didn't know what to do without the sun, so Lui Chun went to ask the advice of one of the elders of the village.

'Can you tell me where the sun has gone?' asked Lui Chun.

'I think so,' replied the ancient man, who was believed to be 180 years old. 'There are demons who live under the Eastern Sea, and it is they who come out only in darkness. The sun is the enemy of the darkness ghosts, and they will do anything to destroy it for they fear it so much. Maybe they have stolen the sun.'

When Lui Chun arrived home, he told his wife of his plan to rescue the sun before the world ended. Hui Niang helped him prepare for the journey. She made him strong sandals from hemp woven into a lock of her hair, and she crafted a special padded coat to keep him warm. As he left the village boundary, a shimmering light flashed down from the sky and a golden phoenix landed on his shoulder. Delighted by his companion, Lui Chun asked the bird if it would go with him. It nodded.

'I shall not return until I have found the sun. But if I die, I shall become a bright star in the sky as a guide to anyone else who looks for the sun.' And so Lui Chun set off on his perilous journey.

For many days his wife, Hui Niang, clambered to the top of Precious Stone Mountain, looking out for the sun to rise over the horizon, but it was

61

always darkness and endless night. Days and weeks passed, and still there was no sign from the sun and no sign of Lui Chun.

Then one day a brilliant shining star rose into the sky and the golden phoenix flew back to Hui Niang, its golden wings tarnished and its head bowed to the ground. Hui Niang fell down in a faint knowing that her husband was dead.

But Bao Chu was born to her while she lay in a trance, and with each breath of wind the boy could first walk, then talk and with the last gentle gust, as the wind disappeared to the east, he grew fifteen feet tall. His mother told him how the sun had been stolen by the demons and the heroic deed of his father in trying to rescue it. So Bao Chu vowed that he, too, would go on the quest for the sun.

He set off with the same golden phoenix, a thickly padded jacket and the sandals woven from his mother's hair. As he left, Hui Niang called to him: 'Follow the brightest star in the eastern sky. This is the spirit of your father, and he will guide you to where the sun is imprisoned.'

'Do not cry for me while I am gone. Any tears that you shed would make me weak and break my heart. You must be strong, and don't believe anything that you are told about me, do you understand?' Bao Chu kissed his mother's cheek as she nodded, and he left with the golden phoenix to find the sun.

For many days they followed the brightest star in the east. They climbed great mountains and crossed many rivers and precipices. At one village where Bao Chu arrived his arms and legs were covered in gashes from the sharp thorns of the mountain bushes. The same thorns had torn his padded jacket to shreds. The villagers gave him pieces of their own coats, which he called the hundred-family coat. Feeling better in spirit and body, he and the phoenix set off again across the great plains towards the distant mountain ridge that seemed unreachable.

Bao Chu came to a great river, wide and fast flowing. Bravely he stepped out into the water, struggling through the terrible currents and the great white waves that crashed over the boulders and rocks. When he reached the centre, a cold wind raged against him and turned the river to ice. He held the phoenix close to him, and the warmth of his hundred-family coat melted the ice around him. Like an ice-breaker, he forced his way slowly through the river, throwing great chunks into the water in front of him. These turned into icebergs and he jumped across from one to another, until he reached the other side of the terrible river.

At the next village the people wanted to give Bao Chu some gift to help him on his journey. All they could offer him was the soil on which they grew their crops. Each villager put a handful of earth into a huge bag, which he then hung weightlessly from his shoulder.

For many years Bao Chu walked on across the plains, through mountains and dense forests, the wilderness of rock plateaux and always in endless night.

The demons would often try to prevent him from finding their land. They sent him along the wrong path so that he arrived in the Village of Lost Souls, and it was only the perceptive phoenix who saw how they had tricked him and his father before him. Determined not to give in, Bao Chu was still unable to send the sun to his mother, but the villagers would walk to the top of Precious Stone Mountain every day, just in case.

Then one day Bao Chu arrived at the Eastern Sea. Remembering the bag of soil, he began to empty it into the sea. As the soil touched the water, a whistling wind stirred the waves of the sea and the soil turned into a chain of islands that carried on across to the horizon. Bao Chu swam from island to island and when he reached the last one, still determined to find the sun, the island suddenly plummeted to the bottom of the sea and pulled Bao Chu down with it.

On the ocean floor Bao Chu saw a huge cave. A great jagged rock sealed the entrance. He was sure that this was where the sun had been imprisoned, but the cave was guarded by the king of the demons and his army. Bao Chu and the evil king fought to the death. The battle was so intense and so violent that great tidal waves swept across the ocean to the lands. The evil king became dizzy and fell back into the depths of the ocean. Taking a chance, the phoenix flew down on the terrible creature and tore out his eyes with his beak. The army of demons vanished in fear and the king fell dead, impaled on the gigantic sharp splinters of rock at the entrance to the cave.

Bao Chu had little strength left, but gradually he pushed the huge rock away from the cavern entrance and found the sun inside. Weak with exhaustion, he managed to lift the sun up through the ocean, higher and higher to the surface, until he reached the air, but at that moment he fell back into the sea and died. The golden phoenix dived down and caught the falling sun in its wings, just before it sank back into the ocean. Then he carried the sun up into the air again, freeing it from the water. Once above the ocean, the sun let go of the phoenix, rising in the sky through its own powerful energy.

The villagers had been watching from their place on Precious Stone Mountain. They saw the light begin to change colour, first to purple then to deep crimson and magenta, then a golden glow shimmered from beneath the horizon and at last the sun climbed into the sky. Its brilliant light turned all the demons to stone.

The golden phoenix flew back to the feet of Hui Niang, and she knew at once that her son had died. Although she was filled with grief, she was also filled with pride and joy, for Bao Chu had become a hero and returned the sun to the world.

The phoenix always rises with the sun for they are true friends. When the morning sky is filled with reds and pinks and golds, the people always remember the man who returned the sun to them so that the world could be fertile again. The people call the bright star that shines in the east just before dawn the Morning Star, Lui Chun, and a pagoda now stands on Precious Stone Mountain where the phoenix returned at the moment the sun arose from the depths of the ocean.

YI AND THE TEN SUNS

CHINA, 300BCE

THE story of Yi and how he shot the ten suns is well known in Chinese mythology. Yi lived during the reign of Yao, not long after the Yellow Emperor. Some ancient records say he was banished from the heavens with his wife Heng-O and exiled to earth. But Heng-O grew tired of life as a mere mortal, and so this myth also includes the sad tale of how Heng-O flew to the moon to hide.

Ten suns mysteriously appeared in the sky during the reign of King Yao, and changed the whole course of nature so that disaster was imminent. The sky was a dazzling blaze of light that came from the fire and fierce heat of the ten suns. There were no shadows and no rain, and no crops grew. Even the rocks began to melt, and the people could not breathe nor could they find food.

The ten suns were the offspring of Di Jun, the god of the east. He lived in the boiling waters of the Eastern Sea, called Yanggu. From the depths of this deep, boiling ocean there rose a great tree, which towered above the world a thousand miles high. From the tree grew nine great branches, which twined up the tree trunk to the one special branch at the top and this spread across the sky like a pathway. Once the dragon-cart had been tacked and harnessed by his mother, one of the children would climb in and travel up the twining branches to the top of the fusang tree. The dragon-cart crossed the same path in the sky every day, and the sun's journey stayed in a regular pattern so that the world could exist as it did. The mother made sure that each son did as he was supposed to with his dragon-cart, and each day the people kept warm, the crops grew, and the cycle of nature seemed assured.

But the ten sons grew bored with the same route every time it was their turn to take a dragon-cart. One night, in the darkness at the bottom of the fusang tree, where the boiling steam swirled hot mist around them, they drank late into the night, daring to rebel against their stern mother and her intolerable routine. By dawn they were in mutinous mood, and in a drunken ecstasy they climbed the great tree together and burst into the sky, dancing and reeling above the earth. They vowed in their intoxicated state to stay together in the sky forever.

After many days King Yao was extremely disturbed by the ten suns in the sky, and he asked the witch, Nu Chou, to use her sorceress powers to banish the suns from the sky. That night Nu Chou cast her spells and made magic potions and incantations, and people chanted and prayed with her throughout the darkness. But the suns still rose at dawn.

Nu Chou stood beneath the ten suns in defiance, but their heat was too powerful and she crumpled on her stone altar, struck dead by the power of the ten suns.

King Yao prayed to the god of the east for help. But Di Jun dared not defy his own sons, even though he was angry at what they were doing in the sky. So he asked one of the lesser gods to go down and help King Yao.

Yi was both a brilliant archer and a lesser god. His skill was known throughout the heavens. His aim and expertise were unbeatable, for he could send an arrow through the wing of a beetle before you could even see the insect in the air. Di Jun gave Yi a new bow and arrow and sent him and his beautiful wife, Heng-O, to stop the terrible annihilation of the earth by the ten wicked suns. 'Threaten my sons with your bow and ten arrows. That will be enough to stop them burning up the world!'

Down on earth Yi was enraged by the behaviour of the ten suns and what they were doing to the people and the world. Completely forgetting the words of Di Jun, all he could think of doing was to destroy them completely. He stood on the open plains in the glare of the burning heat and aimed one arrow at the first sun. The arrow shot into the sky and right into the heart of the glaring sun, which fell like a stone to the earth. As it fell it turned into a crow with golden feathers. Again he lifted his bow and pulled another arrow from the quiver, again a sun was shot right through the heart of its fire. As each sun fell to earth the air became cooler and cooler, and soon nine golden crows clucked and cawed on the ground. But as King Yao watched the nine suns falling from the sky, he remembered how the one sun they had always loved had ripened their fruit, and warmed their lands after the bleakness of winter. At once he realized that without any sun they would all die. Yao ran towards Yi and quickly stole the last arrow from his quiver and hid it under his cloak. As Yi reached for his last arrow his hand grasped nothing but air. He frowned, looked round and seeing there were no more arrows he put down his godly bow. The people cheered and praised him. Concealed under his cloak, Yao snapped in half the last arrow. Yi had left the last sun to shine, to give warmth and light again.

But Yi could not return to the heavens, for the gods were furious at his destruction of the nine suns. His banishment to earth was a nightmare for Heng-O. She hated the mortal world, for the things she loved best were not to be found there. The worst fear for Heng-O was that living as a mortal meant no return to heaven and only a one-way journey to the underworld. Such was her fear of death that she found out about a god who lived on Mount Kunlun.

Xi Wang lived in the earthly palace of the Yellow Emperor. He had tiger teeth, a leopard's tail and wild unkempt hair, which he disguised with a jade hat. He howled like a wolf and guarded the secret of immortality in a big stewing pot of golden liquor.

Heng-O knew that if Yi could obtain some of the medicine of immortality she would be able to escape the terrible fate of all mortals on earth. Yi agreed to journey to see Xi Wang and to beg him for some of the medicine of immortality. If the old god heard the truth about Yi's fate on earth, perhaps he would help them.

Mount Kunlun was virtually impossible for any mortal to reach, but Yi had still some of his magical powers to guide him, and he managed to cross the abyss of death and the fire mountains of eternal damnation, eventually scaling the great Mount Kunlun itself to enter the cave of the great god Xi Wang.

Xi Wang listened to Yi's story of why he had been sent to earth to destroy the ten suns and his subsequent banishment and how his beautiful wife could suffer no more. Xi Wang went to his secret chamber and returned with a small pouch. He placed it on a special stone altar and whispered to Yi. 'Inside this pouch is a powerful potion. It is made from the fruit of the trees of immortality. These fruits bloom only once every three thousand years, and only give fruit once every six thousand years. This is all I have left. If two people drink it they will remain on earth but become immortal. If one person drinks it he or she will become an immortal in heaven. Be careful and guard it with your life.'

So Yi took the potion of immortality home to Heng-O, and told her how they must take it together so that they could remain immortal on the earth. 'We shall make a special time to drink the powerful potion together. If only one of us drinks it only one of us would become divine, and return to the heavens. Then we would be separated.'

Yi went out to hunt, but Heng-O began to dream of her previous life in the heavens. Each day, as she waited for Yi to return, she became more and more obsessed by her desire to return to the immortal world. She began to resent Yi for bringing her to earth, and for what he had done to the ten suns. It was his fault that she could not return to the place she loved.

Angrily she picked up the pouch and realized how easy it would be for her to drink all the immortal potion herself. There was only one thing she had to do, and that was to consult the oracle. She gathered all her possessions and fled into the woods to see the witch of fortune. The witch pulled out of her robes an ancient tortoise, which was covered in strange markings. The tortoise was a thousand years old. Entering into a trance, the witch recited the words of the tortoise oracle: 'Westward you shall go, far into the sky, far from this wretched earth, go now, go now, go with expectations.'

Heng-O was overcome with joy at hearing these words. She touched the tortoise shell, relieved that her return to the divine world had always been fated. That night she sat alone and looked up at the moon. Without hesitation she opened the pouch and gulped down all the potion of the fruit of immortality.

Her state began to change, and she felt as if she were in dream, floating higher and higher into the sky. She felt light, formless and released from the burden of mortality. As she rose in the air, her formlessness soared into the night sky, up and up, towards her divine, heavenly kingdom. But in her peace and serenity a terrible loneliness overcame Heng-O, and she suddenly understood the true message of the oracle. For now she was floating between two worlds, neither heaven nor earth. She was simply floating in the sky. She could not go back to earth for Yi would punish her, and she could not reach heaven for the gods would reject her for leaving her husband. The only place she could hide was on the moon. For many years Heng-O stayed on the moon, wretchedly pale and cold in her loneliness.

Yi travelled the earth looking for Heng-O. He rode on the wind and lived off the plants and the flowers. Doomed to mortality, he became distraught and angry. For many years he searched for Heng-O, and one day the winds carried him back to the palace of Xi Wang, who took pity on him and granted him immortality as the sun-god. So Yi went to live on the last sun, the one that he hadn't shot down with his arrow, the one that is still shining in the skies even now.

He found Heng-O where she ruled the night from her lonely moon palace of great cold. Yi visited Heng-O twice a month, when they would sleep together, and then spend the rest of their time apart. When the moon is full, Heng-O is alone, but when it seems as if only half of her is there, that is when Yi is visiting her from his own sun palace, the Palace of the Lonely Park.

MANI AND SOL

NORTHERN EUROPE, 200CE

THIS version of the Nordic sun and moon myth follows on from the creation of the world from Ymir's flesh (see page 23) and the subsequent aid from the gods. The embers from the over-heated kingdom of Muspel were used to create the sun and moon as well as the stars.

After Ymir had been dismembered and his body used to create the universe, two bright and fiery embers from Muspel, the kingdom of fire, were given special names and special prominence by the gods, Odin, Vili and Ve. One was called Mani (moon) and the other Sol (sun). The gods put the sun and the moon into two special chariots, which were made to cross the sky. But a man called Mundilfari had a bright idea, as mortals do, and called his son after the moon, Mani, and his daughter after the sun, Sol.

The three gods were so outraged that this mere mortal had the cheek to use the names of their own divine creations that they snatched the two children away from earth and bound them to the seats of the two chariots to drive the sun and the moon forever across the sky.

Because Sol was so hot, the two horses, Arvakr and Alsvin, were given special protective armour, and they appeared like war-horses galloping across the sky. At the end of each day they turned the horizon red, their silver armour glowing with the reflected fire and heat of Sol.

Mani had only one horse, Alsvider, which sometimes came so close to the earth that the moon could reach down and touch those who bathed in his light. One night, when the chariot pulled Mani down to the edge of the river, he snatched up from the ground two children who were collecting water. These he kept to be his companions. They were called Hiuki and Bil, and one was the waxing moon and the other the waning moon.

Dag and Nott were day and night. Odin, Vil and Ve gave Nott a wonderful, richly carved chariot in which she could encircle the heavens, drawn by a black horse called Hrimfaxi. When they saw how beautiful and radiant Dag was, they gave him a chariot, too. The horse was shimmering white and its mane gave off such a compelling light that it reflected the fire of Sol and illuminated the world.

But Mani and Sol did not have an easy time in the sky because they were both being chased by wolves. Mani's chariot streaked through the sky in front of Sol, but Sol was always trying to catch up with Mani's chariot because she knew there was a wolf right behind her. Sometimes the wolves caught one of them and dragged it down to the ground so that the sun was blotted out and there was total darkness in the day. When Mani was caught by the wolf, the night became strangely lit by a ghostly haze and people jumped around and made noises to scare the wolves away.

Now everyone knows that the wolves run, but they still fear that the wolves will triumph at Ragnarok.

IDUN AND THE GOLDEN APPLES

NORTHERN EUROPE, 200CE

NORDIC mythology is vastly complex and often confusing. This story is perhaps the only one about the goddess of spring, Idun, who was the keeper of the apples of eternal youth.

As the guardian of the apples of eternal youth, Idun was regarded highly among the gods. Idun kept these golden apples in a magic basket, and they were to be given to the gods only during their feasts and celebrations. Every time she took one from her basket and gave it to a god, there would always be the same number remaining in the basket. Spring always followed winter, and the apples always magically appeared again. But the giants and dwarfs and other mortals who were faced with old age were jealous of the gods and their golden apples and were often trying to find ways to lure Idun out of Asgard. On one particular occasion, because of a shape-changing giant called Thiassi, who usually spent most of his time as an eagle, spring and Idun became dangerously close to being destroyed forever in the frozen arms of winter.

Odin, Loki and Hoenir, three of the gods, were out hunting and came across a wild ox, which they eagerly killed and began to cook. But each time they lit a fire, roasted the massive carcass and sat down to gorge themselves on the meat, they found that the beast remained uncooked. For hours and hours they left the carcass roasting on the fire, but the meat was still raw and unpalatable. Suddenly an eagle, Thiassi in disguise, flew down from the sky and said: 'It is my magic that has stopped you eating the meat. But if you'll let me eat as much of the meat as I want, then you'll be able to eat your dinner too.'

The three gods could hardly disagree, and the eagle removed the spell from the cooking ox, and the carcass was soon succulent, oozing juices and cooked to perfection. But the eagle had a bigger appetite than they had assumed. It ate the rump, the shoulders and all the best meat, leaving the gods with the scrawny neck, the giblets and the guts. Loki was furious and tried to kill the eagle with a huge pointed stick, which he thrust into Thiassi's back. The eagle was powerful and used his magic to fuse Loki's hand to the stick so that he could not let go nor escape. The eagle (Thiassi) flew up into the sky dragging Loki along with him. For many miles they flew into the cold north breeze as Loki screamed for mercy. The eagle agreed to release Loki as long as he promised to help him steal the magical apples from Idun.

'How do you propose to do that?' asked Loki.

'Just bring Idun out of Asgard with her basket of apples then she can be captured.' Loki nodded and the giant, Thiassi, kept his word and let Loki go.

Loki's charming ways did not take him long to convince Idun that he had found a grove of apple trees growing fruit even more magical than those in her basket. Idly, he suggested leading her to them so she might pick some for herself. Idun foolishly followed Loki out of the safety of Asgard. But once she stood alone in the wilderness, Loki deserted her. The great eagle, Thiassi, swooped down from the skies and grabbed the goddess of spring. He carried her far away to his cold, wintery palace and laughed at the gods, for now he had the secret of eternal youth all to himself.

Idun refused to let him have any of the apples, however. He tried to pick them out of the basket, but each time he reached in the apples would disappear and he touched nothing. It was only the power of Idun that could charge the apples with immortality. The breath of spring was also the breath of eternal life.

Back in Asgard things began to go wrong. The gods were sure that Idun had only gone to see her husband, Bragi, but as the days passed and she did not return, age crept up on them. One by one they discovered they had wrinkles and sagging chins and rambling minds. A grey-haired Odin demanded a conference of all the rapidly ageing gods. But Loki was missing. Their addled brains found renewed strength when they discovered that the trickster Loki had been seen leaving Asgard with Idun. Odin summoned Loki and warned him that he might be the first immortal god to die because of the abduction of Idun. Loki was ordered to return Idun and the golden apples before it was too late for them all.

Loki borrowed Freya's falcon skin and flew to Thiassi's grand palace, Thrymheim. He found Idun alone and desperately cold. So he turned her into a nut and, clutching her in his claw, carried her back to Asgard. When Thiassi returned to his kingdom and found that Idun was missing, he transformed himself into an eagle and chased after Loki and Idun. But the gods saw him coming, and as Thiassi swooped down towards the gates of Asgard a great bonfire was lit on the battlements. Flames leapt up and burned Thiassi's wings, and he fell crashing at the gates of Asgard. Then with one mighty blow Thor crushed his skull with the hammer.

Safely back in Asgard, Idun shared out the magical apples among the ageing gods, empowering them with eternal youth. They feasted and drank to celebrate their immortality, for spring had come to Asgard again with the return of Idun. However, fearing retribution from the giants, the gods threw Thiassi's eyes up into the sky to form a constellation to show their respect and honour for the mere mortal who had dared to steal their precious apples.

THUNDER AND THE ELEPHANT

KENYA, 500CE

A SHORT, simple myth from Africa, which tells how thunder appeared in the sky and how humans ended up destroying the harmony of creation.

There were three beings who lived first on earth. They were the elephant, man and thunder. Although they originally got on with each other, uneasy feelings began to grow when thunder noticed the difference between them.

One day he boomed quite loudly to the elephant: 'This is a very strange kind of creation this man. If he wants to turn over in his sleep from one side of his body to the other, or from front to back, then he does it without getting up or waking up. If I want to turn over, I have to get up first, crash through the clouds and bang around on the ground.'

The elephant nodded. 'Yes, it's a similar problem for me. I'm so big that

I can't flick over from one side to another, I have to get up from my resting place, stand up on four legs and then turn round.'

Thunder's paranoia about the man grew steadily each day, and he became afraid of his power. 'I'm going to leave the earth. It's far safer in the heavens,' he bellowed one night.

The elephant just laughed at him. 'Goodness, man is a tiny creature, not even as big as myself, how can he ever hurt you? You're mad to run away.'

But thunder was already rumbling in the distance. 'Because if he can turn over in his sleep, he may be able to do all sorts of other things that we don't know about. I'm off.'

The elephant watched as the clouds rolled across the sky, carrying great thunder with them, his loud boom disappearing into the heavens. Thunder has stayed there ever since.

Man had watched the angry disappearance of thunder and was actually secretly pleased that he had finally gone. The one thing he had seriously been afraid of was thunder. The elephant was the least of his problems.

So man went into the forest and gathered some poisonous plants because he could do other things than roll over in his sleep. With the sap he made poison, and from the stems he made bows and arrows. Then he dipped the arrows into the poisonous sap. He set off back to the kraal and crept up behind the elephant and shot an arrow into his back. As the elephant fell dying to the ground, he wailed towards the heavens, 'Please take me with you, thunder, please I beg of you.'

But thunder didn't care. He had no pity and no feelings. He only laughed at the dying elephant and shouted down to him, 'No you cannot come here with me. You said man was so small he could never do any harm.'

The elephant pleaded, but thunder only shook his head and the clouds turned black. 'It is your stupidity that has killed you.' And he was gone. So the elephant died and man jumped up and down and made more poison, more arrows, and he killed many things that were created. He became the master of nature because he could do more than roll over in his sleep.

AMATERASU AND SUSANO

JAPAN, 700CE

THERE are very few sun-goddesses in world mythology after the dissipation of the female goddess cults by most of the central Asian, European and eastern patriarchal societies. Yet Amaterasu is a highly respected and powerful mythical deity in her own right, and she is still very important in the Shinto religion. In ancient Japanese life, women achieved status as female-warriors and prophetesses.

The powerful interplay between the sun and moon are essential to the fertility of the world in early Japanese mythology. This myth of Amaterasu's conflict with her brother, Susano, her subsequent self-exile to a lonely cave and the gods' realization that they must restore harmony by tempting her back is an excellent example of how things can go wrong if the balance of sun (purpose) and moon (receptor) are out of alignment.

Amaterasu wore a necklace of light that some say was the Milky Way. She clothed herself in jewels and precious stones that sent off sparkling rays of light and prisms of rainbows dancing on the earth. Amaterasu spent most of her time cultivating silk-worms, spinning beautiful threads and weaving the threads into beautiful gowns. She was the goddess of the sun and her consort was Tsukuyomi, the god of the moon.

At first they lived quite happily together in the heavens, but one day Amaterasu sent Tsukuyomi down to earth to eat with the goddess of food. But the food-goddess couldn't be bothered to serve real food for a deity so insignificant as the moon, so she spat out regurgitated food on the dishes and hoped that Tsukuyomi wouldn't notice. Tsukuyomi had magical powers of his own, and immediately knew what she had done. Angered at being given such foul food, he picked up his bow out of the shadows, and killed her with an arrow of silver light.

He returned to the heavens, hoping that Amaterasu would sympathize with his tale. But Amaterasu was furious and sent him to live in a different part of the sky, where they were separated forever by night and day.

Amaterasu sent down to earth a cloud-spirit to make sure that the food-goddess was actually dead. The cloud-spirit returned with the seeds and rice and plants that had sprouted from the dead goddess's face.

'These will grow very well on earth,' said Amaterasu. She sent the cloud-spirit back to earth to plant some seeds around the world. She also kept some for herself and planted these on the great plain of heaven, convinced that the fertility of the earth and heaven would be assured.

But trouble arrived in the shape of her brother, Susano, the god of storms. Susano usually crashed around the heavens and generally misbehaved. One day, he came to visit Amaterasu on her heavenly plain while she was enjoying her first harvest. Susano's behaviour was an unrelieved irritation, and Amaterasu became worried that she would never get rid of him. He spoiled the harvest feast at the great temple by defecating all over the floor, set the horses of heaven free on the fields, and the crops were destroyed. Amaterasu tried to be calm, but her patience was wearing her out. When Susano eventually threw one of the colts of heaven into the air, it crashed through the roof of her rooms, killing her handmaiden, and Amaterasu could bear no more.

She ran from the palace to a great dark cave, barricaded herself in and pushed great rocks across the entrance so that none could enter. But her exile meant that there was no light, and the universe became perpetually dark. Without the sun nothing could live for long and nothing could grow.

So the eight hundred gods held a council on the river-banks of heaven for seven long months as the world began to decay. The god of wisdom, Omoigane, was the only god who thought of a way to entice Amaterasu out of the cave.

Some of the gods were to plant sakati trees outside and around the cave-mouth. Then they hung prayer-scrolls and precious stones, and food and coloured silk strips on the trees. He asked the heavenly jewel-maker to make a necklace of stars and the heavenly coppersmith to make a shining mirror. They hung the mirror on the tree with the necklace of stars, and Uzume, the dancing sorceress, began to dance naked outside the cave. The other eight hundred gods gathered outside the cave and whirled around in a dance of ecstasy, as if they were celebrating some great event. Amaterasu could hear them from inside her cave. She was curious when she heard their chanting, thumping and beating of drums – but why were they enjoying themselves, especially without her presence?

Carefully, she pushed back the great boulder that was blocking the entrance. Her first light, so golden and warm as it emerged through the jagged rocks would always be the first light of dawn. 'How can you be so happy in the darkness without me?' she demanded from the other side of the rock.

Omoigane leaned towards the cave entrance and whispered, 'We have found a god more beautiful than even you Amaterasu. We can at last enjoy ourselves in the light of such a beauty, even though it remains dark in the sky.'

Amaterasu was even more curious now she had a possible rival. Further and further she crept out, until she saw her own reflection in the mirror hanging on the tree. Believing this to be the most radiant goddess of all, she stepped out from the cave to confront her competitor. In a sudden ambush, the strongest gods seized her as she struggled and fought against the tricksters.

'We need you to shine your beautiful light Amaterasu; please stay in heaven so that the fertility of the earth and of the heaven is assured. We will make sure that Susano doesn't bother you again.'

Amaterasu agreed. 'I am the most exquisite of goddesses, and because there is no other, I shall return as you suggest.'

Her return to heaven brought light and fertility to the universe again, and she showed mankind how to spin silk, grow and cook rice. Susano's fate was banishment to earth, but first he was fined, and had all his nails and hair plucked out. From then on he raged and stormed around the world, destroying as many crops as he could every year. But the light of the sun-goddess was always more powerful than the force of his winds and rain.

Tsukuyomi, the moon-god, was alone in the night sky and without Amaterasu's power he could only reflect her light and sometimes hide his face altogether. As a deity, he became to be regarded as a god of prophecy, and those who worshipped him would try to foretell the future by looking at his reflection in huge mirrors. It was believed to be dangerous to look straight at the face of the moon, for although Tsukuyomi could not blind, like the power of Amaterasu, the moon's ghostly light could drive people mad and fill them with delusions and hallucinations.

PELE, THE GODDESS OF VOLCANOES

HAWAII, 750CE

THE goddess of fire is very much a deity of the Hawaiian islands, and she was linked strongly with the destructive image of woman. She represented the constant outpouring of lava that occurs so frequently on those islands. Pele became a highly regarded deity and is an excellent example of the way in which local people develop a divine projection to suit their particular geographical needs. Volcanoes must be there for a reason, and Pele as destroyer and goddess of the volcano must be respected and worshipped as such.

Pele set off from Tahiti to travel across the universe. She tucked her sister Hi'aka under her arm and sailed in a canoe across the ocean with the aim of journeying as far as she could. When they reached the northern islands of Hawaii, lightning flashed and great bursts of energy erupted in the skies above the mountains. Pele canoed across the sea from island to island in her search to find a place to live, but each time she pushed herself down into the earth to make an underground cavern, the sea poured into the cave. Every time water filled her tunnels to drive her out, she became more and more violent and enraged. Eventually she came to the island of Hawaii and nestled down into the great mountain of Kilauea. The mountain was solid rock and there was no sea beneath it, nor water courses running through it, so that was where she lived.

But Pele still hungered for violence and destruction, and she also needed to find a beautiful mortal to be her consort. One night Pele entered a trance-like state and her spirit left her body. She followed the sound of music across to another island's hula dance. There she took on the form of a beautiful young woman and danced with the young chief, Lohiau, who became besotted with her. For three days they danced, and the young chief was enchanted by Pele's eager responses. She promised him that she would send a messenger to guide Lohiau to her, but she had to return to her island to tend to her land.

Hi'aka had a friend called Hopoe, who grew lehua trees in the groves on the side of Pele's mountain. When Pele returned, she told Hi'aka that she

74

must visit the young chief and bring him back. Pele promised in return she would give Hi'aka supernatural powers and look after Hopoe's lehua trees while she was gone.

By the time Hi'aka arrived at Lohiau's island the young chief had died from love for the beautiful and mysterious woman he had met at the hula dance. So Hi'aka used her supernatural power and caught his spirit as it drifted on the wind. With his spirit restored to his body, Lohiau followed the girl to Hawaii.

But Pele began to feel antagonistic towards her own sister and regretted having sent the pretty girl to fetch her lover. Consumed with jealous imaginings and fears that Lohiau would fall in love with her sister, Pele belched out rocks and explosions of lightning into the sky through her volcanic chasm. Red-hot streams of fire poured out all over the mountainside, engulfing Hopoe in burning rocks and molten lava and annihilating the lehua blossom fields for ever.

Hi'aka's own telepathic powers woke her in her sleep, and she sensed that something terrible was happening. Lohiau had by now become infatuated with Hi'aka and said, 'Hi'aka, you know that I love you. Let's return to my island and forget your sister.'

But Hi'aka refused to deceive or betray her sister, whatever the consequences, and she persuaded Lohiau to follow her to the edge of the great chasm of the volcano where Pele lived. When Hi'aka saw the destruction of her friend's blossom fields, the black smoke and the burning ashes still smouldering down across the valleys, she threw herself into Lohiau's arms. 'Take me away, Take me away quickly!' she cried.

But Pele had already spiralled around the two lovers with her flames of burning black fire and killed Lohiau. Hi'aka's powers protected her from the violent attack, and she swirled like a mist out of Pele's burning core and rose like a sliver of smoke into the sky. For many hours she searched for Lohiau's spirit. Then, glimpsing it drifting on the wind towards his island home, she caught hold of it and returned it to his body. Together they escaped from the anger of Pele and went to live on Lohiau's island, far away from her angry fires.

Pele found better amusement for a while and forgot her treacherous sister when the hog-man came to court her. The hog-man had the power to transform himself into a pig, plants or even fish. He had created a great cloak to wear when he was in human form to hide the ghastly bristles on his back and the pink ears that flopped down his cheeks. Pele teased and taunted him by calling him, 'Pig, and a son of a pig', and their conflict and tests became more and more passionate and dangerous. Sometimes she would overwhelm him with her flames and fire, but he would throw fogs and rains over her mountains and send pigs running across her lands. Then, as the rains fell, everything would turn to mud so that her fires were put out.

But the gods intervened when they realized that now only the sacred fire-sticks were left alight, and they told Pele that she must compromise with hog-man. They divided the land between them, so that Pele had places where her lava could always flow down the great gullies of the mountainsides, and hog-man had places where it always rained and where the land was misty and damp and vegetation could grow.

THE SUN TAMER

HAWAII, 750CE

M AUI is the hero and trickster demi-god of Polynesian myths. His father was a god, and his mother was a mortal. The character of Maui has travelled across Tahiti, to New Zealand, Samoa and the Hawaiian Islands. The cycle of myths that reveals his exploits includes this particular tale in which Maui sets out to tame the sun. This myth appears in many versions across Polynesia, and its widespread popularity in different cultures is suggestive of a far more ancient source.

Maui had a problem with the length of the days and nights. He worried incessantly about his mother, because she never seemed to have enough daylight to finish her weaving and prepare the food for dinner. By the time she was ready to finish one task and start another, the sun would quickly scuttle below the horizon and it would be dark again. Maui decided the reason was that the sky wasn't high enough and the sun had far too many legs, running across the sky faster than it should.

The first thing he did was to move the sky so that it was further from the earth. He found a long stick and poked it into the sky, then he pushed it up away from the earth like a tent-pole. Then he propped up the canopy of the sky on all the mountains tops, far enough away from the fertile valleys and the rivers and the places where men and creatures lived.

But life was still difficult for everyone, including his mother, Hina, and Maui angered by the sun, decided to investigate why the sun was still rushing across the sky so fast.

One day he said to Hina, 'Doesn't the sun care about us all down here on earth? If he manages to run so fast, maybe he has too many legs. I think I'll go and cut some off and tame him to be a better sun.'

Hina shook her head, 'Don't think you can trick the sun. He does as he pleases. But maybe you could visit your grandmother and ask for her help.'

Maui went to visit his grandmother. She cooked bananas for the sun's breakfast every morning. Hina had told him to steal the bananas each time his grandmother put the bunches out for the sun. Then to reveal he was her grandson, when she went looking for the thief.

Maui did exactly as his mother had said. When the old lady put out the bananas for the sun, he stole the bunches. The old lady went to look for the thief and found Maui with the bananas. 'Why have you stolen the sun's bananas?' she demanded.

'The sun moves too fast through the sky and nothing grows, and my mother has no time to finish her weaving. I am Maui, your grandson.'

The grandmother was reluctant to help him at first, but then agreed. 'The only way you can tame the sun is to make many ropes and from these ropes make nooses to trap the sun. I have a magic axe, which is greater than the power of the sun, and you must take this too.'

Maui made many ropes from the strongest coconut fibres and used his sister's hair, which was like wet flax and strong enough to make the nooses, which he twisted into the rope. Then he went to the top of Mount Haleakala, where the sun always began his morning journey, to set traps in the top of the great tree.

Rising from his sleep, the sun stretched out his rays to the sky. But the rays were caught in the nooses in the tree and the sun was stuck. He pulled and thrashed around but his rays were caught fast. 'What are you doing? What is going on? I am the sun. I can do as I please!' shouted the angry sun.

Maui called back to him, 'You must slow down, not travel so fast. There is no time for things to grow or for my mother to finish her weaving. The days are too short and the nights too long.'

'I will not listen to this!' cried the sun and began to struggle in the nooses. Maui quickly raised the magic axe and began to chop off some of the sun's rays that had freed themselves from the trap. 'Stop! Stop! you are destroying my rays!'

'Only if you promise to slow down and make the days longer. And then everyone will like you and you will be the most important thing in the sky.' The sun promised immediately, and Maui set free the rest of the sun's rays so that he could travel across the sky. But now with fewer rays the sun could not move so fast and each day became long enough for plants to grow and Maui's mother to finish her weaving. The farmers and the fishermen were pleased and people began to celebrate each new day and even to worship the sun himself.

THE COLD WEATHER LORD

BLACKFEET, NORTH AMERICA, 1000CE

THE Algonquian-speaking peoples lived in the forests and plains around Lake Itasca, the source of the Mississippi River, in Minnesota. This is their story of the god of bitterly cold winds and snowstorms, whose power must be honoured and never provoked.

Sacred Otter was a buffalo hunter with the Blackfeet tribe. With the coming of the cold winds and the cries of the geese as they headed south, the Indians understood that the cold season was imminent. This was the time for the Blackfeet to travel further into the wilderness of the north to find more buffalo to make thick clothes and provide excellent meat, which would ensure their winter survival. Sacred Otter was one of the lucky ones and had killed many buffaloes, knowing that as the winter moon turned pale and cold it would not be long before the snows came.

One day, as he and the other Blackfeet worked quickly to skin the buffaloes and return to their encampment, dark clouds gathered across the northern horizon; the wind began to whistle cold songs across the blades of their knives. Without warning, a black storm gathered above them and wild clouds screeched down like black eagles across the earth. The blizzard drove hard into their faces, and Sacred Otter and his son hid beneath the carcass of a buffalo to shelter from the storm. The snow whipped across their heads and left ice upon their brows. If Sacred Otter could not find a safer place to shelter they would surely perish.

Sacred Otter began to rip apart the buffalo hide and made a small teepee in which they both took cover from the bitter wind and the snow. The snow drifts began to cover up the sides of the little teepee and as the tiny lodge became snowed in, the snow provided them with a wall of warmth so they could sleep.

Sacred Otter began to dream. Far away he saw a beautiful teepee. The pinnacle was the colour of gold, painted with clusters of stars that symbolized the northern sky. The sun's image was painted on the back and attached to this was the tail of the Sacred Buffalo. The bottom of the teepee was painted to look like ice, and on each side were four yellow legs with claws resembling those of the Thunderbird. An angry buffalo was painted above the door, and crow-feathers and bunches of bells tinkled and swayed in the breeze.

Sacred Otter stood before the doorway and gazed at the beauty of the paintings. A voice suddenly spoke, 'Who is looking at my teepee? Please, come in!'

Sacred Otter pushed back the door and saw a white-haired man sitting at the back of the lodge. His face was painted yellow and he smoked a pipe, but he would not look up at Sacred Otter. For a long while he smoked on in silence before he spoke.

'I am the Lord of the Cold Weather, and this is the Yellow Paint Lodge, the snow-teepee. It is I who control the blizzards and the bitter winds from the north. I took pity on you because you and your son were caught in my terrible storm. You must take my snow-teepee and its magical symbols and medicines. Use this mink-skin tobacco pouch and this black stone pipe and you will be safe from the storms.' But as the Lord of the Cold Weather began to tell him the songs and the ceremonies he must perform, Sacred Otter awoke from his dream.

By now the storm had begun to turn to sleet, and the wind was less harsh. Sacred Otter and his son crawled out of the small teepee and began the long walk home through the snow-drifts and the white world. For many cold nights Sacred Otter made a model of the snow-teepee and painted it in the way he remembered in his dream. He collected the plants for medicines and magic, and as spring came he constructed a real snow-teepee and placed all the medicines and the mink-skin pouch inside.

The power that Sacred Otter had discovered in his dream made him highly regarded throughout the Blackfeet. That following winter this power was put to the test.

Out hunting buffalo, Sacred Otter and his companions were caught in a snowstorm and were too far away to get back to camp. They urged Sacred Otter to use the magic of the Lord of the Cold Weather to save them. So Sacred Otter made the men go ahead to make a track for the horses, and he placed the women and children on sledges, which were to be pulled through the snow-tracks. After they had begun their journey Sacred Otter turned to the north and the coming blizzard. He took the pouch and the black stone pipe and began to smoke. As he smoked he blew it towards the north, right into the storm, and he prayed to the Lord of the Cold Weather to have pity. Eventually the black clouds and the searing icy snow began to clear away and the sky became blue. But the people carried on fast down the track knowing that Sacred Otter had only held back the storm to let them get home.

Sacred Otter only ever used his magical power once. For if he ever offended the Lord of the Cold Weather, then who knows what he might do next!

RAVEN AND THE SUN

INUIT, NORTH AMERICA, 1000CE

In the myths of the northwest United States and Canada, Raven is one of the major magic-animal spirits that created the world. Even up in the vast arctic and sub-arctic regions of Greenland and Siberia, Raven carries on his wings a supreme supernatural power. In this particular story, Raven has a brother, Raven Spirit, with whom he quarrels about how the sun should be set in the sky.

After Raven had created the world and everything in it he found that people were killing everything he had ever made. Soon there would be little left of his creations. He had been rather surprised by his first creation, Man. Somehow this formidable creature had arisen out of a pea-pod, walked on two legs and asked many questions. Eventually his surprise had turned to acceptance, and Man and Raven had become friends and lived in the sky together. But the creation of more and more humans had got out of hand and Man, who had the ability to think ahead, pointed out that all the time the sun was shining, people were able to do exactly as they liked and get away with it.

So Raven suggested to Man, 'I'll go and take away the sun. If it's always dark they won't be able to kill the animals and some of them will die.'

So Raven set off to the sun, grabbed it from the sky and put it in his skin-bag. Instantly there was darkness across the earth. He carried the sun to a far distant part of the sky, a cloud-village, where his parents lived. Raven found a cloud-maiden to be his wife, and he kept the sun hidden beneath his bed in the skin-bag.

On earth people became very scared without the sun, and they tried to persuade Raven to give it back by offering him gifts of food and furs. At first Raven was untouched by their pleadings and sacrifices, but eventually, bored with their endless whining, he let them have light for a short while. He would hold the sun up in the sky in one hand for several days at a time. People could hunt and get their food, but then, when his arm got tired, he would put the sun back into the bag. Darkness enveloped the world until Raven decided he would let them have light again.

Raven had a brother who also lived in the village. He was called Raven Spirit, and he wanted to return the sun to the people because they lived in darkness and he feared for their souls. For a long time Raven Spirit thought about how he could restore light to the earth, and then a great idea came to him. First, he pretended to die and his body was carried away in a box to be buried. When the funeral entourage had left the grave, he got out of the box and hid his raven mask and cloak in a tree. Raven Spirit crept down beside the stream and waited for his brother's wife. Soon she came skipping towards the stream to fetch water. As she ladled some water from the stream to drink, Raven Spirit transformed himself into a tiny leaf and fluttered down onto the sip of water she was about to swallow. As it trickled down her throat she felt a tickle, coughed and wondered if she had just drunk an insect. When she got home she told Raven, and he said it was probably just a tiny leaf.

Not long after this Raven's wife had a child called Raven Boy. Raven Boy was energetic and noisy and constantly crying to play with the sun. So Raven would take it out of his skin-bag and let the boy have it for short periods, but he was always careful to put it away again. Once the boy was big enough to play outside, he begged and pleaded to play with the sun every day. Eventually, Raven was fed up with the whining child and gave the boy the bag. Alone at last, Raven Boy ran outside and climbed up a tree, put on the raven mask and cloak and flew up into the sky far away.

He heard his father call after him, 'Don't keep the sun forever in the bag. Sometimes it must be dark, but you must let it out so there is light as well.'

Raven Boy flew on to the highest place in the sky where he knew the sun belonged. He tore apart the skin-bag and put the sun exactly in the right place. Then, remembering what his father had called to him and that there must be dark as well as light, he made the sky revolve around the earth. This made the sun and the stars go round with the sky in a constant cycle of night and day.

Raven Boy picked a blade of grass that shimmered with a brilliant light. Just before sunrise he stuck the blade of grass into the sky. It has stayed there ever since as the brilliant star of the morning.

Back down to earth Raven Boy told the people that the sun was back where it should be and it would remain there forever. Raven Spirit no longer possessed the power to fly back up to heaven. Now that the world was more balanced he was losing his sacred magic. So Raven Spirit took a wife, and all his descendants were able to fly across the land. But they never returned to heaven; all ravens lost their magical powers and became birds of the earth.

GLOOSKAP AND THE SUMMER
ALGONQUIAN, NORTH AMERICA, 1000ce

THE trickster-god Glooskap appears in many of the myths of the North American peoples. This Algonquian myth is a gentle story of how Glooskap, for all his deceit, brought summer to the lands of the north, thus enabling the people to cultivate and establish fertility in the world.

Although Glooskap was arrogant and convinced that he could outwit the mightiest of gods, there was a time when he travelled far into the northern lands and actually caused an unwitting change in the weather.

For many days and nights Glooskap had wandered further and further north, until he began to climb across ice-covered rocks and vast snow drifts, which lured him down to rivers and lakes that were frozen wastes. He began to feel hungry, cold and tired, and he feared he might fall into a heap on the frozen land and never wake up. But then he caught sight of a small light in the distant blizzard, and he struggled on towards its suggestion of shelter and, he hoped, warmth.

As he staggered deeper into the blizzard, the light grew stronger until he could make out a huge teepee, so big that it took up the whole of a mountainside. Breathless and with chattering teeth, he hurled himself through the opening, not caring whether he would be eaten alive or thrown back out in the cold. As long as he felt the warmth on his back for one moment, he could escape any trap set for him.

Inside the tent was a great giant, the giant of winter, who merely shrugged his shoulders at the stranger and invited him to sit beside his huge icy chair.

There was no fire, no warmth and no light, except a sharp beam glinting from a huge icicle that hung from the centre of the tent. It was so intense that it hurt Glooskap's eyes. This was not the pain of sunlight, but the pain of ice in his eyes. Glooskap shivered with cold, but giant winter could only offer him his pipe, which he had filled with some intoxicating tobacco. The smoke drifted around the great teepee. Glooskap took the pipe and began to feel warmer within as the smoke filled his lungs and something flowed through his blood like magical fire.

The giant had many stories to tell, and they smoked and chatted together. But Glooskap did not sense the spell that winter had begun to cast upon him. The warmth Glooskap felt from the pipe was only the illusion of heat. Winter was freezing the air and everything around him as he spoke. Glooskap began to feel drowsier and drowsier, and his head began to drop. He fell into a deep sleep.

For nearly six months Glooskap slept, while winter froze the world and kept Glooskap spellbound. But then, as the days grew longer, the frosty bewitchment wore off and Glooskap awoke to find winter gone.

Setting off southwards, he walked further and further across the plains. The sun on his back felt warm and then hot. Plants and the trees were sprouting into life, and everything seemed to be awake. Inspired by the warmth of the world, Glooskap walked on towards the deep forest to look for summer. For many days he followed a narrow path, which led to a high forest that swept a hood of green across the mountains. As he bent beneath low branches of primeval trees and stumbled across roots gnarled by time, he came across a clearing. The glade was filled with light from the sun, and in the middle danced some tiny people, flickering with light and glowing with some inner magic of their own. The queen of these people was summer, the tiniest, most divine creature he had ever seen.

Glooskap snatched tiny summer up in his hand and tied a lasso around her diminutive body. He ran back into the forest with summer clasped to his chest, and the long cord of the lasso trailing behind. The summer-light elves ran frantically after Glooskap, pulling and tugging on the end of the cord as it disappeared into the forest. The further Glooskap ran, the more the end of the lasso was spun out behind him. The elves were soon left behind, with only the end of the cord to lead them in the direction he had gone.

Glooskap ran fast across the hills and forests where the light was warm and the grass was green, but then he decided to walk north again towards the icy lands and the teepee of winter.

Again he discovered the great teepee on the mountainside, entered the ice-cold tent and was welcomed by the giant. He sat beside the giant, who lit his pipe and passed it to Glooskap. This time, as winter began to tell the stories that had charmed Glooskap into such a deep, drugged sleep, Glooskap was prepared and he, too, began to speak. Beautiful summer lay close to his heart, and her warmth and energy produced such a powerful magic that soon winter began to suffer. The more Glooskap talked, the hotter summer became. Sweat slowly began to trickle across his forehead and drop onto his chest, and gradually he began to melt. Slowly winter thawed. The sweat turned to huge torrents of water, which flowed through the wigwam and out across the land. Then his teepee began to melt too and the land lost its cold, white ice. Green plants pushed their way up through the earth. Old golden leaves of autumn were carried down the streams of winter's melted ice towards the rivers. Nature was coming alive, and the birds began to sing and the ground to rustle with insects and small creatures. So Glooskap left summer behind and once more faced south to return home. The summer-light elves came out of the forest and found summer. They stayed there to keep the land warm and fertile for a while, until it was time for them to go south. Now summer would always come to the north once a year.

THE CHILDREN OF THE SUN

INCA, SOUTH AMERICA, 1200CE

THE Inca empire began in the Cuzco valley high in the Andes in Peru. Like the Romans, the Incas were skilful conquerors. They believed in their sun-god and thought their rulers were gods because they were the sun's children. Before the emergence of their empire, the Incas believed the world was a miserable place, full of wild animals and wild peoples. In this myth the sun-god is a kindly benevolent deity who made it possible for the emergence of the Inca empire.

One day the sun-god drew back the clouds from his heavenly home and gazed down upon the state of the earth. The lands were untended, and the animals and the peoples that lived there were wild and miserable. The people ate only the seeds and fruit they gathered in the forests, and they lived like the wild animals who roamed freely. There were no villages, and the rivers and the mountains were the only beauty that sustained the disorder.

The sun-god realized that earth needed some kind of management for its survival, and he genuinely felt a great surge of sadness at the way these peoples lived. With a sudden jolt of inspiration he decided to send one of his daughters, Mama, and one of his sons, Manco, down to earth to show these people how to improve their condition.

He brought them to him in the sky and said: 'I am the source of the life of those people on earth. I am the light and the warmth and the provider of their food and of their day and night. As I travel across the sky I watch what these people do and how they live, and it brings me great unhappiness because

83

they seem so naïve. These people are ignorant, and they need to be educated or the world will not survive. So you, my children, are to go down to Lake Titicaca and rule these people kindly. Teach them all I have taught you about justice and kindness, and tell them that I am their life-source and will always protect and nourish them.'

The two children nodded and made ready to leave. The sun-god took them as far as the gateway of the sky and handed them a golden rod. 'This golden rod will show you where to build my sacred city. Whenever you stop to camp for the night push this rod down into the earth. If it sinks right down, wherever it does so is the most fertile soil and this is to be Cuzco, the city of the sun.'

So the children of the sun set off to Lake Titicaca, and when they stopped to eat and drink they tried to push the golden rod into the ground, but it would go in no further than an inch. Everywhere they stopped they tried to sink the rod into the ground, but the ground was either too hard, or like mud so that the rod would stick and not sink any deeper.

They climbed into the forests, and as they climbed higher and higher the path became wilder until it disappeared. There were no people but the grass was greener and lusher here than anywhere else they had been. Manco and Mama smiled. Their father, the sun, shone down brilliantly from the blue sky as if they had found the right place. Reaching a beautiful valley hidden between two hills, they somehow knew this place would welcome the golden rod. At the crest of the hill they stopped to eat. Manco and Mama thrust the golden rod into the lush grass. The soil was so fertile that the rod sunk deeply into the ground and disappeared.

Mama said, 'I knew this was the place when our father the sun shone so brilliantly upon us. This is where we must build his city, Cuzco, and where we must rule all his people.'

Manco nodded, 'Now we must gather the people and bring them to this beautiful valley. We'll teach them how to behave like human beings and rule them with kindness and justice as our father told us.'

Manco and Mama set off to the plains and the lakes again and gathered many people to come to Cuzco. When the miserable people from the lowlands and the mountains saw the radiant children of the sun, they gladly followed, knowing that they would be well treated. All these people became the Inca race, and they were educated in everything from farming to irrigation. They worshipped the sun, the father of Mama and Manco, and in his honour built a wondrous temple on the hill where the golden rod had been pushed into the earth. The Inca empire was born and the sun's children ensured that it was one of the most civilized and fertile of kingdoms.

NANTU AND ETSA

THE Jivaros were agriculturists but also warring people. Originally head hunters, the Jivaros believed that they obtained their power against the fearsome spirits of their ancestors by shrinking the heads of their victims. The story of Nantu and Etsa is a small part of a great epic tale of murder, lust and incest, but it reveals the powerful influence of the sun and moon and how closely the cycles of both these celestial bodies were followed in the daily lives of the Jivaros.

Etsa was the son of Kumpara the creator, and Etsa was the sun. So that Etsa should have a wife who was unrelated to him, Kumpara had to devise a different way to create her. So Kumpara took a handful of mud from the moist earth, placed it in Etsa's mouth when he was sleeping and then blew a warm breath across Etsa's face. The lump of mud transformed into Kumpara's daughter, Nantu, the moon.

Nantu's beauty was compelling to all who saw her. Each night, when the moon appeared ghostly silver in the sky, a great bird, the goatsucker, became infatuated with her beauty. Many times he attempted to seduce her, but Nantu was not interested in the goatsucker nor would she let him come near her in her heavenly chamber.

After many years Etsa also fell in love with the exquisite Nantu and constantly followed her about the sky, demonstrating his love and affection for her. But Nantu was shy and would not let him come close too soon. So Etsa found some herbal dye and painted his face to make him even more attractive than his usual radiant self. Nantu realized this was a good chance to escape his drooling heart, and she disappeared by shooting up into the higher canopies of the sky. In her heavenly chamber she painted herself black with *sua* so that her body was the night. She also painted her face so that even now, you can see the strange faint markings on the surface of the moon. She climbed like a mountain jaguar up a steep trail into the sky and across the curving canopy of stars.

The goatsucker, Auhu, saw Nantu perilously high in the sky and realizing that she was probably escaping from the demands of Etsa decided to try his own luck at wooing her. A thick vine hung down from the mantle and the bird began to climb up towards the path that Nantu had taken in the night. When Nantu saw the bird cooing and billing his way up the vine, she cut through the thick woody stem, which fell back into the jungle, tangling up all the jungles of the world. Auhu the goatsucker fell with it, and went to sulk among the trees.

Etsa was furious that Nantu had escaped his advances again, and he decided to chase after her. The only way he could reach the sky was to fly, so he

85

caught two parrots and two parakeets and tied them to his wrists and his knees. The birds flew up towards the moon, and he eventually met Nantu and demanded that she love only him. But Etsa's demands only made Nantu more resolved to go her own way and a terrible quarrel began. The quarrel turned to a fight, and Etsa, full of rage, struck Nantu. This was the first eclipse of the moon. Nantu was strong and fought back, and she hit Etsa across the belly. This was the first eclipse of the sun.

Nantu was exhausted by the passionate antics of the sun, and she began to weep. Etsa said, 'See how much stronger and more powerful I am, and you can only cry.' Now, whenever the face of the moon is red it means that it is going to weep rain across the land.

Nantu believed she had no choice and so agreed to marry Etsa. Their first child was born by the River Kanusa. This was Unushi, the sloth, the first Jivaro.

The sun and moon often meet on earth. They leave the sky for a few nights and then there is no moonlight. This is the time when they procreate. All the children of Etsa and Nantu are born on earth, and the waxing moon indicates the period of pregnancy, and the waning moon is the giving of birth. So the earth was used as a place for all their children to inhabit. Unushi, the sloth, the first Jivaro, was put in the forests that became his home.

One day Nantu returned to earth to sort out a family quarrel. The enraged relative beat Nantu violently, threw her into a deep pit and covered her with earth. A dove saw what had happened and told his old friend, the goatsucker, about Nantu's terrible fate. Auhu, the goatsucker, now had another chance to show Nantu how much he loved he and to prove that he was worthy of her. He painted his face and put on his beautiful beetle-wing earrings. Using a snail shell as a trumpet, he began to blow through the instrument as he walked towards the pit. The shrill sound was so startling that Nantu burst out of the hole and shot straight back up to the sky without even seeing Auhu in all his finery. Auhu called after her, 'Come back, come back!' but it was too late. Nantu did not look back.

So with his love unrequited, Auhu went back to his melancholy lifestyle. This is why on moonlit nights you can hear his mournful song that he cries to Nantu: 'Aishiru, aishiru – Beloved, beloved.'

AG-AG AND KLANG

NEGRITO, MALAYSIA, 1200CE

THIS short account of how the sun and the moon came into being is simple and direct. Like most tribal myths, the undercurrent of why anything is what it is becomes irrelevant, as long as the how is justified.

A long time ago there were a man, who was called Ag-Ag, and his wife, who was called Klang. They lived in a beautiful house built on stilts above the edge of the dark muddy river, and they had a child, Tnong, who took on the form of a dragonfly. Tnong played like any other child, happily flying around under the house and skimming his wings across the water as he buzzed over the mangroves. But one day, in his enthusiasm, the vibration of his wings stirred the house right off its stilts and it flew up into the sky. Tnong carried on flying and buzzing around underneath the house because he was a child and did not know what else to do.

Klang was terrified when she saw the house was flying high in the sky. She ran to the door and looked out and saw how high up they had flown. Klang felt dizzy and began to fall forwards through the door, but as she fell wings sprouted from her back and a beak grew from her head and she became transformed into a hawk. Ag-Ag wondered what was happening, and he too ran to the door and looked out into nothingness. Far beneath him was the earth and the river snaking its way across the rainforests like a worm or a viper hunting its prey. He looked down and saw a hawk soaring on the thermals, and he too fell out and was transformed into a crow.

The house went higher and higher, rising into the sky towards the west. And still Tnong kept circling and playing and skimming beneath the house as it flew towards the ocean. After some hours it gradually descended and dropped gently into the west towards the mouth of a great cavern full of darkness. The house tumbled into the cavern, rolled and tossed around down through the caves of darkness towards the east, to emerge again on the other side of the earth. Again it rose quickly into the sky, shining powerfully as it climbed higher and higher. Tnong the dragonfly decided to stay in the house and play around it forever. He loved to hurtle around the sky and through the deep caverns of the earth, and this was how it became the sun-house.

Tnong enjoyed his life in the sun-house but he was always jealous of the moon who seemed to have all the stars in the sky with her at night. When Tnong was out playing the stars seemed to hide away from him, apart from two that came with him as he rose and left with him when he zoomed down into the dark caverns. So Tnong the dragonfly boy sometimes sends a large moth out at night to swallow up the moon so that he can play with the stars instead. But the people on earth make a noise and dance and bang drums, and the scared moth flies away, and then the moon comes out from the shadow of the moth's wings. However many times Tnong sends his moth to the moon, it is the people who know that the moon must return at night to keep the stars in order, for Tnong would rather just let them play.

THE FINE WEATHER WOMAN

THERE is very little to embellish this lovely myth of the Fine Weather Woman and her divine son. As for many Native Americans of this far northern coastal region, the weather was an unpredictable and often deadly force upon which their lives depended.

The chief's daughter often went down to the beach to dig for shells and stones that could be used for ceremonies and ornaments. One day, as she dug into the soft sand, she found an ordinary cockle shell. She was about to throw it away when a sound of a crying child seemed to come from inside the shell. The chief's daughter looked inside the cockle shell and found a tiny baby. She wrapped the boy carefully up in her sleeve and took him home. For several years she nurtured the child, until one day he began to make signs in the air with his hands, as if he were pulling a bowstring back in readiness to fire it. To make him happy, she made a bow hammered out of her copper bracelet, and gave him two arrows. Even though it was just a toy, he was so happy with the tiny weapon that he went out into the forest to hunt for game. Each day he returned with different birds or small animals to show what a great hunter he might become.

Then his mother married a carpenter, who took them to live in a beautiful house by the ocean. The carpenter had built the house with his own hands and every post was carved and every wall was painted in rich colours and magical designs.

Every day the carpenter took the boy, who was called Sin, down to the beach and made him sit looking out to the great wide ocean. As long as the boy carried on facing the Pacific there was fine weather.

Sin used to go fishing with the carpenter, and one day they went to a fishing ground they had never been to before. When they slowed the canoe, Sin told the carpenter of a magical spell that he must repeat over and over again and they would catch many fish. So the carpenter spoke the incantation. Suddenly the fishing line started to move sharply up and down in the water and the canoe was dragged around an island three times. When it finally came to rest, they pulled in the line and dragged in a monstrous fish covered in thousands of halibut.

Sometimes Sin would put on the skins of the animals he had hunted and caught. One day he cloaked himself with the skin of a wren and his mother watched him soar above her into the sky as if he were a scattering of silver clouds across the ocean. He came back and put on the skin of a blue jay and this time shone across the sky as he hovered over the sea. Lastly, he wore the woodpecker's skin and flew above the horizon like a glowing sunset.

When he came down at last he said, 'I'm afraid that I have to leave you now, mother. I am going away for ever. But when the sky is coloured with blue there will no wind, for I shall be there. Then the time is good for fishing.'

His mother was sad when he left, but heart-broken when the carpenter told her it was time for him to depart also. She had loved the two supernatural beings and knew that they had left her with some of their own power to help her live on the earth.

Sometimes she sits by the sea-shore near the hundred densely forested inlets that weave in and out of the coast. Here, she loosens her clothes as she sits and watches the sea, and the winds eddy along the banks and the waves grow bigger and stormy. The more restless she becomes, the more stormy becomes the sea. She lives on the cold morning winds that come from the sea, and every time she meets the land she makes an offering to her son of fine feathers that rise and fall as snowflakes in the hope that he will soon return. They call her the Fine Weather Woman because her snowy winds remind her son, Sin, to return to the skies above the ocean so that the world can take advantage of the beauty of his golden face, blue eyes and the good time for fishing.

THE MOON

ABORIGINE, AUSTRALIA, first recorded 1600CE

ONCE upon a time the moon was a man. Happy and carefree, he spent most of his time dancing and whistling, singing and playing games. But there were odd occasions when he would fall into a black mood and become most dejected. The reason he felt so low was because he never had much luck with girls.

Although he was funny and lively in their company, enjoyed flirting, and teased the beautiful women around him, he failed miserably when it came to wooing any of them. They saw him as a bit of a fool, and made jokes about him and laughed behind his back because they thought he was fat and slow-witted.

Each night he would travel across the land seeking a partner. But the tribe from which he had originated sent out a message to the rest of the lands warning the other tribes he was coming. 'Watch out, the moon is searching for a wife tonight!'

On one clear and cloudless night the stars shone their usual messages of peace and protection from evil spirits. The moon sang a happy tune as he wandered along the river-bank, shimmering his silver light across the water. Nearby sat two daughters who happened to hear his superb voice. They waited for him to get closer, assuming that a man with such a fine voice must be handsome and desirable, too. But as he approached they saw he was fat, with very short legs and thin arms. This was not the sort of man they wanted to know.

'What a weird-looking man,' the girls giggled, and they ran across to the river and jumped into a canoe. The moon saw them rowing away and begged them to give him a ride across the river. The girls stopped paddling, amused by this strange little man's plaintive request. 'You must be the moon. We've heard you're a flirt and we've been told we must have nothing to do with you. So you'll have to swim across the river by yourself.'

The moon called back, 'But I'm hungry and cold. For the sake of the Pleiades and their place in the sky above, please take me. The stars would be disappointed if you cannot live up to their love of all mankind.'

The sisters nodded to one another, and remembered how the Pleiades shone from the sky to remind them that they must never harm any creature and love all beings. They began to row back to the shore to help the moon.

'Here, you can borrow our canoe, but you must row yourself across the river.'

'But I am unable to row, can't you do it for me?' asked the moon.

Reluctantly, the girls agreed to tow him across, and they plunged into the water. One on either side of the canoe, they grasped the boat and began to struggle across the water. But the moon was having fun, and just about half-way across he began to tickle the girls under their arms. Outraged at this behaviour, the girls tipped the boat forwards, and the moon plunged head-first into the deep, clear river. As he sank further and further down, they could see his shining face, big and white, looking paler and ghostlier the further it sank. Then it became only half his face they could see, and eventually only a thin crescent shape was visible, until his face disappeared altogether into the blackness.

Once the girls had recounted the story of the flirting moon to their mother, the whole tribe spread the news across the country. The crow himself heard the news about the sad fate of the moon and sent out a message to every distant land.

'The moon can no longer shine all the time. He will come from the Land of the Spirits in the west with only part of his face shining. Every night more and more of his face will show until you can see it all. Then it will gradually disappear into the east and he will be invisible for a while. When he comes back in the west he will peep round the corner because he is ashamed of his desire for women. But every month he'll dare to smile his watery smile and try to woo some girl in the full light of his fat face. Then he will gradually fade away because he will always be disappointed. Now everyone knows about the true nature of the moon.'

THREE

DEATH, RE-BIRTH
AND THE
UNDERWORLD

MOST MYTHOLOGY reflects the balance of opposites, of light and dark, of good and evil. This duality is our conscious perception of the universe. These opposites also correlate to the underworld and the upper world; a place where mortals live and inhabit the light, and a place where there is darkness, terror and eternal suffering, run by demons, or deities without faces.

Some traditions believed that this underworld was neither below us nor above us and that it was filled with the souls of dead people awaiting return to the 'real' world. Some believed that the underworld was only a mirror of the world we believe to be real, and both are nothing more than an illusion, or a dream in the mind of one deity or the universe itself.

Death itself was something to which the gods were immune. They were all-knowing, all-seeing and immortal, and although at times they allowed us access to both their wisdom and the art of growing consciousness, they denied mortals the ultimate gift of immortality. The essence of mortality was such that we had no choice but to break rules, manipulate through greed or desire and thus spoil the concept of immortality for ourselves. So death became our personal suffering, and the gods took little interest in it.

Monsters, demons, angels and spirits abounded, and it was they who did take an interest in our afterlife and what did or did not lie beyond the boundary of our mortal span. It seems that for most cultures the quest to enter the realms of the dead and to return alive, as hero or redeemer, set the most important tests for both the 'characters' in the story and for our own endless curiosity to know what lies beyond the apparent one-way door.

INANNA
AND ERESHKIGAL

ALTHOUGH this myth is a direct parallel to the story of Ishtar and Tammuz (see page 189), it carries the same dark and mysterious flavour of the underworld as Persephone's abduction by Hades (see page 102).

Many scholars suggest that these myths are variations on one original source and that the deities concerned are different aspects of the same goddess. This story symbolizes both the same spiritual quest and the same psychological descent into the realms of the unconscious as Persephone's tale does.

The descent to the underworld in all three stories represents the time on earth when there is no growth. In this version, it is through the goddess of light, Inanna, and her twin sister, Ereshkigal, the goddess of darkness, that the balance of life is juxtaposed.

Inanna was the goddess of fertility and sex, and she was responsible for the growth of the plants and creatures of the earth. Her name means 'lady of the sky', and she was the daughter of the sky-god, An. Dumuzi was her consort, the shepherd king for whom she built the city of Uruk. When Inanna and Dumuzi first joined in their passionate love-making to ensure the fertility of the land, Dumuzi appeared like a wild bull, his beard made of lapis lazuli. Inanna's sexual anatomy is also described in great detail in one Sumerian myth, where her genitalia are likened to a 'boat of heaven' or 'fallow land', which she urges Dumuzi to plough. When they eventually consummate their union, plants and vegetation spring up all around them.

Inanna was also the twin aspect of a dual goddess, and as such was the goddess of light. Her twin sister was Ereshkigal, the goddess of darkness who ruled the underworld.

Inanna spent many days and night missing her sister, and she decided that the only way they could be together was to make the terrible journey down into the underworld to visit Ereshkigal. She told her maid, Ninshubur, to set out her finest and most dazzling clothes and to be prepared to help her escape if she had not returned within a certain time.

Inanna dressed in her exquisite robes and set off to the underworld, where only shadows and souls of the dead dwelt. She knocked on the outer Gate of Invisibility. There were seven circles of invisibility, never-ending walls you could not see, and impassable by the mortal body. At each gate Inanna was allowed to enter the next region of the underworld only if she removed one of her dazzling garments or jewels. Symbolically, she began to strip away her life and her own light of fertility. At each gate she passed through, she removed more of her clothes. And at each gate she began to lose her power of light and life, until by the time she reached Ereshkigal at the centre of the underworld and in the darkest, foulest place, she was nothing more than a naked body herself.

When her dark sister gazed upon Inanna's nakedness, still dazzling in its beauty, Inanna finally lost all her power of life. The judges of the dead assumed she had come to take over Ereshkigal's throne, and, dragging her off into the darkness, they hung her up on a butcher's hook for her corpse to rot.

For three days and nights the maid, Ninshubur, waited anxiously for Inanna. When she did not return, she began to pray to the gods as Inanna had told her. As long as Inanna was in the underworld, it seemed that the growth and fertility of life began to decay. Creatures died and plants withered, and love itself was destroyed.

The gods were furious and pitied Inanna's fate. Yet they were confused about what to do. No mortal being could descend to the underworld and return alive. But Enki, the trickster-god, created two beings with neither mind nor sexuality nor internal organs, these being the three components for life. He gave one being a cup of the potion of immortality and the other being a bowl of the immortal food of the gods. Then he sent them to the underworld, and having no life nor soul, they passed through each of the seven gates of the underworld.

They found Inanna rotting on the great butcher's hook in the darkness. Taking her down, the beings gave her the immortal food and drink and she soon recovered. But Inanna knew she must talk to her sister, her only chance she had to leave and return to her world of light. Ereshkigal found some compassion in her heart and agreed that her sister should return to the upper world, as long as she found a substitute to take her place in the darkness. Ereshkigal was lonely, and if Inanna could not find a replacement, Inanna would be forced to return to live with Ereshkigal forever.

So Inanna passed through the seven Gates of Invisibility, back to the upper world. At each gate she put on her robes and her jewels and at each gate her power and fertility and light increased until she emerged dazzling in the upper world. In Uruk she found that her lover Dumuzi had neither mourned nor cared that she had gone. Not only had he usurped her throne, but he had slept with her other sisters. His unfaithfulness and his betrayal were enough for Inanna angrily to banish him to the underworld as her replacement and to satisfy Ereshkigal's conditions. After some time, Inanna regretted her decision and allowed him to come back to earth every year for six months as a god of vegetation to ensure the fertility of the earth and to continue the cycle of death and re-birth.

KA AND BA

EGYPT, 2500BCE

THE *ka* and the *ba* are essential components to ancient Egyptian religious belief in the afterlife.

When a human was conceived, the *ka* was created at exactly that moment by the god Khnum on his potter's wheel. The *ka* lived inside the body all its life. It was a spirit double of the body and could travel outside the body in dreams or in out-of-body experiences. When the mortal body died, the *ka* divided and became the *ba* (the soul) and the *akh* (the spirit).

The *akh* took the form of a human-headed bird, which flew off to the underworld, where it had to know the correct rituals and procedures it must perform to be allowed to stay in the underworld.

The *ba* lived in the tomb with the body but was free to come and go as it pleased. It was given weapons, jewellery, statues and furniture – anything to make its stay a happy one.

As long as the *ba* was on the earth, the *akh* was free to live forever in the underworld. This was a wonderful realm of the dead, where good spirits mingled with the gods and lived a life of peace and harmony. But should the body be destroyed in the tomb, the *ba* would be homeless and both the *ba* and the *akh* would die a second death, a fate much feared by all Egyptians.

This was why they spent so long in their funerary preparations, not only with the elaborate preparations and process of mummification, but also keeping such corpses safe from either animal or criminal molestation. Most bodies were placed in a stone sarcophagus within a walled-up tomb. The tomb would be protected with magical spells and powerful curses. If the tomb was ever robbed and the body destroyed, the *ba* was given an option to stay with the statue of the deceased that was usually placed within the tomb. This statue meant that the *ba* could avoid a second death and thus also the total annihilation of the soul. This whole philosophical and religious tending of the afterlife played a major part in the Egyptian quest for eternal life.

ANUBIS

EGYPT, 2500BCE

BEFORE Osiris changed from being the god of vegetation to being the god of the dead, it was Anubis who was the sole ruler of the underworld. In Egyptian art he is depicted as a man with a jackal's head, symbolically black, representing the afterlife, or perhaps the colour of the corpse after putrefaction. He was sometimes known as the god of putrefaction in earlier times, when burial grounds were scavenged by dogs and bodies were usually interred in only shallow graves. This was long before the time of the pyramids or the deep shafts that were dug for the stone sarcophagi.

As one of the embalmers of Osiris, Anubis came to be the god of all embalmers. He was also best known as the jackal who protected the dead against grave-robbers and was often shown as a dog on guard beside a tomb. In the underworld he supervised the first process of the judgement of the dead, testing their worthiness for the afterlife. As part of the test, Anubis weighed the dead person's heart against a feather, the symbol of Ma'at, the goddess of truth. Thoth wrote down the findings, and then the dead soul had to stand before the forty-two gods and deny that he had committed any of the forty-two sins. The art of how to survive the judgement of the dead was painted inside the tomb and written in 'The Book of the Dead'. If the dead soul passed the test, he was taken by Horus to Osiris, who would give him access to the afterlife. Those who failed were punished with eternal death or had to face Beby, the destroyer.

OSIRIS

EGYPT, 2500–600BCE

THERE are many version of the story of Osiris and Isis. Egyptian myth is concerned with symbols and with finding a way to express religious and philosophical ideas; if the ideas and concepts changed, then so did the myths. The myth of Osiris has evolved and been transformed more than perhaps any other Egyptian concept, from his early associations with fertility cults, through his affiliation as god of the dead, to his resurgence as god of re-growth and re-birth, not just for mortals but for all living things.

The mummification of Osiris by Isis and her sister is probably the first ever to be recorded, and it mythically represents both the first stage of eternal life and the obsessive fear of eternal death. Mummification was perfected by about the fourth dynasty (2600BCE), and it usually took as long as seventy days to complete all the processes.

The Osiris cult, carrying with it the belief of life after death and the judgement of the dead, continued down through the Egyptian dynasties as a distinct form of Egyptian religion. Eventually, however, Osiris's character began to absorb more of the solar features of the sun-god.

Between 2500 and 1500BCE Osiris was considered to be as important as Ra. A festival was held annually at Abydos, where Isis had found Osiris's head. This became an important location for wealthy Egyptians to be buried, for it signified the door to the underworld and the place where the dead soul would be judged and either allowed access to the underworld and an afterlife or sentenced to eternal death.

In the last 600 years BCE the Osiris cult outshone all others in Egypt. The mystery religion spread throughout the Mediterranean. The story of Osiris and his resurrection was closer to people's hearts than any of the other deities who seemed neither untouched by human suffering nor to have a sense of the human soul.

When Osiris was born it was said that singing was heard in the heavens and rejoicing spread throughout the land, for this was the birth of a great and wise king.

It seems that Osiris was indeed a king as well as a deity. His grandfather was the great god Ra and his father was Geb. Before his reign Egypt was full of nomadic tribes who were always warring. He established order to these peoples, civilizing them and teaching them the arts of agriculture, laws and building. He also introduced them to new rituals and religion to show respect for the gods. With his sister, Isis, he showed people how to grow crops of wheat, how to bake bread, how to raise vines and make wine and how to brew beer from barley. He built temples decorated with statues and fine paintings. He encouraged these peoples to be noble, just and wise like himself. This was a golden age, when people began to work together in peace. As an ideal model-king he began to travel further away from Egypt with Thoth and Anubis in the hope of civilizing the rest of the world. When he ventured on these travels he left Isis behind to rule over his kingdoms.

But while Osiris was away, his brother, Seth, became envious of Isis's power and position and tried to take over the throne for himself. Isis had known intuitively that Seth was up to something and quickly defeated his rebellion. As Seth was her brother, too, he was allowed to keep his freedom, which would prove to be fatal for Osiris.

Osiris continued to carry his message of peace and gentle persuasion across the world. His army marched to the sounds of music, and many countries began to benefit from his invasions. When he eventually returned to Egypt he found that Isis had done a good job of running the country in his absence and the land was prosperous and peaceful.

But Seth became even more driven by envy, and with the assistance of the queen of Ethiopia he plotted to overthrow his brother and sister. One night, while Osiris slept, he crept into his bedchamber and secretly measured the king's body. Then, with his carefully chosen conspirators, he began to make a carved cedarwood box that would be big enough for the king to sleep inside. It was exquisitely painted and rich with jewels, and its dimensions were such that it would be the right size only for the king himself. When the box-bed was finished, Seth held a feast in honour of Osiris and invited him to try out the bed. The other guests at the feast were, of course, all his allies.

The box was brought before the assembled party with great ceremony. The guests pretended to greet the box with cries of delight and admiration and Seth jokingly said that whoever fitted inside the box would be able to take the box away as a gift. One by one the guests eagerly lined up to try the box. Each would attempt to lie down in it, but none was just right. Each was either too long or too short, too wide or too thin. Finally, Osiris unsuspectingly took his turn and climbed into the box and lay down. He was an exact fit. As soon as he lay down the conspirators pulled out a hidden lid and slammed it down on top of the box. Nailing it firmly in place, they poured molten lead over the box to seal up the cracks. The beautiful box-bed had now become a deadly coffin.

The box was carried down to the Nile, weighted with lead and thrown into the river, where it quickly sank from sight. But the box was washed out of the mouth of the Nile into the open sea, and it eventually became lodged in a myrrh tree in Byblos. The roots began to grow around it so that it was hidden right inside the heart of the trunk, and the divine spark of the god's body made the tree grow bigger and stronger than any other tree and its scent more fragrant than any other scent.

News of Osiris's death soon reached the ears of Isis. In deep despair she immediately set out to search for her brother's body, knowing the dead could not rest without proper ceremonies and rituals. She searched throughout Egypt, walking from town to town in hope of some clue to Osiris's fate. Reaching the sea, she was beginning to give up hope when she met some children playing in the sand. They told her they had seen a box cast adrift in the sea by Seth. Isis consulted the oracle and learned that the chest had indeed been washed ashore on the coast of Byblos.

Melcarthus, the king of Byblos, was impressed by the huge tree and commanded that it be cut down and used as a pillar in his royal palace. Unaware that the trunk concealed the wooden chest, the king used the great tree trunk to support the palace roof. It exuded such a hypnotic and powerful perfume that people came from miles around just to see the tree.

Isis travelled to Byblos and sat outside the king's palace by the fountain. Each day the queen's handmaidens arrived for water and the goddess spoke kindly to them. She braided their hair and perfumed them with the fragrance of her own breath. When these handmaidens returned to the queen she was curious to meet this strange woman who had such great skills. Queen Astarte was impressed by Isis and eventually asked her to be her child's nurse.

Before long Isis revealed her true identity to the queen. She told her that she was the goddess Isis and that Osiris's body was in a chest hidden in the middle of the myrrh tree. The king was also moved by her story, and he cut down the great tree trunk and removed the wooden chest from the heart of the tree.

Isis took the chest back to Egypt, but she could not wait to see Osiris's body and she forced open the coffin. When she saw Osiris, pale and still in death, she used her magical powers to try to revive him. Transforming herself into a hawk, she fluttered her wings over his face, attempting to fill his lungs with air. With her magic spell she brought Osiris temporarily to life, enough time for her to have sexual intercourse with him and conceive a child. Isis then buried the box in the desert before she escaped to the delta region. Seth's spies were now combing the countryside for her, and Isis became a fugitive, giving birth to her son, Horus, in the delta region.

But Seth was also searching for the coffin, and one night, while he was hunting in the desert, he found where the chest had been buried. Seth was overjoyed. He removed the body and cut it into fourteen pieces. He scattered thirteen of these around the provinces of Egypt, but the fourteenth, Osiris's penis, was thrown into the Nile and eaten by a fish.

Isis once more set off to search for the different pieces of Osiris's body. With the help of her sister, Nephthys, and the god, Anubis, she found the thirteen pieces and began to reassemble them. They used wax to join the pieces together and then brought a long cloth of linen, smeared it with ointments that would preserve the body, and began to wrap Osiris's body in the anointed bandages. Then they buried the body.

Now it was time for Horus to bring his father back to life. He led Isis down to the world of the dead, where they found Osiris. Isis and her sister spoke magical incantations to resurrect the body. With the help of Ra, Horus made a ladder that reached right up from the world of the dead to the world of the gods. When Osiris had climbed the ladder and rejoined the gods, Ra made him king of the gods and ruler of the dead. He was to live in the underworld and judge the dead souls, after they had left their bodies in the mortal world, bandaged and anointed as his had been.

Horus eventually defeated Seth to become ruler of Osiris's kingdoms, and, like his father, he established law and order. Horus was also chosen to be the ambassador between the living and the dead, and before their deaths, men and women would pray to Osiris to ask that he would resurrect their souls after death.

YAMA

INDIA, 900BCE

TOWARDS the end of the Vedic period, around 900–550BCE, when early Hinduism was still evolving, the search was on for a supreme deity. This was the Brahmanic age, when the hierarchy of the Vedic gods was confused and there was a feeling that a new deity, Brahma, might be considered not just as a manifestation of one of the older gods but as a worthy universal supreme deity.

During this period beliefs developed into the more structured doctrine that universal time is a never-ending cycle of creation and destruction, each complete cycle being represented by a hundred years in the life of Brahma. However, one day in the life of Brahma is equivalent to 4320 million years on earth. When Brahma is awake the three worlds of heavens, middle and lower regions are created, and when he sleeps they are reduced to chaos.

Yama appeared as the first man in part of the creation of the human race in this great Brahmanic philosophical system, but was later identified in Hindu mythology solely as the less benevolent god of death.

Yama and his sister, Yami, were the first man and woman. Once the human race had been established, Yama became its explorer. He was the first to travel into the hidden regions and discover the road that led the dead to heaven. Perhaps because Yama discovered it, not only did he become the first man to die but he also became the king of the dead.

In the beginning the dead merely had to walk along this route to heaven just as Yama had done. But eventually Agni, the god of fire, watched over the 'path of the fathers' and as the dead were cremated, he was able to distinguish the good and the evil in each mortal from the colour of the flames. The ashes that remained represented evil and imperfection, and the fire carried the rest of the body into the heavens. The soul was carried on a golden chariot or by golden wings to rejoin the purified body, and it was greeted in heaven with festivities and glorification by the forefathers who lived a riotous life in Yama's kingdom.

This was a wonderful place for an afterlife. Desires were fulfilled, and eternity was spent enjoying every pleasure imaginable. But Yama also had the power to judge the dead, and not all mortals were allowed to stay in his heaven. Those that did not pass the test were either annihilated or sent to the realm of darkness, called Put.

Yama would pass the days and nights of eternity by playing his flute and drinking *soma* with the other gods. As the dead approached, he would give believers and the truly faithful cups of *soma* to drink to achieve immortality. This was a place of lightness and laughter, of music and happiness, but then came the era of rival gods and their own heavenly realms.

Varuna had once been Yama's main ally in judging the entrants to Yama's heaven, but Varuna now had his own heaven, as did Indra. Varuna's heaven was filled with water deities, spirits of the sea, river-sprites and the spirits of the mountains and the landscape. Indra's heaven was filled with saints, sages and major gods, a heaven without sorrow or suffering, and a place for warriors and heroes with intelligence and honour.

Yama's heaven soon seemed less sophisticated with the growth of these two other heavens and their more mortal associations with reward for virtue. Yama's heaven had merely been a place where the dead had to go as the abode of their ancestors. But to be welcomed into a heaven where you were honoured began to make Yama's heaven look less and less attractive.

Eventually Yama's heaven became linked with hell and suited only to those who were sinners or evil rather than to those who were wise, kind, honourable, benevolent do-gooders. It was about this time that Yama himself began to be seen as a figure of terror.

Torture began to be an integral part of Yama's kingdom, and the number of different hells to be found there ranged from seven to hundreds of thousands, one for every soul that passed through. Torture was dished out to suit the individual requirements of the sinner's offence. Those who killed a mosquito would be tortured by sleeplessness; oppressive kings would be crushed between two giant boulders.

The common belief held that the good and virtuous went on a path upwards towards the sun or moon, to the heaven of the fathers, and became the food of the gods. From the gods the souls were defecated as clouds and rain and so returned to earth to renew life. The stars were the souls of dead saints, heroes or women. The wicked, on the other hand, went down to one of Yama's hells or were re-born as serpents or worms, moths or spiders – anything that justified their own previous miserable life as human beings.

In Hindu belief, Yama carries on his evolved traditional role as the ruler of hell and is no longer associated with his original form as the welcomer of the dead to heaven. Yama now lives in his dark, foreboding palace, Kalichi, in the lower regions of the world. He keeps a great book of destiny, in which is written the timespan allotted to each human. When Yama reads the book and sees that a man must die, he sends his messengers to fetch him. All souls must pass before him, and his recorder, Chandragupta, reads aloud the virtues and sins of the dead. The soul may be sent to one of his many hells or returned to face another life on earth. Sometimes Yama sets out on a buffalo with a noose and a mace. He lassoes his victim and drags them off to the underworld, shrouding them with his blood-red robes and glaring at them with his shining copper eyes.

Many tried to avoid Yama's book of destiny and elude death. One young man, Markandeya, was a worshipper and devotee of Shiva's phallus. In the book of destiny his allotted span of life was sixteen years, and when he reached that age, Yama sent his messengers to fetch the youth. But in his fear, Markandeya hung on to Shiva's phallic statue for dear life, and the messengers dared not touch him, such was his propitiation. The furious Yama came along on his buffalo and with his noose tried to prise the boy away from the great phallus. Unable to separate the boy from the statue, he simply put the noose round both the boy and the lingam and began to drag them both down to hell. Shiva immediately appeared in person and, enraged at this affront to his own worship, beat Yama to death. Subsequently, all human beings became immortal and there was no god of death.

But the world became overrun with too many people and life was miserable for those who were good and virtuous, so the gods decided to restore Yama. Hell returned and mortals lost their one chance at immortality.

HADES AND THE UNDERWORLD

GREECE, 750BCE

THE ancient Greeks held a similar belief to that of the Ancient Egyptians that the realm of the underworld lay to the west and the setting sun. The Greeks also shared the same idea that neither the underworld nor its ruler, Hades, was particularly malevolent or evil in intent, unlike Christianity's notion of Satan. The underworld was as necessary as the upper world, and it is probably the myths of Persephone's abduction by Hades and Orpheus's search for his wife, Eurydice (see page 204) that glamorize this dark and shadowy place more than any other in Greek mythology.

Hades means 'unseen', and as the son of Kronos and Rhea and the brother of Zeus, Demeter, Poseidon, Hera and Hestia, Hades was made the ruler of the realm of the underworld after the overthrow of their father and the war between the gods and the Titans.

Hades was also known as Polydegmon because he welcomed so many millions of guests who had died and come to his kingdom only out of necessity. Hades also ruled all the precious stones and metals and the wealth that was buried in the earth. In this aspect he was also known as Pluton or Pluto (the rich one).

But Hades ruled the dead as Zeus ruled the living, and although he was not evil by nature, he was represented as a dark and grim deity who was by nature reclusive and left most of his ruling in the hands of his able assistants. This enabled him to stay hidden in the shadows and darkness of his deep underworld caverns. With his reputation for an aloof and impenetrable invisibility, those who worshipped Hades would avert their eyes when making sacrifices for fear of seeing him in all his radiant darkness.

Hades visited the upper world only when he was searching for a consort or was overcome by desire. He seemed to have little choice but to abduct the beautiful Persephone, or Core as she was then known, who became his queen of the underworld for six months of each year. But he also was overcome by lust when he saw a nymph called Minthe and would have seduced her if it were not for Persephone, who, during one of her stays in the upper world, saw what Hades was up to and changed poor Minthe into apple-scented mint before he could have sex with her.

The underworld itself was known as Tartarus. When a soul descended to Tartarus it was common for the relatives to leave a coin under the corpse's tongue, so that the dead soul could pay Charon to ferry it across the terrifying River Styx on its one-way journey. Charon was the son of darkness and night, and his leaky boat was so fragile that he refused to carry the living, unless they bribed him, as the heroes Heracles and Theseus did. Those souls who had no money to pay their way would have to wait forever on the near bank. On the far bank lived the great fifty-headed dog Cerberus, who guarded the shore and devoured any mortal who tried to enter or any soul who tried to escape.

There were several regions of Tartarus. The first was the Asphodel Fields, where ordinary souls would twitter forever like birds and bats. There was also the Pool of Lethe, where the ordinary souls would drink to wipe out all memory of their lives. Some souls avoided this water and chose to drink from the Pool of Memory instead. The souls who had lived evil lives were sent to the Punishment Fields, while those who had been virtuous to the orchards of Elysium. Elysium was a land of perpetual day and happiness. These inhabitants could chose to be re-born, and souls who were re-born three times were allowed to go to the Fortunate Isle.

Erebus was the lowest region of the underworld and here lived Hecate, the goddess of black magic and the queen of ghosts. She was accompanied by the Furies or Erinyes, three sisters who were monsters and whose job it was to decide on the torment of the wicked souls. It was thought they were born out of the blood spilled when Kronos castrated his father, Ouranos. Their names were Megaera (jealous rage), Alecto (endless) and Tisiphone (punishment). They were ghastly old hags, with dog's heads, bats wings, blood-shot eyes and snakes for hair. It was unwise to mention them in conversation because they were able to visit the upper world to hunt down mortals in nightmares or those who had committed crimes or evil deeds. They hounded their victims relentlessly and would appear as black clouds and storms or even as swarms of stinging flies and bees.

Nemesis was also no stranger to the underworld. She was the daughter of night and sister of the Fates. Her name means 'retribution', and in the upper world she would hunt the guilty down and make sure that any crime committed by god or mortal would be punished. In the underworld she accompanied the judges of the dead souls, making sure that the punishment fitted the individual crime. As each soul came before her, she would assume the form that suited each criminal's conscience and mirrored its deeds. Thus judgement was passed for each soul according to its crimes on earth.

Hecate was more feared than any other of the underworld deities, and she would dance across the fields of Tartarus with a pack of ghosts howling after her. She was sometimes seen on moonlit nights by lonely travellers, and became known as the goddess of the crossroads, and her statues and sacrifices could be found at such places in daylight. Hecate has been confused with other goddesses – Selene (the moon) and Persephone herself. It also seems in some accounts that when she was living in the underworld Persephone preferred Hecate's company to that of Hades.

DEMETER AND PERSEPHONE

GREECE, 750BCE

DEMETER was the daughter of Kronos and Rhea and the sister of Hades, Zeus, Hera, Hestia and Poseidon. Demeter was gentle-natured and her only interest was in tending the earth, ensuring that each year new crops grew and seeds were sown. She was not interested in males and was worshipped mostly by females. Yet according to some accounts, her brother Zeus raped her and she gave birth to the beautiful Core, later known as Persephone.

Core was the most desirable goddess in Olympus and every god craved her. She was safe only because Demeter was so watchful and protective, perhaps remembering her own seduction by Zeus. But Zeus himself was overcome by lust for her, and one day he turned himself into a great serpent and had sex with her while coiling his snake-form around her. Demeter realized that the snake was Zeus. She took Core away from Olympus, placed her on an island on earth and changed her name to Fersefassa, Persephone, which means 'teller of destruction'. So Persephone was now safe in Sicily, where she spent her days tending the flowers and singing in the meadows.

But Hades had spotted the enchanting Persephone and made a rare visit to his brother Zeus to ask him if he might have permission to marry her. Zeus did not want to offend his brother, even though he knew that Demeter would refuse to allow Persephone to live in the dark world of Tartarus. Zeus, therefore, could not commit himself either way. There was only one thing for Hades to do, and that was to abduct Persephone.

Not long after Hades's discussion with Zeus, Persephone was picking her favourite flowers in the water-meadows when she saw a rare and exquisite flower and bent down to smell the fragrance. As she leaned forwards, the earth split apart like a chasm beside her, and Hades's golden chariot surged up from the underworld, his black horses foaming at the mouth. He snatched Persephone from the field, and took her back down into the darkness. The earth closed together again, and the flowers grew back and filled the land with fragrance as if nothing had ever happened.

Because Hades had been wearing his helmet of invisibility, the only sign that Persephone had disappeared was the roar of a storm and an earthquake. When Demeter could not find her daughter, she became frantic and set off to search for her in every corner of the world. For nine days she walked, with no food or drink, calling Persephone's name wherever she went. Eventually the sun-god Helios, who sees everything there is to see in the world, confessed that he knew it was Hades who had abducted Persephone and taken her to his land of darkness. When Demeter also heard that Zeus had known about Hades's desire for Persephone, she became even more furious and refused to have anything do with any of the gods or to help Zeus again.

She set off on her wanderings and disguised herself as an old woman until she reached Eleusis where she was welcomed, so she decided to stay. But after her travels as a mortal and not as the goddess of fertility, when she had protected nature, decay and degeneration began to appear everywhere. The trees and the crops began to die, and the ground grew barren and infertile. Nothing would grow, and people were near to starvation. Zeus sent the messenger-god, Iris, to agree to some compromise with Demeter. If she would bring back life and fertility, Persephone would be released by Hades. For all Hades's dark aloofness, he was capable of fairness and pity, and he sadly agreed to let her go, knowing that Zeus had made one condition, that she must not have eaten any of the food of the dead. It was an unbroken law of the gods that to do so, meant you must stay in the underworld forever.

So Hades sent for his chariot and his horses and said farewell to Persephone, who had, in her own way, come to love him. He gave her one last gift, a pomegranate. As she rode away on the chariot she ate a single pomegranate seed and broke the law of the gods. Now there was a terrible conflict, because Persephone was bound by law to stay with Hades in his kingdom. Yet she also felt great pity for the world of mortals and her mother, Demeter, and wanted to help them. It was again Zeus who had to intervene.

Hades and Demeter agreed that for six months of the year Persephone would live in the upper world and bring fertility, growth and sunlight, spring, summer and autumn to the world. The other six months she would live in the underworld as Hades's queen and help him rule the world of the shadows. From that day on, the pattern of the cycles of the seasons was set ironically by Persephone, who had not totally rejected Hades in her eating of the pomegranate seed. The interchange of darkness and light were balanced by a simple choice.

VALHALLA AND THE VALKYRIES

VALHALLA (hall of the slain) was Odin's great feasting hall for the Einherjar, the heroic dead who had been slain on the battlefield. Those warriors who had been slaughtered while performing heroic acts were brought to Valhalla so that they could enjoy a glorious afterlife.

Valhalla itself was gigantic. Its roof was made of shields, and its walls of spears. It had over 500 doors and each was wide enough to accommodate 800 men marching abreast. The newly fallen heroes were admitted to Valhalla through a door called the Valgrind (the sacred barred gate of the slain), but before they could enter this gate they had to undergo a series of obstacles, which included crossing a torrential river of air.

Once inside Valhalla, the great heroes were cured of their wounds and lived an endless life of hedonistic indulgence, pleasure and fighting. Each morning they had to wear their armour, go to the practice ground and fight one another. If they were killed they would be brought back to life, obviously enduring all the agonies of their original combat on earth over and over again. But each evening they were restored to life and returned to Valhalla to begin their drinking and feasting. The meat came from a huge boar called Sahrimnir, which was re-born every day, only to be slaughtered and boiled eternally to provide the ravenous warriors with endless meat. The mead was supplied by the udder of a goat, and the warriors drank it from the skulls of their enemies.

Because the Vikings believed this to be the perfect existence, warriors who were not slain on the battlefield during their young and active years would even fall on their own spears in order to be welcomed into Valhalla and enjoy the eternal bliss of wine, food and women.

The Valkyries were the beautiful but deadly young women who were the warrior-servants of Odin. They rode over the battlefields, selecting the heroes who would go to Valhalla and probably choosing the ones they most desired. They originated from earlier goddesses of slaughter, who took great delight in using the severed limbs, intestines and blood to weave a tapestry. On the battlefield they were sadistic and terrifying, but in Valhalla they became desirable women to the fallen warriors. Each morning, after a night of rampant sex, they would be re-born eternally virginal, appearing in their white robes and combing out their long golden hair.

They were also assistants to the god of war, Tyr, and rode on panting white stallions (sometimes wolves) across the skies above the battlefields,

106

swooping down to pluck their chosen heroes. Sometimes they rampaged across the earth, seizing sailors from ships, then spraying the earth with frost or early morning dew, which came from the drowning men's soaking clothes and falling tears.

Several of the Valkyries were renowned for their more serious relationships with mortals or gods. Brynhild was the unfortunate lover of Sigurd. She threw herself onto his funeral pyre when she realized that he had not betrayed her at all. Freya was the leader of the Valkyries and also the goddess of sexual desire.

RAGNAROK AND THE DEATH OF BALDER

NORTHERN EUROPE, 100CE

RAGNAROK is the final battle of the gods. In Nordic mythology it is something that has not yet happened, and when the time comes, a series of events will lead to the final battle between good and evil. This has a similar parallel to the Apocalypse, but unlike the Christian triumph of good over evil, after Ragnarok there will be a re-birth of a new pantheon of gods and new life on earth.

Loki, the trickster-god, had angered Odin by arranging the tragic death of his beautiful son, Balder. In Niflheim, the world of the dead, Balder's brother pleaded with Hel, the ruler of the dead, to bring Balder back to the upper world. Her reply had been that if the whole world wept a tear for him, then he would be returned. So every tree, plant, creature and mortal cried for Balder, all except an old woman who hid in a cave and refused to shed a tear. This was Loki in disguise. So Balder the bringer of beauty was doomed to remain in Niflheim until after Ragnarok, the end of the universe.

When the gods discovered that the old woman had indeed been Loki, they punished him, tying him down in an underground cave where he was forced to lie beneath the endlessly dripping venom of a snake that fell on his face. Loki's wife sat beside him with a dish and caught the drips so that his suffering would not be so intense.

As Loki writhes in agony, the death of Balder means there is no beauty in the world, and more and more evil is created.

One day Loki, who has for a long time plotted the downfall of the gods and revenge for his punishment, will be free and he will join the frost-giants to fight the gods. Surt will lead the fire-giants across the rainbow bridge and gather on the plains of Asgard to fight the powers of light. But first will be a savage, year-long winter, during which snow will fall endlessly in every part of the universe. The wolves who have been chasing the sun and moon will catch and devour them. Fenris, the wolf, and Hel's dog, Garm, will break their tethers and attack the gods. The dragon, Nidhug, will succeed in gnawing through one of the roots of the great world tree, Yggdrasil. The world serpent, Jörmungand, will rise from the depths of the ocean and engulf the world, and on this tidal wave Loki will sail his ship.

The dead warriors from Valhalla will join forces with the gods, and there will be a great battle when evil destroys good, and good destroys evil. Odin will be killed in his duel with Fenris, and only Surt will survive to burn the corpses in a huge fire that will engulf creation and drown the universe in a sea of cataclysmic chaos.

Yet things will come into being again. The world tree, Yggdrasil, will survive, and the daughter of Sol will drive the chariot across the sky again, accompanied by Balder, who will at last be re-born. The first two mortals will be Lif and Lifdrasir, and they will populate the earth with mortals. Balder will rule the children of the gods and it will be the beginning of another cycle of the ages of the universe.

XIBALBA – THE PLACE OF PHANTOMS

MAYA, MEXICO, 500CE

THE second book of the *Popol Vuh* tells the story of the two hero-gods, Hun-Apu and Xbalanque. This extract tells the story of their descent into the underworld, the realm of Xibalba, and the way in which they managed to trick the lesser demons of this dark and dreadful land of the dead.

A long time before the hero-gods Hun-Apu and Xbalanque were born, two of their ancestors were playing a game of *tlachtli*, a kind of hockey that was popular throughout ancient Mexico. These two ancestors were unfortunate enough to lose their ball down a tunnel that led to the underworld or the dreaded realm of Xibalba. When the owl-faced princes of the underworld saw the ball, they thought it would be amusing to challenge these two ancestor demi-gods to a game of *tlachtli*. But the world of Xibalba was also a world of deceit and treachery, and the two gods were fooled into entering the underworld at the cost of their lives. Eventually they were imprisoned in the House of Gloom, where they were sacrificed and buried.

The head of one of the ancestors, Hunhun-Apu, was hung from a gourd tree, and in its putrefied way it looked not unlike one of the crop of gourds.

Throughout Xibalba none was allowed to eat the fruit of the tree. Yet a princess of the underworld, Xquiq (blood), one dark timeless moment, picked a gourd as she passed and found in her hand the head of Hunhun-Apu. The god spoke to her through the froth of death in his mouth and told her she would soon become a mother.

Xquiq fled from the underworld, for the demons of Xibalba had heard that she had picked a gourd from the tree and demanded her death. She stayed with Hunhun-Apu's mother, and eventually gave birth to twin sons, the hero-gods Hun-Apu and Xbalanque. These two hero-gods lived with their grand-mother when Xquiq returned to the underworld, her mission complete.

On one of their many adventures, a rat related to the hero-gods the story of how their ancestors had heroically entered the underworld, then been defeated by the powers of Xibalba. The rat also told them where the game of *tlachtli* had been played, and the two hero-gods set off to try out the wonder-ful game for themselves. But the watchers from the underworld, seeing the heroes playing the same game as their ancestors, resolved to trick them to come down to the underworld, too. They sent out a challenge to the sons, not realizing that the twins knew about the terrible fate of Hunhun-Apu and Vukub.

Keen to meet the challenge of the demons, the two gods followed the path that led down to the River of Blood and the entrance to Xibalba. They sent an animal called Xan as a scout to prick every being it encountered with a hair from Han-Apu's leg. If the beings were made of wood they knew they would be led down the wrong pathways. First, they avoided the Seat of the Red-hot Stone, and although they entered the House of Gloom, they passed on unscathed.

The gods of Xibalba challenged them to a game of *tlachtli*, and because the twins were severely beaten, they were sent to the Garden of Shadows to pick the flowers as an offering to the underworld spirits. The Garden of Shadows had no real flowers, but the twins called out to a swarm of ants in the dark earth who went back to the upper world and returned with gar-lands of scented hibiscus. The anger of the underworld demons intensified, and the heroes were thrown into the House of Lances, where spirits thrust sharp spears into their bodies. But the boys bribed these lesser spirits and escaped.

Xibalba was relentless in its afflictions, for it was a place of horror and danger, not one of mere punishment. The two heroes were forced into the House of Ice, where they escaped a dreadful death from icy fingers that spread across their skin to freeze them. They buried pine-cones and lit a fire and the ice-demons began to melt. In the House of Tigers and the House of Fire they again outwitted the spirits of the underworld.

But they were not so lucky in the House of Bats. Here they tried to avoid the whirring bats that came with terror to blind them or eat out their eyes or drink their blood. One of the bats wrapped its great leathery wings around Hun-Apu's face and with his sword-like claws ripped off his head. But a tortoise crossed the ground and touched the severed head. Carrying the magic of the god's eyes to the decapitated body, the tortoise transformed itself into Hun-Apu's head and he arose again from the ground.

The only way the gods could be saved from this eternal nightmare was to prove that they were in fact gods and therefore immortal. First, they arranged for their resurrection and invoked two sorcerers, Xulu and Pacaw, to help them in their re-births. The two heroes stretched out on stone slabs and died. Their bones were ground up into fine powder and thrown into the river. Within five days they appeared as men-fishes and on the sixth day as senile and ragged men, who killed one another and then restored each other to life. The demons of Xibalba demanded they burn the Palace of Darkness and restore it to its great dark splendour, kill and resurrect the Hound of Death and cut a man in pieces and bring him to life again.

The hero-gods did all this, and then smiled to each other as the underworld rulers demanded to experience death and resurrection for themselves. The demons of Xibalba were finally outwitted when the two gods having declared their own immortality, now reminded the underworld rulers that they could only ever die and never be resurrected because they were not gods. The dark shadows and phantoms of the underworld cowered in the light of the immortal gods, condemned to the underworld forever. Their power soon waned and they were especially forbidden ever again to play the noble and honourable game of *tlachtli*.

The souls of Hunhun-Apu and Vukub, the first adventurers into the Land of Darkness, were sent up into the heavens as the sun and moon, and the heroes returned to the world to remind people of the immortality of the gods and their triumph over the land of shadows and the dead.

THE LAND OF GHOSTS

BANTU, AFRICA, 500CE

THE cult of the dead is the core of Bantu religion, for it is the ghosts and the spirits that live on after the death of the body that can influence those who are still living. There are different classes of ghost. Family ghosts, kungu, who are honoured and propitiated throughout the generations until they lose their individuality and merge into a host of spirits known as vinyamkela or majini. The vinyamkela are usually more friendly than the majini, but both are more powerful than the family kungu ghosts. These ghosts are usually invisible, but have moments when they appear with half a human body and nothing on the other side.

The ghost country is usually found by way of holes and caves in the ground, but variations obviously occur depending on the immediate geographical locale. The huge distances in Africa permit great changes and evolution of the practicalities of where to find the land of ghosts, as well as the kind of ghosts that inhabit these places. On Kilimanjaro, for example, the ghost land is reached by throwing oneself into a deep pool (as in the following myth); for the peoples of the Transvaal the gateway to Mosima (the abyss) was via a great ravine.

Few of these ghost lands are above ground, However, especially in East Africa, sacred groves are found in forests as well as on gently sloping mounds called spirit hills. The trees of these burial ground are never cut down, and great care is taken to protect them from bush-fires.

Marwe and her brother were hungry. They had been ordered to watch over their parents' bean-field and scare away the monkeys who came to feast on the beans every day. But they had decided to dig up the rat burrows instead, kill a few rats and roast them for a delicious dinner. Rat meat makes you thirsty, so after their tummies were satisfied they ambled off to the deep pool to drink. When they returned they found the monkeys had visited the bean-field and stripped it bare. Marwe knew the consequences of their actions and, terrified of her parents' anger, could think only of throwing herself into the pool.

But her brother shook his head. 'Let's go home, listen to what our parents are saying in secret, and then decide what to do.'

They crept back to their hut, climbed on to the roof and listened to their parents through the thick thatch of banana leaves.

The parents had by now heard of their empty bean-field and were enraged. 'What are we to do? Beat them? Or shall we just strangle them!' shouted their father.

The terrified children refused to hear any more and Marwe rushed back to the deep pool and threw herself in. Her brother's courage stopped him at the last moment, and he ran back home to tell his parents. By now the parents had totally forgotten and forgiven both children for leaving the bean-field and ran quickly to the pool to save their daughter.

'Marwe come home! All is forgiven, we can replant the bean-field, please come back!' But there was no reply, not even a ripple upon the still, dark, deep pool, for Marwe had already dived down into the depths of the pool and entered the Land of Ghosts.

She entered the Land of Ghosts from the deepest, bottomless part of the pool. Here, great rocks, sparkling with crystal, guided her towards an opening garlanded with the skeletons of deep-water fish. There was a tunnel with sheer rock that shone like gold, and the water was so clear she could see through the shoals of transparent fish and beyond to the gates of the Ghost

Land. The gates opened for Marwe and she came into a land where light and dark did not exist and the sounds she heard and the sights she saw were at the same time the sights and sounds that those who were living saw at that moment. But this parallel world was filled with ghosts who had neither form nor age.

She came to a ghost hut, where a woman sat spinning fine threads into thicker twine. The woman said she could stay, and she helped gather firewood and cook the food. But Marwe never ate the food, for to eat the food of the dead meant you could never leave that land again.

Marwe became homesick and asked the old woman if she might now return to the land of the living. The old woman nodded and then said: 'To return home you must make a choice. If you are wrong you will stay here forever. Here are two pots of water, one is so cold it is almost ice, the other so hot it is almost boiling. Which will you chose that will hurt you the most? Into which pot will you plunge your pretty hands?'

Marwe considered this for a moment. Those with a conscience would always chose the most difficult and most testing choice, for those who had a conscience would know the right answer would also be the most painful.

Marwe plunged her hand into the icy water, for the cold would burn her as it froze around her skin. The old woman told her to draw out her hands, and suddenly they were now covered with sparkling golden armlets and bracelets. She was then told to stand in the water, and as the pain seared her feet, she was told to jump out and found her ankles draped with silver chains and rich stones. The old woman gave her an exquisite skin-robe, covered with deep blue stones and beads, and she said: 'Go back to the land of the living. Your future husband is called Sawoye, it is he who will carry you home.'

So Marwe returned to the pool and the silver fish and the deep crystal rocks and swam to the surface. As she broke through the still water of the pool and took a big breath she found herself sitting on the bank as if she had never been away.

But time had moved on in the land of the living and there was a famine now in the country. Two herdsmen found Marwe sitting in her rich clothes and fine jewellery and could not believe their eyes. They returned to the chief of the village and told him about Marwe. The whole village went to inspect her, wondering if she was sent to bring them the food and the riches they needed to survive the terrible famine.

But Marwe would not let the chief carry her back to the village, she would only go if one man came for her, Sawoye. The villagers pushed Sawoye forward and laughed at him, for he was disfigured with a terrible skin disease and no woman had wanted him for a husband. But Marwe, in her fine clothes and shining bangles said, 'That is my husband', and allowed him to pick her up and carry her back to the village.

They were soon married and bartered the bangles and jewels for a herd of cattle and built a house. They irrigated the land and brought water down from the gullies that led from the pool. Some of their neighbours were envious when Sawoye's disease disappeared and he became the most handsome man in the tribe. The chief was jealous of Sawoye's good fortune and one night Sawoye was mysteriously killed in his bed. But Marwe had brought back more than bangles from the land of ghosts. Her incredible visit had also given her the power to restore his life. Sawoye was ready and waiting when the murderers came back to abduct Marwe and take her for the chief's wife. He killed the abductors, and the treachery of the villagers was avenged forever.

Marwe and Sawoye continued to drink the water that trickled down the stream from the deep pool. This was peaceful time.

THE SNOW SPIRIT

JAPAN, 700CE

IN Japan there is an old belief that those who die in the snow and the cold winter become spirits of the snow. The ancient deity, Yuki-Onna, is the lady of the snow, and although snow-time in Japan is full of beauty and a favourite theme for both poets and artists, Yuki-Onna, is far from being a benevolent or even graceful spirit, and she has none of the charm of freshly fallen snow. This is a spirit of destruction and doom, for Yuki-Onna represents death and has perhaps closer connections with vampires than with snowflakes. Japan is a country of contradictions, where beauty contrasts with deformity, and good really sparks off the harbingers of evil.

There was once a carpenter called Mosaku, who travelled with his apprentice, Minokichi, to the forest quite some distance from their home village. They had heard a rumour that trees with wood the colour of ochre and branches the size of towers were to be found there. If such a place existed they would surely never be out of work with such prize timber. As they approached the distant forests, the chilling wind turned directly onto their faces from the north. Darkness suddenly came, and the great heavy clouds above warned them of a coming snowstorm. Mosaku wanted to press on and reach the forest for shelter, but racing forwards in an attempt to beat the driving snows, they found themselves staring at the cold, swirling water of a torrential river. There was no possibility of swimming across, and the ferryman had long since abandoned his job at the onset of winter. Mosaku suggested that they spend the night in the ferryman's tiny hut, with no time now to turn back to the village. If they slept through the snowstorm, they might perhaps reach home in the morning.

The tiny hut was bare except for two mats on the floor. Mosaku lay down and immediately fell asleep, his great coats pulled round him and his head covered in sacking. But Minokichi could not sleep as easily. He felt disturbed, restless and unusually fearful of the night ahead. For a long time he lay listening to the wind howling across the thin rafters and the hissing snow as it blew against the door and the sides of the hut. Finally, he could not keep his eyes open any longer and fell asleep.

After what may have been seconds, minutes or hours – Minokichi could not tell – suddenly something woke him, a shower of snowflakes falling gently on his face and the sound of the wind whipping across the floor. He sat up and stared at the door, which had blown open in the gale. It banged against the shed, and the snow poured in through the doorway. Then he saw her, and Minokichi drew back against the wall in terror. For there stood a woman dressed in dazzling white garments, her hair was covered in snow and her face was paler than the snow that blew across her face. She bent over Mosaku and seemed to kiss him for some minutes, and then as she drew back her head, Minokichi gasped in horror, for from her icy blue lips ran trickles of the blood she had drunk from Mosaku's neck. Her ice-cold breath was like white smoke in the tiny hut. Droplets of ice formed as she breathed out and then shattered into slithers on the ground. She turned to approach Minokichi. The ice-rain that fell from her lips was like music, but the colourless eyes and the mouth of death that grinned as the woman came nearer was like hell itself. The woman hesitated when she saw him and then leaned over his body. He tried to cry out but her breath was like a freezing wind that held him transfixed to the spot where he lay.

'You have beauty on your side,' she smiled and licked the blood from her chin, 'I would have drained your life-blood too, but I am enchanted by your youth. You must swear on your master's blood never to tell anyone what you have seen of you will die, too.'

Minokichi nodded quickly as his hands began to go numb under her frozen breath and icicles began to form from the tears that fell from his eyes. Then suddenly she vanished in a gust of ice and snow. The door slammed and he was suddenly alone. He called out to his master, 'Mosaku, wake up, wake up! What has happened to you?!' There was no reply. Minokichi crawled across the floor of the dark hut and found his master's hand. It had turned to ice, and his master was dead.

The following winter Minokichi was returning home from the woods when he met a pretty girl called Yuki. She told him she was on her way to Yedo to find work as a servant. Minokichi was infatuated with the girl, and when he found out that she had no other suitors he asked her to marry him. So Yuki and Minokichi had ten adorable children with unusually fair hair and skin the colours of swans' feathers.

One night the light of the paper lamp threw strange shadows across

Yuki's face as she sat sewing. Minokichi remembered the terrible night in the ferryman's hut fifteen years before and somehow Yuki's face resembled the ghostly white face of the snow spirit. He could not help himself, and he told her the story.

'It's strange, Yuki, but you remind me of a woman who was as white as the snow she seemed to arrive with. She killed my master with her ice-cold breath and drank his blood. I am sure she was a demon, or spirit, and its strange how you look just like her tonight.'

Yuki stood up and threw down her sewing, there was a terrible smile on her face and she bent over Minokichi and he remembered how she had done so once before, 'Yes, it was I, Yuki-Onna who came to you and killed your master! You stupid mortal, you have broken your promise to keep our meeting a secret. If it were not for our sleeping children I would kill you now!' the spirit shrieked, 'If they should ever complain about you I shall hear it, wherever I am, and on the night when the snow falls I will certainly kill you!'

Minokichi cowered in the corner of the room as Yuki-Onna, the lady of the snow, changed into an ice-white mist. Frost formed on the windows as the mist spiralled around the room and rushed up through the chimney into the winter sky. Minokichi heard a terrifying shriek as the spirit vanished into the cold night, and he knew she would never return in mortal form again.

So Minokichi was always good to his children in fear for his life, and each year, when the winter came, he dared not go out if the snow fell. Whenever he saw one snowflake he would not look up to the sky, just in case he saw the lips of death come down to steal his life-blood from him.

YOMI

JAPAN, 700CE

IN Japanese Buddhist myth Emma-O was the great ruler-judge of the underworld, Yomi-tsukumi. Yomi meant the land of gloom, or the darkest part of the night, and was originally merely a mirror-image world, with no light, no beings, just nothingness. Izanami's escape to Yomi (see page 29) brought with it the creation of demons to live in the underworld, tormenting all those who died, and subsequently Yomi became a place of ordeal and torture rather than just a netherworld of no-form.

Emma-O lived in a palace with never-ending halls, corridors and tunnels teeming with dead souls who could never find a way out to the light. As the judge of all who came to Yomi, Emma-O would sit at his great desk made of jewels and precious metals cast out of the earth, and judge the male souls, while his sister would judge the female souls. These souls were transported in great chariots of fire or brought once a year across the sea of darkness. Those who were deemed innocent would be returned to the upper world to a new incarnation. The wicked would be punished before returning to another life. No one could change these punishments unless they were blessed by the goddess of mercy at the last moment. The dead would be tied to planks of wood on which their crimes were written, and marched before Emma-O. Those guilty or punishable were tormented by the cruel demons, 80,000 red- and green-skinned warriors, who would inflict either physical torture or mental agonies suited to the individual's crimes in his past life.

PO

POLYNESIA, 750CE

THROUGHOUT Polynesia were many different variations of the otherworlds. The ones that appear most are the underworlds of Po, where the soul would probably not wish to linger after death, and two spirit worlds, called Polotu in western Polynesia and Hawaiki in eastern Polynesia. Just to be confusing, Hawaiki was also the name given to the ancestral netherworld in the west – a place where spirits could return, but the living could never find. This became the desired destination for souls, and depending on which part of Polynesia you inhabited, it would be either on an island, in the sky or even below ground, where again it became confused with the underworld of Po.

Po, like many of the other netherworlds, was divided into different regions. The most ominous region of Po was ruled over by Miru, who waited in the underworld with a huge net in which he caught the souls of simple people, those who had done wrong in their lives and those who had the misfortune to be killed by sorcery. As the souls leapt out of the 'real' world into the otherworlds, he scooped them up with his net and then threw them into his great ovens, where they were to experience oblivion. It was not that they believed in eternal punishment or reward for their behaviour in this life, because wrong-doers did not suffer eternal torture for their sins, simply complete annihilation.

Those who were privileged enough to have friends and support for the correct funeral rites were usually given access to join their ancestors in the spirit world that mirrored this one. But some were not so lucky, and would be stuck between this world and the netherworld, so that their spirits became locked in a twilight zone where they became evil and enraged at their persistent state of liminality.

PARE AND HUTU

PARE was a beautiful young woman who was of such high and pure lineage that she was seen both as sacred in her tribe and also as untouchable by any man. Pare was set apart from the other young women of her own age as a *puhi* (a high-born virgin), who would have to wait until a man of high enough ancestry and rank was found to marry her.

Pare lived alone with her servants in a house that was surrounded by three beautiful palisades. Every time food was sent to her it had to pass through each enclosure and each level of rank of servants.

Pare's house was filled with most exquisite flaxen floor-mats; her clothes were made with the finest threads; and she perfumed the rooms with fragrant grasses and saps. Once the season changed into the time of games and joy, a young chief, Hutu, of great nobility, came to the village to play darts and spinning tops. Hutu was highly skilled and won all the competitions, so that most in the village admired his talent, his bravado and his charm. When Pare heard the people cheering and singing and praising the stranger she became restless and longed to escape the confines of the house.

Pare waited near the gates of the outer enclosure and watched the games. When she saw Hutu's good looks and how skilled a player he was, she instantly fell in love with him. Hutu threw his darts again and this time one fell close to the gate where Pare crouched. Quickly she grabbed the dart through the wooden gates and hid it within her skirt. As Hutu approached she stood up. Hutu's request for his missing dart was denied and Pare instead invited him into her house.

Fraught with her own desire for this incredible young man, she could not think of anything else. Hutu agreed to enter the house, knowing that he was of a lower rank than she and telling her that he had a wife and child in his own village. Here he was a stranger, alone in the middle of her tribe, and it was neither correct nor proper for him to enter the house of a puhi. But Pare pleaded with him, begging him to make love to her, and when he again and again rejected her and demanded that he be allowed to leave, she hung her head and looked to the floor sadly nodding, tears flowing across her cheeks and her heart completely broken.

The tormented Hutu ran away from her house as fast as he could, not daring to look back. In some way she had aroused his own passions and he was running mostly for his shame, not because of his feelings. But it was too late for Pare. In her humiliation at losing her dignity to this man who had rejected her, she returned to the house, now no longer beautiful, no longer sacred, spoiled by her own desire. In her terrible sorrow she hanged herself, and her soul descended to Po.

When the rest of the villagers learned of Pare's death and heard from the servants that Hutu had entered the house, they believed the worst. Hutu had been overcome with lust for her, ravaged her and she had hanged herself with shame for losing her bodily virginity and spiritual sacredness. The villagers followed Hutu, seized him and brought him back to the village to learn his fate. When Hutu heard that she had killed herself he offered to descend to the spirit world to find her.

He found Great Hina sitting in Te Ringa, the threshold of the under-world. Here she would wait, the guardian of the pathway that leads to Po, and direct those who came, knowing which path they should go down. First, she tried to send Hutu down the path for the spirits of dogs. But when he offered her his magical greenstone dagger she relented and showed him the pathway by which the souls of men descend to Po. Hina gave him food in a basket and warned him not to eat the food that might be offered him in the underworld, for then he would never be able to return.

'I advise you to bow your head as you enter Po, for a wind will lift you from the ground, and you must make sure your feet touch the ground first when the wind places you back down.'

In Po, Hutu found Pare in a village that mirrored the one in the upper world. But she refused to acknowledge him, she would not appear and she would not watch as he played darts, spun tops and threw spears in every effort to win her to him. His heart became heavy and he began to think of other ways to attract Pare's attention. Hutu invented a new sport. He bent down a great long tree to the ground, climbed on the branches then catapulted up in the air as the tree was released.

Pare was intrigued by this new game, and when she eventually emerged from her darkness and saw Hutu, they could not resist one another. Together they swung higher and higher on the tree, and with Pare clasping on to Hutu's back they eventually were thrown high enough for Hutu to grab hold of the roots of the trees of the upper world. Scrambling up through the roots at the entrance to Po, they climbed into the world of light through a cave in the hill-side not far from Pare's village.

Hutu guided her spirit to where her physical body still lay and forced her soul up through the soles of her feet. The villagers cried with happiness to see their beautiful puhi again, and agreed that Hutu must be a man of great power and that it would only be right that he should marry Pare.

SAYADIO

SAYADIO was a young brave who still mourned every day the tragic loss of his young and beautiful sister. For a girl both innocent and cherished to die so young seemed unfair, and so Sayadio resolved to find her in the Land of Spirits. For many moons he searched the plains and mountains of his homeland for the Land of Spirits, but although he met many strangers and experienced many adventures, it seemed that the lost world would always elude him.

He grew weary and tired and was about to abandon his quest when he met an old man who sat down with his pipe and spoke at length about the spirit world and the difficulties in reaching it. Before they parted, the wise Indian gave Sayadio a magic gourd. He told Sayadio that with this gourd he would be able to catch the spirit of his sister if he ever found the Land of Spirits.

It was not long after this encounter that Sayadio found himself in a deep cavern. The cliffs above him were sheer rock, and there was no sound except his own breath. He walked down through the narrow gorge, further and further down into darkness it led, until the light of the sun was gone and the blue sky had turned black. This was the Land of Spirits.

Sayadio quickly noticed that he was surrounded by whispering spirits. But as he approached them they fled, either melting into thin air or swishing across the rock faces like birds in flight, their misty forms echoing only a gasp of air in the caverns. The more he tried to communicate, the more they would disappear or whirl themselves into eddies of terror and frenzied spiralling dances. Sayadio was miserable, now convinced he would never find his sister. The spirit master was brave enough to come forward and asked him what was wrong. Sayadio recounted his story, and the spirit master felt sorry for him. 'You must visit the great festival of the dead, where the spirits dance and celebrate the changing seasons, just as they had done on earth. It is there you might find your sister.'

'How will I know her?' Sayadio asked.

'She will appear to you, because you are related by blood. She will be the only spirit who will take the image of a mortal form.'

In the part of the cavern that joined the entrance to the deeper Land of Spirits there came dancers; these were swirling mists and wisps of air that seemed to fly around Sayadio's head. Entranced, he watched as they formed clouds shaped like faces, or bodies attired in showers of golden dust, then as the circle of spirit-dancers rose on the wind he saw one face emerge, one glimpse of a shape that was his sister. As he tried to catch hold of her she dissolved into the darkness. Again Sayadio asked the spirit master how he was to catch her.

'Take this magic rattle. It has the power to draw the spirits to you. Then you may be able to grab her.'

The music began for another dance and the spirits formed a bigger circle. Sayadio's sister was intoxicated by the music, so he began to shake the rattle in time to the rhythm. She was closer to him now, and as the dancers whirled even faster he scooped his open gourd up around the misty vapour and fished her out of the mist, then shut the gourd's lid firmly down upon her.

But the captured soul did not want to return to the land of the living and struggled inside the gourd to escape. Sayadio ran back along the cavern, upwards through the rocks until he began to see a glimmer of light again and the world that he knew. Without much difficulty he found his way back to his village, as if it had only been a moment's walk away from the Land of Spirits.

He called on his friends to come and see his sister restored to life. The girl's corpse was brought from its resting place in readiness for her spirit to be reabsorbed. Ceremonial robes were placed across the dead girl's body, and the tribe began to dance as Sayadio brought the gourd and placed it beside his sister's corpse. But another Indian girl was curious, she had always wondered what a soul might look like, and she foolishly peeped inside the gourd. As she lifted the lid, the tormented soul flew out from the gourd. Up into the air it swirled and swished until it vanished into nothing and was gone. Sayadio was heartbroken. For some hours he sat alone with his sister's corpse, believing that her spirit might return of its own accord, but it did not. In his despair he now believed that he could never bring back her soul. He fell dead to the ground; the only way he could ever be with his sister again was for his own soul to join hers.

SEDNA

INUIT, NORTH AMERICA, 1000CE

THE ancestors of the Inuit peoples of the Arctic regions that extend from Greenland to Siberia can be traced back over 900 years. It was the neighbouring peoples who called the Inuit people 'Eskimo' – meaning 'eater of raw meat'. Sedna is part of the oral tradition of the Inuit. She is the daughter of the creator-god Anguta, but she functions as the go-between for the Inuit people and the animals they need to survive. Sedna represents the undersea forces of nature, and as long as she is appeased, order and the stability of the food chain will remain.

In a land far from Sedna's lonely home there lived a seabird who was too arrogant and too conceited ever to consider marrying one of his own kind.

Eventually the petrel decided that he would choose a wife from the human race and especially from the Inuit women, who appeared to be hard-working, strong and very beautiful.

He spent many weeks flying across the Inuit lands looking for the right woman and at last came to the lonely shore where Sedna lived with her father. As soon as he saw her he knew this was the woman he wanted to be his wife. The petrel made himself a strong kayak to withstand the wild and rough seas, and he stitched together a strong sealskin coat to cover his bird-form, sure that he could win Sedna in the guise of a man. The petrel set off on his journey across the wild icy seas and found the lonely land where he had spotted Sedna on his flight.

Sedna, however, had so far refused to marry any of the suitors that her father had brought for her. She was like a spoilt child, constantly hungry, and spending most of her time eating and ignoring her duties. That morning as she looked out to sea she saw a kayak bobbing up and down in the water. The bird-man called across the waves and sang an enchanting song, which impressed Sedna.

'Come live with me in my beautiful home,' he sang. 'Come sleep on the softest skins, in the warmest tent, with the most splendid food you can ever imagine. Come marry me and enjoy the light and the warmth of my heart and my home.'

For Sedna the idea of endless food, warmth and luxury was irresistible, and besides this charming stranger had dark eyes and a haunting voice, not unlike a bird's.

She ran back to her tent, told her father she was going to marry this bird-man, and there was nothing he could do stop her. So Sedna joined the petrel in the kayak, and they journeyed across the rough, icy seas to the land of the seabirds. But Sedna found that the petrel had deceived her. For the land of the seabirds was cold and dark. They lived in tents made of fish-scales, and the floors were covered in old sealskins that were so rough she could not sleep. There were no luxurious items, and the food was raw fish, and more raw fish, which the seabirds dropped on the ground so she had to scrabble among them to take a piece for herself. But the petrel loved her as only a seabird could and had no reason to believe that she was not happy.

Soon it was spring, and the misery of winter in the seabird land had made Sedna determined to escape. Sedna's father, Anguta, had also ventured out in his kayak, anxious to see the home of the bird-man who had captivated Sedna's heart. When he found Sedna in her wretched state, he killed the petrel with his harpoon, then, grabbing Sedna, he sped off in the kayak back to their homeland.

The seabirds were enraged that Anguta had killed their best loved friend, and they flew out to sea to punish Sedna and her father. Swooping down on the little kayak, they stirred up a storm with their wings so the boat would capsize. The waves grew bigger and bigger until the kayak was tossed and thrown around in the sea and began to turn over. Both Sedna and her father were thrown into the icy water. Anguta managed to haul himself on to the spine of the kayak, but realizing that he would drown if Sedna came back on the boat, he refused to let her climb aboard.

'You have angered me! Look what you have done! Let the seabirds have you, let you go to your fate at the bottom of the sea!' he cried, in fear of his own death.

Sedna clung on to the side of the kayak as the petrels returned, bringing with them bigger waves and piercing icy winds. There was only one thing left for Anguta to do. He pulled out his seal-knife and began to chop off Sedna's fingers one by one as she clung miserably to the side of the boat. Each finger that fell into the sea became the whales, or the seals or the walruses, but then, with her fingers gone, she slipped under the water and sank to the depths of the great ocean.

Sedna lives at the bottom of the sea. This is the underworld where she rules over the dead, and is queen of the monsters and the demons. The animals created from her fingers are the first of all the animals that live in that part of the sea, and the storm petrels still cry and shriek across the skies in case she should ever rise up out of the ocean again.

If the Inuit people disobey her taboos, she becomes angry, the ocean rises above her to create storms that drown and destroy all who try to survive on the surface of the sea. So the Inuit shaman must make a yearly journey to her underworld home. Here, he combs the tangles out of her hair, and unravels the knots filled with creatures and serpents of the deep. Only then will she restore calm to the sea.

THE RESURRECTION
OF PAPAN

MEXICO, 1500CE

THE curious but well-documented myth of how the Princess Papan rose from the dead to prophesy her brother's doom and the subsequent fall of his empire at the hands of the Spaniards is both alarming in its prediction and extraordinary in its accuracy.

The irony of the strange story of Papan's resurrection is that not long after Montezuma's self-imposed isolation, the Spanish conquistadores arrived in Mexico. One of the first people to welcome the Christianity they brought with them and one of the first to be baptized was the Princess Papan.

Montezuma's rule had been long and unopposed. His sister, Papan, had been married off to one of his most trusted advisers, who had been presented with his own palace, surrounded by superb gardens, waterfalls, rock pools and baths for the royal court that resided there.

Papan lived a wonderful life, and after the death of her husband she took over his role as governor and performed royal functions and duties that would be expected of someone more powerful, like her own brother, Montezuma. Her supremacy was both great and also revered, and so when it came about that Papan died, the greatest funeral ceremony ever took place. Even the emperor himself attended, along with every notable and important person in the whole kingdom.

Papan's body was placed in a stone tomb and interred in a subterranean vault in the palace grounds, not far from the royal baths. Here, with great solemnity and mourning, the entrance to the vault was sealed by a stone slab, and the attendants, guests and royal party left the palace and returned to their chambers to grieve privately.

The following morning, one of the royal children, a young girl aged six, went out into the gardens to search for her governess. As she pushed her way through the bushes towards the royal baths she saw the Princess Papan standing alone as if in a trance. The princess beckoned to her and told her to bring her governess to her. The child ran back into the palace and found the governess preparing for their journey.

'Come quickly,' she cried. 'The Princes Papan is alive, and she wants to speak with you, you must come!'

The governess was not particularly amused by this childish fantasy, but agreed to follow the girl into the garden to put her mind at rest. When the governess saw Papan sitting on a rock beside the pool she immediately fainted with terror. The child ran to her mother's apartment to tell her what had happened. Together, with two attendants they returned to the royal baths and found Papan still there.

Again, the woman was frightened but Papan called to her, 'Don't fear me, for I have only returned to tell you something of great importance. I must tell my brother Montezuma, for only he will be able to do anything to stop what is prophesied.' The woman nodded and took her into the palace and hid her in her apartment.

The resurrected Papan was given the opportunity to meet Montezuma before he returned to his own palace. When he heard the story that she was indeed alive and anxious to speak to him, he rushed to the apartment fearful of what he might find. When he saw Papan standing before him he shouted out, 'Are you really my sister, or are you some demon who has taken her likeness and come to harm us?'

'It is only Papan who stands before you, your majesty, you must believe me. No demon could speak to you, or tell you what I am about to tell you.'

123

So Montezuma grimly nodded for her to be seated before him, and she told him and his closest courtiers her terrible prophecy.

'I was dead and buried yesterday, but my ancestors have sent me back to the upper world from the dwelling of the dead to inform you of this prophecy. The moment after death I found myself in a great valley with no beginning nor end. There were mountains all around that seemed to reach up into nothingness for eternity. As I walked on I found a path which led to more and more paths. The noise of a torrential river enticed me to walk down one path until I found myself beside a raging stream. Beside the stream there stood a young man dressed in a long robe that was fastened with a shining diamond like the sun. On his forehead was a mark, a sign, like a cross. His hair was fair, and his eyes gleamed like emeralds, he had wings upon his back with golden feathers and some the colours of the rainbow. He smiled and took hold of my hand. "You cannot cross the river of eternity yet, it is not time for you."

'He led me back between the skeletons of dead men, their skulls filled with worms, and their bones dried pure white in the sunlight. I saw some other strange creatures who were dark like shadows, with horns on their heads and feet like deer. Across the water there were many ships filled with men with grey eyes and strong features. They carried banners and flags in their hands and wore strange helmets to cover their heads. They were called the sons of the sun.

'The beautiful youth turned to me, and told me that it was the will of the gods that I should return to the upper world and not yet cross the river because I was the one chosen to see the future with my own eyes and to take the faith that would be offered to me by the strangers who would come to this land. That the bones of the men I had seen were those of us now who had died in ignorance of that faith and had suffered great torture and agony in their disbelief. That the dark shadow people were all that was left of those who had battled with the strangers. That I was the only one destined to return to my land and tell you the true faith so that you might make ready for their coming and save yourselves.'

The princess then arose, and bowed to her brother, Montezuma. He could not speak, for he was deeply troubled by her words. Were they indeed true, as her presence here was true? Had she ever died, or had her resurrection some deep and significant meaning for them all? Montezuma then left without a word and returned alone to his apartment, plunged in deep despair.

THE JOURNEY TO THE LAND
OF THE GRANDFATHER

IN many myths of the South American peoples it is the journey that the soul must take to the afterworld to achieve an afterlife that is fraught with danger, rather than the actual afterworld itself.

In this particular myth, from the Guarayu peoples of Bolivia, if the soul manages to escape all the trials and tests on its long and arduous journey, it may enter the Land of the Grandfather and join its ancestors to enjoy eternal youth and to indulge in the kind of activities it preferred while on this earth. This afterworld in the west was ruled over by Tamoi (grandfather), a mythical ancestor and hero of these peoples.

Once the burial of the body had been completed, the soul was immediately confronted with two paths, one wide and apparently easy, and the other narrow, dark and dangerous. If it chose the easy way, then it was certain to spend the afterlife in eternal darkness and death. It was the hard path that a soul must chose, for only by being severely tested did a person have the right to an afterlife at all.

First, the soul had to cross a wide and dangerous river. The only way across was on a ferry, and unless the soul took with it the bamboo musical pipe buried with the body in the grave, the ferryman would refuse to carry the soul across. If the soul attempted to try to cross the river without the help of the ferryman, it would certainly never reach the other side. Once across this river, the soul had to cross a raging torrent, which could be traversed only by jumping on a tree trunk. This rushed haphazardly and violently from bank to bank in the white water. If the poor soul fell into the surging foam, it would be devoured by the palometa fish, whose great sharp teeth and foul-smelling breath would provide a slow and painful eternity.

If the soul succeeded in crossing this river it now had to pass through the house of Izoi-tamoi (the worm grandfather). This particular worm-like ancestor grew bigger and bigger if the soul had been virtuous in its lifetime, and smaller and smaller if it had committed any crimes or sins. If the soul had been evil in any way, Izoi-tamoi would instantly split it into two pieces with his sharp tongue.

Any virtuous soul would now have to carry on and walk through a land of darkness, carrying only a bundle of straw that could be burned to show the way. This straw was left in the grave together with a spark of fire to light the straw. Once it was out of the darkness, the soul must stop at the ceiba tree where humming-birds hummed all day in the branches. This trial was to pluck

125

a million feathers from the darting birds without disturbing their nectar-gathering and then to offer the feathers to Tamoi for his head-dress.

But an even more dangerous test faced the soul as it now passed through a steep-sided gully. Here two rocks crushed together across the path as each soul tried to walk through. If the soul knew the right code word, the rocks would hold back and let it pass to safety.

Yet more dangers faced the weary soul, as it must now be examined by the gallinazo bird to ensure it had the perforated lips and nose that every Guarayu must have to enter the afterworld. But if for some reason they were absent, the bird would lead the soul astray with magical potions and halluci-nating drugs until it went into a frenzy of eternal madness.

Next it must be tickled for a day by a monkey and not laugh, walk past the speaking tree and not listen, but neither hold its hands to its ears nor make any sounds to drown the tree's voice. Then it must gaze upon the most beau-tiful thing it had desired in the 'real' world and not want it.

If the soul could survive these trials it would at last arrive at the land of Tamoi. The soul would be welcomed and would then bathe in a pool of eter-nal youth to carry on its activities much as it had done in the 'real' world.

DUBIAKU

GHANA, recorded 1700CE

DUBIAKU is a trickster-hero of the Asante peoples of Ghana, but this short tale shows how he delights in playing games with death itself. How to cheat and outwit death has been one of the greatest dilemmas of human consciousness.

Dubiaku was the eleventh son in a very poor family. He was called Dubiaku (number eleven) because his mother had become so tired with producing chil-dren that she had given up naming them after the fifth. Dubiaku's mother was also miserable because they had no money and never enough food. The eleven brothers ate so much grain and bread that there was never enough for their mother or father.

One day, after the eleven boys had gorged their way through all the corn-bread and bowls of root-broth, Dubiaku's mother begged Sky-Spirit to ask death to come and take some of the boys. Sky-Spirit nodded and went to find the boys who were out swinging in the trees like monkeys and not doing a stroke of work. Sky-Spirit joined them in the trees, and the idea she planted in their heads was to perform a dare. The boys were to visit death in her hut. To prove to Sky-Spirit they had been there, they were to collect four gold items – a chewing stick, a whetstone, a snuff box and a pipe.

The boys eagerly ran off to death's hut. Death welcomed them quite kindly into her home and set out eleven sleeping mats. When it was night-time she placed one of the boys on each mat next to one of her own children. She wanted to wait until the guests were fast asleep and then eat them.

Dubiaku's brothers soon fell into a deep sleep. Death hurried to the smallest brother. She was hungry and wanted to get on with her grand feast of children, but when she looked down she found that Dubiaku was still awake.

'I want a pipe of tobacco before I sleep,' said Dubiaku. So death fetched him her golden pipe.

'But I need a pinch of snuff, without that I really cannot rest.' So death fetched him a pinch of snuff.

Then he asked for a chewing stick and something to eat. Death began to get angry, yet she couldn't attack the boy for fear of waking the others with his screams. Instead, she went outside and lit a fire with her golden whetstone to cook some broth. Some of the golden sparks landed on Dubiaku's mat and he picked up the pieces of whetstone and crammed them in his pocket. A few seconds later he woke all his brothers. They crept out of the hut, leaving their clothes in bundles where they had slept on the mats and taking the golden objects with them.

Death gave up her night-time cooking, sure now that Dubiaku must have fallen asleep. She slithered back inside the hut and began to eat all the children on the mats. These were, of course, her own children. When she realized what she had done, she ran screaming and shrieking out into the bush.

With death chasing after the boys, there seemed little they could do to save themselves. But Dubiaku made them all hide up in the trees so that she couldn't see them. Breathless, death stopped to think right under the branch where Dubiaku was perched. Dubiaku peed on the top of her head and she instantly went into a frantic trance and began to shriek out a falling-down spell.

One by one the boys fell to the ground like ripe nuts and died. But Dubiaku had already jumped down before she had sung the spell, and he lay hidden in the long grass while death pulled up her skirts and clambered into the trees to find the missing boy. As soon as she was caught up in the branches, Dubiaku called out the falling-down spell and brought her crashing down out of the tree. She shattered on the ground like a split watermelon. So death herself was dead like Dubiaku's ten brothers.

Dubiaku found some water of life and threw it across the boys' faces. The boys all revived and so did death because accidentally Dubiaku had splashed some water on her face too. Death chased them down towards the river, and the first ten swam quickly across the raging torrent. But Dubiaku couldn't swim and was left standing on the bank, death approaching him like a herd of rhinoceroses. Quickly, he turned himself into a stone, and in her rage death

127

picked up the stone and threw it at the boys on the other bank. Dubiaku landed safely on the other side, far away from the hands and jaws of screaming death.

FOUR

HEROES, WARRIORS AND THEIR QUESTS

EVERY CULTURE OR CIVILIZATION throughout the history of world mythology has produced a hero, great mortal or semi-divine warrior. Whether it is a divine quest, the search for enlightenment, the desire for vengeance or fulfilment, the hero is a necessary catalyst for our consciousness. Many of these myths are long-winded and elaborate, for they often involve stories that encompass more than just one single hero and his immediate problem. The myths may involve tests of man's strength or mortal acclaim, such as in the epic and oldest known Babylonian tale of Gilgamesh. Nearly all heroes are mortal, or at least part-mortal, part-god, and the tales are generally male dominated – most of these myths originate from a time when patriarchal societies had already dissipated the earlier cults of the great goddess.

Heroes seem rarely to question themselves, apart from such thinkers as Odysseus or Arjuna. In a sense, it is the story itself that presents a form of quest with which we can all identify. Often the tale poses a question that has no expectations about its hero's ability to come up with a solution. Rather it is we, the readers, and the story-teller who must do so.

GILGAMESH

THIS is one of the oldest surviving stories in the world dating back to about 3000BCE. One form of this tale was written on twelve tablets of clay, each containing 300 lines of verse, for the library of King Ashurbanipal, c.600BCE. One of the tablets contains an even older story of the great flood and the only survivor, Utnapishtim, who was subsequently granted immortality. There are various scholars who believe that Gilgamesh was a real person, a king of Uruk who ruled c.2700BCE, and that this epic story is based on real events.

Gilgamesh is probably the earliest recorded human being to achieve heroic status, and his story reveals how the so-called boundaries of time and space are, in fact, unbound. The questing of human nature, whether for wisdom and insight or for immortality, are clearly part of our psyche, whether set over 4000 years ago or today. Perhaps it is someone as ancient and as solitary as Gilgamesh who answers those questions about who we really are. The hero is the one who sets out on a quest, but it is only the question itself that carries the answer. The heroes of later myths are more concerned with social status or proof of their identity. They accept what they have been born into, but Gilgamesh questions all. It is wisdom he seeks, and he learns both wisdom and the ability to find answers only in the seeking.

Gilgamesh was one-third mortal and two-thirds god. His mother was the sky-goddess, Ninsun, and his father had been a demon who had disguised himself as the king of Uruk. But because he was a mortal he shared the fate of all human beings, that of death. Gilgamesh soon succeeded to the throne of Uruk as a young man, proved his courage and daring by hunting and fighting, and his worth by building a wall around Uruk with 900 towers.

However, inside his fortress palace he behaved like a wilful and spoilt child. He made men his slaves and, with an insatiable hunger for sex, raped most of the young women. He wrestled for money and cared nothing for his subjects or what others thought of him. His unruly behaviour earned Gilgamesh a bad reputation, while his drinking and debauchery only made the people of Uruk more determined to stop him.

The people of Uruk prayed to the gods and asked for their help. When the gods heard their pleas, Anu, the father of all gods, persuaded Ninhursaga, mother-earth, to create a giant: 'This giant will be called Enkidu, and he will be so strong and powerful that he will fight with Gilgamesh and put an end to all his boasting. Gilgamesh's humiliation should extinguish his own tyranny.'

So mother-earth formed in her mind an image of a giant man who was called Enkidu, and she placed him far away from civilization with the wild beasts in the mountains. He was covered in hair and he clothed himself in skins when it was cold. He ran with the gazelles, and he drank water at the same watering holes. He was not aware that he was a human being, and believed he was a beast of the night.

The other gods put an image of the wild giant Enkidu into Gilgamesh's mind one night as he lay restless and disturbed by terrible nightmares. In the dream a heavenly being fell to earth at Gilgamesh's feet, blocking his way. Gilgamesh tried to move the being, but it was so strong that he could not shift it, and the people of Uruk kissed this being and he came to love it like a friend. The next night Gilgamesh had another dream of a giant, so tall and strong, so wild and untamable, that he longed to capture the giant and add it to his playthings around the citadel.

Knowing that this giant must really exist, Gilgamesh refused to hunt him nor bring him to Uruk by force. Instead he sent a woman priestess to lure him out of the wilderness. When Enkidu saw the woman he was enchanted. He had spent so long alone in the wild that he didn't know what to think of this strange creature, only that he was beginning to feel different instincts and urges. The priestess taught him many things, about sex, about cleansing his body, and about drinking and eating. She taught him about human civilization, and after a week Enkidu was ready to follow her anywhere. The woman took him to the great walled citadel of Uruk where the feast of Ishtar was in progress. She told him that he might have to fight Gilgamesh to be acknowledged and accepted into Uruk.

Gilgamesh was ready. He had seen in his dreams that Enkidu would come, and as Enkidu entered the gates he swept off to meet him. The nobles were elated, at last here was a mortal who would match the tyrant Gilgamesh! The giant, already warned that he must fight Gilgamesh, instantly began to wrestle with him. But as they fought they began to admire one another and respect each other's strength. Exhausted, they fell to their knees, embraced and kissed. From that day on they were the closest of friends, and Gilgamesh's people now had two strong and petulant rulers instead of one.

So the people once again prayed to the gods for help, and once more the gods put an image in Gilgamesh's mind to send him on a quest. They also made Enkidu bored with living such a lethargic life in the city. He longed for the wilderness, to run with the beasts and to use his strength. His arms were becoming fat and his muscles were weaker. Gilgamesh had now seen in his dreams that he must destroy the great monster, Humbaba. The gods were convinced that both Gilgamesh and Enkidu would be massacred by the monster and Uruk would be peaceful again.

Humbaba (the fire-breather) guarded the cedar forest. Gilgamesh knew that if he succeeded in killing the great beast he would not only rid the land of all evil but it would surely put him on the road to fame and glory. A hero to be honoured among his people!

In the cedar forest, the monster Humbaba was not as ferocious an adversary as the gods had anticipated, and after a fierce fight, Enkidu held the monster down while Gilgamesh stabbed it in the neck. The beast fell to the ground, the great crash of its body echoing through the cedar trees for miles. Gilgamesh and his men continued into the deep forest and cut down all Humbaba's cedars to take them back to Uruk.

On his return, Gilgamesh was hailed a great hero. He put on fine clothes and washed his skin of grease and sweat. His handsome face glowed with pride, and the women-priestesses could not stop themselves from desiring him. Ishtar, the goddess of desire and fertility, fell into a faint of lust when she saw him. She tried to seduce him, but Gilgamesh rejected her by reminding her of all her past terrible deeds. Ishtar ran to her father, Anu, and pleaded with him to send the bull of heaven down to Uruk to kill Gilgamesh for his insults. Anu reluctantly agreed, and the bull raged through the citadel, killing hundreds of people. Enkidu and Gilgamesh wrestled with the bull and tore its heart from its body. When Ishtar saw that Gilgamesh had killed the bull, she asked the gods if she could destroy Enkidu and Gilgamesh herself.

Enkidu was not a problem. She arranged for him to be struck by the plague. He lay for many days in a coma before dying, and Gilgamesh wept days and nights by the giant's bedside, not realizing that he was, in fact, dead. It was only when a maggot dropped out of his nose that Gilgamesh realized he must bury the body. He covered the giant's body with a veil and wailed before the people, insisting that they mourn this great hero as one of their own. In his misery, Gilgamesh now vowed to grow his hair and roam the wilderness, clad only in a lion-skin.

But Gilgamesh was not prepared to die like his friend. Now he seriously needed to find the answer to the one great mystery in life: how could he avoid death?

He found himself, probably at Ishtar's instigation, on a quest to seek out Utnapishtum, the man who had everlasting life. He travelled a treacherous journey across grassy plains, where he saw no one except the birds, and across scorching deserts, where he met no one except the scorpions. When he came to the sea he met a fish-woman to whom he bemoaned his fate. 'I fear death old woman. This journey is to find the secret of everlasting life. I believe that Utnapishtum can give me the answer. Do you know how I can find him?'

The fish-woman shook her head. 'I do not know where he is, and I doubt you will ever find the answer, even if you find him. Ask the boatman, he may know.' She pointed down the shore and Gilgamesh found the boatman, who rowed him across the sea to Utnapishtum's island.

Utnapishtum listened to Gilgamesh's long story about his heroic conquests and the sad death of his friend Enkidu. He listened to Gilgamesh's desire to learn the secret of eternal life, and how he feared death. Utnapishtum stood up and pointed to the sky: 'There is no way for a mortal to cheat death, because to be mortal is to live and to die. All that I can do is give you the secret of eternal youth until you die. Do you wish to have this everlasting youthfulness in your life?'

Gilgamesh nodded. If he could not be immortal, then at least he would live happily until he died.

'So Gilgamesh, you must pick a plant that grows at the bottom of the sea. It is the only flower whose scent can be smelled in water. You must make a potion from the flowers, then drink this elixir, and it will keep you young forever.'

Gilgamesh weighted down his body by tying great stones to his legs and then plunged into the sea. The stones dragged him to the bottom of the ocean, and he found the scented plant growing among the rocks. He picked the plant, slashed the ropes to release his legs from the stones, then returned to his boat, now intent on sharing his secret with all the people of Uruk.

The journey across the sea was long and arduous. On the distant shore he set down the plant carefully in his clothes while he went to bathe and wash the sweat from his skin. The intoxicating scent of the plant drifted across the land. A serpent glided out of the water, lured by the fragrant petals, and swallowed every piece of the plant.

Gilgamesh returned refreshed and ready to continue his journey, but he found the plant gone and the serpent with a shining new skin. His anger turned to rage, and his rage to despair as the serpent slithered quickly back into the sea. He would never be able to find another plant now in the depths of the ocean. For some hours he cried to himself. Now he had nothing for himself, nor his people.

But as he walked on homeward his heart began to grow stronger. In losing what he desired so much, he had begun to learn to live with who he truly was. As he approached the great walls of Uruk he recalled how strong they were, how beautiful were the temples and how impressive was the citadel with its 900 towers. No one would ever be able to forget this achievement; this was his immortality. He wrote down on tablets the stories of his travels and placed the tablets on the walls of Uruk to share his wisdom and be remembered as one who had come to understand why he was only a mortal.

SEKHMET

SEKHMET was the consort of Ptah and a goddess of the Memphis triad. She was a defender of the divine order, not a creator of it, and she became associated with her father, the sun-god Ra. One of her other titles was Nesert (flame), which emphasized this attachment. Sekhmet means 'the powerful' or 'the mightiest', and she became a feared war-goddess, represented in sacred art as a woman with the head of a lioness carrying a fire-spitting cobra.

When she was in war mode she was highly destructive towards the enemies of Ra. She was considered to be the eye of Ra, representing the powerful rays of the sun. Fiery arrows flashed from her red eyes, and she breathed flames and scorched her enemies before devouring their blood. Another of her titles was 'the lady of the bright red linen', which may refer to the colour of the earth or the blood-spattered clothes of her enemies. She was feared by many, and even the great serpent Aapep and the demons of Seth cowered in her presence.

Ra had originally taken human shape as one of the pharaohs, so that he could be worshipped more easily by mortals. But Ra's biggest problem was that in mortal form he also aged. His people began to worship other deities, like Aapep, the world-snake, while Ra became withered and haggard, and not much like the sun he was supposed to be. So Ra sent Sekhmet as his eye (other versions suggest Sekhmet was sent as Hathor) to punish the human race.

The furious Sekhmet was uncontrollable, searing the earth, scorching the crops and feasting on the blood of those that she swept up like a raging inferno. She slaughtered everyone who worshipped Aapep and even turned on the innocent or those still loyal to Ra in her wrath and anger. She might have annihilated the human race if Ra had not realized that unless she were stopped there would be no one left to worship him. So Ra used a trick, and while she was burning her way across the Delta region he sent out messengers to the island of Elephantine to gather red ochre from the soil. Ra's servants fetched huge vats of beer from the stone cellars and mixed the alcoholic brew together and spread it across the land. When Sekhmet came flaming down to this part of the earth she thought the red mess was blood and began to drink it. She became so intoxicated that she fell asleep like a dozing lioness and slept while Ra put out the fires. In celebration of this great saving of mankind, orgiastic and debauched festivals were held in her honour.

But Sekhmet was also known as a healer. From the moment that Ra had restored her to a more dispassionate nature, she focused her rage mostly on the Nubians, the real enemies of Egypt, turning their land into a great desert.

Ironically, because she had caused so much plague and pestilence people turned to her to appeal for help. Her healing skills were widely regarded, for her ability to see into the depths of the supernatural empowered her with extraordinary magical strength. Not only could she cure her subjects, but she could also root out the demons that possessed them. These powers eventually evolved into a following of priests, who became an important dynasty of healers specializing in heart disease. She was worshipped everywhere in Egypt, and her temples and statues can be found throughout the country.

RAMA

INDIA, 900BCE

FROM the great *Ramayana*, a Hindu epic story compiled in the eleventh to sixth centuries BCE, comes Rama and his quest to destroy the terrifying demon Ravana and save his love Sita. The *Ramayana* tells in part the story of the time when there was a golden age. Harmony abounded, and women, gods, goddesses and men all lived in peace. Rama's story reveals the workings of destiny, through the desires and adventures of a god who incarnates as a mortal and finds out what life is really all about.

Rama's real name was Ramachandra (Rama the moon). In Hindu myth he was the seventh incarnation on earth of the god Vishnu. The gods had decided that Ravana, a demon-king of Sri Lanka, had become so invulnerable and so invincible that someone must be created on earth to destroy him. Not only was he destroying mortals, but he had also turned his attentions on the gods themselves. Because Ravana had been too conceited to ask for immunity from humans, it would only be a mortal who could actually kill him. So the gods decided the only way to deal with him was for one of their number to assume mortal form and destroy him.

Vishnu volunteered to go and rid both man and gods of the dangerous demon. He went down to earth with a jar of his beloved soma, the food of immortality, and let the three wives of King Dasaratha drink from it. The first son to be born was Ramachandra, a mortal with half of Vishnu's divine powers, then each of the other three sons had lessening degrees of supernatural strength. The four princes grew up together and were good friends, and Rama was particularly close to his brother, Lakshmana.

One day a sage called Vishvamitra came to visit them and asked if they would help him to destroy a demon-queen called Taraka. Rama was very reluctant to kill a woman, but he was an excellent bowman, and it didn't take much for the wise man to persuade Rama to show off his skills. Rama killed Taraka, and so Vishvamitra introduced the boy to the court of King Janaka.

Here Rama met the king's daughter, Sita, who was the most beautiful woman on earth (as well as being an incarnation of Vishnu's wife, Lakshmi).

Janaka had organized a contest to find a suitor for Sita. Each man had to try to bend a bow Janaka had been given by Shiva. Whoever could do so would win Sita as his bride. All the suitors failed to bend it, except Rama, who bent the bow so far that it snapped. So Rama married Sita, and not long after they had returned to Rama's own palace, King Dasaratha decided to abdicate in favour of Rama.

Dasaratha's second wife resented Rama taking precedence over her own son, Bharata. She tricked the king into making Bharata an absent king, and Rama exiled himself to the forest for fourteen years. Rama wanted Sita to stay behind at the palace, but she insisted on going with him and together they set off for exile. The old king died of grief a few months later, and Rama's devoted brother, Lakshmana, joined them in the forest.

Bharata had been away all this time, and when he returned and found out that he was supposed to be king, he blamed his mother for his father's death and searched the forest for Rama, to persuade him to return. But Rama, from a sense of duty, refused to go back, so Bharata reigned as his viceroy, and kept a pair of Rama's shoes on the throne, to show who was the rightful king.

In the forest of exile Rama met Ravana's sister, a demon called Surpanakha. The demon-princess fell instantly in love with Rama and insisted that Rama marry her, but Rama resisted her advances and told her he was happily married to Sita. Rama suggested that Lakshmana might be looking for a wife, but he, too, rejected the great demon-woman. Surpanakha was so furious that she swelled to a gigantic size and chased after Sita, intent on swallowing her alive. But Rama and Lakshmana caught up with the demon and cut off her nose, her breasts and her ears. Bemoaning her fate, Surpanakha angrily returned to her brother, Ravana, who sent out an army of 14,000 demons to destroy Rama.

Rama, however, killed the entire army, so Surpanakha now sought vengeance through her powerful brother, Ravana. She knew that Ravana would be easily seduced by the thought of Sita, and so she planted the idea in his mind that he must capture her. Filled with lust, Ravana's passion for Sita grew more intense with every day that passed. Soon Ravana was so hungry for Sita that he resolved to kidnap her and have her for himself.

Ravana knew the true identity of Rama, and realized that he would get anywhere near the beautiful Sita only by trickery. So Ravana sent an enchanted deer into the forest. Every day Sita went to her favourite clearing beside a pool to meditate, and every day the deer would appear on the far side of the pool. Sita fell in love with the beautiful creature and wanted to adopt it. She asked Rama and Lakshmana to catch it, and they duly followed the deer deep into the forest. Further and further away from Sita they rode, until they were totally lost. Ravana took his chance, and snatching Sita as he rode past in his sky-chariot, carried her off screaming to Sri Lanka. On the way the vulture king, Jatayu, tried to stop Ravana and was fatally wounded. He managed to flutter back to Rama and tell him what had happened to Sita before he died.

In Sri Lanka Ravana attempted to have sex with Sita but she rejected him, so he tried to threaten her into lying with him by telling her that he would eat her alive if she did not. But Sita was saved by the knowledge of one of Ravana's other wives, who reminded him that he was under a curse that if he ever seduced or forced another man's wife into having sex he would be doomed to die.

Meanwhile, Rama had sadly cremated the great Jatayu and now began to make plans to save his wife from the terrible hands of Ravana.

Rama had already helped Sugriva, the monkey king, recover his kingdom from his wicked half-brother. So Sugriva gave Rama an army of monkeys and bears led by the great god Hanuman, the son of Vayu (the wind). The army marched south towards Sri Lanka, and Hanuman flew on ahead through the sky, crossed the great sea and found Sita alone in the garden of Ravana's palace. After giving her Rama's ring as a sign that he was on his way to rescue her, Hanuman spied out the enemy defences and the plan of the fortress and island. Lanka was a great fortress built for the god of wealth, Kubera, and the city was built mostly of gold. It was surrounded by seven moats and seven great walls of stone and precious metal.

Rama soon discovered the difficulties in crossing the strait that separated the island from the mainland. But even though the dark demonic creatures of the sea tried to devour the armies, the monkey leader, Nala, built a huge bridge. Nala had the power to make stones float on water. (The gods later anchored the rocks to the sea-bed. The remains of a massive construction still exists and is known as Nala's Bridge or, sometimes, Rama's Bridge.) The army crossed the stone causeway, and a huge battle was fought at the gates to the city, one of the biggest ever struggles for cosmic power. The gods still could not intervene because only a mortal could destroy Ravana. They watched from the heavens as the great giant Kumbhakarna, Ravana's brother, began devouring monkeys so fast that he did not have time to chew them up. Hanuman flew quickly to the Himalayas and returned with a magic herb to cure Rama's wounds. The monkeys and bears retaliated and inflicted heavy casualties on the demons. One by one the demon leaders were killed, until the battle could be resolved only by single combat between Rama and Ravana.

The earth trembled as they approached one another, the gods daring not to intervene, for Rama was their last hope. Then Rama began to shoot his arrows at Ravana's many heads. As each arrow struck one of Ravana's heads, one by one they rolled to the ground. But as each one fell another grew in its place. Rama drew out a magic weapon that had been given to him by a renowned magician, Agastya. It was shaped like an arrow, but it was infused with the power of all the gods. Its point was the fire and the sun; its shaft was

Mount Meru, the core of the universe; its feathers were the wind. Rama drew back his bow and fired the magic arrow straight into the heart of Ravana. Ravana fell dead as the arrow shot out through his back and returned to Rama's quiver. At the moment of Ravana's death, the gods showered Rama with flowers and rejoicing and resurrected all the monkeys that had fallen in the battle against evil. The gods sent down a million servants to toss all the demon corpses into the underworld, for now peace could be restored.

But Rama was not as victorious as had been hoped. The evil energy of Ravana had sown confusion in the great hero's mind. Now, reunited with Sita, he began to have terrible doubts about Sita's promises that she had been faithful to him all the time she had stayed with Ravana. Although Sita seemed to love him more than ever, there hung in the air a cloud of suspicion that for weeks and months Rama could not get out of his head. Sita swore over and over again that she had never slept nor had sex with Ravana, but Rama refused to believe she could have prevented the demon from having his way. Nor did he know of the curse that had prevented Ravana from doing so.

Sita carried on declaring her virtue and her innocence, and in despair and as a way of showing her faithfulness, she determined to prove it by the ordeal of fire. She sent Lakshmana to build a fire and light it, and then she threw herself on it, trusting to the gods to proclaim her innocence. As the flames leapt around her, Agni, the god of fire, led her away and took her before Rama, telling him that she was as true as her word. Rama felt sure now that she was innocent, and they returned to Ayodha, where Rama was restored to his throne.

For sometime all was well, but the last threads of Ravana's magic had still yet to be broken. The people of the kingdom gossiped and wondered about the innocence of Sita, and although she became pregnant, Rama decided to send her into exile. For fifteen years she stayed at a hermitage in the forest until her two sons were old enough to demand to see Rama. When he recognized the boys as his own sons, he knew he must take Sita back and show publicly that Sita was indeed innocent.

Sita returned to the palace, and Rama gathered together a great assembly of people. Sita asked the gods for a sign to prove that she was pure and that her children were those of Rama. As an answer mother-earth gaped open beneath her and swallowed her alive, then closed around her so that she was gone. Rama was heartbroken. He realized that everything she had said was true and his only wish now was to follow her to eternity. Not long after her death, he walked into the River Sarayu ending his own human life and returning to his divine form as Vishnu. His mortal quest as the destroyer of Ravana had been tragically completed.

139

PERSEUS

GREECE, 750BCE

T HE Greek myths contain probably more heroes and inspirational individuals and gods than those of any other culture. These heroes were usually
renowned for their ability to overcome any adversary against all the odds, or
they were champions in war, concerned only with blazing their way through
every adventure and enduring every torment and action. These rather male-
dominated and chauvinistic individuals, however, portray the ideal talent or
quest that was the core of Greek culture. Few of these heroes had much time
for self-questioning, but two seem to embody both empathy and a smattering
of psychological awareness – Perseus, for his ability to fall, like any human
being, passionately in love, and Odysseus, for his lonely wanderings that
allowed him to perceive the nature of mortality.

Acrisius, the king of Argos, had no sons and only one daughter, Danae.
Desperate to conceive an heir to his kingdom, he asked an oracle how he
could bring a male child into the world. But the prophecy was not the one he
had expected. Acrisius was told that he would never have any sons and any
male child of Danae's would grow up to kill him.

Acrisius was terrified of this oracle and imprisoned Danae in a bronze
tower to prevent her from ever having sex with any mortal or god. But Zeus,
in one of his highly amorous moods, turned himself into a golden shower,
rained through the window of the tower and made passionate love to her. The
result was a child, a son named Perseus.

When Acrisius heard that Danae had given birth to a male child he
would not believe that Zeus was the father. He accused Danae of having sex
with his brother, Proteus, then he pushed Danae and her child into a deep
wooden chest and threw it into the sea.

The wooden box drifted with the tides towards the island of Seriphos,
where a kind fisherman, finding the mother and child inside, took them to his
brother, King Polydectes, who brought up Perseus as his son. Once Perseus
was grown up, Polydectes tried to force Danae to marry him. But Danae had
no interest in becoming his wife, and so it was Perseus who often had to intervene and come to his mother's rescue. There was a constant undercurrent of
rivalry between Perseus and Polydectes, but it was enough for Perseus to boast
that he could win Polydectes any thing in the world, even the head of Medusa,
one of the Gorgons, as long as he did not marry Danae. The ecstatic
Polydectes instantly ordered him to do this, and Perseus was sent to cut off
Medusa's head and bring it back.

There were three Gorgons, Medusa, Euryale and Stheno. Luckily for
Perseus, the goddess Athene hated Medusa and, having overheard the

conversation on Seriphos, decided to help Perseus in his quest. She gave him a polished shield that dazzled like a mirror and told him to never look directly at Medusa who could turn men to stone with a single glance. Hermes gave him a sickle made of diamonds, and the Stygian nymphs gave him a pair of winged sandals, a magic bag and a helmet of invisibility that had belonged to Hades. Wearing the winged sandals, he flew west to the far side of the ocean guided by Athene.

The Gorgons lived in a vast underground system of lairs and tunnels, freezing cold and dripping black water. The entrance to the caves was guarded by the Gorgons' sisters, the three Graeae, who had one eye and one tooth between them, which one would use while she was on watch and the others slept. Perseus took his chance. Wearing his helmet of invisibility, he snatched the eye and tooth and ran into the caves, leaving the Graeae blind and speechless.

The Gorgons slept together in their lair among the stone shapes of the men and wild beasts that Medusa had petrified. Some were beginning to be eroded by the dripping black water, but some were fresh from the outer world, their faces almost as white as the flesh they had once been. Perseus worked slowly; he turned his back on the sleeping Medusa to avoid facing her and to make sure he never looked once in her eyes. He looked into the reflection of the polished shield and, reversing all his actions and movements, he gradually crept up on the snoring snake-headed Medusa. Then, with the diamond sickle, he cut off her head with one stroke.

The head rolled onto the black, slimy ground. Still turned away from it and watching in his shield, Persues reached behind him and picked up the ghastly head by one of the hissing serpents, then pushed it into the magic bag. Blood had spurted out from Medusa's severed neck, and where it splashed to the ground sprang a winged horse, Pegasus, rearing and stamping its hooves. Perseus leapt on the great horse's back and flew away before the other two sisters awoke, his helmet of invisibility still on, as he flew southwards and away from Cisthene.

On his way back to Seriphos Perseus landed at the feet of Atlas, the great giant who had been condemned to support the sky forever. Perseus showed him the Gorgon's head and he was instantly transformed into stone, and became the Atlas Mountains, which still support the heavens. Perseus dropped the tooth and eye that he had stolen from the Graeae and they fell into Lake Triton in Africa.

After visiting Egypt, Perseus rounded the coast to the north and saw a naked woman, Andromeda, chained to the foot of a cliff, and he immediately fell in love with her.

Andromeda was the daughter of Cassiope (or Cassiopeia) and Cepheus. Cassiope had once boasted that she and her daughter Andromeda were more beautiful then even the sea-nymphs, Poseidon's maidens. As punishment,

Poseidon sent a great sea-monster to prowl the waters of Philistia so that none could fish and all mortal men would be devoured. The monster would relent only if Cepheus sacrificed Andromeda to it.

Perseus saw Cassiope and Cepheus screaming with fear on the sea-shore and asked them what had happened. They begged him to save Andromeda, offering that she should be his wife if he did so. Perseus flew down to the crashing waves on Pegasus and, with his diamond sickle, plunged it into the sea-monster just as it was about to devour Andromeda. Perseus unchained Andromeda and took her to her parents. She had fallen in love with Perseus and asked that they be married.

But Cassiope and Cepheus had deceived Perseus, and insisted they had been forced into making a rash promise of Andromeda's hand only because of her desperate situation. But both parents pretended to relent and agree to the marriage, knowing full well that it would never happen. Cassiope then summoned Agenor to the wedding feast. Agenor had long claimed Andromeda for himself, and the deceitful parents announced that Andromeda's marriage to Perseus was void because Agenor had always been meant to be her husband. Cassiope turned on Perseus and insisted he must die. In the fight that followed Perseus reluctantly picked up the magic bag, drew out Medusa's head and turned every man and woman to stone.

Perseus and Andromeda flew back to Seriphos on Pegasus to return triumphantly with Medusa's head. But another problem awaited them. For while Perseus had been away, Polydectes had tried to force Danae to marry him. In fear of his threats of physical violence, she had shut herself in Athene's temple. Polydectes and his men had formed a great circle around the temple, waiting for her to emerge. Perseus was furious when he saw the ring of men surrounding the temple. As he and Andromeda soared overhead on Pegasus he pulled out Medusa's head, looked away and turned them all to stone. There is still a ring of stones at Seriphos today.

Perseus returned the winged sandals, wallet and helmet to Hermes and gave Medusa's head to Athene, who fixed it to the front of her shield.

Perseus set sail for Argos with Danae and Andromeda. But Acrisius heard he was coming and fled to Larissa. Not long after Perseus was invited to compete in a contest and the prophecy that Acrisius would be killed by Perseus came true. While Perseus was throwing the discus in the games, it was carried off course by the wind, striking Acrisius in the neck and killing him. Perseus was deeply grieved at the death of his grandfather and, too ashamed to rule Argos, left for Tiryns.

He founded Mycenae, and for long after his death the people of Seriphos and Mycenae worshipped him almost as a god. When Perseus and Andromeda died, Athene placed them both in the sky as constellations. The horse, Pegasus, served Perseus well throughout his life, and after his death flew to Mount Helicon to live with the Muses.

THE EARTH-BORN GIANTS

THE giants born from the blood of Ouranos's severed penis were created at the same time as the Furies, but they were quite different from the Titans. (The Titans, the oldest generation of the gods, were led by Kronos, who was Zeus's father.)

The twenty-four earth-giants were creatures or monsters of air and rock. They had human shape except for their lashing, snake-like tails, which were attached to their legs. When the earth-giants attacked Olympus, the gods stood their ground, but knew they couldn't win. Hera had prophesied that the giants could not be killed by gods but only by a single, lion-skinned mortal. If they died these giants would simply dissolve into the earth and grow straight back into huge monsters again, especially if they were near to the place of their initial birth. So to avoid anything more than bodily disintegration followed by re-birth, the giants attacked Olympus from their own birthplace and searched for the magic herb that would heal the wounds of anyone that chewed its leaves.

Some of the earth-giants went in search of this herb, which was called ephialtion, and others began piling up huge rocks and boulders into a great tower, high enough for them to jump on to Olympus and destroy the gods.

Zeus, meanwhile, was also frantically searching for this healing herb. Advised by Athene, he enlisted the help of Heracles and forbade the sun and moon to shine while he scurried around in all the secret places on earth looking for the magic plant. Finally, Zeus found it in the darkest, most unknown of caves, and he hurried back to Olympus to the battle.

During the great battle between the giants and the gods it was Heracles who played the decisive part. Every time a god succeeded in outwitting, stoning, scalding with burning metal or singeing with torches one of the giants, it was always Heracles who had to finish off each opponent with his own poisoned arrows. The two peaceful goddesses, Demeter and Hestia, stood around twiddling their thumbs in great anxiety, but the Fates were far more useful and beat the giants off their stone tower with pestles and mortars from the heavenly kitchen. Eventually, the giants fled down their stone tower and ran back to Phlegra. However, the gods stubbornly refused to give up, and hurled islands and mountains after the giants' rumbling retreat. The giants made one final stand near Trapezus, but they were no match for Heracles's poisoned arrows and were destroyed. The giants were buried deep beneath volcanoes so that if they ever tried to get to the earth's surface again they would burn themselves up in the heart of the molten lava.

ODYSSEUS

ODYSSEUS was the relentless heroic wanderer, who has been portrayed throughout literature in many different guises, although it is perhaps only Homer's *Odyssey* that does the hero real justice. Here, he faces not only hardship, adventure and true suffering but also his own shadow and his own inner journey. The philosophical and psychological perspective that allows some sense of self-searching is a vital part of the *Odyssey*. The *Iliad*, on the other hand, portrays Odysseus as simply a heroic adventurer. He is arrogant and ruthless and seems to possess no deeper human qualities. Perhaps feeding off both these sources, Odysseus encompasses all facets of human nature, from unscrupulous deceit to the honesty and integrity of a real hero. It is the light and the shade of such a character that illuminates our own sense of who we are and the particular journey we are presently following.

YOUTH

Odysseus means 'angry'. This angry young man was the son of Anticlea and Laertes, the king of Ithaca, or, some say, the trickster Sisyphus. The centaur, Chiron, brought him up, and his father Laertes abdicated as soon as Odysseus was old enough to rule the kingdom of Ithaca. Odysseus was not unlike every other young hero in that he wanted desperately to marry Helen of Sparta, but to avoid being rejected, he astutely married Helen's cousin, Penelope, instead.

Some say that Penelope actually pursued and seduced Odysseus after try-ing out all Helen's suitors herself. While he was in Sparta, Odysseus advised Helen's father, Tyndareus, to make all Helen's suitors swear an oath whereby they would support whoever eventually married her, otherwise civil war would break out. Tyndareus did exactly as Odysseus suggested, and all the Greek heroes who had been Helen's suitors swore to support any man that married her. So when Paris abducted Helen, it was this oath that compelled every Greek hero to help King Menelaus and subsequently join in the Trojan War.

But Odysseus was so devoted to Penelope that after they had settled in Ithaca he was most reluctant to leave her to take part in the war. Perhaps this was also an unconscious reaction to an oracle that had informed him he would be away for twenty years and would return only as a beggar. Odysseus pretended to be raving mad when recruitment for the war began, yoking an ass and an ox to the same plough and sowing his fields with salt as any mad man would. But Palamedes, *en route* to the war himself, tricked Odysseus into proving he wasn't mad by dropping Odysseus's own baby son right in front of the plough. Odysseus stopped immediately to prevent the child from being trampled to death, and Palamedes declared this act was something no mad man would do. Odysseus was now forced to go to war, but he never forgave Palamedes for tricking him and later brought about his untimely death.

TROY

Odysseus was a noted strategist, and he used cunning and intellect to help the Greeks, rather than brawn and the impulsive heroics of warrior haste. The Greek king, Agamemnon, placed great belief in Odysseus's cunning as both counsellor and schemer. Odysseus even crept through the drains of the city and seized the statue of Athene that symbolized Troy's luck and showed the Greek leaders where Achilles had hidden himself on Scyros as a woman. But he made as many enemies as he did friends, because for heroes to think rather than simply to act was suspect. The end of the war came about through the use of the Trojan horse, probably at Athene's suggestion. Odysseus led the forces that hid inside the hollow wooden horse, which the Trojans dragged into their city at night because they had been wrongly told that the offering from the Greeks would bring them divine protection. It appeared to them that the Greek forces had sailed away, but during the night Odysseus and his men emerged from the horse and surprised the Trojans.

Because of his divided support among the gods as well as among mortals, Odysseus's return to Ithaca after the ten-year-long war seemed ill-fated and took ten years. Poseidon in particular had turned against Odysseus. He had rebuilt the walls of Troy that Odysseus had destroyed, and it was Poseidon who saw to it that Odysseus suffered and was the last Greek leader to return home. His whole journey was thwarted with conflict, and the long period of wandering he suffered was filled with adventure, love, heroics and danger. He faced supernatural forces and was carried by the ebb and flow of the sea to many strange lands. Odysseus defeated his enemies and the dangers of these weird places by cunning, bravery and strategy.

THE WANDERINGS

His exact route remains a mystery, but he first set sail to Thrace. Here he lost many of his men in a bloody battle. Storms and bad winds blew him across the ocean to the land of the lotus-eaters. These strange people lived on the sandbanks on the edge of a great tidal estuary on the coast of North Africa. Because of the changing tides, the sandbanks also changed their features, and once you had left them you could never find them again. These people ate the fruit of the lotus, a plant resembling a bean with a long taproot that grew far down into the underworld and was nourished by the waters of the River

Lethe. Drinking from this underworld river destroys all memory, and thus the lotus fruit in the upper world had the same effect. The lotus-eaters lived a timeless existence, aware only of the here and now. They had no memory of the past nor any thought for the future.

Odysseus landed on the sandbanks and sent out three of his men to explore this empty land. The men came across the lotus-eaters, were offered some of the fruit and instantly lost their memories. Odysseus went to look for them and found them in a senseless daze. He dragged them back to the ship, and the lotus-eaters just stared after the departing crew, not remembering who or what they were.

Next he outwitted the king of the Cyclopes, Polyphemus, whose father was Poseidon. Polyphemus had sworn that he would destroy every member of the human race after losing the only nymph he had ever desired, Galatea, who in turn had chosen only ever to love a mortal.

When Odysseus landed on Sicily he made a camp in Polyphemus's empty cave and sent out his men to hunt for food. But when Polyphemus came back and found his home besieged by mortals, he blocked the cave-mouth, grabbed two of Odysseus's men and ate them alive. The following day Odysseus sharpened a green olive branch to a sharp point, brought some large jars of wine from his ship and waited for Polyphemus to return from his shepherding. The great monster returned and ate two more of Odysseus's men, but then agreed to taste the wine, something he had never tried before. The ghastly creature drank every jar and fell into a drunken stupor, but not before asking Odysseus his name. 'Nobody,' Odysseus had replied. As soon as the Cyclops was snoring, Odysseus took the olive wood spear, heated it in the white ashes of the fire and seared out the Cyclops's eye. The pain was so intense that Polyphemus screamed with terror. The other Cyclopes appeared and called out into the dark cave, but Polyphemus could only cry, 'Nobody's hurt me!'

The following morning Polyphemus removed the boulder that blocked the cave-mouth to let out his sheep, but now he could not see and could only feel each one as it passed out of the cave. Odysseus and his remaining men clung to the undersides of the sheep. As each sheep passed Polyphemus felt only the fleece and was convinced the men had not escaped.

Safely on board his ship, Odysseus teased Polyphemus. As they set sail he shouted out to him, 'Never forget that the Nobody who has tricked you is really the greatest hero, Odysseus of Ithaca!'

The travellers next arrived at the floating island of the ruler of the winds, Aeolus. Odysseus was given a present, a bag full of winds to help him on his voyage. But his men became curious about the contents of the bag, and opened it, thus dispersing all the winds, which could now help no one as they blew off in every direction.

At the island of the enchantress Circe, Odysseus resisted her spells and, with the aid of the god Hermes, restored his men to human form after they had been turned to pigs. He stayed some seven years with Circe, delighting in her charms and enjoying a deeply sexual relationship. They produced three children, but soon the gods decided it was time for Odysseus to leave, and on Circe's advice he sailed to the far western edge of the sea, to Oceanos, where he met the ghosts from the underworld. These included the soul of Tiresius, who warned him not to offend Helios or his return home would be thwarted with loneliness for many long years.

Odysseus set sail east again and managed to avoid being bewitched by the Sirens' songs by tying himself to the mast of his ship and filling his men's ears with wax so they could not hear the magical songs. He also escaped from Scylla and Charybdis, the two sea-monsters who devoured anything and everyone who sailed through the narrow strait between Italy and Sicily. He did, however, lose some of his crew who were swept into the great whirlpool of Charybdis.

The long sea journey had began to take its toll, and with very few men left, Odysseus reached the island of Thrinacia as Tiresias had prophesied. But the men had become mutinous and hungry for home and good food, and despite his warnings they set out in the night while Odysseus slept. They killed some of Helios's best cattle and roasted them, feasting on the meat throughout the day. Eventually they deserted Odysseus, and Poseidon drowned them in a terrible storm for their evil deeds.

Now alone, Odysseus drifted to the wonderful island of Ogygia, where lived the beautiful sea-nymph, Calypso, the goddess of silence. Odysseus was washed up on the shore, and Calypso immediately fell in love with him. She desperately wanted to marry him and offered him immortality and a ranking among the gods. Not even such tempting gifts could seduce him, for he longed only to return home. But Calypso's spell drew him deeper and deeper into her heart, and their passion for one another grew more intense with every day. Odysseus stayed with Calypso for seven years, but each morning he would slip away from Calypso's generous heart and warm embrace, to gaze across the sea towards Ithaca and the wife and son he thought he would never see again. In his moments of being alone, he began to yearn for Penelope, but was still torn apart by the tormented desire he had for Calypso.

The gods eventually took pity on him, and Zeus ordered Calypso to set him free. With a wretchedly broken heart, she sadly agreed and helped Odysseus to make a raft. She gave him wine and food and watched with tears in her eyes as he sailed away forever. From then on, Calypso turned back to her silence and solitude to become more of a recluse than ever before.

Odysseus drifted across the sea alone, was nearly drowned but was washed up on the shores of Phaeacia where Princess Nausicaa rescued him. After recounting his stories to King Alcinous he became an honoured guest and was given a ship and crew to take him home to Ithaca.

THE RETURN

His wife Penelope had been loyal to him for the twenty years of his absence, believing him to be still alive. She had been courted by many suitors, who insisted that she must marry again and give up on Odysseus who would surely never return. Penelope had at first put off their advances, but as the twenty years approached, she had to make more and more excuses. As a last resort, she pretended that she would not marry anyone else until she had finished weaving a linen shroud for her father-in-law, Laertes. Once the last thread had been woven, she promised she would chose a husband. Every night she unpicked what she had woven during the day to make sure that she never finished it. Many months later one of her maids betrayed her, and she was forced to finish the shroud.

So Penelope agreed to marry whoever could bend and string Odysseus's great bow and fire an arrow through twelve tiny loops of leather tied to the ends of twelve axe-heads set upright into the ground. Many of the suitors attempted the challenge, but all failed. Then an old beggar asked to have a turn. This was, of course, Odysseus in disguise. He strung the bow and fired the arrow straight through all twelve loops. With the assistance of Telemachus (his son), he turned on the suitors and fought a fierce battle until all the suitors were killed. The treacherous maid was hanged. Odysseus then revealed his true identity, and Penelope and the people welcomed him back as their king.

But Odysseus was soon tested again by the gods in a different way. To appease his anger, Poseidon demanded that Odysseus must find a country where no one had ever heard of the ocean and build a temple to Poseidon there. Alone again, Odysseus set off on another journey. He rowed to the mainland from Ithaca, and walked inland, carrying only an oar over his shoulder. He travelled for nearly ten years, and everywhere he went people would say, 'Why are you carrying an oar?' Eventually he reached a place where the people said, 'Why are you carrying a winnowing fan?' He knew that he had found the right country, and he planted the oar in the ground of Thesprotia and built Poseidon's temple.

Freed finally from Poseidon's rage, Odysseus set off for Ithaca. On his way he consulted the Delphic oracle and was told that his own son would kill him. On his return home, therefore, he banished Telemachus, who eventually went to marry Circe and founded a whole new dynasty. But Telegonus, Odysseus's son by Circe (a son he had no idea he had fathered) happened to visit Ithaca. Telegonus also had no idea who his father was, and he had been travelling around the world in search of his father. He landed quite by chance in Ithaca, and Odysseus assumed that he and his men were pirates and fought them on the shore. But Telegonus killed Odysseus with a poisonous spear made from a sting-ray's spine, and the oracle came true. In some accounts Telegonus then married Penelope and ruled Ithaca.

GASSIRE AND THE SINGING LUTE

THE Fasa were an aristocratic people of the southern Sahara, who lived around the third century BCE. They displayed courage in combat, but would fight only those who were their equals. Like most other mortal heroes, Gassire, both hero and warrior, wanted everlasting fame. The problem was that what was best for him was not necessarily best for his local people, and his desire for fame and glory became his undoing.

King Ngaanamba was an aged king, and his son, Gassire, was getting old and grey himself. Gassire longed to inherit his father's shield and have an opportunity to rule the kingdom, so he yearned for the old, old man to die. His impatience was so intense that every day he would search for some sign that his father was near death. Just as a lover looks to the sky for something to be written in the stars, so Gassire would look to the heavens each night for some sign that he would one day soon be king. But night after night and week after week the old king refused to die. Every day Gassire would ride into battle and achieve fame as a great hero, and each night he would listen to his fellow-warriors praise him for his feats. Yet he would sleep restlessly, for his heart was eaten up with envy and desire for his father's kingdom.

Gassire's greed and lust for power turned eventually into rage, and one night as he tossed and turned in his bed he could not stand the anticipation any longer and went to visit the wisest man in the city. He asked the wise man when he would become the king of the Fasa. The wise man replied, 'Your father may die, but you will not inherit his shield. You will carry a lute.'

Gassire was outraged. 'You're lying, obviously you're not as wise as I thought.'

The old man shrugged. 'You may not believe me, Gassire, but your path in life is not that of a king, nor that of a warrior and hero. When you hear the partridges in the fields, then you will understand, for they will reveal the true nature of your journey.'

Determined to prove that he was better than any other warrior and still a hero among his men, Gassire decided to ride alone against the enemy and scatter them like birds. He fought like a madman and put fear into the hearts of the Burdama until they retreated. His heroic status was notched up a few more points, and the men gathered around to rejoice and praise him.

Not long after enjoying this glory, he walked into the fields and heard a partridge singing of its battle with a snake, 'Eventually all creatures must die, and turn to dust; even myself, but my song will live forever, and the song of my deeds will never die. Each generation will sing my song, long after the heroes and kings have died.'

So Gassire returned to the wise man and said, 'The partridge in the field sang a song of its deeds, which will always be remembered. Is it possible for men to sing great battle songs so that they can never be forgotten?'

The wise man nodded. 'Long ago the Fasa lived by the sea and they were heroes too. They fought other men, and bards played the lute and were remembered long after the battle for their music and singing. It was their names that lived on, unlike those men who had been warriors. You, too, will be a singer of great battle songs, but never a king.'

So Gassire visited the smith and asked him to make a great lute that would sing.

'Here is a lute for you, Gassire, but it can never sing alone. You must take it into battle with you, until it has drawn in the heart of your own true courage. Only then may it begin to sing. The lute can only ever sing your songs, and it can only do so by absorbing the blood of your wounds and your deeds. It must absorb the life blood of your sons so that it truly feels as you feel. Then it will be truly a lute on which you can play battle songs. But your father is not ready yet to die and leave you his shield.'

So Gassire set off for battle the next day with his eight sons to fight the Burdama. His first son was killed and he carried him home on his back, the boy's blood oozing across the lute. For the next week Gassire took his sons into battle with him. Relentlessly he fought, and grimly each day one of his sons would die and he would return with another corpse across his back. Soon all his sons had been killed and each had stained the lute with his own blood.

But the people of Fasa believed that Gassire was going mad. He had become obsessed with his desire for fame and glory and did not care for his sons' deaths. People began to stay away from Gassire, and one night the heroes gathered in a circle and told Gassire that he must leave the city. 'We want fame and glory, too, but we choose life before fame. To allow your sons to die because you want only your own glory is not our way.'

Gassire found only the support of a couple of his men, his wives and his youngest son. So, with the lute on his back and his few companions at his side, he rode off into the desert, an outcast in his own kingdom.

That night, camping out under the bright stars and wrapped up against the cold desert air, he could not sleep. He gazed upon those who slept and then turned to touch the blood-stained lute that lay beside him. Then, as he plucked the strings, the lute began to play the most beautiful of battle songs. At the same moment, in his far away home, his father the old king died. The lute began to play again, and this time Gassire's anger left him and he wept for both grief and joy. The song he sang and the music he played was the most exquisite ever. For the grief was for his dead sons and his dead father, and this was the true music of his soul and the real pain of his deeds. The only happiness he felt now was that he would be remembered for his battle song, long after any of the heroes or warriors were remembered for their valiant deeds.

THE GREAT YU

CHINESE heroes have much to prove to raise them above the level of ordinary mortals or lesser gods. Yu is one such hero. He is considered by most sources to be the first king of the Xia dynasty, 21–16BCE, and he was, in fact, a real person who became transformed into a legendary figure. His sense of duty and honour, and his leadership and strength proved to make him the ultimate Chinese hero.

In the reign of Yao a great flood came to the land and caused terrible tragedy. The world became one huge ocean, and the creatures were either drowned or had to swim to higher ground on the peaks of the mountains. Many people died and were swept away by the swirling waters. Each day the water rose higher and higher, until the only safe places were on the highest peaks.

King Yao became increasingly worried as hills and valleys disappeared and the ocean seemed to be engulfing every mountain top around him. 'What can we do to stop this?' he asked his advisors.

The officials had a meeting and after many hours agreed that they would ask Gun, the god of the white horse, to help them.

Yao shrugged. 'He is wise and brave, but I fear he is the Yellow Emperor's grandson and as a god he will not come down to earth to help us mere mortals.'

Gun had, however, already decided to help the people on earth. He was angered that his grandfather, the Yellow Emperor, had neglected the world. He had tried to persuade him to stop the flood, but the Yellow Emperor had ignored his pleas. So Gun went down to earth to help the people and conquer the flood. On a mountain high above the rising waters he sat and wondered how he could prevent the great seas from engulfing the world. Then he saw a tortoise and an eagle, who came to sit with him on the high peak.

'What is wrong, Gun?' they asked.

'I have to rid the world of this flood, but I don't know how.'

'We can help you. It's not difficult to get rid of the flood if you can steal some magical substance called endless earth.'

'What is this endless earth?'

The tortoise smiled. 'It is a small lump of earth, but when it is dropped from the heavens on to the world it grows into mountains and dams.'

151

Gun felt better. 'But where can I get this endless earth?'

'It is to be found only in the divine palace of the Yellow Emperor. It is one of his most treasured possessions.'

So Gun set off back to the heavens and stole the endless earth from the Yellow Emperor while he slept. Gun dropped the endless earth on to the world, and soon mountains sprang up and the earth grew and soaked up all the water. Mud turned to earth, and valleys, hills, land and sea soon became how it was always supposed to be. Yao's people celebrated and hailed Gun as a hero for bringing them back their land, and for a while the world was a happy place. But the Yellow Emperor found out that his own grandson had stolen the endless earth and he was outraged. He sent the god of fire down to earth to kill Gun and to return the endless earth to the heavens.

The fire-god found Gun on Mount Yushan and killed him with one blow to his head and then stole back the endless earth. The floods returned and Yao's people again had to fight for their lives and journey up into the high mountains. Many were drowned and the seas rose faster than they had ever done before.

But Gun's spirit could not rest. His body lay on the mountain top for three years, but as the months passed a new life grew inside Gun's belly, nurtured by his own divine power.

The Yellow Emperor was concerned when he heard that Gun's body still lay on the mountain top, and he sent another official to go and cut open the belly of the corpse, in case an evil spirit had possessed it. The official went to Mount Yushan and as he slit his knife into the corpse's viscera, out flew a great golden dragon, with magnificent horns and the strength of a thousand men. This was Yu, Gun's son. Gun, too, was transformed into a yellow dragon and went to live in the abyss at the end of the world. But Yu took all Gun's power, and it was he who now had to complete his father's quest, to save the world from the terrible flood.

As the golden dragon flew through the sky, the Yellow Emperor's heart softened, knowing that the spirit of Gun had been passed on to Yu. It was perhaps a sign that the people on earth had suffered enough. The Yellow Emperor decided to help Yu return the world to its previous form. He gave Yu the magical endless earth and sent him a thousand dragons to help him fight the flood and regulate the flow of the rivers.

But one of the gods was angered. This was Gong Gong, the god of water. He had been given the honour of creating the flood in the first place, and he didn't want his power to be diminished just because of a golden dragon-boy called Yu.

Yu resigned himself to a face-to-face battle with Gong Gong. Gathering the dragons and spirits of the earth to Mount Huiji, Yu totally overpowered the god of the water and then prepared to tackle the flood.

Yu ordered the giant turtles to drop little lumps of the magical endless earth everywhere they went. If they saw people drowning, the turtles would scatter the magic soil over the water and land instantly formed beneath their feet. Yu travelled the earth changing the oceans to mountains and deserts, to land and small seas, and he directed the course of the rivers so that the flood water flowed down towards the oceans.

The dragon, Yin Long, dragged his tail across the earth and scoured the land with deep scratch marks with his claws. The spirits dug shallow gullies along the scratches and the waters filled these narrow beds. The flood waters were channelled towards the sea, creating the great Yellow River of China and all the other rivers of the world.

Yu regulated many rivers and created many mountains, but the work was hard and took many years of dangerous setbacks and wasted moments.

One year Yu was working with his dragons when a terrible storm blew up. Rocks flew in the air and the cliffs began to fall like avalanches around them. Strong currents arose in the water and created huge waves and the people fled. Despite his powers, Yu could not control the storm. But Yao Ji, one of the fiery emperor's goddess daughters, saw Yu's disaster and flew down to help him. Her powers enabled him to direct the thunder and lightning to forge a tunnel right through the mountain, and the tidal waves drained into the earth. Yao Ji also gave Yu a red jade box inside which was a magical scroll to help Yu to change the courses of all the flood waters.

For many years Yu worked hard, and when he reached the age of thirty he decided to marry a girl called Nu Ji, who had fallen desperately in love with his heroic antics. Yu travelled away from home for many months, and Nu Ji became lonely and homesick. He built her a great tower so that she could gaze across to her old home town, but she hated the tower and decided to follow Yu instead.

One day they reached a treacherous mountain range. Yu told his wife to stay behind in the valley until he had finished his work. 'I shall beat on the drum when it is safe for you to come to the edge of the cliff and bring me some food.'

Yu could transform himself into other creatures, and to clear the great boulders from the mountain he turned himself into a black bear with huge claws. Yu started to dislodge the boulders from the mountain, creating a chasm through which the waters could flow. But as he was digging, some of the stones flew through the air and hit the drum. Nu Ji decided that it was safe to give her husband his lunch, but when she reached the cliff's edge she saw a terrible black bear, not her husband. Terrified, she dropped the food and began to run back down the mountainside. Yu ran after her, forgetting he was still in bear-form, and as she fan faster and faster she grew stiffer and stiffer until she stopped. At the foot of the mountain she turned, petrified at the sight of the bear still chasing her, and changed into a rock. Just as she did so, Yu called out to her, 'What about my son? Leave me a son!' The north face of the rock cracked open and from it fell a baby, Yu's child. Yu picked up the child and, remembering his own strange birth from his father's corpse, he said: 'You are to be called Qi.'

Yu's final battle was against the nine-headed monster. This was one of the water-god's officials who had prowled around the earth after his master's death seeking vengeance on Yu. Whatever it touched turned to poisonous swamps filled with slime. With nine heads it could feed on nine different mountains simultaneously, and its breath stank of fumes so powerful that it could turn anyone to a muddy puddle. Yu decided to rid the world of this dangerous monster, but every time he stabbed it and cut off one of the nine heads, the stinking blood swirled across the earth, polluting the land and the rivers. Yu made dams to stop the sludge from spreading, but it kept breaking through the earth. So he dug a deep pit at the bottom of the mountain and formed a huge bottomless pool of the revolting creature's blood.

Yu created the new world as his father had wanted to do so, and after being offered the role of ruler of the kingdom, he was honoured by his people. He had conquered the flood and for more than thirteen years had travelled the entire land regulating the rivers. They say that his skin was covered in callouses and he had no nails or body hair. They say, too, that he never stopped for a rest and nothing, not even the cries of his baby, would make him give up on his mission. He would limp across the land, his body weak from the freezing winters and his skin parched and wrinkled from the wind and the hot summer sun.

No one knows what really happened to Yu after that. Some say he died and was buried on Mount Huiji where the first spirits and dragons had gathered. His spirit ascended to heaven, where he lived eternally as a god.

CÚ CHULAINN

CELTIC, 100BCE

CELTIC myths have a reputation for being obscure and often rather confusing, mostly because of the wide scattering of the Celts themselves throughout Europe. From Scandinavia to Ireland, their culture went with them and was modified to suit the needs of the individual communities. This is why the names of the gods and mortals have changed so frequently, especially since the onset of Christianity and the rewriting of myths in the Middles Ages. Perhaps the purest form of Celtic myth survives in the hero-tales of Ireland and Wales. The following story of Cú Chulainn is perhaps the best known.

Heroic single combat was the main means by which the ancient Celts settled their disputes. This was because of the acute shortage of men to fight lengthy battles, and chosen champions duelled to the death on behalf of their kingdoms. Cú Chulainn is one example of such a champion, who would fight continual combat for many days against all kinds of warriors, even harassing the great armies with his sling in between these mammoth duels.

Setanta was the son of the sun-god, Lug, and a mortal woman, Dectera. For many years, until he grew into a fine youth, he was brought up by Dectera's sister who had a child of her own, Conall. Setanta was impatient and boisterous, and when he was old enough he was sent to the court of King Conor. There he was brought up like the other sons of nobility and chieftains.

Setanta was not renowned for his obedience, and one day was left behind when Conor and his court were travelling to a feast held by a wealthy smith called Cullan. Setanta watched them disappear into the forest and knew he was supposed to catch up with them. However, he was rather keen to finish a game of hurley with his companions first. The royal party arrived at sunset, and Cullan welcomed then into his massive fortress. With night falling fast, he clanged the great gates shut and let loose his ferocious hound, who guarded the approaches to the hall. As the evening progressed the merry feast turned into a drunken one, and even the king forgot Setanta had chosen to be left behind.

But as the ale flowed and the roasting spits turned, a howl from outside the fortress walls pierced the room with an eerie and chilling sound. Cullan's hound howled and bayed at someone approaching the gates. The warriors rushed out, remembering now that Setanta might have arrived, and Cullan cursed and swore thinking the dog might rip the boy to pieces.

Reaching the gate, Cullan's fears turned to dismay when he saw the youth with the dead dog at his feet.

'What have you done?' shouted Cullan, mortified that his dog was killed.

'The dog flew at me, he tried to tear me to pieces so I seized it by the throat and threw it against the wall.'

The king's warriors cheered at Setanta's feat, but Cullan could only mourn the death of his dear friend. The dog had been his only companion for many years. When Setanta saw Cullan's misery, he said, 'Find me another young hound and I will train it to guard your fortress. Meanwhile I shall guard you and your hall, until it is time for the hound to take over.'

Everyone was impressed by Setanta's pledge. They gave him a nickname, Cú Chulainn, the Hound of Cullan, which he was called forever after.

As he approached adulthood, Cú Chulainn was summoned before the king and asked what he wanted to do with his life. Cú Chulainn had been born to fight and could only think of one thing, to be a great warrior. The king gave him two great spears, but he merely shattered them to bits as he took them in his hands. He was given chariots to drive, but his feet broke them to pieces as he raged across the countryside. Finally, he was given the king's own chariots, spears and sword, and these he could not destroy and so he kept them all.

Cú Chulainn was a handsome youth, and many women were entranced by his beauty. He was aware of his good looks, however, and found few of the women he met attractive enough to equal his own glamour. Except one. This was Emer, the daughter of Forgall. The moment Cú Chulainn saw Emer he fell in love with her and wanted her to be his bride. But at Forgall's house, Cú Chulainn found Emer difficult to woo. 'My older sister must marry first, before I am even allowed to take a husband,' she confided to him.

'Do you know how much I desire you, Emer? Do you know the pain I feel when I know you cannot yet be my wife?' he confessed.

Emer laughed. Even Cú Chulainn could not persuade her to lose her virtue. 'There are few men who can ever be my mate, let alone prove their love to me. The man I choose to wed and to love must be someone who has slain many men and completed heroic deeds. This is the only kind of man who would ever be good enough for me.'

Cú Chulainn left, frustrated by her initial rejection of him but even more determined to have her.

He had heard of a woman-warrior called Scáthach who lived in the Land of Shadows and had trained many young men to be great heroes. He set off across the seas to the Plains of Ill-luck, managed to escape the monsters that lurked in the Perilous Glen and reached the Bridge of Leaps, the gateway to Scáthach's land. But the Bridge of Leaps was a barrier that he had not anticipated. Here he met many sons of Irish princes who had come to learn how to fight and to become famous warriors. But none had dared to try to cross the bridge. One of these youths was his old friend Ferdia.

'It is good to see you, Cú Chulainn, but even I dare not try to jump this bridge. For Scáthach reveals the secret of how to jump it only in her last lesson, and so no one had attempted to cross.'

But Cú Chulainn could think only about Emer. As night fell and with his strength restored, he took four great strides and leapt onto the high bridge. It was narrow and swung in the air like a tightrope but he stayed balanced and with one final leap, jumped across to the land of Scáthach. When the warrior woman saw his agility, she allowed him to remain as her pupil. For a year and a day Cú Chulainn learned all her skills, including the deadliest of all – how to use the gae bolga, a terrible barbed harpoon, which was thrown with the feet. This fearful weapon could tear a man's insides to shreds, then fill him with a million spikes that would never be removed.

Cú Chulainn grew impatient to return to Erin, to show off to Emer the powers he had acquired and the warrior skills he had learned. But first he had to prove himself and become a hero.

On the borders of Connacht and Ulster there were constant battles, and

Cú Chulainn resolved to test his strength and challenge the greatest fighting families to combat. Now that he had become such a powerful adversary, his temper had increased along with his passion for battle, his vision of becoming a famous hero and, of course, his love for Emer.

First, he went to the fortress of the great sons of Nechtan. Near the outer walls was a great stone inscribed with ogham, a magical language. Cú Chulainn took hold of the great stone pillar and forced it from the ground, a sacrilege to the sons of Nechtan. Their fame as the brawniest warriors in the land had prevented many from attempting to challenge their strength, but Cú Chulainn had only the desire for conflict in his heart. His eyes bulged with anger, his legs swelled with powerful muscles, and his mouth drooled with the thirst for battle.

The first son to emerge was Foill. Cú Chulainn had shrewdly arrived with his charioteer, which irritated Foill because he did not kill messengers or drivers. Cú Chulainn himself looked like a mere youth, whom Foill decided wasn't worth the effort, and he shrugged and stomped off back to the fortress. But Cú Chulainn raised his sling and fired a ball of iron straight through the great warrior's head. Cú Chulainn decapitated Foill, tied the head to the side of his chariot and drove round and round the fortress, teasing the other sons of Nechtan. Unable to resist his taunts, the warriors hurtled out of the fortress, intent on killing Cú Chulainn. This was how he liked to fight best, and one by one he massacred them with his sword or spear. Each blood-thirsty battle increased Cú Chulainn's rage, until his head bristled with the blood of his victims and his body shook with a terrible frenzied passion for more destruction.

Cú Chulainn continued on to Emhain Mhacha, intent on fighting with anyone he met, now that his addiction had got hold of him. Conor saw him driving his chariot towards his castle, the heads of the three sons of Nechtan swinging from the sides and blood flowing down the sides of the wheels. Conor realized that this was no time for reasoning with Cú Chulainn and sent out a troop of naked women to stand in his way. When Cú Chulainn saw them he bowed his head in embarrassment, the one chance Conor's men had to seize him. They tied his arms and legs and brought out three vats of water into which they threw Cú Chulainn. The first was only luke-warm and so the warrior was able to burst through the sides. The second was so hot it boiled over with the heat of Cú Chulainn's own anger. The last vat was filled with ice-cold water, and it was only when the men plunged him into the freezing water that at last Cú Chulainn's rage was subdued. The young hero was temporarily tamed.

Calmed again, Cú Chulainn set off to the fortress of Forgall the Wily to show Emer that he was not only a hero but also a famous warrior. He leapt up on to the high ramparts, and the men of Forgall attacked him. But he lashed out with his sword and each time he brought his sword down, he killed three men with a single blow. Forgall himself jumped off the ramparts to escape Cú Chulainn's rage and fell to his death. Emer was besotted with the heroic antics of Cú Chulainn, and now, seduced by his strength and daring, she agreed to be his wife.

But Cú Chulainn had not anticipated a skeleton in his cupboard. When he had stayed with Scáthach he had become lover to Scáthach's sister, the wild and impetuous warrior princess, Aífa. Before he left the Land of Shadows, Cú Chulainn had given Aífa a gold ring and had made her promise that if she ever bore him a son, he was to be sent to Erin to find Cú Chulainn as soon as his fingers were big enough to fit the ring. He had also told Aífa that the boy must travel incognito and never refuse combat.

Not long after Cú Chulainn had married Emer, King Conor sent for him to do battle against a mysterious youth who had arrived in Ulster on a bronze boat with gilded oars. This youth had so far defied the power of the land. Emer realized who the youth must be, but even her pleas to Cú Chulainn not to kill his own son were not enough to stop him.

Father and son met on the white sands of the Ulster shore. The boy refused to tell Cú Chulainn who he was or where he came from. They fought long and hard until both fell into the sea and Cú Chulainn began to sink under the waves. His anger and rage gave him one last chance, and he reached for the gae bolga. He drove the barbed harpoon into the boy's belly, ripping his flesh to pieces. The boy shouted out, 'Scáthach never taught me this!' and died. Cú Chulainn saw the ring on his finger and knew he was his son, and he laid him down before Conor and the lords of Ulster to show his loyalty to them.

After being acclaimed as the champion of Ulster in a beheading contest, Cú Chulainn became renowned for his unstoppable combat. But that did not deter the terrible Queen Meb of Connacht from invading Ulster to seize a famous brown bull. Her timing was immaculate. Cú Chulainn had recently been cursed by a witch's spell and now suffered from one withered shoulder and hand. The Ulster heroes were unable to fight for five days and nights because of another curse upon them. Cú Chulainn had also lost the support of the goddess Mórríghan, because he had rejected her sexual advances. Yet he fought bravely and slowed down Meb's powerful warriors until the Ulster heroes had regained their strength and the curse had been shaken off.

Cú Chulainn was severely wounded in the stomach, and even the help of his father the sun-god, Lug, could not heal the wound. Cú Chulainn knew he was dying and Mórríghan, the goddess of death, would never help him again. He tied himself to a pillar stone so that he could stay upright and fight until his last breath. As soon as he died, Mórríghan took the form of a crow. She sat on the dead hero's shoulder as his enemies cut off his head and his right hand, and the other crows came to eat his remains. Cú Chulainn's refusal of Mórríghan's deathly style of loving had surely sealed his fate.

His foster-brother, Conall, found the missing head and Ulster mourned the loss of their extraordinary champion, whose fame and exploits set a precedent and may well have influenced many of the myths of Arthurian Britain and France.

CONAIRE MÓR

CELTIC, 100BCE

FOR Irish warriors, kings or heroes, the violation of their *geasa* meant the turning point in the narrative, and the moment when the hero's great victory would be fated to end in tragedy. A *geis* was like a spell, a taboo or a highly personal magical bond and talisman that, if transgressed, would bring about certain disaster to that individual. Every Irish chieftain had his own personal *geis*, which was both sacred and obligatory, but no one knew who imposed it or even how anyone found out their magic taboo in the first place. In this myth, the great Irish king Conaire Mór breaks more than one *geis* in his life and thus falls victim to his sadly woven fate.

Conaire Mór was the son of a cowherd's foster-daughter, Mess, and the bird-god, Nemglan. Mess was actually the daughter of Etain Oig and Cormac, king of Ulster, but Mess had been thrown into a pit because he had been so angry at not having produced a male child. The baby girl had been saved by two servants who took the child to a cowherd to be brought up.

The high king of Ireland, Eterskel, had been told in a prophecy that a strange woman would bear him a wonderful son. When Mess grew up, her beauty was so extraordinary that the king decided to marry her. But the night before she was to leave for the court she slept with the bird-god, Nemglan, who flew down to her and took on the form of a stunning youth. Mess fell instantly in love with him and they spent the night together. From this union was born Conaire Mór, who the king of Ireland believed, quite naturally, was his own son. Before Nemglan left Mess's bed, he told her that the child she was to conceive was never to kill any bird.

Eventually King Eterskel died, and the right of succession in this particular realm was not naturally passed on to the son. Someone had to be appointed. This was done at a bull feast. The chosen diviner would eat his fill, drink the bull's blood then go to bed, where a truth-compelling spell would be chanted over him. Whoever the diviner saw in his dream would become king. In this particular dream the sleeping diviner saw a naked man walking along the road to Tara with a sling in his hand.

At the time of the feast, Conaire Mór was some miles from Tara. He was heading back to the great palace when a flock of birds flew around him, startling his horses and daring to soar and dive towards his chariot. Conaire forgot his promise never to kill birds. He was full of spirit and wanted to test his powerful sling, but when he raised the sling to fire, the birds suddenly lost their feathers and were transformed into armed warriors. One of the birds was finer than the others, and he alighted beside Conaire to protect him.

'I am Nemglan, the god of birds. You must never cast your stones at birds, for they are your ancestors and your kin. I am your father and will help you to become king. But for your penance for raising your sling at these birds you must walk naked to Tara tonight. You must also know your *geasa*. Listen carefully. You must not go righthand-wise around Tara nor lefthand-wise round Bregia. You must not sleep in a house from which firelight shows after sunset or one in which light can be seen from outside. No three reds must go before you to the Red House. After sunset no woman or man alone may enter the house you are in. Do not forget these, your *geasa*.'

So Conaire Mór walked into Tara naked and, as the god of birds had prophesied, he was made high king.

At first peace and prosperity characterized his reign. Conaire Mór had made sure that none would raid cattle nor kill others from different clans, yet his evil foster-brothers forced the countryside into disorder and were soon sliding back into clannish disputes. It was around this time that Conaire Mór was forced into breaking, one by one, all of his *geasa*.

On returning to Tara he found the countryside lit up with the glare of fires and shrouded in clouds of smoke. Convinced that raiders were attacking from the north and to escape the searing fires, Conaire's men had to circle clockwise round Tara and then anticlockwise round Bregia. They found to their horror that the fires and the smoke were only an illusion caused by the spirits. Next Conaire Mór had to find a rest-house for the night. He came to a roadside hostel where he caught up with three strange horsemen, clothed in red and riding red horses. He remembered his *geasa* and sent a messenger ahead to ask them to wait until he could get in front of them, but they shrugged and galloped on ahead of him, tied their red stallions to the hostelry and sat down inside for beer. The hostel was called Da Derga's hostel, and *derga* means 'red'.

Conaire was now extremely concerned, for each of his *geasa* was being broken. Then came night, and the glare of the fires lit by the giant Mac Cecht glowed through the chariot wheels that stood before the open doors of the hostel. It was as if the spirits of night and the fates of day were conspiring against him.

Again another *geis* was transgressed as the king prepared to sleep. A lonely woman came to the door and wanted a bed and shelter for the night. But Conaire remembered his *geis* and shook his head, knowing that to let anyone in after sunset would mean he was doomed to a tragic fate. Not realizing that this was Mórríghan, the goddess of death, he was overcome with pity for her as she begged to be let in or find someone who had more generosity than a king.

Knowing full well that he would be breaking another *geis*, he opened the door for the woman. The moment she had entered the hostel, Conaire's enemies attacked. The rebels surrounded the house and three times the building caught fire and was put out until every drop of water was used. A druid accompanying the rebels put a spell of thirst on the king, and knowing there was no water in the hostel one of Conaire's companions travelled far away to find some. By the time he returned, the king was dead from thirst, and Conaire Mór's head lay decapitated on the ground. The loyal friend picked up the head and began to pour water into his mouth. And Conaire Mór's last words from the parched lips of his head were: 'Thanks, kind friend, this *geis* is now quenched with water.'

SIGMUND AND SIGURD

NORTHERN EUROPE, 100CE

THE Nordic gods and warriors were famed for their spirited fighting, their acceptance of death on the battlefield and the great doom of Ragnarok, which would mark the end and the re-birth of the universe. Whatever it was that drove them on, the heroes of the Nordic myths sought exclusive fame and deeds of great courage to prove their worth. They had little time for self-questioning or psychological awareness, for death was accepted as part of life. To stop and reflect upon oneself was far from the instinctive consciousness required to live in the harsh conditions of northern climes and the needs of survival.

The following two stories are the basic myths as told in the Norse Volsunga Saga. Richard Wagner was inspired to write his music-drama 'The Ring of the Nibelungs' from both a later Germanic version of the Sigurd myth, and also elements taken from the earlier *Volsunga Saga*. He filled the shell of a great myth with a level of consciousness that incorporates both psychological drama and deeper threads of meaning. Sigurd's confusing tale of the cursed ring and the tragedy of the two lovers is included here because it carries the seed of the heroic actions of Sigmund.

SIGMUND

Sigmund was the son of Volsung, and his twin sister was the beautiful Signý, who had been betrothed to the king of the Goths, Siggeir, whom she did not want to marry but had no choice. At their wedding feast, Odin saw through the corrupt Siggeir. He stuck a magical sword into the heart of the Branstock, a huge oak tree that grew right up through the middle of Volsung's hall. Then he told the wedding guests that whoever could remove the sword from the tree would become the greatest hero ever known.

Siggeir tried to remove it first but could not shift it even an inch. Volsung himself did no better. Then Sigmund's nine other brothers tried, but none could remove it. Sigmund was the last to try and the sword instantly slipped out of the tree as if it had been standing in honey, not solid oak. Sigmund was now declared a hero, much to the anger of Siggeir, who tried first to bribe Sigmund to give up the sword, but Sigmund, as any hero would, refused to part with it.

Siggeir plotted to kill all of Sigmund's family. In a great battle Sigmund's nine brothers were murdered, and Sigmund escaped only because of Signý's quick-thinking. The ten brothers had been bound to the trees in the forest, and each night a wolf would come and devour them, one by one. Signý smeared Sigmund's face with honey, and the wolf licked his face instead of biting his flesh. Sigmund caught the wolf's tongue in his teeth and was able to tear out the insides of its mouth and escape. But he had already lost his magic sword.

Signý was determined to bear a great son, but the two sons that she had with Siggeir turned out to be wimps. Signý quite astutely realized that it was probably Siggeir's fault, as he wasn't exactly of warrior status but was a conniving, scheming weakling. She decided to have Sigmund's son, so she changed her shape by magic, seduced Sigmund and slept with him for three nights and days continuously, before disappearing. The resulting child was Sinfjötli, who was, she claimed, Siggeir's to avoid any harm to the child.

When Sigmund met Sinfjötli they became great friends, and charged around the countryside killing terrible monsters and evil people. On one of their many journeys they discovered two men fast asleep. The men had left a pair of wolfskins hanging on the wall of their hall, and Sigmund and his companion tried on the skins to amuse themselves. Their amusement turned to tragedy when they found themselves transformed into werewolves, running through the forests and eating anyone who got in their way. The two werewolves turned on one another, and Sigmund, in his werewolf form, killed his own son, Sinfjötli. Sigmund watched two weasels fighting, and when one killed the other, it placed an oak leaf on the breast of the dead weasel, which miraculously restored its life. So Sigmund did this to his dead son, and Sinfjötli was restored to the land of the living. They threw off the wolfskins and decided never to take on animal form again.

While they were trying to avenge the terrible Siggeir, both heroes were captured. Signý found Sigmund's lost magic sword and, freeing themselves, they set the great hall on fire so that none could escape. Sigmund wanted Signý to come with them, but she remained in the burning palace, sacrificing herself as a penance for her incestuous adultery.

Sigmund eventually married the princess Hjördis, and they had a son called Sigurd. But Sigmund preferred battles to child-raising, and when the time came for him to leave the world and go to Valhalla, Odin destroyed the magic sword by smashing it to pieces. Hjördis picked up all the fragments and gave them to the smith, Regin. She also gave Regin the care of her son, Sigurd, and when the boy was old enough Regin re-forged the magic sword so that he could also become a hero like his father.

SIGURD

Sigurd was brought up by the astute and wise smith Regin, who taught him music, the carving of runes, the forging of metal and many other attributes of warriors and heroes. When he was old enough Sigurd was given the opportunity of choosing his own war-horse, and he acquired the great horse Grani, a descendant of Odin's own horse Sleipnir.

Regin told Sigurd about a hoard of treasure that contained the total riches of the universe. This treasure had been owned by a dwarf, Andvari, who had also crafted a fabulous golden ring with the power endlessly to create more and more gold. A long time before, the treasure had been stolen by the trickster-god Loki and given to Regin's magician father. Regin's brother, Fafnir, had turned himself into a dragon to guard the golden hoard. Unfortunately, unknown to anyone, the ring had been cursed by Andvari so that it would destroy anyone who owned it. The ring was part of this treasure, and it was the treasure that Regin wanted. Fafnir still guarded the hoard of gold in his lair, and Regin asked Sigurd if he would be willing to fight the great dragon and recover the treasure.

Sigurd instantly agreed to go and slay the dragon, so Regin began to forge a magical sword using the fragments that had been collected from Sigmund's sword. Together they set off for Fafnir's lair. The dragon had just eaten and was gorged with food and could hardly move. Sigurd hid under a bush beside the stream where the dragon always came to drink, took the magic sword, stabbed him from below and ripped his belly apart. Once the dragon was dead, Regin asked Sigurd to remove the dragon's heart, roast it and eat it. But while the heart was cooking some of the blood dripped on to Sigurd's fingers. He licked them and found he now had the power to understand the language of birds and animals. The twittering birds were trying to tell him that Regin intended to kill him and take all the gold for himself. Sigurd quickly stuck his sword into Regin's back, took from the treasure hoard a single gold ring and set off to continue his heroic quests. Sigurd, however, did not realize that the ring he had chosen was the one cursed by the dwarf Andvari.

Crossing the rainbow bridge, Bifrost, he found on a hilltop the beautiful Brynhild, asleep in her palace surrounded by a ring of fire. Brynhild was a Valkyrie who had been banished to earth by Odin because she had refused to

163

have sex with him. He had punished her by placing her in a ring of fire where she would sleep until a hero came who would be courageous enough to cross the fire and wake her. Her love for this hero would destroy them both.

Sigurd did exactly this. He leapt across the ring of fire, fell instantly in love with Brynhild and gave her the stolen ring as a sign of their betrothal and undying love, knowing that he must continue his journey. As he travelled to complete his quest, his fame as a dragon-slayer spread across the land. Arriving at the hall of King Gjúki, he seemed a highly desirable suitor for Queen Grimhild's daughter. Princess Gudrun fell in love with Sigurd and his kindness and great deeds inspired all those who met him. The queen had heard rumours that Sigurd had already pledged his love to another, but she was determined that he should marry her daughter and so she bewitched Sigurd with a magic potion that would make him forget his love for Brynhild. At court he was under such a powerful spell that he was now compelled to marry Gudrun.

Yet Grimhild was still not satisfied. The only way she could be sure that Brynhild did not find out about her own deceit was to arrange for her son Gunnar to marry Brynhild himself so that she could feed Brynhild with lies about Sigurd.

Gunnar was also put under a magic spell, and, full of desire for a woman he had never seen, he set off to capture the heart of Brynhild. He was no hero but felt sure that he could cross the ring of fire. Gunnar failed miserably. Sigurd, still also spellbound, agreed to disguise himself as Gunnar, and crossing the ring of fire for the second time he unknowingly betrayed his own love for Brynhild.

Disguised as Gunnar, Sigurd spent several nights with Brynhild declaring his love for her. But Brynhild could not forget her true love, Sigurd, and was now confused about whom she should marry. But Sigurd (as Gunnar) insisted that he had ridden through the flames and reminded her that it was her destiny to marry any man who did so. She had sworn to Odin a sacred oath that she would marry whoever rescued her and dared to wake her. Sadly Brynhild remembered this oath. Sigurd had now been gone so long that she had resigned herself to being abandoned by him. After all, wasn't this man Gunnar here now to take her away from her loneliness?

Sigurd (still apparently Gunnar) offered her his ring, and asked for one from Brynhild to show that she would marry him. Reluctantly Brynhild exchanged rings, giving Sigurd (as Gunnar) the cursed ring of Andvari. The very same ring that Sigurd had given her as a pledge of his love.

The real Gunnar changed places with Sigurd on their journey back to Gjúki's court and married Brynhild, who, it seemed, hardly noticed the difference between the two men such was her sadness at losing her true love. Sigurd set off back to the palace alone, while the happy Gunnar and the miserable Brynhild journeyed together.

On his solitary return and still under the queen's powerful spell, Sigurd gave Gudrun the golden ring. The queen had reminded him that, after all, Gunnar had no need of Brynhild's ring now he was married to her. Sigurd should keep the ring as a reward for his help. Idly, Sigurd had then given it to Gudrun in an attempt to keep her happy.

But on the arrival of the newly married couple, Brynhild saw with horror that her true love, Sigurd, was married to Gudrun. Worse still, the ring Sigurd had given to Brynhild in their love tryst was now firmly placed on Gudrun's finger.

As Brynhild lay twisted with despair in her chamber, Gudrun knew there was only one more lie to place in her heart. Brynhild must believe that she had been utterly betrayed by Sigurd. One night, Gudrun visited Brynhild in her chamber. She whispered in her ear that Sigurd had pretended to be Gunnar to win her on Gunnar's behalf only so that Brynhild would not get in the way of his own marriage to Gudrun. Fraught with jealousy, Brynhild was now convinced that Sigurd had purposely deceived her, had pretended to be Gunnar and had taken back the ring so he could give it to Gudrun. Believing that Sigurd had betrayed her, she turned against him, and in her despair arranged for her brother-in-law, Gutthorm, to murder the innocent Sigurd.

But even after Sigurd's death, she was not released from her love for him, and with the realization that Sigurd had never betrayed her but had been doomed by the jealousy of Gudrun and her mother, Brynhild threw herself onto Sigurd's funeral pyre and killed herself. The curse of the ring had come true.

VAINOMOINEN

FINLAND, 300CE

THIS Finnish hero is god, trickster, shaman and tireless explorer. As the main hero in a great Finnish epic, the *Kalevala*, this character is a highly unusual form of hero, capable of losing some of his struggles and yet still becoming a vigorous and wise old man, who eventually sets off to sail on a voyage for eternity.

Before the existence of the universe there was nothing except Luonnotar (daughter of creation), her mother, Ilma, and the primordial ocean. Luonnotar wandered through the air, her mother, for eons of time until she became exhausted by the nothingness. Restless for change she slipped into the primordial ocean. For 700 years she floated on the gentle waves as the sea lapped her body, making her endlessly fertile and also pregnant. But Luonnotar did not know that she was pregnant and the child inside,

165

Vainomoinen, had grown to adulthood inside her womb after taking 700 years to reach maturity.

Vainomoinen sat inside her womb for thirty more years and reflected upon life and how he could come into being. Luonnotar had no idea that she had a child inside her, and Vainomoinen became more and more desperate to get out. He called to the stars and the sun and moon to help him to get out, but no one could hear him. Boredom eventually got the better of him, and he hauled himself out of his mother's womb, clambered along her vagina and popped out like a jack-in-a-box, before diving into the sea.

For many weeks Vainomoinen swam towards a distant shore, and he was washed up on the beach of a country that eventually became Finland. Because Vainomoinen was mature, he quickly set about using his magic to plough the land, to thaw the glaciers and to fell the great forests so that the land could be used for farming. Every day he sang songs and chanted spells. A frost-giant, Joukahainen, who ruled the far north, began to fear that his empire was on the verge of changing, and he took his sleigh and set off from the edge of the coldest tundra to find the stranger and stop his magic. The frost-giant sang his own songs and spells to make the sea and earth shake with fear, but Vainomoinen was totally unmoved. He simply sang his own spells louder and outwitted the giant by turning his horse into a boulder, his sword into lightning, and his bow and arrows into rainbows and birds. Finally, he froze Joukahainen into a column of ice and planted him in a great icy swamp right up to his neck so that he couldn't move. But the frost-giant had one last chance and quickly suggested that Vainomoinen could marry his frost-giant sister, Aino, if Vainomoinen set him free.

The one thing that Vainomoinen hadn't bargained for was that Aino was repulsed by the attentions of such an old man. For although Vainomoinen thought he was young, he had been born thirty years old, and didn't realize that to others he might not appear to be quite the youth he felt himself to be. Aino could not bear the sight of him, and she threw herself into the sea and drowned. So Vainomoinen set off to the land of the ice-giants to find himself another, more stable wife. Now that he had been rejected by such a young and beautiful woman and been the cause of her death he was more determined than ever to marry and create children, fearful that he was ageing faster than he had imagined.

On his way to Pohjola, the frosty wastelands of the far north, Joukahainen, who was still vengeful for the death of his sister, ambushed Vainomoinen's boat. He was thrown into the freezing sea, surrounded by great breakers of ice and floating glaciers. For eight days he swam, growing weaker and weaker. Sometimes the icebergs grabbed him with their icy fingers, sea-creatures nipped his toes for signs of death as he floated on in a daze, his body temperature falling below zero, further and further into oblivion.

But a sharp-eyed eagle saw his body drifting near land and swooped down to grab him like a fish. The eagle took him to the shore but finding that his prey was not a tasty herring after all, abandoned him on the icy wastes. Day after day Vainomoinen's health improved as he lived on a diet of fish and ice. Soon he was walking and set off northwards, until he came to the great palace of Louhi, the witch-princess. Many suitors had visited the princess's palace to court the exquisite icy daughters of the north. But Louhi gave each suitor impossible conditions so that none would leave with his heart's desire, and if these conditions were not met she generally sent out her army of frost-giants to kill him.

When Vainomoinen arrived at the palace, Louhi offered him one of her daughters, if he would make a magic device that would ensure prosperity for whoever owned it. This was called a sampo, and it could provide endless salt, flour and gold from each of its three magic orifices. But Vainomoinen shook his head – he knew no one as yet had ever made the sampo. It was an impossible task. Louhi persuaded him to return to Finland and create this magic device, for only the person who was able to make it would have her daughter's hand in marriage.

Vainomoinen had no choice but to do as he was instructed. Louhi reminded him never to look up to the sky on his way home nor to stop for any man or beast. These conditions would assure his safety so that he could fulfil his quest. Doubts and fears racked his head as he travelled into the forests again, and just as he was about to turn back he heard the most enchanted singing in the world. He looked up to the sky and saw Louhi's daughter sitting on a rainbow, spinning gold threads into golden pouches. Numbed by desire and enchanted by her cold-hearted spell, Vainomoinen pleaded with her to marry him without the magic sampo and offered to do anything in the world for her.

The witch's daughter had her own set of tests for the love-sick Vainomoinen, and after he had completed the first three the fourth proved to be the most arduous. This was to carve a boat from her shuttle. But each time he tried, evil spirits forced him to give up and eventually he resorted to his magic spells. Every time he wielded an axe it only inflicted injury upon himself, and although he could remember every spell for carving the wood, fixing the wooden bolts and joining the pieces, he could not remember the spell that would make the parts join up to make a completed boat. He began to search everywhere for the assembly spell – in the forests, across the plains and even down into the underworld, where he just escaped being captured in an iron net and getting drunk on the beer of oblivion.

But it was the giant, Antero Vipunen, who had the secret of the binding spell to finish his boat. Luckily, a kind shepherd directed him to where the sleeping giant lay. This giant had slept for hundreds of years just under the surface of the earth, using the soil as his blanket. Trees and plants had rooted themselves above him, and he had been there for so long that some of the oldest trees had died and seeded new trees in his skin. Worms crawled through his hair and kept it shining and as clean as if it were washed in spring water, and his nails were kept short by mice or voles, who would burrow down and gnaw at the ends of his fingers.

Antero Vipunen knew every spell that had ever been sung or chanted, and so when Vainomoinen found his body heaped over with earth and trees he tried to wake him. First, he hacked down the trees and pulled out the roots that had grown from his body. Then he stuck a stick down the giant's throat. But the giant yawned, and as he closed his mouth again he swallowed Vainomoinen whole, and went back to sleep. Vainomoinen was still undeterred, and he organized the inside of the giant's huge belly into a smithy. The hammering and working of iron woke the agonized giant, who threw up the contents of his stomach, which included, with Vainomoinen, all the spells he had ever known and the binding spell for wooden boats.

With the magic song firmly implanted in his mind, Vainomoinen set off to finish making the boat for Louhi's daughter. But in his haste to get the ship finished, Vainomoinen delegated the task of making the magic sampo to his brother, a blacksmith named Ilmarinen. Ilmarinen was a master-forger of iron, and he poured, mixed and stirred all sorts of concoctions in his alchemical smithy until the magic sampo appeared in the flames. In his excitement, he took it straight to Louhi, and she kept her promise: whoever made the sampo would marry her daughter. And so it was Ilmarinen who married the daughter of the witch, not Vainomoinen.

But Louhi's daughter had been cruel to one of her servants, Kullervo, who was also, unbeknown to her, a dab hand at magic. In his anger, he turned her cattle into wolves, which turned on the newly wed bride and killed her. So Ilmarinen returned to Finland, renewed his friendship with Vainomoinen and together they decided to return to Pohjola and steal the magic sampo. If there were no frost-giant wives for them, at least they could bring back the mill of prosperity for the people of Finland.

Accompanying them was the womanizer and hero Lemminkainen. Together the three gods sailed in the magic boat to Pohjola. Vainomoinen caught a great fish from the ocean and after eating it, he used its backbone to make a zither. This magic instrument had the power to lull everything to sleep – rocks, animals, mountains and the sea. By using the zither, the three heroes managed to enter Pohjola and steal the magic sampo while the frost-giants and the witch-princess slept. As the ship sailed away again on the turning tide, Lemminkainen couldn't resist shouting out their triumph, and his voice awoke Louhi's possessive heart. She sent icy storms and great winds to destroy the ship and drown them. The howling gales blew the zither across the icy sea, and it sank to the bottom beneath a great iceberg. After the storm had passed, Vainomoinen found fragments of the smashed sampo attached to the sails. Collecting the scattered pieces, he joined them together with his binding spell to provide enough magical prosperity for the people of Finland.

Vainomoinen had now completed his quest, and as a last offering, he blew the breath of light and warmth into the forests of Finland, so that when Louhi came to attack the country with ice and freezing winds, the spring would always follow to restore life.

Vainomoinen built himself a bronze boat and sailed away on the shafts of sunlight on his endless journey between heaven and earth. It is said that if the people of Finland ever need him, he will sail back on the morning sunlight before he continues his never-ending voyage.

THE ADVENTURES OF RATA

POLYNESIA, 750CE

THERE are many versions of Rata's adventures throughout the islands of Polynesia. Rata is part of one of the great cycles of dynastic myths, the Tawhaki cycle. This version relies on the beauty of the unusual and the simplicity of a powerful imagination. There is a classic and well-known Maori version that is perhaps superior in style and content but much of the underlying depth of human emotion is lost because of the emphasis on the actual adventure rather than on Rata himself. In this version from the islands of the South Pacific, it is Rata's quest for vengeance that is so directly brought to life.

Wahie-roa was one of the gods of the sky, a comet that travelled quickly across the heavens. He took a wife called Matoka, and she gave birth to a son, called Rata. Not long before Rata was born, Matoka had a terrible craving for a delicacy called koko, a kind of over-fat bird with meat as rich as venison. Wahie-roa set off with his servant to catch this bird but unfortunately could not find one in his usual hunting grounds and had to travel further than he wanted to. This meant trespassing on land belonging to Matuka, a cruel mortal. For some time Wahie-roa and his servant followed the trail of the koko, but it led them straight into the trap that Matuka had set for poachers. Wahie-roa was instantly killed and Matuka carried off the terrified servant to be his slave.

When Rata grew to be a young man, he naturally asked his mother about his father. She explained how her desire for koko had led Wahie-roa to Matuka's lair and his subsequent death. Rata determined to avenge his father's tragic end. 'So where is this Matuka now?' he asked one day.

'He lives in the direction of sunrise across the sea. It is far away and you cannot go there, for you have no boat.'

But Rata was now desperate to go; the need for justice was so strong in his heart that nothing would stop him from finding Matuka.

One day his mother went to the forest to gather firewood and found a tree that she knew could be made into a canoe. It was the only one on the island, and she pulled some branches from it and excitedly took them home to Rata. Matoka told him about the tree and where to find it, and for several days he searched the forests until he eventually found the magical tree. But his axe was blunt, and he could not fell it.

His mother told him to go and see one of his ancestors, Hine-Hoanga (daughter of the whetstone). When she heard his story and saw that the axe he had brought belonged to one of his ancestors, she knelt down and told him to draw the axe across her back. 'Kia koi, kia koi, kia koi – Be sharp, be sharp!' she cried, and instantly his axe was sharp.

So Rata returned to the tree in the forest and felled the top half of it to make his canoe. The next day he returned to hollow out the trunk but to his alarm he found the tree standing again, rooted to the spot as if it had never been cut down. Again he cut down the tree, but on his return the following day he found that the tree had once more been returned to it place. This time, after he cut it down, he decided to wait and see what would happen and hid behind some bushes.

A strange light glowed through the clearing and then began to diminish until a darkness descended around the tree. Far above the treetops was sunlight, and across the sparkling sea Rata could make out a cloudless sky. Yet here in the depths of the forest a strange transformation was taking place. He heard a rustling, not of leaves but coming from the air above him, then he heard music and songs, but not of birds or humans, not of tangible things, only the sounds themselves. He listened to the music and the songs, and as the dim light thickened like a mist he saw the tree stand upright. The mist slowly disappeared and he just managed to glimpse the spirits of the forest vanishing into the tangled copses of the wood.

Rata angrily ran into the clearing. 'So it is these spirits who have put back my tree, who have made a fool of me and who have undone everything that I wanted to do!' He rushed after the spirits and seizing them, demanded they explain their interference.

'You must only perform the ceremonies to the great god Tane, for this is his sacred grove. Return to your home and make a sacrifice, perform the ceremonies and we, your ancestors, will do what is necessary here for you.'

So Rata agreed, and as he walked away from the clearing the leaves of the toe-toe drooped to the ground and the tips of the great ferns dropped their fronds as if in fear of Rata's anger when he seized the wood spirits. These plants have done so ever since.

When he returned home, his mother remembered that it was true that he should perform these rituals. So Rata made sacrifices and offered flowers and chanted songs, and the following day he went back to the tree. But the tree had gone, and in the middle of the clearing lay a canoe, hollowed to the correct shape and ready to sail. The spirits came and helped Rata to take the canoe to the sea, and when it was launched, it rode the waves with the magical energy of the woodland grove.

Rata named the canoe Niwaru, and with his trusted men he sailed away to find the island of the evil Matuka. First, they came to Poua's land. Poua was a terrible goblin, who recited strange incantations that made the men lethargic and mesmerized them so that they gave up their quest and returned home. Rata could hear none of it and asked them, 'What is his spell? What does he say to enchant you?'

'He calls us little-heads, and then it seems our strength is drawn out of us.'

So Rata said, 'I have a spell more powerful than this goblin, trust me.'

As they approached the shore, again the great ugly goblin shouted out his spell, and the men immediately began to grow weary.

Rata shouted back, 'Big-face, spread yourself across the whole of heaven!'

The confused goblin retreated to his dwelling. Quickly the men jumped on to the shore, and Poua sensed he had an equal mind to contend with. Thinking perhaps he could outwit this youth and devour the lot of them, he offered them food. But Rata had warned the men what to do when they entered his dwelling. Instead of entering through the doorway, they cried 'Big-face' and broke down one of the walls. When Poua told them to sit on the mats, Rata stopped them and told them to sit on the floor where there were no mats. Each time Poua tried to overpower and enchant them, Rata had a more powerful magic.

They sent Poua out for water, and while he was gone Rata used his power to force the water in the well to recede each time Poua was about to ladle some out so that would take him longer than usual to return.

Rata took the water from the exhausted goblin. 'You must be hungry, dear goblin, after spending so long fetching water. In your honour I have prepared some food for you.' Poua was certainly hungry and opened his mouth in great delight at the thought of nourishment, but the dish that Rata served was burning stones. Heaving them from the fire with wooden tongs, Rata and his men threw all the stones into Poua's great gaping mouth. The stones popped and burst inside him as they slid into the depths of his belly, and within minutes the great goblin Poua himself burst all over the island. His entrails were spread everywhere, and with them every man, boat and weapon that Poua had ever devoured.

They found Tama, the servant who had been with Rata's father when he died. Tama had been given to the goblin by the great Matuku on his way to his own inner sanctuary. Luckily for Tama, he had been eaten whole by the hungry goblin, and he was one of the first to burst out of the erupting stomach. Rata was pleased to find him: 'Can you tell us where Matuku lives?'

'He sleeps deep in the cavern on the island of Kai-whaia. He eats only men, and anyone who sets foot there has never returned.'

'Could he be lured from his cavern?'

'Only when there are men nearby, for his hunger is never satisfied.'

'Then we shall go there and call to him,' said Rata, for he knew that his power must surely be greater than that of Mutuku.

They landed at the island of Kai-whaia, and climbed the great mountain towards the caverns of the terrible monster. Rata made snares and traps around all the openings and warned the men not to pull on the ropes until Matuka was right in the middle of the snare. The men were fearful but Rata reminded them that his power had already saved them from the goblin.

Rata stood at the lip of the cavern and called down into the dark tunnel, his voice echoing eerily in the blackness, 'Matuku, Matuku, come and see the offerings we have for you!'

They soon heard a rumbling as the great Matuku bellowed back, 'You are foolish whoever you are, to disturb the sleep of the great Matuku.' The grotesque giant stumbled up through his deep dark caves. The smell of mortal flesh awakened all his other senses, and he began to murmur a magic spell to ensure a good feasting on the meat of men. He was half-way out of the cavern when a noose was suddenly drawn tight around his body.

'You can't kill me, I am impregnable!' he bellowed.

But Rata and his men threw themselves upon him and hacked off his arm. 'You cannot destroy me!' he screamed. They chopped off another arm, but still he cried that he was indestructible so they chopped off his legs and then, lastly, his neck until he could scream no more. But his words were true, for his body changed into a bird, the bittern, and his voice is still heard across the marshes where he lives, lamenting his fate.

Rata then asked Tama where his father's bones were kept.

'They are hung from the ridge-pole of the house of the wise men of Ponaturi. They have special powers, and they use them for their charms and incantations.'

So Rata quickly left his men and arrived at Ponaturi at nightfall. The wise men had gathered to chant their powerful spells and sat around a fire, beating human bones together while they sang. As Rata listened he realized that the charm they were invoking was powerful enough to destroy any enemy, however powerful he might be. He also knew that the bones they were beating together were the bones of his father. When he saw that this power was also his own, he rushed forward into the circle and began to shout war-cries and attack the surprised gathering. After defeating them as if they were nothing more than sand-flies, Rata gathered up his father's bones and returned to his men. Quickly they put to sea in their canoe and set sail for home.

The next morning the Ponaturi found their wise men were dead and the bones of Wahie-roa were missing. They suspected that Rata had been there and vowed to avenge the deaths of their seers.

Rata saw the fleet of the Ponaturi approaching across the horizon three days later. It seems that there was nothing Rata could do to prevent the furious enemy from attacking in great force. His men were driven back further and further and many were slain. The strength of the sea-avengers was so relentless that Rata began to doubt his own powers. Then he remembered the incantation of the wise men and his father's bones. He began to chant and immediately strengthened his men and weakened the enemy. Soon the Ponaturi were pushed back to the sea, and they turned and fled to their canoes. But Rata's men made sure that none would escape, and every one of them was slaughtered as they tried to leave. Even the dead warriors of Rata sprang to life, and the bones of Wahie-roa rattled and swung in the breeze that had lifted off the sea.

With the death of his father finally avenged, Rata had the great canoe drawn up on to the shore and placed under a sacred cover to protect it from the weather.

AHAIYUTA

ZUNI, NORTH AMERICA, 800CE

THE Zuni of the New Mexico desert are a peaceful, agricultural people, who still live today in much the same way they have been doing for centuries. Their concerns are with the weather, for drought is a constant threat in the southwestern United States. This myth describes a heroic, god-like being whose task is to restore fertility to his people. A simple hero with a simple task, but a mission of grave importance to the Zuni people.

A long time ago there was a drought in the land. The sun shone incessantly and there was not a cloud in the sky, so the land became baked and parched with too much heat and no rain. It became clear to everyone that the cloud-eater, a monster who lived at the top of a great mountain, was responsible for the state of the land.

This monster had a particular desire for devouring clouds. Each day he would stand on his mountain top, open his huge mouth and swallow any cloud that appeared in the sky. He was so addicted to eating clouds that not one drop of rain ever got a chance to form, and so the land became drier and more and more barren. Many people realized that the monster was responsible for their drought. The fields were full of dead corn, and any food that had been stored was soon used up. The people knew that someone would have to go and slay the cloud-eater.

The sun had a child called Ahaiyuta who lived with his grandmother on Corn Mountain. When he grew up to be a youth he could run as fast as a deer, and he could fight the most fearsome of beasts. His strength was greater than even his father's, and he shone twice as brightly at dawn. One day Ahaiyuta overheard his grandmother complaining about the drought to her friend the crow, and he just happened to hear her accuse the cloud-eater of causing their troubles.

Ahaiyuta ran to her. 'I'll go to the mountain in the east and kill the cloud-eater, then we shall have rain again and we will have food and crops and peace.'

His grandmother was not happy about his decision. 'You must be very careful. The cloud-eater is a dangerous monster, and many brave warriors have never come back from his mountain.'

But Ahaiyuta merely shrugged and set out with the belief that he alone could destroy the monster. He took with him the sleekest arrows and the strongest bow. As he was on his way down the track, his grandmother shouted after him: 'Here are four feathers to protect you and give you a safe journey. The red feather will show you the right path; the yellow feather will make you as small as the tiniest creature; the blue feather will let you talk to any animal you meet; and the black feather can give you all the strength you need to perform any task.'

He placed the red feather in his hair and the others in his pocket and set off towards the east. For many days he walked and found nothing. The earth was dry and the green fields were now brown and full of dead corn. There was silence in the land: birds were dying and would not sing, and the animals were becoming weaker and weaker. The sun was scorching hot, and Ahaiyuta could not keep his eyes open. Many times he nearly fell exhausted to the ground. He became hungrier and thirstier, but still he walked on relentlessly, sure that he would get to the cloud-eater and end this terrible drought. After a while he stumbled into a hole in the ground and out of it popped a gopher. He quickly put the blue and yellow feathers into his hair and shrank down to the gopher's height.

The gopher was friendly enough. 'Hey, what are you doing wandering around in this heat? And how do you have such amazing powers to make yourself so small?'

Ahaiyuta explained why he was there and about the feathers. Gopher said, 'Come into my hole, and I'll show you a secret passage that will take you to the cloud-eater's mountain. I can lead you to the terrible monster's lair, and on the way you can eat and drink and become strong again.'

Gopher began to tunnel his way through the earth, and as they dug further and further into the side of the mountain it grew damp and clammy, and Ahaiyuta felt cooler. He found springs of water to quench his thirst, and mossy vegetation that the gopher said was all right to eat. For many hours the gopher tunnelled and then he suddenly stopped. 'Shhh, do you hear what I hear?'

Ahaiyuta stopped eating the moss and nodded. Far below them they could hear the rumble of the sleeping monster as he snored in his mountain lair.

'Stay here,' said the gopher. 'I'll go and make a tunnel right to the edge of his heart.' The gopher tunnelled through into the monster's cavern and began to gnaw at the fur that covered the cloud-eater's heart.

The cloud-eater woke up suddenly and yawned at the gopher: 'What are you doing here?'

'Sorry grandfather. I've just taken some of your warm hairs for my nest – you won't even know they are gone.' In a flash he shot back up his tunnel towards the waiting Ahaiyuta.

'Listen, you must go now, very quickly. Follow the tunnel down to the sleeping monster and shoot your arrows straight into his heart. I've gnawed away the fur above the centre of his heart, aim your first arrow there and it should kill him instantly.'

Ahaiyuta ran quickly into the tunnel, placed in his hair the black feather that would give him the strength to accomplish any task and, taking careful aim, he pulled out one of his best arrows and drew back the bow. The arrow hit the centre of the monster's heart. An agonizing bellow roared through the whole mountain until it shook with the vibration. The gopher and Ahaiyuta were thrown backwards; rocks and rubble crashed down around them as the tunnel began to collapse. The cloud-eater's heart turned yellow, and every drop of rain that he had stolen from the sky, and all the clouds that he had devoured swirled up into a gigantic typhoon that forced its way out of the mountain top and gushed out as a great torrential river down the side of the mountain. The monster lay dead. Ahaiyuta and the gopher cheered and ran back down the tunnel away from the avalanche of water and mud that was beginning to seep into their hole.

'The cloud-eater can never eat the clouds again, the rains will come now that the typhoon has called the clouds back to the sky!'

As they emerged from the other end of the tunnel, it seemed as if darkness had come early to the day. But then gopher pointed across to the sky in the west and they saw dark clouds of rain covered the sun, not night.

Ahaiyuta began to walk back to the west with his friend the gopher. He felt huge drops of rain on his face, and black clouds scudded across the whole of the sky as the rain fell, heavier and heavier. The path soon became a stream of gurgling water, and the landscape was filled with pools and rivers. Torrents flowed down the mountainside, making fresh lakes, and the rain fed the hungry plants and every creature of the earth.

Ahaiyuta returned happily to the Corn Mountain, and on his arrival the people came to greet him and praise him. He would always be treated as their hero, but he never forgot to include the gopher in his story whenever he remembered the days of killing the cloud-eater.

BEOWULF

IT is believed that this extraordinary epic poem was written around the eighth century CE in Old English, probably by a monk or poet in an Anglo-Saxon court located north of the River Thames. The writer was most probably a Christian who was inspired by the pagan heroics of the Anglo-Saxon tradition still interwoven into the culture of the time. It is believed that the original manuscript may have been lost during the ninth-century Viking invasions of Anglia in which many of the Anglo-Saxon monasteries and libraries were destroyed. The Beowulf manuscript was not discovered until the seventeenth century, and although it was written in Old English by an Englishman, the story takes place in southern Sweden and Denmark, probably from where the ancestors of the writer originally came.

Beowulf gives its hero psychological awareness and also reveals the social and cultural heroic value of the pagan warriors and peoples of its time. They believed in the inevitability of death and in fate, which they called Wyrd, but not in an afterlife. Fame and glory could be achieved only in this life to provide any sense of immortality after one's death. Beowulf's creator has done just that for himself. But it is Grendel, the 'foul' monster and a symbol of the dark, unconscious shadow of our psyche, who perhaps touches a chord of human compassion in us, something that, ironically, few heroes seem able to do.

The Danish king, Hrothgar, ruler of the Spear-Danes, had recently built a great hall for his warriors. The palace was splendidly filled with treasures, and it was a feasting centre for those who deserved to enjoy their success as warriors in battle and as a reward for their courage and valour. The glamorous hall was called Heorot, and many champions came to feast under the gabled roof, receiving their prizes and trophies from the generous king. But unknown to them all, their lurked an evil and gruesome monster.

Grendel was a foul and loathsome creature who dwelt on the misty moors and marshes beyond the palace walls. Hate and malevolent thoughts filled his mind by day. He was spiteful and full of vengeance, having been subjected to evil himself as the result of a murderous curse from his cruel ancestors. Grendel had been banished from love and from enjoyment of life, and he lived alone in the dark swamps with only his hungry heart, his wicked mother and the other monsters of this deep and dreadful place.

One night Grendel's greed led him to the hall of the Spear-Danes. Peeping in through the darkened windows, he saw a group of sleeping warriors, drowsy from mead and too much food and snoring in a corner. The grim and greedy monster put his great arm through the iron gates and grabbed two of the sleeping warriors, then threw them over his shoulder to return to his deep lair to feast upon their bodies.

Each night the monster came to devour more and more of Hrothgar's men, his hunger for flesh becoming an obsession. Whatever the great king offered the beast he rejected, desiring nothing else except to eat flesh and to prove his great power over the land.

For many years the dreadful demon monster stalked the moors and haunted the woods, many warriors died and many ran away terrified by Grendel's devouring sport. Stories of Grendel's grisly greed travelled far and wide, and bards sang of his terror and the Spear-Danes' never-ending struggle against him. The news travelled to the southern coast of Sweden, where the Storm-Geats lived. Beowulf was the greatest of these warriors, and when he heard about Grendel he was determined to help rid the Danes of the terrible beast.

When Hrothgar heard of Beowulf's arrival in his land he was overjoyed. He had known him as a child, and many rumours had grown up that Beowulf had the strength of thirty men just in the grip of one hand. He welcomed Beowulf into his hall and they discussed how best to rid the land of Grendel. Beowulf convinced the king that he should stay the night in the great hall and wait for the beast to come. He would slay him with his bare hands, for Grendel had no weapons either.

That night Beowulf and some of his companions remained in the great feasting hall. Some fell asleep but Beowulf lay awake, ready and waiting. As the moon fell behind some clouds, Grendel slipped out of his dark cavern among the swamps of the moor and made his way towards the hall. He saw the lights still glowing and knew warriors were sleeping off their fine banquet. His mouth drooled and his lips turned to a grin at the thought of such succulent meals ahead of him. Sneaking into the hall, Grendel found a sleeping warrior. He seized him by the throat, tore his body to shreds and then began to bite into the flesh. The corpse soon ran with blood, which Grendel drank like water, tossing away the bones. Grendel was about to snatch another warrior when Beowulf jumped up from his pretend sleep and seized the great monster's arm in his own mighty grip. The monster was frightened, he had never met a living being as strong as himself. His courage left him, and he wanted to escape and return to his own dark, dank cavern to hide, but Beowulf held on to him. Clutching his hand Beowulf pulled him back, and as he pulled on the monster's arm it began to tear away from the shoulder and Beowulf ripped Grendel's arm from its socket. Grendel ran way from the palace shrieking in agony. He managed to drag himself back to his swampy home and there, with his own blood swimming around him and the life-force draining from his evil heart, the great monster died.

To prove his success, Beowulf hung the ghastly arm from the rafters of the great hall so that all who came to feast might see it.

Hrothgar insisted on having a ceremonial banquet. He ordered that the hall be cleansed and that Beowulf should receive many gifts and treasures for his bravery and courage. And for that night at least, they drank, enjoyed themselves and slept in peace. But it was not the end of terror in the hall of Heorot.

Grendel's mother, a water-witch, had grieved deeply at the death of her terrifying son, and as she sat alone in the darkness beneath the swamps and moors she began to weave her own spell of evil revenge on the warriors of the great hall. That night she surged up from her underwater lair in anger and broke into the great hall. She grabbed one of the king's favourite comrades in her teeth and then snatched from the ceiling Grendel's revolting arm.

Grendel's mother returned to her lair deep in the underground caverns and waters of the swamp.

Again Beowulf agreed to challenge this monster, but this time he knew he would have to follow her down to her lair, for now that she had retrieved Grendel's arm she might never return to the surface. Beowulf dived into the black, bubbling swamp and swam like a seal into the dark depths of the underground waters. He found the water-witch in her lair, and the terrible battle began. Yet the sword on which Beowulf had decided to rely to kill her was useless, and he began to struggle under her fearsome power. But then, just as she drew her own dagger to slay him, Beowulf saw sticking out of the rocks an ancient sword, encrusted with the barnacles of time. Its golden hilt glinted, willing him to reach for it, and impulsively he grabbed at the blade. The sword came instantly to his hand as if by some supernatural power, so he thrust it between the witch's eyes, sliced it down through her head, and completely chopped her body in half, as if she had been a slab of butter.

He swam back to the surface of the black waters carrying the monster's head and the bejewelled hilt of the magic sword. His return to Heorot was glorious, and so he became one of the most honoured and renowned of warriors. Then Beowulf returned to Sweden and ruled his people in peace and honour for fifty years.

But many hundreds of years before Beowulf had gained fame as a hero, a fire-eating dragon had taken up residence in a stone-barrow at the base of a cliff, far below the surface of the earth. Here the dragon guarded a secret hoard of treasure, which had been left under the curse of a lone warrior a thousand years before. The dragon loved its hoard and would gloat day and night over its possessions, not interested in anything else or even in eating anyone, until the fateful day when it was disturbed.

One of Beowulf's servants stumbled by accident upon the secret path that led down to the underground cavern. The servant was terrified when he saw the dragon, but he was also tempted by a golden goblet that lay near the dragon's head. The servant snatched the goblet and ran quickly away to prove to his friends that he had found the treasure trove.

The dragon made a daily count of all its bits and pieces, and finding a golden goblet had gone missing it puffed itself up and frantically searched everywhere for the cup. Dragons are not known for their tolerance of mankind, and it set off up the path, sure that someone had been down and robbed it. Now only vengeance was in its mind, and not even the safe return of the cup would satisfy its disturbed head. For a whole day the dragon savaged the villagers, burned their buildings, then flew back to its nest and safety.

Beowulf was by now over seventy years old, but he was determined to destroy the dragon who had burned his own gift-hall and killed many of his people. With only his trusted companion, Wiglaf, he descended the steep path down the cliff face into the depths of the earth and the dragon's lair. The servant had eventually owned up to Beowulf how he had accidentally found the barrow. It did not take long for Beowulf and Wiglaf to destroy the dragon, but Beowulf was mortally wounded in the terrible fight and died from his wounds.

His body was cremated on the cliff top above the great dragon's lair. The huge treasure hoard was laid out all around him so that when the fire was lit he could be honoured from far across the sea. With the ashes of his bones and the dragon's hoard, the warriors built a barrow on the headland to keep his fame remembered for always. His immortality was now assured, and the thread of the Wyrd had been woven for Beowulf.

HUITZILOPOCHTLI, GOD OF WAR

AZTEC, CENTRAL AMERICA, 1200CE

HUITZILOPOCHTLI was one of the most important gods of the Aztec pantheon. Not only a god of war, he was also the god of fertility, responsible for both the lightning season and the season of growth of both crops and fruits of the earth. The Nahua peoples believed he could grant them fair weather for their crops, and thus they developed a deep connection between war and their food supply. If war was not waged every year, the gods would be without mortal flesh to devour and they themselves would be destroyed. Ultimately, if there were no gods, the crops would fail and there would be famine and the end of the human race. War was more important than anything else, and this rather potent and impulsive war-god, not unlike Mars in Roman myth, represented both the power of the midday sun and the aggressive instinct in humankind.

Huitzilopochtli means, 'blue humming-bird on the left'. The Aztecs believed that the souls of dead warriors turned into humming-birds and flew to the left to enter the underworld.

Under the shadow of the mountain called Coatepec near the city of Tollan lived a goddess called Coatlicue. She had many sons and one daughter – some people believed she had 400 sons who were the night stars. One day as she was going about her devotions, a brilliantly coloured ball of soft feathers fell into her lap from the sky. She was pleasantly surprised and decided to keep it as an offering to the sun-god. The different colours shone like a rainbow, so she placed the ball in her cleavage for safe keeping. Soon Coatlicue found that she was to give birth, and her terrible sons and equally vicious daughter decided to kill their mother because of her mysterious conception. But the unborn child spoke to Coatlicue and told her that he would save her and not to fear their anger.

So the children dressed in their war robes and carried their bundles of darts towards the great mountain, intent on murdering their mother. But the unborn child, hearing their approach up the mountain, was born fully grown, flourishing a shield and a spear of bright blue. He was painted for war, with his face and limbs striped with blue bars; he had golden feathers on his legs and a plume of humming-bird feathers on his head. He shattered the daughter with a flash of lightning from his spear, and then chased the others four times around the mountain. When Huitzilopochtli finally cornered them, he cut out their hearts and gave these to Coatlicue to hang round her neck as jewels.

Celebratory festivals, such as the Toxcatl, were held in his remembrance, and human victims, or their hearts, were offered to him and to his mother, Coatlicue, in very bloody sacrifices. This ensured both fertility of the crops and the rainy season to the lands. Sometimes these also included daily sacrifices of blood to make sure the sun-god rose in the sky.

CHACOPEE – WHITE FEATHER

SIOUX, NORTH AMERICA, 1500CE

IN the depths of a great forest, in total isolation, lived an old man and his grandson. Many moons before, the child's ancestors, a proud and arrogant tribe, had foolishly believed that they would beat the giants at a great race. Unfortunately the giants had won, and the forfeit for losing the race was the deaths of all the children of the tribe, as well as the deaths of the adults themselves. It was only luck that this one child had escaped. His name was Chacopee, and his grandfather had run off with him into the forest to raise him, teaching him to hunt and fish.

As Chacopee grew older he became more curious about the world beyond the dark, damp forest, and one day he decided to wander further than usual. He came to the edge of the prairie and the traces of an old encampment. He returned quickly to his grandfather to find out how the camp could have been there. For all the boy knew was that his grandfather refused to speak about his relatives or ancestors. Now, maybe, there was some way of finding out about them.

But the grandfather curtly ignored his questions, and told him it was all in his head and that he had imagined the rotten tent poles and the white ashes of fires.

Chacopee resolved to go back. This time he took a different path and found himself confronted by a stranger. He nearly turned and ran, for he had never met any other human being in the world in his boyhood apart from his grandfather. And this weird stranger was wooden from the neck down – only his head made of flesh.

'Wearer of the white feather, it is good to meet with you,' smiled the head on the wooden body.

Chacopee did not understand. His grandfather had not yet informed him about his tribe's ancient belief that a brave and heroic man would rise up in their family and prove to be the mightiest and bravest of them all. He would be called White Feather. Just as he was about to turn back for home the stranger spoke again: 'You do not wear the white feather yet. But soon you will. You must go home and sleep, for then you will dream. You will dream of a sack, a pipe and a long, white feather. Then, when you wake you will find these things beside you. You must put the feather on your head so that you are the greatest of warriors, and if you need to prove this, you must take the pipe and smoke it, and the smoke will turn to white pigeons.'

'But how am I to believe you?' asked Chacopee.

'I know of your family. Your mother and father were very brave, but they were part of a tribe who thought they could win a race against the giants. But the giants won the competition and the tribe was killed except for you, who escaped with your grandfather. Now you must avenge your ancestors' deaths and seek out the giants. Here is a magic vine that will make you invisible, and will also trip up the giants when they run a race with you. Go now, and dream.'

So Chacopee returned to his home in the forest and things began to happen just as the Man of Wood had prophesied. Chacopee put on the white feather and smoked the pipe, and the smoke turned to a flock of white pigeons, which flew out of the house and alarmed Chacopee's grandfather. But when grandfather saw the white feather on Chacopee's head he remembered the old prophecy of his tribe; one day a great warrior would emerge wearing a white feather. Fearing the worst, he knew that Chacopee must carry on his quest to slay the giants.

The next morning Chacopee left the house in the forest, stumbling through the dark canopy of trees, which led further and further into places that no man had ever seen. Here he came to a great, dark lodge where the giants lived. They had heard that Chacopee was coming from their spirit guides and pretended to greet him affably enough, but secretly they rubbed their hands with glee at a new opponent and another tasty meal.

Chacopee's insight was deeper than even that of the giants, and he was not deceived by the welcome and their courtesy. Soon a race was planned between Chacopee and the youngest giant, and the winner was to chop off the head of the loser. With the help of his magic vine, Chacopee won and killed the small giant. Next morning he came again, and killed another of the mighty giants, and repeated this each day until all but one of the giants were dead.

On the seventh morning he met the Man of Wood, who warned him about a beautiful woman whom he must not trust. 'You must pay no notice of her, for she is there to kill you,' said the Man of Wood. 'You must turn yourself into an elk and run away.'

So Chacopee carried on his way and not long after met the most beautiful woman in the world. He remembered what the man of Wood had told him and instantly turned himself into an elk so that he could run into the forest. But the woman burst into tears when she saw him and cried, 'I have travelled so far to find you, because I wanted to be your wife, and now you have turned yourself into an elk. This is surely the end of my happiness.'

Chacopee was, as any young and naïve man would be, instantly besotted with her sad, tear-stained face, and he immediately resumed his own shape and tried to comfort her. Eventually he fell asleep with his head in her lap. The beautiful woman resumed her form as the terrible giant. The giant took his axe and broke Chacopee's back, then turning Chacopee into a dog, he stuck the white feather into his own head-dress, thinking that whoever wore the magic feather would carry its powers. But he was wrong.

The giant married one of two daughters of a great chief. They had heard the rumour that whoever wore the white feather was the bravest and most famous warrior in the country. The older sister had married the giant, and the younger had taken the dog to her home and looked after it with great kindness. It soon became obvious that the dog had magical powers and the giant did not, and when the chief found out that the giant could not even bend a bow and the dog was able to perform the most magical of tricks, he sent a group of hunters to bring them both to him. When the deputation arrived at the younger sister's house they found not a dog but a handsome warrior. Chacopee had been given his human form but he had not been given back the power of speech.

So the chief set a test for the giant and the young warrior, and even though the giant wore the white feather he could not do anything with the magic pipe. The warriors took it in turns to smoke, then the giant and finally Chacopee. The smoke rising from his mouth turned into white pigeons. At this moment he recovered his speech, and the warriors and the chief heard his strange story. The tribe demanded that the giant be punished, and he was sent like a dog to their camp and stoned to death.

Chacopee proved himself with other examples of his magical powers, producing a whole herd of buffalo out on the prairies for the warriors to hunt. His white feather was placed again on his head and his reputation as one of the great magical warriors was rewarded with the hand of the chief's daughter who had taken so much care of him when he had been placed under the spell by the terrible giants.

SIMPANG IMPANG

BORNEO, 1500CE

THIS is a simple tale of a mortal's quest to restore order to himself and the natural world. Nature, in the form of storms and changing weather could be cruel to the Sea-Dyaks of Sarawak, but it was infinitely fertile in its growth and lush plant life. The cultural closeness to such natural phenomena and the people's dependence on the seasons and rainfall make this character more of a social hero than one with egotistic aims to acquire fame or immortality.

A hunting party went out in search for game one night. The roamed deep into the jungle but could find nothing. Weary and hungry, they decided to rest beside a fallen tree trunk. The huge tree trunk stretched across the length of the clearing, so the men huddled on either side of it and made a small fire. One of the huntsman stuck his knife carelessly into the tree bark to mark his place for sleeping, and as he did so, it was not sap that gushed from the tree's wound, but blood.

The men sat up startled, but before they could run, whatever it was they had been sitting upon encircled them and attempted to choke them all to death. It was the king of the pythons. The great snake coiled round them, but they managed to overcome the great beast, slashing at it with their knives and spears. Eventually the dead snake was chopped up into pieces and they cooked some of the best bits over the camp fire. As the oil from the python's flesh dropped into the flames and hissed and spat, the rain began to fall upon the great leaves of the surrounding jungle.

The drops turned into bigger globules of water. The rain fell more and more heavily, until the men were forced to shelter under the trees to finish their meal. The rain was relentless, turning first to a downpour and then to a torrential storm. It flooded the clearing, washed away the huntsmen and the remains of the python. Then the rain flooded the valleys, washed away the villages and drowned the inhabitants. Except for one woman.

This woman managed to escape to the top of a mountain with her dog. As the rain plummeted down, the dog sniffed out a place for them to shelter – an opening in the edge of the cliff beneath a hanging rock. Throughout the deluge the woman huddled there with her dog, while a creeper swung in the wind, scraping its branches against the rocks. The friction soon produced some sparks, so the woman made a fire to keep herself warm. Then the creeper took the form of a man-spirit and one night they had sex together. A child was soon born, but it was only half-human. One half was like the creeper, and the other half consisted of a mortal leg and one arm.

The child, called Simpang Impang, hobbled around on one leg and scrabbled around in the dirt looking for food, grains and seeds with his one hand. He found some grains of rice left at the entrance of a rat's hole and put these out to dry in the sun now that the rains had cleared from the mountain top. Finding his grains of rice had disappeared, the rat angrily accused Simpang Impang of stealing them.

'You have robbed me of my only food, now my children will rob your children for ever!'

But with the changing weather came another, more malicious force for Simpang Impang to deal with. He replaced the rice on a leaf and waited for the sun to come out again. But it was the wind that suddenly came by and scattered the rice across the valleys, gusting around the mountain top on its way to the west. Simpang Impang was furious. He hopped on one leg after the cruel wind, which had by now already crossed many mountains and valleys.

Simpang Impang was determined to find the wind and get back his grains of rice. He was not only hungry for food; he was hungry for revenge, just like the rat. For many miles, through torturous jungle, he struggled on his leg. Tired and desolate, he eventually came to an ancient tree that seemed to have few leaves and many distorted branches. Birds sat on the higher boughs pecking off insects and eating each new green bud the tree managed to unfurl. Simpang Impang asked the birds if they knew they way to the wind's house. The birds ignored him, but the tree creaked and groaned.

Simpang Impang looked up and saw the great tree twisting round its roots and bending its branches in one direction as if it were pointing the way. 'Tell the wind for me,' it creaked, 'to come and blow me down. I am tired of these terrible birds and of the hot sun and of the searing rains.'

So Simpang Impang promised the tree that he would tell the wind, and he followed the path he had been shown. Soon he came to a foul-smelling lake filled with stagnant water. It was covered in green and yellow scum, rancid and dangerous. He approached cautiously, then the surface of the water began to pucker and speak to him, the words bubbling onto the surface in great ripples of speech. 'You must tell the wind to come and blow fiercely through my outlet stream, because it is blocked by a piece of gold.' Simpang Impang agreed to give the lake's message to the wind, and he hobbled on along the lake's shore towards the wind's home.

The path led him down between sugarcane and banana plants, which grew well in the valleys beneath the mountains, and the plants called to him: 'Ask the wind to give us some boughs like other plants so that we can embrace the wind too.'

For many hours he travelled further downhill. Then, spreading before him, he saw the bare landscape of the plains. This was where the wind lived. The wind saw him coming and rushed quickly across the dry rocks and whistled into his ears, 'Why are you here? Why are you here?'

Simpang Impang replied, 'I want my rice back. You stole it from me.'

The wind rustled in his ear, 'Then follow me, follow me. See if you can follow me!' He dashed off across a deep river, rippling waves across the surface. Simpang Impang couldn't hop across such deep and dangerous waters, so a friendly fish swam after the wind, who thought it was Simpang Impang following him.

'So, you can keep up with me across water, now see if you can follow me in the air!' The wind swirled upwards into the air, gushed across the tops of the tallest trees and raced along the side of the hills. This time a swallow soared into the sky and chased the wind. Like the wind it circled and swept back down to the ground. The wind was sure Simpang Impang had chased him.

'You are quicker and faster than I thought,' whispered the wind, 'Now see if you can whistle through a blowpipe, as I can do!' So this time when the wind swirled through the tiny hole in the blowpipe, a friendly ant scuttled through the same tunnel in Simpang Impang's place.

The wind sang softly now around Simpang Impang's ears. 'You have passed three tests and you must be proud, and you must be congratulated, too. But I can never find your grains of rice for they have scattered far and wide.'

Simpang Impang was angry, for the wind seemed to be unstoppable. So he called for help to his father, who had once been a creeper, and his father gave him fire. With the firestick, Simpang Impang set light to the wind's great tail as he swirled up in the sky. The wind howled and shrieked in pain and turned into a whirlwind, so that the dust and fire sparks lit up the sky like a volcano. The wind cried out, 'Put out the fire, my plumage is on fire. Put out the fire and I will make you a whole man!' Simpang Impang lifted his one and only hand and suddenly the fire went out.

As he looked down at himself, Simpang Impang saw that he now had a complete human body, two hands, two feet, a right side and a left side, a back and a front. He had hair on his arms and hair on his head, and two eyes and two ears. Overjoyed at finding he was a complete mortal, he agreed to make friends with the wind and forgot the grains of rice.

He gave the wind the messages from the tree and lake, and the banana plant and the sugarcane, and the wind said he would do his best, like Simpang Impang who had become a complete human. The wind did blow down the tree and unplug the lake, but he could not give the sugarcane boughs nor the banana tree proper branches because he was after all, only the wind.

FIVE

LEGENDARY LOVERS
AND
DIVINE DESIRES

*L*OVE AND LOVERS, whether in human or animal form, have played an integral part in many myths as a projection of our search for self. The tragedy of love affairs, the pain of loss, the separation of 'twin-souls' or unrequited love are different aspects of the human need to relate and to find out what this mysterious thing, love, is all about.

Not only is the question 'What is love?' repeated over and over again in the evocative myths of passion and romance, but also the question 'Why is love?' The power of love and of transformation within is reflected through the imagery of passionate gods and goddesses and their myths. The divine desire that connects us to the unity of nature and beyond the duality of our perception can be glimpsed via these wonderful transformations of love in mythical guise.

This collection of myths reveals the universal energy of love. For thousands of years humans have sought to reconnect to the soul, to the very source of life itself, through myths that reflect our own personal tales of emotion.

Love is a mystery to be lived, and it is only in myth that the mystery can become truly alive for each of us. Once we are 'in love' we are slaves to our own subjectivity. There is no way out, only further and further in, until either the image dissolves and we reclaim our love of self, or the pain becomes unbearable, the image is shattered and we turn to another mirror to reflect our soul again. The paradox is that by being 'in love' we are, in fact, falling in love with ourselves, and the chance is offered us to truly know ourselves in the eyes of another. Love and myth go hand in hand, for myth is the most exquisite mirror of all for the reflection of self.

ISHTAR

ISHTAR was the Babylonian goddess of sex and was the evening star. She was known throughout the Mesopotamian region by her other names, which included Astarte, Inanna, Ashtart and Ashtoreth. It is also highly likely that the cult of Aphrodite originated from Ishtar, as astrologically Ishtar was also identified with the planet Venus.

The myth that describes her best is perhaps that of her descent to the underworld to find her husband Tammuz, which is similar to the Sumerian story of Inanna and Ereshkigal (see page 93). Although this particular story, from around 4000BCE or earlier, has many similarities to Inanna's own journey to the underworld, Ishtar is more concerned with restoring sexual activity to the world through the balancing act of love.

Ishtar was not only the goddess of sex but also the goddess of music. She would bathe in a sacred lake of purity each evening to restore her own virginity. She was highly promiscuous, having many consorts in many different forms. But it was only to Tammuz that her real love was promised.

Tammuz was a sun-god of the springtime who accepted mortality so that he could live on earth and concern himself with the growth of nature, the trees and plants. But Ishtar's love for Tammuz destroyed him. For once the summer sun rose high in the sky, the heat of the sun and of Ishtar's intense love killed Tammuz in his fresh innocence and his spring-like growth. So, as a mortal, Tammuz died and Ishtar was heartbroken. She knew that the only way she could restore their love would be to travel to the underworld, Aralu, and try to bring him back.

Angered and enraged by her own destructive passion, Ishtar threatened to break down the gates of Aralu if she was not admitted instantly. The gatekeeper rushed to inform the mistress of the underworld, Ereshkigal, that Ishtar had journeyed to the underworld to find her husband. Ereshkigal was Ishtar's sister, and was furious that she was at the gates. But because they were related she allowed Ishtar to enter, but only if she underwent a test at each of the seven gates.

At the first gate the keeper took away her crown, at the second her earrings, at the third her necklace, at the fourth her ornaments, at the fifth her girdle, at the sixth her bracelets and at the seventh her clothes. Ishtar was allowed to pass into Aralu, and she stood naked before the goddess of the underworld who showed her no mercy. She was tortured and imprisoned by the plague-demon Namtar and left to suffer alone, without light, and without Tammuz.

But because she was now imprisoned in the underworld there was no love

189

on earth, and all sexual activity ceased. The earth seemed to be held in suspension, so that no animals or vegetation would grow and the fertility of the earth was under threat.

The messenger-god, Papsukal, decided to visit the underworld and find out what was going on. When he saw the terrible suffering of Ishtar he told Shamash the sun-god about her incarceration.

'My lord, without Ishtar nothing will grow, and there will be no love on earth. You must do something to bring her back,' confided the messenger.

So Shamash visited Ea and Sin, the gods of the earth and the moon, to beg for their help. Because Ea was of the earth she created a mortal being called Ashushu, whom the gods sent down to the underworld to demand the release of Ishtar. But Ereshkigal was enraged that the gods should demand such a thing from her, and she cursed Ashushu and placed him a dark dungeon with only the filth of the underworld as his food.

But the gods reminded Ereshkigal that she was not as powerful as they, and if she kept Ashushu in the underworld surely she would at least release Ishtar as an exchange. Ereshkigal could not refuse, and Ishtar was led back through the seven gates of Aralu. At each gate she was given back the clothes and jewellery that had been taken from her, and eventually she arrived back in the upper world. The gods decided to allow Tammuz to return to life once a year to meet his beloved Ishtar. So Tammuz spends each spring with Ishtar, and fertility and love are restored until Ishtar's passion destroys Tammuz, and he returns to the underworld for another six months.

KRISHNA AND THE COWGIRLS

VEDIC, INDIA, 1000BCE

KRISHNA was the eighth incarnation, or avatar, of Vishnu and entered the world solely to destroy the demon-king, Kansa. However, his popularity as a deity made him, for many people, the supreme god, and he later became the object of *bhakti* worship. His sensuous and lustful nature inspired artists and writers alike, and although he was known for his passionate indulgence for milkmaids, he was perhaps the one god who seemed to possess a genuine ability to love only one mortal, Radha. Krishna became known as the 'stealer of hearts', Hari Krishna, and his love for Radha was celebrated in one of the most beautiful and evocative poems called the 'Gitagovinda'.

Krishna enjoyed a highly amorous lifestyle as he grew up into manhood. His early childhood days had been idyllic. Surrounded by cowgirls and gossiping women, he would flirt, tease and play jokes on everyone and often blame the other children for his mischief. By the time he was changing from boy to man, the cowgirls had begun quite naturally to fall in love with this handsome mortal. He would spend the evenings playing his flute in the water-meadows, and at sunset the milkmaids would run down to the river and dance provocatively in front of him.

One day a group of love-struck girls decided to bathe in the river to attract his attention. Krishna watched them from behind a tree, heard them shouting out his name and laughing about their desire for him. Krishna stole their clothes, hid them in a tree and refused to return them unless they came out one by one to worship him. He told them that Varuna inhabited the river, so they were no better off trying to hide their nakedness under water. Varuna was the god of water who could see all, and retrieving their clothes from under the tree would be far less embarrassing. So each of the girls walked across the bank to fetch her clothes. Krishna no doubt ogled at their beauty, then merely sent them all away again, promising he would dance with them the following autumn.

Autumn came, and one moonlit night Krishna took his flute and ran into the forest to call the cowgirls. These girls were all now married and slipping away from their husbands made the whole experience a highly exciting and daring adventure. For some time Krishna teased them, for there was no easy way for one man to dance with all of them at once. But Krishna multiplied himself a hundred-fold, and each girl thought she was dancing with the one and only Krishna, and each girl believed that he was her own lover. The girls fell into ecstasies of passion, and Krishna not only danced through the night in his many forms with each girl but had sex with each as well.

Krishna became truly bewitched by one cowgirl out of all the others. Her name was Radha, and one summer evening he slipped away with her into a beautiful garden beside the river, while the other cowgirls carried on dancing with his illusions. For many nights they made love, but the girls became suspicious of the strange 'hologram' Krishnas and set off in search of the real thing. They followed footsteps and found Krishna and Radha together. But Krishna had grown tired of Radha's assumption that she was better than the other girls, especially when she had demanded that he carry her in his arms to the spot where they had sex.

Krishna was so annoyed that he abandoned her in a rage and returned with the other cowgirls to take up the erotic dance again. The girls became frantic with desire, and the dance went on for six months, ending with the whole group bathing in the River Jumna.

The girls returned to their husbands, but it was as if they had never been away. Time did not exist in Krishna's arms. Radha was totally lovesick by now and could only think of Krishna. He, too, regretted his intolerance, and when he eventually returned to find her in the garden alone, he knew that he was still passionate about her. Their idyllic relationship lasted until the time Krishna began his epic struggle against the demon-king, when marriage and heirs were more important in the struggle of gods and man than the passions and physical desires of true love.

Krishna seemed to be as promiscuous with his marriages as he was with his early lovers. During his great battle against the demons he married eight wives, and as each marriage was opposed by one demon or other, he was able to conquer a flow of evil forces through these very marriages. Later on, when the demon armies had been massacred, Krishna married another 16,101 wives, all virgins who had been imprisoned by the enemy. When he returned with them to Dwarka he agreed to marry them all, as every one of them had fallen madly in love with him. Krishna lived with all 16,101 wives and managed to pleasure them all simultaneously so that each one eventually bore him ten sons and one daughter. Even with so many wives, he was able to attend to their every desire, need and irritation. A seemingly perfect husband.

BITIOU

EGYPT, 1300BCE

THIS short but blood-thirsty love and vengeance myth dates from the thirteenth century BCE, and the reign of one of the greatest pharaohs, Rameses the Great. Some sources suggest it dates back even further, to 4000BCE or even earlier. It reveals how the shadowy depths of human experience can be sparked off from simple betrayal, and how revenge is sometimes sweeter than we dare to believe.

Just before the sun set below the horizon a boy named Bitiou led his cattle into the barn for the night. But the cow in the lead suddenly stopped at the door and began to make a lowing noise. The boy could understand what she was trying to tell him. 'Watch out! Your brother, Anapou is waiting behind the door! He has a knife!' Bitiou saw the shadow of Anapou flash beneath the door just as the last rays of the sun swept a golden sheath of light across the stone ground.

He turned quickly and began to run for his life. The brother, Anapou, saw him disappearing into the dust and ran quickly after him, knowing that he was stronger and faster than Bitiou. But the sun-god, Ra, took pity on Bitiou. Ra saw everything and knew everything that happened in the world, and he intercepted the chase by creating a huge, deep river that suddenly flowed and gushed its way between the two brothers.

Bitiou caught his breath and stopped, realizing that Anapou could no longer catch him. He stood defiantly on the other side of the raging river, waiting to hear insults and abuse from his brother. Anapou cursed the river and shouted across to Bitiou: 'You deserve to die, I should have killed you and I still will if I ever catch up with you again. My wife says you raped her!'

Bitiou couldn't believe what he had heard. He had never touched Anapou's wife nor even given her one glance of desire or lust. There was no reason why Anapou should have said such things about him. In his anger and horror he cut off his own testicles and threw them into the river for the fish. 'Your wife is a liar! I am going to travel far away so that I never see either of you again. I am ashamed to know you as my brother and that you believe these things she has said about me. But if you ever find the beer in your cup is clouded over, you must come to find me.'

Anapou was overcome with guilt over his own accusations. How could his wife have accused his own brother of such a thing? Distraught and filled with grief that Bitiou had vanished across the other side of the river, he ran home in a frenzy. The knife he had sharpened to kill his brother gleamed in the sunlight. Ra had saved his brother for a reason, but the knife had to find a home. Anapou crept back into his house and before his wife could turn round to face him he pushed the knife deep into her neck.

Bitiou travelled for many days. He had become more and more distressed about the behaviour of his brother and the accusations of his brother's wife. His feelings were wounded, and he vowed that he would never allow anyone access to his heart again. So he took his feelings and his heart and hid them in the trunk of an acacia tree, knowing that no one would ever find them there.

The potter-god, Khnum, felt sorry for Bitiou in his loneliness and decided that he needed a bride. As a potter it was easy for him to make an artificial girl out of clay. He placed her near the river and because she smelled so beautiful, when she washed her hair the river became perfumed with the most wonderful fragrance, like the blossom of the acacia tree. Bitiou was instantly enchanted by the beauty and the overwhelming scent of the clay girl and she became his bride. Because he trusted her he showed her where he had put his heart and his feelings for safe-keeping inside the acacia tree.

For many months the girl would wash her black hair in the river, and for many months the perfume drifted downstream towards the palace of the pharaoh. The pharaoh became fascinated by the lingering perfume and decided to find out who it was that was casting such a powerful spell over him. As each day passed he yearned more and more to find the creature who was making him swoon with desire.

The pharaoh and his court took the barge and rowed up stream for many days, further and further into the wilderness. Many wanted to turn back, but the pharaoh's only passion now was to find the girl who had enchanted him. When he eventually found the clay girl, he decided there and then that he would marry her. The girl, artificial and filled with desires for riches, wealth and power, could see herself now only as the pharaoh's queen.

Bitiou had gone further up the river to catch the pearl fish that they ate for breakfast. The artificial girl knew she would have to act quickly before he returned: 'Pharaoh, I would gladly be your bride, but I cannot unless you cut down that acacia tree. For I am bound by its power.'

The pharaoh took an axe from the barge and began to hack at the great tree trunk. Sweat ran down his back, down his forehead and into his eyes, and with each swing of his body the tree began to creak and tremble until it toppled over and hit the ground. At the moment it was felled Bitiou died, for his heart and his feelings had been destroyed. Yet at the same moment, many, many miles away, Anapou was drinking his favourite beer. The beer clouded over and Anapou knew that his brother was in danger, or worse, was already dead.

Anapou stood up and walked away from his drinking friends, vowing he now had to find his brother. It was time to make amends for all the unhappiness and sorrow he had caused Bitiou.

For seven years he travelled across Egypt, through the baking hot desert, across the barren countryside and over the wilderness, searching for his brother, and one day he came to a river where an old tree had been felled. Along the water's edge were the dried acacia berries from the tree. Anapou sensed this was where his brother's heart lay, and he picked up the one berry that smelt still so fragrant, and placed it in a cup of water. A white light began to glow from the water, until the berry, the cup and the light were transformed into a great white bull, pure and radiant. This bull was Bitiou.

Bitiou had no other choice but to go to the palace of the pharaoh and confront the artificial girl. He didn't want her back, but he had trusted her with his secret and she had betrayed him.

But the artificial queen saw the white bull arriving at the palace gates. She recognized him immediately as Bitiou and was terrified that he had come to seek revenge. She ran to the great pharaoh, knowing that he would do as she asked because he loved her so much.

'Will you do anything for me, anything in the world, and if I ask will you promise to do it?' She said breathlessly.

'You know I will do whatever your heart desires,' he said, entranced by her beauty.

'There is a great white bull that has come to the palace. You must sacrifice it, for it has come as an offering to Ra.'

The pharaoh nodded. He did not want to kill the unusual beast, but he had no choice but to honour his promise to the girl. So the pharaoh took his knife and slit the bull's throat. The blood gushed across the ground and with it two seeds of the persea tree. Within a few years these trees grew so tall that people began to worship them as if they were divine. The shade of these two trees became a powerful place for all the pharaoh's subjects to make sacrifices and honour their gods.

The queen was not happy, for she knew that in the trees lay the soul of Bitiou. This time she did not ask the pharaoh to help her. She sent for two foresters and ordered them to cut down the trees. As she stood watching, the light of her inimitable power dancing in her eyes, a tiny chip of wood flew from the foresters axe and landed between the queen's gloating lips. At that instance she conceived a son, and when he was born he was none other than Bitiou.

So the artificial queen gave birth to the husband she had murdered in his first incarnation as a man, had murdered again when he was a bull and again as a tree. So the years passed and she did not know that her son was Bitiou, and when the pharaoh died Bitiou became the pharaoh.

Bitiou knew he could not trust his mother, the artificial girl, and so he sent for his brother, the only one he could believe in, the only one whose love was beyond doubt.

He made Anapou prince of the Nile, and he brought his mother to trial before all the people and told them how she had tried so many times to destroy him because all she had wanted was wealth and riches and had never loved anyone. She was a woman ravaged by greed, and the price she would now have to pay was her execution.

APHRODITE

GREECE, 1000BCE

APHRODITE was the goddess of desire in Greek mythology. She was also the goddess of love, beauty and fertility and probably evolved out of much earlier goddesses in Sumeria and Babylon, such as Innana and Ishtar. Aphrodite was by no means pure, and her role as goddess of sexual love was particularly consistent with her appetite for both mortals and gods. The origin of her name is usually given as meaning 'foam-born', relating to the method of her birth.

Aphrodite emerged from the surge of foam that was created when Kronos castrated his father, Ouranos, and threw his severed penis into the sea. She was blown across the ocean by the west winds, which carried her across to Paphos, Cyprus, where she was washed up on the beach.

Aphrodite was married to Hephaestus, the crippled smithy god, and was eternally unfaithful to him. Aphrodite was more interested in self-gratification and her own desires than in anyone else's. She was constantly seized by the desire for a particular god or mortal, whom she would enchant and seduce. If goddesses stood in her way, she would have no compunction in ruthlessly disempowering or disposing of them, and she was incredibly jealous of any woman or goddess who might challenge her beauty.

Aphrodite's jealous streak was clearly in action in the story of Psyche and Eros (Cupid). Psyche was a mortal, whose beauty was comparable with Aphrodite's. When Aphrodite heard that the people were more adoring of a mere mortal than of herself, she sent her son, Eros, to fire one of his arrows of desire at Psyche so that she would fall in love with the first and ugliest creature she saw. Unfortunately for Eros, he fell in love with Psyche as soon as he saw her and forgot what he was supposed to do. He warned Psyche never to look upon him, but when she could resist him no longer, he fled in fear of Aphrodite's revenge. It was only the intervention of Zeus that permitted them to be united and for Psyche to be made immortal.

Aphrodite's affairs in heaven were with Ares, Dionysus and Anchises. When Hephaestus found out about her affair with Ares, the god of war, he was so outraged that he made a net of gold and caught the lovers in bed together. He sent for all the gods on Mount Olympus to come and see them caught in the act, but they merely laughed at his own shame and Poseidon managed to persuade Hephaestus to release them from the net.

One of Aphrodite's greatest loves was for the beautiful young Adonis. As soon as she set eyes on Adonis she was besotted with him. She gave him to Persephone to bring up, and unfortunately Persephone fell in love with him, too. Calliope, one of the Muses, settled their dispute by allowing Adonis a third of the year to himself, a third with Aphrodite and a third with Persephone. However, at the end of her four-month long orgy of passion with Adonis, Aphrodite seduced him with her girdle of desire, and he swore that he would stay with her forever.

When Persephone heard this, in a pique of jealousy she told Ares he had a mortal rival called Adonis. So when poor Adonis went out hunting one day, Ares disguised himself as a wild boar and killed him. Now that Adonis was dead, Zeus decreed that Adonis was allowed to spend six months of the year with Persephone in the underworld, and could come back to life for six months to be with Aphrodite. They had three children, two mortal and beautiful, and the third an ugly immortal called Priapus, who was so sexually promiscuous that the gods refused to have him in Olympus.

Aphrodite is perhaps best known for her part in a beauty competition and the subsequent start of the Trojan War. Paris was a young, handsome prince, the son of Priam, king of Troy. Paris was also renowned for his sexual expertise and ways with women. He was asked by Zeus to judge a beauty contest between the goddesses, Hera, Aphrodite and Athene. The prize for this contest would be a golden apple. Paris astutely tried to evade having to make a choice between the three of them at all, knowing full well that whichever two he turned down might seek some kind of revenge. But mortal compromises were not welcome and every idea he came up with was immediately rejected.

So the three goddesses paraded before him. Hera promised him a position of worldly power and wealth if he chose her as the most beautiful; and Athene offered to give him prowess and wisdom in the art of war if he chose her. But Aphrodite promised him nothing. All that Aphrodite did was loosen her girdle of desire and Paris was instantly lusting after her.

Aphrodite's reward to Paris was to offer him the most beautiful mortal in the world, Helen of Sparta, who was already married to King Menelaus. However, this kind of mortal predicament proved to be no difficult task for Aphrodite, and Helen and Paris conveniently eloped and were quite innocently instrumental in starting the Trojan War.

THE LOVES OF ZEUS

GREECE, 1000–750BCE

APART from being the leader of the gods and ruler of the universe, Zeus had a remarkably big appetite for women. He is perhaps the most promiscuous of all mythological deities and embodies the archetypes of desire and power as well as the human need to play.

His mother, Rhea, gave Zeus to some mountain-nymphs to bring up so that Kronos could not eat him. Kronos had already devoured Zeus's other siblings, for the Titan had been told that his children would one day overthrow him. Rhea substituted a stone wrapped up in clothes for the baby Zeus. Kronos duly popped it down his throat, thinking now he had no cause to worry and the prophecy could never come true.

Zeus grew up in Crete with Amalthea, who nursed and suckled him. She was half-goat, half-mountain spirit. When he was old enough, one of his sisters, Metis, the goddess of wisdom, told him how to rescue the rest of his siblings from Kronos's belly. Zeus made sure that Kronos vomited up all his other brothers and sisters, who were, of course, now fully grown gods. This resulted in the battle between the gods, led by Zeus, and the Titans, led by Kronos. Once Zeus and the gods had won, he exiled his father Kronos to Tartarus.

Zeus married twice. Because Metis had helped him initially in his struggle against Kronos, he made her his first wife. Metis was the goddess of wisdom, but when she became pregnant Zeus was told that if the child was a boy he would be destined to become greater than Zeus himself. Obviously, Zeus had great reason to fear this particular prophecy, as Kronos had castrated his own father, Ouranus, for the very same reason and was now overthrown himself. Zeus was extremely worried by this, and as the child grew within Metis's belly, he became more and more fearful.

So Zeus thought up a contest to see who could become the smallest creature. Metis always liked a challenge and immediately turned herself into a fly. Zeus grabbed her out of the air and swallowed her, and her immortal wisdom merged into the body of Zeus as he digested her fly-form. But Zeus's trick backfired on him to some extent. For later that evening he developed a terrible head-ache. The sounds inside his own head were so violent that he called Prometheus and Hephaestus to help him. Prometheus held his head while his blacksmith son, Hephaestus, performed an emergency operation and split his head open with a wedge and hammer. Suddenly out sprang Athene, the goddess of wisdom and war. But because she had not been born the normal way, nor was she male, Zeus had nothing to fear from her. In fact, Athene provided the strongest support to Zeus and never betrayed him.

His second wife, Hera, was a different matter. Hera was also his sister, but she had been distinctly unhappy about not having any share in the initial division of power of the universe. Hera skulked off to Mount Thornax where she lived in the wilderness and sulked alone. For many months she saw no one, but as spring came and the mists rose she found a bedraggled cuckoo. She took pity on it and put it to her breast to warm it up. At that moment, the cuckoo turned into Zeus, who instantly made love to her. He persuaded Hera to come to his kingdom as co-ruler and be his consort. But Hera was constantly jealous of Zeus's wandering eyes and also acutely aware of the trick he had played on her at Mount Thornax.

The only time she ever had more power over Zeus than he did over her was when she borrowed Aphrodite's girdle of desire. This made any mortal or god who saw the wearer instantly infatuated. Zeus enjoyed Hera all the time she wore the girdle. But Hera could never forgive Zeus for his promiscuity, and she began to detest him. Eventually, she persuaded Poseidon and Apollo to conspire to overthrow him. So that he had no time to get hold of his mighty thunderbolts, the two gods crept up while he slept and tied him to his bed with ropes of cattle hide. These were unbreakable, and not even the mighty Zeus could escape. But this ridiculous trap caused chaos on earth, and Thetis, the ocean-nymph, visited the underworld and released the hundred-handed giant, who disappeared up to Olympus and set Zeus free.

Zeus's revenge on Hera was predictable enough. He tied her upside down by golden chains to the sky, and weighted her with anvils so that her limbs stretched and her body ached. He left her for over a year and eventually cut her down and forced her to grovel at his feet.

Now that his throne was secure and he was sure of being the supreme ruler, he left the running of the universe to all the other gods and spent most of his time in hot pursuit of beautiful mortals. Each time he spotted someone who took his fancy he would take on some appropriate disguise so that he could have sex. In fact, Zeus mated with Titans, birds, animals and even the clouds and running water, and his offspring from mortal women were the ancestors of the human race.

Early Christian saints were scandalized by Zeus's promiscuous behaviour. They calculated that Zeus began seventeen consecutive generations of mortal women. Hera was constantly bitter and resentful, and would often pursue Zeus's lovers, either seeking vengeance on their offspring or on the woman herself.

Some of Zeus's lovers are described below.

CALLISTO

The forest-nymph, Callisto, was Artemis's companion. She loved Zeus and bore him a son, Arcas. But she was changed into a bear, either by Hera in a fit of jealous rage or by Zeus himself to save her from the evil deeds of Hera. Unfortunately for Callisto, while she was in bear form, she was shot by her own friend, Artemis, in the forest and was placed in the constellations as the great she-bear (Ursa Major) by Zeus as a sign of his love for her.

EUROPA

Europa was another of Zeus's lovers. She was the daughter of Telephassa and the King of Agenor in Phoenicia. One spring day she went out in the fields to pick flowers with her maids near the king's cattle. Zeus disguised himself as one of the bulls and let the girls play with his horns and fondle him. Europa was precocious and daring and decided to ride the bull. But the bull plunged into the sea with Europa on his back, and disappeared across the ocean to Crete. Zeus took her on to the sand, raped her and left her no longer a virgin. She bore three sons – Minos, Rhadamanthys and Sarpedon – and then married the local King Asterius. Asterius, however, was not too pleased with marrying a woman who was not a virgin, and so Zeus agreed to give him a great bronze man called Talos to defend his kingdoms, as a compensation for Europa's 'imperfection'.

DANAE

Danae's encounter with Zeus was more of a life-saver. She had been imprisoned in a bronze tower by her father, the king of Argos. He had been told by an oracle that Danae would be the cause of his death because he would be killed by his grandson. So to prevent Danae from ever having a child, the king of Argos locked her away in the bronze tower with no food and only one slave to bring her water.

But Zeus's lusty eyes could see and know everything. He spotted Danae in her bronze tower and immediately decided she was in need of his attention. He came to her as a golden shower of rain that poured through the roof of the tower. After a night of rampant sex Danae conceived and had a son,

Perseus. But the slaves heard the baby crying and told the king of Argos. Fearing his life was in danger from the child, he ordered that Danae and the child be put into a wooden box and thrown into the sea. But the box was under the protection of the gods, for no mortal can destroy Zeus's child unless Zeus so wills it. Perseus and Danae were safely guided across the sea by Poseidon to the island of Seriphos. A fisherman, Dictys, caught the box in his net and took Danae and Perseus to live with the king of the island, Polydectes. After many adventures, Perseus did kill his own grandfather by accident when throwing a discus in a competition.

SEMELE

Zeus was tempted by the sight of Semele, the daughter of Cadmus and Harmonia. He sent her a message saying he wanted to make love to her, promising her any reward she wanted. To confirm that this was a genuine pledge, he made a vow in the name of the River Styx. Gods were forced to obey this promise and never to break their word. This would be such a pow-erful gesture of intention, that Semele would feel suitably honoured to accept.

But Hera found out about the message and intercepted it before Semele could answer. Hera took the form of an old servant, Beroe, and advised her to demand a very high price for this intimacy. The only way she would submit to Zeus was if he came to her in his full immortal radiance and splendour, not disguised as just an ordinary mortal creature. Semele was suitably excited about meeting the god in person, and sent back a message stating these terms. Zeus agreed to this. When he appeared to her in his full immortal glory he was like the very sky itself, thunder and lightning radiated down, and fire shot through her body and entered her like a thunderbolt as they made love. This was just as Hera wanted, for Semele was incinerated by the fire of Zeus's own passion. In Semele's dying moments, Zeus managed to snatch the growing embryo from her womb and save it from the raging inferno of his own fire. This child was Dionysus, who, once he was elevated to the status of god, placed his mother in heaven as a star called Thyone.

LEDA

Leda was married to the king of Sparta. She was one of the most beautiful mortals that Zeus had ever seen, and when he spotted her bathing in the River Eurotas he was instantly filled with lust. But Leda was already carrying the Spartan king's child and was known to be incredibly faithful. There was only one way to ravish her, and that was to trick her into making love with him.

Zeus asked Aphrodite to help him. He transformed himself into a swan and Aphrodite changed herself into an eagle. Together they soared across the sky like the hunted and the hunter until they came to the clouds above Leda's river. Zeus swooped down and fell on the water as if he had been chased by the eagle, and the eagle swooped down and then soared back up into the air as if it had been cheated of its prey. Leda took pity on the swan and took it into her lap where she stroked and comforted it. As soon as Zeus felt she was languidly mesmerized by petting the swan, he had sex with her then took off into the air and disappeared. After a while Leda gave birth to two swan eggs. Out of one hatched Clytemnestra and Helen, and the other Castor and Pollux. It was not known exactly who was the father of which child. But Clytemnestra and Helen became mortals and stayed on earth, while Castor and Pollux were treated as immortals and were taken up to heaven. When Leda died she was taken to heaven and merged with Nemesis, the goddess of retribution.

IO

Io was a river-nymph and daughter of the river-god Inachus. She was a virgin priestess to Hera, at the temple in Argos. When Zeus first set eyes on this beautiful nymph he arranged for Io to be sent away from Argos so that he could seduce her without any problems from the watchful eyes of Hera. He changed Io into an exquisite cow, but Hera guessed immediately what he was up to, and asked Zeus to give her the cow as a present. He could hardly refuse without revealing the truth, and Hera's first punishment for Io was to keep her tethered among all the other cows in the muddy fields. She sent the hundred-eyed Argus to keep guard over the cow and stop Zeus from rescuing Io. But Zeus was not to be stopped from having the river-nymph, and he persuaded Hermes to go down to the fields and sing and play a lullaby to Argus, who eventually fell asleep. Hermes stole Io from the herd and gave her to Zeus.

But Hera was mad with rage and jealousy when she heard what had happened, and she sent a gadfly to sting the cow so that it would never stand still again. Io went mad from the constant pain of the stinging fly and ran around the earth trying to escape the terrible agony. She wandered even as far as Mount Caucasus, where she saw poor Prometheus chained to a rock for stealing fire from the gods.

Her punishment lasted for many months, but at last her torment ended when she came to Egypt and Zeus made love to her on a cloud. She returned to her normal form and the fly disappeared. Surprisingly, Hera eventually forgave her, and she bore a son to Zeus, called Epaphus, who was a calf-child.

KAMA AND RATI

IN Hindu myth Kama is the god of desire and Rati is the goddess of sexual passion. Kama's name was also known in the Vedas and was identified with the creative force that grew inside Purusha when he was alone in the cosmic ocean at the beginning of time. Kama's first emanation was desire itself, and his second the power to create desire in others. Later on in Hindu myth he became a less powerful god and was relegated to being the god of sexual desire and the abstract process that passes between two people when they fall in love. The erotic book Kama Sutra was named after Kama.

Kama would carry a bow made of sugarcane, strung with rows of humming bees. He would fly around everywhere, shooting his five arrows of desire at both mortals and gods. These arrowheads were tipped with flowers that had been chosen by his friend Vasanta (spring), who decided which flower would be most suitable for which victim. Kama was incredibly handsome and would swoop around the skies on a parrot accompanied by his beautiful wife, Rati, who was just as frivolous as Kama. Her other name was Mayavati, which means deceiver, but she was faithful to Kama.

Kama loved to roam between mortals and gods and quite indiscriminately shoot his arrows at whoever that day took his fancy, inspiring both their own desire and his in the process. His favourite victims were usually innocent maidens, married women and celibate monks. But Kama suffered from his art.

The gods were convinced that the great Shiva should marry again. He was in no mood to do so as his first wife, Sati, had only recently thrown herself on her father's sacrificial fire. The gods decided that Sati should be reincarnated as Parvati, and when she came of age she was sent to the Himalayas to attract Shiva. Shiva had by now turned to a totally ascetic life. Like a savage, he wandered around the mountains dressed in rags and deep in meditation. Observing that Shiva was interested only in meditation and disinterested in the wonders of love, the gods sent Kama to arouse some passion in Shiva's heart.

Kama travelled to Mount Kailasa where he found the great Shiva in deep silence, impervious to everything around him. He seemed even to be part of the great rock that he sat upon. Kama hid for a while and watched as Parvati caught sight of Shiva among the trees and walked towards him. At that moment Kama pulled an arrow from his quiver and sent it hurtling towards Shiva with the greatest flower of passion at its tip. As it struck, lust surged through Shiva's heart and loins the moment he saw Parvati. But as the arrow reached its target, Shiva saw Kama in his hiding place and was filled with outrage at Kama's game. As punishment, he burned him to ashes with a single glance from his third eye.

The arrow of desire worked very slowly. For many years Shiva would not give way to his desire for Parvati, and he fought against the pull of his physical longings by hardening his own ascetic way of life. However, Shiva knew he would find no peace until he married Parvati.

As Kama lay dead, love disappeared from the world and Rati, too, refused to enflame passion in mortals or gods hearts. Eventually, after many years, Shiva married Parvati. Rati immediately went to see Parvati and pleaded with her to help her bring desire back to the universe. Together they implored Shiva to allow Kama to be re-born.

Shiva reluctantly agreed. He was spellbound by the beautiful Rati, and seeing that there was no love on earth, he allowed Kama to return as Pradyumna, the son of Krishna and Rukmani.

A great sage, Narada, had also advised Rati to take shape as a mortal woman and marry a man called Shambhara, for only in this guise would she ever be able to rejoin her beloved Kama. Shambhara was a demon in mortal form, and he had been told by Narada that Pradyumna was destined to kill him. Shambhara was furious and stole Pradyumna, throwing the child into the sea, where he was quickly swallowed whole by a great fish.

For many months Rati waited for Pradyumna to appear to her, but he did not come. She began to give up hope and disbelieve all that Narada had told her. One day Shambhara brought home a great fish he had bought at the fish market for supper and as she gutted it she found inside the child, Pradyumna. At this moment Narada appeared to her and told her who the child really was.

'This is your first husband, Kama, reincarnated. I give you the power to make him invisible so that you can bring him up yourself without your husband knowing he is here. For it is your husband who wants to destroy him.'

So Rati looked after Pradyumna until he was a young and beautiful man, and one day told him about his true identity and how she loved him. Pradyumna was horrified and could not believe her. Rati had always been like a mother to him, not a lover. But Rati made him a bow and some arrows tipped with flowers, and told him to aim one into his own foot. He did so and immediately fell in love with Rati again. Eventually, Rati became pregnant so Shambhara began to beat her, believing her to be unfaithful. Pradyumna finally threw off his cloak of invisibility and killed Shambhara with his bare hands. Narada's prophecy had been fulfilled.

The couple were free, and once Pradyumna had shaken off his mortal form, Rati and Kama resumed their original forms as the god and goddess of desire and sexual passion.

ORPHEUS AND EURYDICE

L EARNING to let go is one of the most difficult lessons we face in love and relationships. But it is only when we finally do relinquish the pain that we can allow something or someone else to enter our lives and move another step forwards in our journey. The Greek singer and musician, Orpheus, the son of Calliope, had to face this particular test. The story of his love for Eurydice shows that even when the most dark and painful experience comes into our lives it can sometimes be a means to a better way forwards.

Orpheus was a poet and musician, and his beautiful songs and inspiring music made the trees uproot themselves, boulders melt and rivers change their courses. The wild beasts of the forests and hills would listen as he idled along, playing his lyre and reminding all of the eternal dance of nature.

Orpheus went to Colchis with the Argonauts. His singing and music kept his colleagues light-hearted and spirited and hopeful that they would return from their great battle. When he returned he married the nymph Eurydice, the woman of his dreams. Aristaeus was the son of Apollo and the river-nymph Cyrene. He was also the cousin of Orpheus and knew Orpheus had recently married one of the most exquisite of all women. But Aristaeus was also a bit of a wanderer, who knew how to keep bees, to make cheese and to blend herbs and olives. He travelled across Greece, teaching these skills to anyone he met, and one day he came across Eurydice bathing in the River Peneus. Eurydice was naked and without doubt one of the loveliest women he had ever seen. Aristaeus couldn't stop his lusty thoughts taking over his conscience, and he threw himself into the river and attempted to rape her. Eurydice escaped and ran up the riverbank in panic, but as she did so, she trod on a snake, which sank its fangs deep into her foot. Within minutes she was dead.

When Orpheus heard of the news of Eurydice's death he ran to where she had supposedly fallen from the snake-bite, but unknown to Orpheus Hades had already taken her to the underworld. Unable to accept the tragic death of Eurydice, Orpheus set off at once to find her. He travelled across Greece looking for her soul, or believing that she had been taken from the riverbank and hidden in some dark cave. He played his lyre everywhere he went in the hope that she would hear him and come to him. But it was Hermes who eventually took pity on him and told Orpheus that she had indeed been taken to the underworld.

Orpheus could not bear the finality of his beloved's death and his grief turned to unbearable and wretched longing. He set out to do what no man had ever done before: he boldly plunged into the dark tunnels and passageways that led to the underworld. When he reached the River Styx he played his lyre and sang sweet music and songs to lull and seduce the ferryman, Charon, to take him across the river. When he met Cerberus, the three-headed dog who was the watchdog of the gate to the underworld, he also charmed him to sleep with his music, along with the three judges of the dead. When he eventually arrived in the heart of the darkness, all hell's torments and pain momentarily ceased because of his beautiful music.

He was met by Persephone and Hades, and they asked him to play to them. Not usually known for their benevolence, they allowed him to stay and play so that the dead were soothed and all who heard him wept for the upper world as Eurydice did. But Orpheus's plaintive words and poignant music touched even the souls of Persephone and Hades, and they agreed to his pleas for them to release Eurydice back to the upper world.

But there was one condition. Orpheus could lead Eurydice back to the upper world and her life with him again, as long as he never looked back at her nor even glanced once into her eyes until they were in the upper world. For living eyes to gaze upon a soul in the underworld would condemn Eurydice to eternal death, and they would surely never be able to meet again. Orpheus agreed, but his love was so intense that the thought of not looking at Eurydice until they reached the light of the upper world was tearing his soul apart. What if Hades had played a trick on him? What if this being that stepped so softly behind him was not Eurydice but some ghastly tortured demon that followed him to the light to always plague him and torture him about his true love? These thoughts spun in Orpheus' head. He couldn't trust his instincts and began to analyse and question the situation he had got himself into, until he had no intuition left to trust.

Hermes guided Orpheus back through the dark tunnels and dank caverns of the edges of the underworld. As they walked further and further towards the light, Orpheus became more fearful that whoever it was that walked behind him and the soft hand that he held in the darkness was not that of Eurydice. But Orpheus's own mistrust and his own perception of what he was doing were his downfall. As they reached the very brink of the upper world, as the first chink of light sparkled through a crack in the rocky cavern, Orpheus could not resist looking back to see who it was that walked behind him and to make sure that it was Eurydice that he was taking back into life.

As he turned around to look and saw her there for a second, he knew he should have trusted himself, and at that moment as they gazed into each other's eyes Eurydice dissolved into thin air, along with Orpheus's hopes for fulfilment and completeness. Orpheus could not believe what he had done. How could he have not trusted in himself? Where was Eurydice now? He searched the tunnels of the underworld for seven days and nights, overcome with grief and anger, and when he came to the River Styx this time the old ferryman Charon would not ferry him across the river. He blundered his way

205

back up to the upper world like a man drunk on grief. For Orpheus could now never forget the terrible memories of the underworld or his love for Eurydice.

Orpheus went to live a hermit-like existence on Mount Peangaeum, where he climbed the peak each night to worship Apollo as the morning sun arose. His inner state would not allow anyone near him, and he refused the company of women.

Many people heard that he had travelled to the underworld and had returned alive. Male followers came to hear his secrets of beyond the grave, but his worship of Apollo aroused the anger of Eurydice's fellow-nymphs. Some of these had become the Maenads, the female worshippers of Dionysus, the god of ecstasy and wine. They came one night to the cave where Orpheus was teaching his disciples and took the knives and weapons left at the entrance to the cave. In their anger and madness, they hacked Orpheus to pieces and threw the parts of his body into the sea, nailed his head to his lyre and tossed it into the river. But the lyre and the head floated downstream without sinking, still singing and playing plaintive songs, calling for Eurydice wherever it went. The head floated out to sea, and when it arrived at Lesbos the islanders buried the head in the temple to appease Dionysus's rage and Apollo hung the lyre in the sky as one of the constellations.

Yet Orpheus's death meant that he could be reunited with Eurydice in the underworld, and they could now gaze into each other's eyes as they could not do when Orpheus was chained to his life in the upper world, and she to hers below.

POMONA AND VERTUMNUS

ROME, 600BCE

VERTUMNUS was the Roman god of the woodlands. He was shy and sensitive and feared rejection, which was why he rarely courted any of the nymphs whom he saw every day as he worked. His job every autumn was to turn the leaves from green to bronze, brown and gold, and then to send them drifting to the ground so that new buds could appear on the trees. He sent the insects and the grubs to burrow around in the leaves, and the worms to come up through the soil to eat at the rotting vegetation. He was the guardian of the leaves that would be returned to the earth and produce new fertile soil for the trees. Vertumnus was the gardener of the gods, but his bashful and secretive lifestyle meant that he seemed doomed to living a life without love.

Pomona was a beautiful wood-nymph who lived in the orchards on the Palatine Hill. She would dance and sing among her trees and tend the fruit. She removed parasites from the bark of trees and picked the greenfly off the buds or saved new shoots from early spring frosts. She was happy being busy and never really had time for the tree-spirits and satyrs who pursued her.

Vertumnus had little to do when it wasn't autumn time, so he would spend many months watching Pomona from behind his trees as she skipped and laughed and enjoyed herself with the other wood-nymphs. But he didn't dare pluck up courage to speak to her. Each time she even glanced his way, perhaps to watch a bird fly into its nest or a bee to buzz around a flower, he darted back behind his trees for safety.

Over a thousand times Vertumnus nearly had the nerve to declare his love for her, but each time he withdrew at the last moment, so sure that he would be rejected. Wasn't it safer to keep guarded, to not reveal his feelings, and make his love for Pomona only a fantasy? In wretched torment and his feelings torn apart, he asked advice from the goddess Pales, who looked after the pastures and hills.

'I am in deep despair,' he wept into her shoulder one day. 'Every time I feel ready to speak with Pomona, I run away again and hide my feelings. What can I do?'

The kind goddess took his hand and said, 'If you can change the leaves from green to brown on the trees each autumn, then surely you can change yourself from shy to bold? Maybe Pomona will see you in a different light, and you can declare your love to her.'

So Vertumnus disguised himself as many different mortals, hoping that one of these transformations would attract her. But whether he was a farmer, a plough-man, a soldier or a bee-keeper, he was still himself underneath and the beautiful Pomona was not in the slightest bit interested in these bold images that paraded before her each day. She did not even turn her head to look at the many different gifts that he left behind in her orchard.

As a last resort he disguised himself as an old woman and hobbled into the orchard in the heat of the day carrying a cup of cool water. He offered her a drink, but Pomona merely drank from the cup, said thank-you and then danced off into the pools of sunlight that filtered through the trees. But for Vertumnus this was the closest he had ever got to her, and the following day, his heart still fluttering, he returned to the orchard again dressed as the old woman.

This time Pomona smiled when she recognized the old woman coming and they sat together on a grassy bank. Vertumnus began to tell her a story. 'Have you heard the tale of Iphis?' he asked carefully as she drank from his cup again.

'No please tell me. Is it sad?'

'Very sad,' he whispered in a low voice. 'Iphis was a poor peasant boy who fell in love with a princess called Anaxarete. But because he was poor she refused to have him and turned her own heart to stone so that she could have no feelings for him. In his pain and anger he hanged himself from a tree. When Anaxarete found his body, her stone heart transformed the whole of her body into stone too, and she became a statue in the garden where he had fallen dead. Don't you think that is a very sad tale?'

'Yes, indeed,' said Pomona, 'I am very saddened by it. But I now must go and tend to my fruit. And you are old and frail and must go home before dusk.' Pomona smiled and began to leave.

But Vertumnus was now in despair, believing that Pomona had no heart either. She would never love him if she could not see how bold he was to hide behind such a disguise. In a rage he threw off the old clothes and began to walk dejectedly away through the trees. Pomona turned to wave good-bye at the old woman, saw the tattered clothes lying on the ground and frowned. She ran back to where they had been talking.

'Wait a minute! Who are you really?' she called. Vertumnus was already running into the woods, but she chased after him and caught hold of his arm. He breathlessly turned to face her and she smiled, realizing who he really was.

'I didn't know it was you!' she said, 'Now I can see you as you really are!' She ran to his arms and they gazed at one another, transfixed with desire.

From then on, Vertumnus and Pomona were inseparable. They worked together in the woods and orchards, ripening fruit and changing the seasons just as easily as Vertumnus had changed Pomona's feelings for him, once she had seen the truth of his heart.

ETAIN AND MIDIR

CELTIC, 100BCE

In Irish mythology Etain was one of the Tuatha Dé Danann (people of the goddess Danann). These 'people' were supernatural inhabitants of Ireland and were the last gods to rule before the mortals took over their kingdoms. This is the story of Etain's reincarnation and how two beings, a mortal and a god, fought for her beauty and love.

Midir was the son of the Daghdha, father of all the gods. Midir had been married to Fuamnach for some time when the beauty of the princess Etain overwhelmed him with desire and he decided to marry her, too.

Fuamnach was jealous of the younger woman and, using her invincible magic, turned Etain into a butterfly. The first storm winds that gusted across the palace blew Etain, the butterfly, out into the wilderness of Erin. For many years she was at the mercy of the wind as it blew her fine fragile wings further and further away from Midir. One day a gentle breeze lifted her fluttering form into the palace of an Ulster chief called Etar. Etain fell into the drinking cup of Etar's wife who unknowingly swallowed her, and she grew again in Etar's womb. Etain was born as a mortal and knew nothing of her past life as a goddess or as Midir's virgin bride. She grew up to be a beautiful and much admired young woman.

About this time the high king of Ireland, Eochy, was himself beginning to look for a suitable wife to be his queen. He heard about Etain's beauty and that she was the most exquisite woman in the land. One day Eochy travelled far afield in his vain hope of meeting the girl. After many miles on horseback, he grew weary and stopped to rest beside a pool. He heard laughing and singing, and the voices of women giggling beyond the trees. Fearful that he might alarm the women, he crept along the side of the pool, his curiosity tinged with a feeling that he was at last going to find the one woman had been searching for. When Eochy saw Etain and her two friends swimming and diving in the deep end of the sunlit pool, he fell instantly in love with her. Her hair was like golden sheaves down her back and her skin was whiter than the most fragrant of lilies.

For some weeks Eochy stayed near Etar's palace and courted her in the accepted way. Soon she became quite fond of him. Not long after, Eochy married Etain and took her back to Tara.

But back at Tara, Eochy's brother, Ailill also fell instantly infatuated with Etain. He became so love-sick for her that he fell gravely ill and was very near to death. Eochy had many travels to make that summer throughout Ireland, and he asked Etain to look after his brother and nurse him, in case he died while he was away. Etain visited Ailill the next day and found to her surprise that the man was wretched with desire for her.

'It is moments like this Etain, when you are so close to me, that I feel I must surely die if I cannot have you in body and in soul.'

Etain took his hand, her warm heart felt compassion and sadness for this dying man. She knew she was not in love with Ailill, but neither did she want him to die of his love-sickness. 'How can I give you my love, dear Ailill? Eochy is away. This may be the only chance that I can return your love; tell me what it is you want from me?'

'Meet me tomorrow in the enchanted copse. No one will see us, and there we can become one.'

Etain nodded, but as she left him, the joy of saving his life did not stay long with her. The guilt of her betrayal to Eochy began to weigh heavily in her heart. But Etain's doomed rendezvous became a far more mysterious and dangerous affair. For Ailill fell into a deep enchanted sleep on the day of their meeting and a strange spirit took on his form and went to meet Etain instead.

Etain made her way through the tangled wood towards the enchanted copse. She had heard of its magical powers when she was a child and that here, even if you did not love someone, you would be cast under such a powerful spell that you would have to love them back.

The sunlight glinted through the dancing leaves. The magic seemed to be broken for Etain's heart sank when she saw the young Ailill standing beside the tree. Yet as he spoke she sensed something was not right.

'Dear Etain, it is good that you came. But my fever, my wretchedness is nothing to do with you. I have been wrong to mislead you, and I am sorry to have hurt you. This is wrong for you as it is for me. Do you forgive me?'

He smiled and took her hand, and as Etain looked deep into his eyes she could only see that he lied.

'Of course I forgive you. But you must rest, and perhaps we can at least be friends. Perhaps I can visit you again tomorrow and make sure you are well.'

'That would be wonderful, Etain. Come to me in my chamber again and I will make you some food and we will talk.' He kissed her hand and she fled quickly, for fear that the magic place might suddenly hold her in some tight net of love for him.

Etain began to feel uncomfortable each time she visited Ailill, almost as if it was not he that she was nursing but something or someone much more dangerous and powerful. To begin with he had made her food and showed her his books and journals. Each day he progressively grew ill with fever again, and yet there was always a strange glint in his eyes that he could not hide.

One day as Etain washed his sweat-sodden clothes and made a potion to cleanse Ailill's body, Midir could no longer shroud himself in Ailill's physical form, and appeared before her as himself. The bold and dashing god transformed himself before her eyes, and she knew that the glint in Ailill's eye had been the glint of a supernatural desire.

Etain tried to run from the chamber, realizing she had been falling in love with a god, not a mortal.

'Wait Etain, you must listen to me. Do not leave in haste for you must know why I have come here in this guise.'

Etain turned and flashed her fiery eyes at him for an explanation.

'You are Etain, daughter of Danann. You are a goddess by right. Yet you were turned into a butterfly and must now live out this incarnation as a mortal.'

'I don't remember this, how can I remember this? Are you lying to me?' she cried, not wanting to know the truth nor daring to question her own disbelief.

Midir begged her to return to the Land of Youth. 'Come back with me Etain, you loved me once, you were my bride. But we never made love because of the treachery of my first wife. Please return with me, because it is only you that I long for.'

Etain shook her head, not knowing if he was telling the truth, nor even if she wanted to leave. But as Midir told her more and more about her past life, the memories of their love slashed at her heart like a knife. She was now in a terrible predicament. If she visited the real Ailill again, he would still be passionately in love with her, for the spell that the god had cast over him would be shattered if she did not go with Midir. And what of Eochy? She loved him with all her mortal heart, but her feelings had intensified for Midir, too.

It seemed to Etain that the only way to ensure that she was not to be torn between Eochy's love and Ailill's despair, was to return to her life with Midir, but there had to be one condition.

'My lord,' she began, knowing that he would be angered by her refusal, 'There is only one condition that I ask. I shall return with you, but only if Eochy agrees to my departure. He is my husband and I love him like I once loved you. You must allow me that right.'

Midir nodded. He pulled Etain to him and kissed her without saying a word, then vanished into the mists that had risen outside the palace walls. But as the days went by and Etain had not yet dared to ask Eochy if she might go, Midir became passionate for Etain to return, especially as her jealous rival, Fuamnach, was now dead. His own aching longing for Etain grew so intense that he could wait no longer. Forcing Eochy into agreeing to Etain's departure was the only way out for him now.

Midir came to King Eochy on the Hill of Tara and asked if he would like to play a game of chess. Eochy was excited – he loved playing chess, and enjoyed gambling with his own wealth, mainly because he usually won. Midir was unusually ineffective and allowed Eochy to win every game. In payment for all his losses Midir was over-generous with his magical powers and vowed to restore pathways, reclaim lands and clear the forests of Tara. Eochy began to believe that he was the better player and announced rather recklessly at the beginning of the final confrontation that the stakes would be decided by the winner, but not until the end of the game. Midir nodded. This time he won, much to Eochy's horror.

Eochy sighed, knowing he had been foolishly over-confident. He had no choice: 'What is it that you desire from me?'

Midir laughed. 'Only that I can hold Etain in my arms and have just one kiss from her beautiful lips.' The king was angry, but he could only nod his head, 'This will be granted to you, but do not come until one month from this day.'

Eochy spent the next four weeks planning how to keep Midir out of his kingdom. He sent armies of his men to surround the palace, and, feeling sure that one man could never infiltrate the most powerful army on earth, he organized a celebratory feast. Etain sat beside Eochy, and as she sipped the wine, her lips looked like liquid jewels of desire. But it was not for Eochy that she smiled.

Suddenly Midir appeared at the table, even more radiant and glorious than ever before. When Etain saw him she had remembered how she loved him. Now her own predicament had come to haunt her. Eochy or Midir, how could she ever chose between two such powerful and passionate partners? Midir clutched his spear in one hand and with the other hand suddenly pulled Etain to him and kissed her on the lips in front of the feasting guests. As Etain turned to acknowledge his embrace, they rose together in the air like white eagles and soared through the high arched windows out into the swirling mists. Eochy and his warriors ran outside to try and stop them, but all they could see were two white birds flying through the sky across the mountains.

Eochy was heart-broken and would not accept the fact that Etain had gone forever. For many months he travelled wearily across Ireland, looking for her in vain. He was relentless in his search and summoned the druid Dalan to use his magical powers to help him find Etain. Dalan made three wands from a yew tree, and on these wands he wrote magic spells until the yew bark burned away to reveal the place they could find Etain. The words that burned across the yew wands spelt out Bri-Leith, the palace of Midir.

Eochy gathered his great armies together in a massive attack to destroy the palace of Midir at Bri-Leith. When Midir heard that his palace was to be invaded, he offered to give up Etain only if Eochy could chose the right Etain out of the fifty women he would send out beyond the palace walls. When Eochy saw the fifty identical Etains walking towards him he was heart-broken; how could he ever chose the right Etain when they all looked the same?

But Etain's mortal love for the king shone through her eyes when Eochy's horse pranced before her. Eochy jumped down off his stallion and took Etain into his arms. The spell that Midir had cast was broken. Now that Midir knew he could no longer break the bond of mortal love between Etain and Eochy, he vanished from sight to return to the land of Erin. Etain would always love Midir and knew that one day she would be with him again, but first she must go to Tara to finish her mortal life with the great King Eochy.

FREYA, THE GODDESS OF SEXUAL DESIRE

NORTHERN EUROPE, 100BCE

FREYA was not virtuous; nor was she particularly interested in her duties as a goddess; rather she was the object of sexual desire from gods, mortals, giants and dwarfs and, in turn, enjoyed sex quite freely and openly. However, her promiscuity was not frowned upon in the primitive Viking society, and Freya was one of the most respected of deities. Perhaps this ancient pagan goddess, who was still being worshipped in thirteenth-century Scandinavia, was an enigmatic equivalent to the male gods of the Nordic pantheon in her role as goddess of sex.

Friday was named after her, and she became a favourite subject for goldsmiths and silversmiths, who used her image frequently in jewellery. Her own necklace of desire, the Brisingamen, was often used in literature and art as a symbol of the power of sexuality.

Freya was the twin sister of Frey (see page 214). She would ride around Asgard in her chariot, which was pulled by the boar, Hildisvini, or by a troupe of cats. She kept a coat made from falcon feathers, which she used to fly her around the world disguised as a bird. Horses were included in her sexual cults, and she would often send parties of Valkyries down to the battlefields to fetch the dead warriors and their steeds and to bring them back to her realm to enjoy the orgiastic fruits of the afterlife.

Od, the god of sunshine, was her first husband, but he left her without a trace one day and she wept tears of gold, which covered the floor of Asgard. She was so grief-stricken – or so overjoyed – at her release to freedom that she never married again and set full steam ahead on a life of promiscuity.

Her most infamous exploit was with four dwarfs. One dark and dull night Freya was out with her chariot exploring the many possibilities of lust and desire when she saw a dim light in the distance. She followed the light to its source and came across the smithy of the Brisings, four dwarfs who made beautiful ornaments. At the moment she knocked on their door they were engaged in making the most exquisite necklace in the kingdom. This was called the Brisingamen (necklace of the Brisings). When Freya saw this extraordinary piece of jewellery she immediately wanted it. The precious stones glinted, and the metal gleamed as if it were on fire. Her desire to cherish and own this necklace was so intense that she would do anything to get it.

The dwarfs raised their eyebrows and went into a huddle. The treasure would be hers if she agreed to spend a passionate night of lust with each of them in turn. For Freya this was not a problem and she quickly agreed.

However, Loki, the trickster-god of lies, had followed Freya out of Asgard that night, and when he saw what Freya was willing to do, he rushed back to tell Odin of her wickedness. The king of the Æsir was furious and extremely jealous. He had desired Freya for a long time and to find out that she was about to sleep with four dwarfs hurt his masculine pride. His emotions were combustible, but his anger was directed towards Loki for bringing him such hurtful news.

Odin ordered Loki to steal the Brisingamen from Freya or he would be severely punished. Loki tried to plead with Odin that it was almost impossible to enter Freya's hall without her permission, but Odin refused to listen to his excuses and told him that if he didn't bring back the necklace he would suffer an even worse fate.

But Loki was also a shape-shifter and could take on any form that he so desired. He found a tiny crevice in the wall of Freya's hall, Sessrumnir, and like an ant squirmed his way through the crack. As he tumbled out onto the floor he realized he was in Freya's bed-chamber. Freya was sleeping naked on her bed but was lying on her back, so that the clasp of the Brisingamen was behind her neck and he could not possibly take it without waking her. Loki tapped his tiny ant feet and fidgeted until he thought of what to turn into next. A flea.

He jumped off the floor, landed on Freya's breast and bit her so nimbly that she turned over to scratch herself and he removed the necklace. Loki instantly returned to his own form and let himself out of the great hall with the Brisingamen carefully hanging around his own neck.

Loki took the necklace to Odin and when next morning Freya awoke to find the Brisingamen gone from her neck she realized that it could only have been Loki who had stolen it. She stormed off to Odin to complain about Loki, but Odin was ready for her and reminded her that Loki's behaviour was no worse than her own. She had taken the necklace in exchange for sex, and Loki had merely stolen it. Its possession had enhanced her sexual powers, but the dwarfs had lost their powers of reproduction, leaving them only with the lust for gold and not for sex. Odin said that Freya could have the necklace back as long as she guaranteed universal fertility. Freya nodded, for there was no way she could argue with this. Her desire for the necklace was so intense that even her daily presence under the branches of the Yggdrasil to ensure universal fertility seemed a small price to pay for having the power of the necklace and sexual desire returned to her.

FREY

NORTHERN EUROPE, 100BCE

FREY was the twin brother of the goddess Freya (see page 213). Both were fertility deities, she the goddess of sexual desire, and he the god of insatiable lust. Freya ruled the female genitalia, and Frey was associated with phallic symbols, which can still be found all over northern Europe in the form of chalk carvings of male phallic figures on hillsides or Frey's phallic image carved into the wood of lintels and doorways. His original cult seems to have been pretty unpleasant and involved both sexual initiation and human sacrifice.

Frey was considered one of the most important of Norse gods, but there are very few stories about him. The best known concerns his love for a frost-giantess called Gerda.

Gerda lived with her father, Gymir, a grand frost-giant in his hall in Jötunheim. Frey had gone to live in Asgard with his father, Njörd. One day he discovered Odin's great throne, a magical spot where everything in the universe was visible. From this incredible vantage point he saw the most beautiful female pulsating with a sexual aura. This was Gerda, and Frey was, as usual, struck with instant lust for her. For days he pined and yearned for her. Realizing how much he was suffering, Njörd decided to do something about it and put his son out his misery. He sent his trusted servant, Skirnir, to Gerda to woo her. Skirnir agreed on condition that Njörd lend him his sword and his horse. He also took with him eleven of the golden apples of eternal youth as well as Odin's magic ring.

At Jötunheim Skirnir found the frost-giant's hall was surrounded by a ring of white-hot fires. But Skirnir kicked the horse on and they leaped through the flames unharmed. At the gates of the hall were ten terrifying hounds, which began howling and barking. Gerda heard the racket, and when she saw Skirnir, guessed that he had been sent by Frey. A long time before, Frey had murdered her brother, Beli, in a brawl and she had never forgiven him. Nevertheless, she politely asked Skirnir in for a horn of mead before sending him away. Skirnir had other ideas, however, and immediately began to flatter her. He tried to bribe her with the apples and with the horse, but she refused outright and said quite openly she would never agree to marry Frey.

Skirnir now realized that he must resort to less subtle means and informed her he would chop off her head if she refused to come at Frey's bidding. But Gerda merely laughed and wouldn't be threatened in her own hall; besides, her father would never let such an insignificant servant escape. So Skirnir resorted to his most deadliest threat. On his staff were carved magic runes, and he began to chant a magical curse over her that was so powerful that he knew she would have to give in. Refuse, and ever after Gerda would be filled with an insatiable lust that would never be satisfied because she would have to remain celibate; she would be consumed by a constant hunger, but find that no food could ever satisfy her; be confined by Hel's gates and be forced to watch the dead arrive, knowing that she was slowly becoming a repulsive hag herself. To avoid this terrible fate, she must do as Frey had commanded.

Gerda had no choice and agreed to marry Frey, on condition that she did not meet the god for nine nights. Frey managed to wait his nine days and nights in a tangle of sexual pain and desire. After they married it seems that she came to love him, bore him a child and was apparently the only female in creation able to put up with his incessant desire for copious sex.

THE HERDSMAN AND THE WEAVER GIRL

CHINA, 300CE

ALTHOUGH this story could be included with the myths describing the creation of heaven and earth, it sits better here because it is a gentle and beautiful story of eternal love. It is the tale of Altair and Vega, the two stars of the Milky Way and how they came to be there.

There lived in the sky a weaver girl who wove all the clouds into different colours. It was her job to make these 'clothes of heaven' and hang them in the sky. She had to weave many different colours for all kinds of weather. It could be pink and peach for warm, sunny days in springtime, red and crimson for sunset in the autumn, or black, violet and grey for the winter storms and rainy days. This part of heaven, which was called the Silver River, was a shallow stream that ran across the sky and just touched the earth in one place where reeds and rocks created a heavenly pool. Across the heavens, at the far end of the Silver River on earth, lived a young herdsman who had been orphaned when he was a child. He worked all day long in the fields with only his ox as a companion.

One day, when the boy had just become a young man, the ox spoke for the first time. He told Ni Lang about a weaver girl and her friends who bathed each day in the Silver River. They came from heaven, and the weaver girl was one of the most beautiful creatures ever to be seen. The ox went on to tell Ni Lang that if he could steal the girl's clothes while she was bathing in the river pool she would be his wife. So the herdsman travelled down to the bank of the Silver River as darkness fell and hid among the reeds and the tall bulrushes that grew close to the still, shallow water. Not long after dusk the weaver girl and her friends arrived to bathe. They threw their clothes on to the rocks and jumped happily into the clear water. The still water of the stream sparkled as it ran off their backs and on to the rocks. The herdsman was hypnotized by the radiance of the weaver girl. Entranced, Ni Lang watched them for a while, then, realizing that they would soon be coming back to the rocks for their clothes, he quickly dashed out from the reed bed and snatched the weaver girl's bundle. The other girls heard the noise in the bulrushes and were terrified. Naked, they began to run away but the weaver girl stayed all alone. She was curious.

'Come out,' she called softly. 'It's all right, I won't harm you.'

The herdsman crept through the long reeds and with his face down – he dared not look at her nakedness – he said, 'Here are your clothes. I'm sorry, but my ox told me to steal your clothes for then you would become my wife.'

The weaver girl laughed. 'Yes, you shall have to be my husband now you have seen me without my clothes.'

Ni Lang looked up and instantly fell in love with the weaver girl and they were married. For many years they lived happily, Ni Lang working in the fields and the weaver girl weaving her clouds. They had two children and a happy home, and it seemed that nothing could come between them. But the perfect union they had found on earth could not be.

The god of the heavens and his consort found out that the weaver girl had stayed on earth, and they demanded she return immediately to the palace of heaven to be punished.

One day, after working in the fields, Ni Lang returned home and found she had been abducted. The herdsman was devastated, and placing his two children in panniers on a pole across his back he set off towards the Silver River to the place he had first found her, hoping that she might be there. But when he reached the rocks there was no river and no pool. The angry queen of the heavens had taken the river up to the sky as well as the weaver girl. As the sun set below the horizon Ni Lang looked up and saw the bright band of the Silver River now far away in the sky so that mortals and gods could never meet again.

All night he tossed and turned in his despair. In the early morning the ox came to his side. 'I am dying, herdsman. Once I have departed this form wrap yourself in my skin and you will find that you can get to heaven.'

The ox died that day, and Ni Lang wrapped himself in the animal's heavy skin and suddenly felt that he had wings, that he was lighter than air. He put the children in his panniers and pushed a ladle through the two baskets so that he could carry them behind him as flew up into the sky. Beyond him were beautiful stars and shimmering gleams that filled the Silver River with light. On the other side of the Silver River the children saw the weaver girl and called to her, 'Mother, mother we have come to you!' But the herdsman was unable to cross the river. The great goddess of the heavens had scored a great gash down the middle of the river with her long hairpins, so that it changed from a shallow gentle stream to a raging torrent. It was too deep and too dangerous for anyone to cross it now.

Ni Lang wept with despair, but his daughter said, 'Take the ladle Father, and drain the river until there is no more water in it!'

So the herdsman and his children took turns with the ladle, scooping the torrents of water out of the river. The god of heaven had watched them trying to reach the weaver girl, and he felt sorry for the poor herdsman. 'You may visit the weaver girl once a year, but that is all I can do for you.'

So the weaver girl and the herdsman lived on different sides of the river. She is Vega, and the herdsman is Altair. Every seventh day of the seventh month of the lunar calendar the herdsman crosses a bridge that is made by flocks of magpies that soar across the Silver River. The herdsman and his children cross the bridge and Ni Lang makes love to the weaver girl again. When they meet, the weaver girl cries and her tears fall to earth. The women on earth know she is crying because her tears fall like soft drizzle from the clouds she has painted grey.

So Vega and Altair are on different sides of the river, and the four bright stars beside Altair are the shuttles of the weaver girl's loom, and the two stars either side of him are his children. Beside the weaver girl are three bright stars, which are the messages from Ni Lang. And when these bright stars are seen in the autumn sky it is a reminder of the eternal love between the weaver girl and the herdsman.

TRISTAN AND ISEULT

CELTIC/FRANCE, 500CE

T HIS is probably one of the best known myths of romantic frustration and doomed love. Although known as a Celtic legend, it originated in Brittany and eventually became attached to the Arthurian stories of England. As a myth it shines out from many others in its painful account of betrayal and self-destruction when love becomes too unbearable a test in life.

Tristan was an orphan. His mother, the queen of Lyonesse, had died in child-birth, and Tristan (sad soul) had been sent to Tintagel to the court of his uncle, King Mark of Cornwall. He lived there happily, but although Mark wanted to proclaim him as his heir, the courtiers and barons objected to such a lowly successor. It was decided that the king should marry and produce his own sons.

Mark was in the middle of dealing with the giant Morholt, the brother of the queen of Ireland, who had come to try to collect tribute from Cornwall with his band of raiders. At this time there was constant warfare between Ireland and Cornwall, and so Tristan left for Ireland, resolved to fight and destroy Morholt. Although Tristan was badly wounded by the champion fighter, he succeeded in killing him and left a fragment of his sword in Morholt's head.

Tristan's own wound was nearly fatal and it was Iseult and her mother, the queen of Ireland, who tended the wound and nursed him back to health, not realizing who he was or that he had just killed the queen's brother, Morholt.

When Tristan returned to Tintagel, his wound healed, the king told him that he could not be made heir to the throne. To appease the great lords who were still nagging him to have sons, Mark agreed that he would marry the girl whose golden hair had just been dropped in his palace courtyard by a swallow. Tristan recognized the hair instantly as that of the beautiful Iseult, the queen of Ireland's daughter.

Tristan offered to go back to Ireland and ask for Iseult's hand on Mark's behalf, for while he had been in Ireland he had heard that whoever could slay the dragon would be able to take the hand of the Princess Iseult as a reward. If he slew the great dragon that was terrorizing the country perhaps the queen of Ireland would look more favourably on Mark's proposal, especially as it might bring peace between the two kingdoms.

Tristan disguised himself as a Cornish trader and set out to slay the Irish dragon. He spent many months searching for its lair and eventually found the great beast in the caves beneath the mountains. He fought for many hours to kill the dragon and at the last thrust of his blade the dragon fell dead. But the dragon's breath was so poisonous that it weakened Tristan and he fell down unconscious.

A passing merchant, who had seen the great conflict between the two, decided to take Tristan's place and say he had been victorious. The impostor insisted that he had just slain the dragon so that he could win Iseult's hand, but the queen and Iseult discovered the young Tristan lying nearby and realized that the merchant had tricked them. They took Tristan back to their palace to nurse him again. But one morning Iseult entered his bed-chamber before he woke and saw that his sword had fallen to the floor. As she put it back on his bed she noticed that a piece of the gleaming metal had broken off. This missing piece was exactly the same shape as the piece they had found in Morholt's head.

Realizing that Tristan had killed Morholt, Iseult wanted revenge, but something in her heart stopped her from exposing him, especially as she now believed that she would have to become Tristan's wife. He had slain the monster and she could not harm him. So as the days passed and they spent long hours in each other's company, a passionate bond formed between them that could not be broken.

It took many days for Tristan to recover, and when he told Iseult that he was there on behalf of King Mark and not himself she was heart-broken. Her father had already agreed to the marriage because it might patch up the quarrels between Ireland and Cornwall, but Iseult was deeply unhappy. She had begun to feel something deeper in her heart for Tristan than she could ever imagine. The queen noticed her daughter's great unhappiness and assumed it was because she was to marry a man she did not know. She sent for one of Iseult's maids, Brangaine.

'Brangaine, you must take this magic potion with you to Cornwall, and slip it into the wine that Iseult and King Mark will drink on their wedding night. They will both fall in love with each other instantly, and my daughter can be happy.'

Brangaine hid the philtre and accompanied Iseult and Tristan on the boat to Cornwall. Restlessly pacing the deck of the ship one night, Tristan tripped over the magic potion that Brangaine had hidden carelessly in a sack. It was a clear and moonlit night, and as Tristan sat on deck, watching the stars above he heard someone else's footsteps near him. He turned and saw Iseult, her golden hair glimmering in the moonlight but her face sad and longing for home.

'You look lonely, Iseult. Is it Ireland you yearn for or is it the thought of marrying King Mark that makes you sad?'

Iseult came to sit by him, but she did not dare to tell him her desire for him. 'It is nothing. The trip is long and tiring. Yes, I miss my home, but yes I am very unhappy about marrying the king, because I love another.'

Tristan picked up the philtre and, thinking it was only wine, offered to share it with Iseult. So, through the night they drank the magic potion and as each drop fell into their mouths, their love grew stronger and stronger for one another. Both knew that Iseult still had to marry Tristan's uncle, but now, unable to hide their feelings for each other, they made passionate love beneath the stars as the ship rolled through the waves towards Cornwall.

On the wedding night Iseult could not go through with her union with the king. She asked Brangaine to take her place in the royal bed so that Mark would suspect nothing. He was drunk, anyway, on wine and happiness and spent the night making love to Brangaine, until she slipped away before dawn to Iseult's chamber, leaving the king snoring in a stupor of love and alcohol. But Tristan and Iseult had met secretly that night, there was nothing now that could keep them apart. For many months they met in the orchards outside Tintagel, until the lovers took too many chances and they were discovered.

Many of the other courtiers were jealous of Tristan's position, and when they found out that he was having an affair with Iseult, they did everything they could to expose him. Whispers became nightmares for the king, and his suspicions began to grow as each day Iseult seemed to be less and less able to return his love. One day Mark was out riding in the woods when he came across Tristan and Iseult sleeping side by side. Between them lay Tristan's sword. Mark was filled with rage and jealousy, but he loved them both so much that he could not bring himself to kill them. Instead, he exchanged Tristan's sword for his own so that the lovers would realize they had been discovered.

When they awoke Iseult guessed that the king had been merciful. Tristan was overcome by remorse for what he had done, and he forced Iseult to agree to stay with Mark while he would leave the country in self-imposed exile. Tristan went to Brittany, where he married in an attempt to settle his feelings and forget Iseult. But he could not forget her, nor even consummate his marriage. Every day was a nightmare of desire and passion for Iseult. On many occasions he disguised himself and returned to Cornwall where the lovers secretly met, but the many wars and expeditions in which he became involved meant that he had less and less time to visit Cornwall.

Kaherdin, Tristan's brother-in-law, found out the lovers' dark secret and when Tristan became seriously wounded in battle, Kaherdin was sent to Cornwall to fetch Iseult to heal him. Kaherdin agreed that if he were to be successful in bringing Iseult back to France he would raise a white sail on the ship, but if he failed to bring her, he would raise a black sail.

Tristan became too ill to watch for the ship's return and asked his wife to look out for the boat. She had always been suspicious of Tristan's trips to England and knew that he had once had a lover in Cornwall. When she saw the ship coming towards the shore with a white flag raised she ran back to the palace and found Tristan lying half-unconscious on his bed.

'The ship returns, my lord, but the flag is black,' she said in a fit of jealous rage. After she had stormed out of the bed-chamber, Tristan lost the will to live. Now that Kaherdin was seemingly returning without Iseult he could find no strength to heal himself. In a moment of complete despair and long-ing for Iseult he threw himself on his sword and died. Finding Tristan dead when she ran into his bed-chamber, Iseult was so overcome by grief that she died of a broken heart.

King Mark understood their tragic ending and took the bodies of Tristan and Iseult back to Cornwall to be buried side by side, the only way they could ever be together. He planted two trees over the grave and as they grew, the trunks began to lean towards one another and the branches intertwined until there grew only one tree that held the secret of the lovers' embrace locked in their tangled boughs.

THE CONVOLVULUS FAN

JAPAN, 700CE

FANS have played an important part in Japanese life and in the nation's leg-ends and mythology. The fan that folds up on itself symbolizes life, the rivet being the beginning of the journey, and the radiating parts made of paper are the road of life itself. A gigantic fan was used in celebration of the great sun-goddess in Ise. But fans were also used by lovers inscribed with love-poems and messages on the back. These would often be swapped and trea-sured for ever.

This is the tale of Asagao, who was blinded by her own love for a mer-chant, and by chance it was their exchange of messages on the fan that brought them together again after many years.

Fireflies glimmered between trees and on the banks of the river, and the ladies of Kyoto would spend the evenings trying to catch the tiny insects. They would place them on their hair or just let them rest for a moment on the tips of their fingers before they let them fly back to their business. It was on one such night that Komagawa, the merchant, happened to take a boat out on the river to relax and watch the ladies at their play.

As Komagawa drifted idly downstream and the fireflies landed on his own robes like drops of silver rain, he saw a lady in great danger. Her boat was about to get tangled up in the mighty reeds beside the waterfall. He rowed quickly across and pulled her boat from the strong current and towed it to the other shore, back to the laughter and the fireflies. As soon as they saw each other, they fell in love, so they stayed for a while beside the river, talking and forgetting all around them except their own desire.

As was the custom, the two lovers agreed to pledge their love for one another by exchanging fans. The lady was called Miyuki, and on her fan was a painting of a convolvulus, asagao. So Komagawa wrote a poem on his own fan about the beauty of the asagao, and they exchanged fans. They both knew that the convolvulus was the key to their love and that they must meet again.

The lovers eventually separated and met again a few days later before it was time for them to return to their homes. Miyuki knew that Komagawa wanted her for his true love, and she was filled with happiness. But when she reached her parents house they told her that she was to marry an honourable man, someone that she did not even know. The marriage had been arranged, and Miyuki had no choice.

Miyuki was heart-broken. She could only do as her parents said, but was tormented all night by the knowledge that she loved someone else. In desperation she left the house early the next morning, dreaming of fireflies and the love of Komagawa. She hurried down to the river, hoping that he would return one more time to take her away, but he did not come. The dawn had jangled the air with an early breath of cold air, and the fireflies had vanished. Alone she cried into her fan, and for many days drifted around the countryside weeping her salt tears everywhere she went. But because she cried so much she could not see. The salt tears took away her sight completely, and she was now blinded by her own despair.

Miyuki had to carry on living with the pain of her blindness. Her one talent was her voice. So that she did not become a wretched beggar, she visited tea-houses and stood in the streets to sing her enchanting songs for money. Her voice was so perfect that she became famous. People would cry as soon as she sang a few notes, and her audience grew steadily in number. She loved to sing best the poem that Komagawa had written on his fan. So the people who grew to love her voice called her Asagao, the convolvulus.

She made a friend called Asaka. Asaka would lead her from place to place and from town to town. They journeyed together for many months, but a band of thieves attacked them and Asaka was killed. Now that Asagao was all alone, she would travel across the countryside from village to village, and all who heard the tapping of her stick knew that she was coming to sing them a haunting song. What kept her alive was the thought of Komagawa, and that one day they might meet again.

A few years passed, then one day Komagawa, the merchant, came to a place on his travels with his friend Takita. Takita was tired and wanted to stop and spend some time at the tea-house. So they entered. Takita was not an inspiring companion and had little conversation. Komagawa idly began to look around at the painted screens as they sat crossed-legged on the floor. Suddenly he jumped up, for there before his eyes was the love-poem he had given to Asagao, convolvulus. He asked the owner of the tea-house how he had acquired the poem.

'The poor blind girl ran away from her parents' house because she could not be with the man she loved. She looked everywhere for her lover but could not find him and she sings this song everywhere she goes in the hope that she will find him. But you're in luck sir, because this lady is currently in my tea-garden.'

'Would you bring her to me?' asked Komagawa.

So the tea-house master brought Asagao into the apartment, and Komagawa saw how lovely she had become even though she had cried so many tears. Her peaceful waiting had created its own inner beauty. Asagao sang to him. Komagawa longed to touch her to tell her who he was and to reveal how much he loved her, but his friend Takita was still in the room listening. When she had finished singing he made a polite thank you and dismissed her with her payment.

Yet Asagao had been stirred by the stranger, as if she had been deeply affected by his presence, even though she did not understand why. On the following day Komagawa gave a fan to the tea-house master and said: 'Give this fan and money to Asagao. She will understand. I will be back for her one day.' So Komagawa and Takita continued on their travels, and as they set off into the hills and valleys Komagawa felt a deep wrench at leaving her, but there was nothing he could do until he was free to return on his own.

The tea-house master gave the fan to Asagao. 'The gentleman you sang to last night? He has left you this fan and money.'

Asagao eagerly grasped the fan. 'Is there a drawing of a convolvulus on it?'

'Yes, there is. How did you know?'

Asagao was full of joy when she realized that she had been with Komagawa. 'Do you know where he is now?'

'No, only that he will return. But I'm afraid there is bad news from your parents. They are to send a servant to take you back home so that you can marry the man of their choice.'

Asagao wouldn't listen. 'I will never go back there!' she cried. 'You must help me, you must help me find my true love so that we can be reunited.'

The old tea-house master nodded. He knew what he had to do. Many years before he had betrayed Asagao's father and would have been punished with death if her father had not taken pity on him and allowed him to run the tea-house. Now, still guilt-ridden, he could only do what he thought best for them all. If he committed seppuku, his liver could be used to restore Asagao's sight. So the tea-house master killed himself and the old medicine man took the still warm liver from the body and made a potion for Asagao to drink. Within minutes her sight was restored and she was overwhelmed with both grief at the tea-master's death and happiness at the restoration of her sight.

That night, accompanied by two loyal servants, she set out in a fierce storm to find her lover. She walked down stony tracks and through fields of stubble until her feet were bleeding and her heart became heavy. But she would not give up. Again and again the belief that she would find Komagawa pushed her own. She would not sleep and would not stop until she had found him.

As the sun rose she looked up at the mountain range before her, and it seemed as if it were no longer an obstacle, but only a warm hill filled with flowers. Then she heard her name called. 'Asagao! Asagao!' She turned round and saw Komagawa running towards her and at last happiness came to her.

The flower of the convolvulus lasts for only for a few hours, and as they fell into each other's arms they knew that their love might not last for ever, for sometimes it fades as fast as the convolvulus flower.

SCAR-FACE

ALGONQUIAN, NORTH AMERICA, 1000CE

SCAR-FACE was one of the best younger hunters in the tribe. But all the braves teased and taunted him because he had an ugly scar across his face. This had ruined his good looks and the Indian girls refused to look at him. The scar had been the result of an encounter with a grizzly bear. Scar-face had killed it, but although he was left with this sad disfigurement, he had at least the reputation of being a mighty hunter.

Scar-face had fallen in love with the chief's daughter. Most of the young hunters in the tribe wanted to marry this beautiful girl, and many had declared their love to her, but Scar-face did not dare do this. Why should such a wonderful girl like her want such a poor and disfigured man like himself?

One day Scar-face walked past her as she sat weaving outside her lodge. He stopped and looked deeply into her eyes, hoping that she might return his gaze. She gave him one quick look from behind her long eyelashes and ran down towards the river, terrified of her own feelings for him. One of her previous admirers, whom she had rejected, saw the exchange of glances and followed Scar-face down to the edge of the encampment. He strode up to Scar-face with a sneer on his face.

'Hah, Scar-face, so you want to marry the chief's daughter do you? Now's your chance to have a go at wooing her, but you think you've got more chance than I have, do you?'

'I may have a blemish up my face, but not in my heart,' replied Scar-face and left to find the girl. He ran quickly down to the river where he knew she would be pulling rushes to make baskets.

Scar-face sat down beside her and spoke quietly. 'I may be poor, but my heart is filled with love for you. I've got no furs, no riches, but I live by my bow and spear. Would you marry me, and live with me in my lodge?'

The girl looked at him directly now, and he felt as if the sun was shining out of her eyes. But she hesitated. 'My father has much wealth, it is not necessary for my husband to be rich. But the sun-god has decreed that I shall never marry anyone, for I am to be his own sun-maiden.'

Scar-face was sad. 'Is there nothing you can do to change this arrangement?'

'There may be one way,' she said. 'You must find the sun-god and persuade him to release me from this promise. If he agrees to this, he must remove the scar from across your face as a sign that he will give me to you.'

Dejected and confused, Scar-face left the girl. He couldn't believe that the sun-god would ever give up such a beautiful woman as this. Yet he knew that he must at least try to find the sun-god – it was his only hope of ever marrying the girl.

For many moons he travelled across the plains and the forests in search of the home of the sun-god. He crossed many rivers and lakes and climbed the highest mountains, but it seemed that he could never find the golden gates to the sun-god's lodge. He asked many creatures on the way, the wild animals of the forest and the plains, but none seemed to know the way to the sun.

He eventually met a wolverine who had been there once himself, he said. The wolverine offered to show Scar-face part of the way at least. Together they travelled for many miles until they came to a huge area of water that was both too deep and too wide to cross without a boat. Scar-face was distraught as the wolverine shrugged his shoulders and said good-bye. 'This is as far as I can go,' he said.

Scar-face was about to turn back, but just as he felt the sun shimmer with warmth across his face, two white swans appeared on the water and told him to sit on their backs. He jumped on one and threw his bow and spear on the other, and the swans glided across the great lake to the furthest side. He travelled for some time in the direction suggested by the swans and came across a bow and arrow lying beside the rock-face. He wondered who was the owner but was not tempted to take them. As he walked further and further into the rocky terrain he came across a handsome young man who asked, 'You haven't seen my bow and arrows have you?'

Scar-face told him where they were, and the youth, overwhelmed by his honesty, decided to befriend him.

'Where are you heading?' he asked Scar-face.

'I am trying to find the sun-god, I've been told that he's not far from here.'

'I am the son of the sun-god,' said the boy. 'My name is Apsirahts, and I am the morning star. Come with me. I will take you to my father.'

So Apsirahts and Scar-face set off across the stony hills until they climbed up onto a wide rocky ledge and looked across to the golden light that shone from the sun-god's lodge. It was the most beautiful lodge that Scar-face had ever seen, decorated with dazzling colours and unusual art. Kokomis, the mother of Apsirahts, waited at the entrance to welcome him in. She was the moon-goddess.

The sun-god himself appeared and a most extraordinary power exuded from his golden light. He, too, welcomed Scar-face warmly and suggested he stay, be their guest and hunt with his son for as long as he wanted. He warned

225

them not to go near the great waters, as there were big savage birds there that could kill Apsirahts.

So Scar-face stayed with the sun-god for many moons, knowing that one day he must ask the question about the chief's daughter. But there never seemed to be a right time, and he had to feel sure that when he did ask, his request would be granted.

One day Apsirahts ran off into the forest as they were hunting together. Scar-face guessed he had gone down to the great waters to kill the huge birds and ran after him, arriving just in time to save the boy from the terrible bird monsters. The sun-god was so grateful to Scar-face for rescuing his son that he asked him if there was anything he could do, any request that he might be able to grant.

So Scar-face told him why he had come to the sun-lodge and about his love for the chief's daughter and how she could not marry him while she was under the power of the sun-god himself.

The sun-god nodded. 'You have saved my son. How can I not grant you this request? Go back to the woman you love and marry her, and as a sign that I have granted this to be so, I now make you whole again.'

The sun-god raised his golden hand, and instantly the scar disappeared from the youth's face. The sun and moon gave Scar-face many rich clothes and ornaments to take back to the earth world. Now that his disfigurement was gone, his arrival back at the encampment was greeted with awe and wonder for no one recognized this richly dressed Indian whose face was as beautiful as the sun itself. The chief's daughter could hardly believe her eyes, but when she saw that the scar had disappeared from his face she hugged him to her and within a few days they were married.

Scar-face became known as Smooth-face, and together he and the chief's daughter built a medicine lodge in honour of the sun-god in the sky.

RAKIAN AND THE BEES

BORNEO, 1500CE

ALTHOUGH human passion is symbolized by myths of lovers and desire, this has never stopped myth-tellers from incorporating animals and creatures of different species into a love story. The creatures involved may represent archetypal qualities that could not be described in any other way than in their most basic animal form.

There was a man called Rakian who lived with the Fusun people of Borneo. His job was to go out into the forests and gather wild bees' nests. One day the elders from his village sent him further into the jungle than usual. The canopy of trees was so dense that he could neither see the sky nor glimpse the sunlight through the leaves. There were few birds, and only the cries of the birds of paradise far away in the clearings reminded him how near he was to his home.

The trees here were taller than the ones where he lived, and he could just hear a buzzing of bees from the topmost branches. Rakian was an excellent climber, and with the help of his knife and twine he scrambled up the tree like a monkey. As he reached the top, the light began to filter through the high branches and soon he was dazzled by the sunshine again. At the top of the tree was a nest very unlike any he had ever seen before. He watched, fascinated by the unusual colour of the bees as they came and went from the nest. These bees were completely white.

Rakian began to cut down the nest from the branches, but as he hacked his way through the tangled boughs of the tree a strange cry came from inside the nest. He frowned and put his knife away. Gradually, he began to free the nest with his fingers, untwining each branch and each creeper that held the nest to the tree. Once it was released, he put the nest in his basket and set off back down the tracks towards his home.

Back in the village he stored the nest above his bed and the bees did not seem to mind being there at all. The following morning he went to work in his own rice field. Tired and weary, he returned to his hut just before sunset and to his astonishment found rice and fish cooked and prepared for him on the table. He ate the food gratefully, unsure who could possibly have made such a delicious meal.

The next day he went to work in the rice field again. When he returned there was food on the table, and even fruit and vegetables cooked in a way he had never known before. For the next few days the same thing happened, and he became more and more puzzled. There was only one thing for him to do and that was to spy on his own house and see what happened during the day. So on the fourth day he pretended to go to the rice field but came furtively back and hid behind the tree at his home.

It was not long before a beautiful woman appeared through his own front door. Carrying a jug, she ambled down to the stream to fetch some water. Rakian dashed into the house, sure she was something to do with the nest above his bed. He pulled it down from the rafters, and hid it under the wooden slats, and pulled the bedclothes over himself.

After a while the beautiful girl returned and saw that the nest was gone. Strangely all she shouted was, 'Who has taken my sarong!'

Rakian could not hide himself any longer and emerged from under the bedclothes. 'What are you doing in my house? Are you here to steal my bees' nest?'

The woman just ignored him and would not answer. So Rakian told her to cook his dinner but she shook her head and sulked. After a few hours Rakian began to ignore her and was ready to go back to the fields, hoping she would be gone by the time he returned. But she ran to the doorway and stopped him. 'Where is my sarong? You've hidden it haven't you? All my clothes and possessions are in that bees' nest, and I need them.'

Rakian smiled. 'Yes, I did hide the bees' nest, but I don't want you to have it, because you'll just hide in it again, and I won't be able to see you.'

The woman shook her head and smiled for the first time, too. 'I promise I won't hide from you. I have been given to you by my mother because I have no husband among my own people, and you have no wife among yours.'

So Rakian got up and took the bees' nest from under the bed and placed it high above his bed so that the woman could get her sarong and her other possessions. She thanked him, but added: 'You must never tell anyone that you are married to a bee-woman; if you promise this I will stay and cook for you and be your true wife.'

Rakian promised that he would never tell a soul, and so the bee-woman stayed. For over a year they lived happily together and had a child. But it was not long after the birth that Rakian became very drunk one night and gave away his secret.

All the villagers were shocked when they found out that Rakian lived with a bee-woman, and because everyone laughed and insulted Rakian each day as he went to the rice fields, the bee-woman's shame became too much for her, and she turned into a white bee and flew away. Rakian picked up the child and ran after her, following the tiny speck of white that darted through the trees into the deepest jungle. For many days he travelled wearily through the forest until he came to a long-house next to a river-bank.

He heard the familiar sound of bees and crept slowly up the long-house steps. The sound of busy bees became louder and he bravely pushed open the door. Inside were millions of bees, all white, swarming around the roof beams. There were many passages leading off the first hall. These led to more rooms and more bees. It was just like the biggest nest he had ever seen. He began to search each room for his wife, but the bees all looked the same and he began to sob piteously. His child cried too, and he feared that the bees would swarm down upon them and sting them to death.

Further and further he crept into the bee-house, calling out, 'Bee-woman where are you? Have you no love for our child or for me?'

But the bee-woman could not hide from him any longer, and filled with love for Rakian she appeared to him in human form. The bees that had clustered around the roof and among the rafters flew down to the floor and turned into people. The bee-woman welcomed him and so did the bee-people. The only thing he could do was to become a member of this bee-tribe so that he could be with his wife and child. So Rakian became part of the bee-people, and his own tribe never saw him again.

SIX

TRICKSTERS

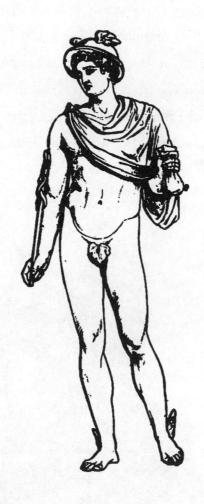

RICKSTERS WERE NEITHER GOOD nor bad. They were morally neutral and often helped to create mankind, including both its corruption and its goodness. Tricksters were also responsible for posing questions to humans about their own mortality. Some magicians were spirits who set the world in order, and some spirits were magicians who changed the course of events on earth. Many of the early trickster-gods eventually became separated from the very myths from which they originated. Their gradual shift towards a more 'mortal' characterization inspired folk-tales and heroic anecdotes through the centuries. The irony of this is that the tricksters themselves are the ones who have transformed themselves to fit in with changing social and psychological consciousness – the craftiest trick of all.

ISIS

ISIS, or Aset, was one of the most popular of all Egyptian deities, and in Greek-Egypt a cult following grew up around her called the Mysteries of Isis. She was worshipped under the name Isis in the Greek-Egyptian towns of the Nile delta, where she was regarded as the great goddess herself. In addition, she had associations with Demeter, Hera and Selene. Isis was not a trickster-deity but a sorceress. Her magical powers were honoured by all who worshipped her, for Isis had found out the secret of immortality and the ultimate power of magic.

Osiris and Isis were the children of Nut and Geb, and they had a dual roles as fertility-gods. Isis was responsible for love and the union between mortals, while Osiris was the god of growth. As husband and wife, they ruled Egypt together and became the most respected and best loved of all gods and together assisted in civilizing the people of the Nile. Isis taught healing, spinning, weaving and the grinding of corn. Osiris would travel out of Egypt to teach what he knew and spread his creed of civilization.

Osiris was drowned and dismembered by his jealous brother, Seth, who threw the pieces of Osiris' body into the Nile. Isis and her sister, Nephthys, later found them. Knowing that their only hope to restore Osiris to life was Isis's own medical and healing skills, she began her great task. With her great insight she realized that if she could not bring him back to life, at least she could become pregnant by him. In some accounts she changed into a bird, brought him back to life just long enough for him to have sex with her. In other accounts she impregnated herself with the last drop of semen from her husband's penis and set to work to reassemble the parts of his body.

Whichever method she chose, the magical insemination worked and she became pregnant with Horus. However, all her attempts to restore Osiris to life failed. The gods refused to allow him to return to the world of mortals, and he was sent to rule the underworld.

Isis was now intent on destroying Seth, and she goaded Horus to take every possible opportunity to kill him on her behalf. But Horus struggled against the mighty Seth, and it was not until their last duel together that justice was done and Horus castrated Seth.

Isis's knowledge of the magical arts was vast, but she still did not have the same degree of power as her grandfather, Ra, the sun-god. She was jealous of his amazing wizardry and, of course, of his secret of immortality. As time went by and Ra became older and frailer, Isis was sure that he would never reveal his secret power, and she would be denied access to it. Ra was immortal but, as he was also subject to growing older, he might reach a point when he would forget what his secret was. Isis knew the only way she could retrieve such secrets was by a trick.

As an aged man, Ra often dribbled and drooled saliva from his lips. One day he dribbled on to the sand. Isis quickly gathered some of the saliva and mixed it up with the sand where he had walked. In her hands she moulded the mixture into a water-snake, a venomous serpent. Then, using her own powers, she transformed the serpent into an arrow.

As dawn rose, Ra and his fellow-gods, as usual, crossed the same place in the sky. They approached the turning point on the horizon and Isis hid the magic arrow just where Ra would walk. Sensing the great Ra above, the arrow suddenly turned into a serpent and plunged its fangs into Ra's leg. Ra fell down in great pain. Never before had he been in such agony, and he began to be concerned for his own life. As an immortal god, surely he could not die from a snake bite? The other gods were worried, too, seeing him in such pain. As father of all things, how could he have created something that would kill himself? He begged for the gods of magic to use their own powers to cure him. But all who came were unable to do anything, and Ra became weaker and weaker, knowing he was under a powerful and fateful spell. Finally, he asked for Isis to come to his side and to try out her own healing skills.

She eagerly arrived and whispered into his ear: 'Dear grandfather, I can cure you from this terrible affliction, but only if you will reveal your true name to me.' Isis knew that the key to immortality was in his name.

At first Ra refused, and kept telling her different names in the hope that she would believe him. He said his name was 'creator of the heavens' or 'the one who made the waters flow and caused the air to move' or 'lord and master of the Nile' or 'the originator of all time'. He was 'Khepri' in the morning, 'Ra' at noon and 'Atum' in the evening. With each false name he gave, the suffering and the agony increased, and his reluctance to tell Isis the magical word ended. Instead of opening his lips, however, Ra caused his name to move from his own heart into the heart of Isis, without speaking one word. Isis now knew the most powerful magic word in the universe and instantly restored Ra's health and removed her own spell.

From that moment Isis became the most powerful of the gods with her knowledge of the word of immortality and with it the secret of the universe.

ENKI

MESOPOTAMIA, 2500BCE

ALTHOUGH Enki was a creator-god he was also a bit of a trickster. His chief role was as sustainer of life on earth, but he also became known as a prankster, who irritated the other gods and demons and outwitted giants, solely for his own amusement. However, it was his earth-goddess wife who made sure his lustful eyes received a dose of his own medicine.

Enki lived in a paradise known as Dilmun with his earth-goddess wife, Ninhursaga. There was only this wonderful paradise and nothing else in the universe, but Enki's wife began to feel the stirrings of desire. She wanted Enki to make love to her and once he had been seduced into the art of sexual passion, he couldn't stop himself and began to want to have sex with everything. He enjoyed himself so much that he even had sex with his grandchildren. Eventually he began creating the land that became the earth; all the rivers, the mountains, the valleys, the animals and the creatures of the sea and land, simply in order to gratify himself.

Creation happened all over the place because of his highly virile and fertile libido. But Ninhursaga was jealous of her rampant husband, who wanted to have sex with any goddess or mortal woman he met.

Enki had recently had sex with the spider, so Ninhursaga gathered some of Enki's sperm that lay in the spider's womb and planted the seeds in the ground. The sperm grew into spider plants, which were highly poisonous, but Enki had never seen such plants before and decided to eat them. Of course, Ninhursaga made sure he ate enough of the foul leaves to make him very ill, and as he lay writhing on the ground in agony, he eventually died. Ninhursaga had not really wanted to cause his death, so she buried him in her womb and gave birth to him again.

From then on and with his libido tamed, he became less concerned with the evolution of the earth and spent most of his time playing tricks on gods and demons, as a way of avoiding the wrath of Ninhursaga.

HANUMAN

INDIA, 900BCE

HANUMAN, or Hanumat, is a trickster in Hindu mythology, but with one important difference from many of the other trickster-gods: he is a monkey. There are many animal gods and goddesses throughout the world's mythology, but Hanuman's antics seem neatly to encompass the dual roles of trickster and jester in his image as the monkey with the heavy jaw. Hanuman is a major character in the Ramayana and also appears as the monkey, when he accompanies Tripitaka on his journey from India to China.

Hanuman was born of the monkey-queen, Anjana, and the god of the wind, Vayu. As soon as he was out of the womb, Hanuman was ravenously hungry. Catching sight of the sun, he thought it must be something wonderful to eat and leaped after it. The sun ran away to Indra's heaven, and Hanuman chased after it. But Indra intervened and threw a thunderbolt at Hanuman, which knocked him back to earth and smashed and deformed his jaw. Hanuman's father, Vayu, was so angry that he slid into every god's belly and gave them terrible colic until Indra apologized to Vayu and agreed to grant Hanuman immortality.

Some accounts, however, suggest that Hanuman was given immortality because of his loyal support of Rama. He was agile and strong and became an invaluable ally to Rama in his war against the demon-king Ravana. He could fly at the speed of wind and had the strength to uproot mountains. He could alter his size and change form, and even make himself invisible. He was cunning and terrified his enemies with his golden skin and enormous tail. He could sometimes grow taller than a tower.

Hanuman went to Lanka as a spy for Rama in his battle against the demon-king, and also to deliver a message to Sita, Rama's wife, whom Ravana had kidnapped. Hanuman was anxious that he would not be able to cross the strait dividing Lanka from the mainland. He had been told by a vulture that it was a hundred leagues wide. Angada, another monkey, thought he might be able to leap it but would never have enough strength to get back again. Hanuman was worried that he would ever get across, let alone get back, and he disappeared up into the mountains to meditate on the mission. As he sat his body began to grow until it was the size of a mountain. He leaped across the skies, roaring and flashing his red eyes. In mid-air, he was stopped by a female demon, Saurasa, who opened her great jaws, and Hanuman could do nothing to stop himself being engulfed by the gaping mouth. He instantly shrank to the size of a thumb-nail and, once inside Saurasa, swelled up even larger than he had been before, bursting right through her belly so that she disintegrated into a thousand pieces across the skies.

When he reached Lanka, Hanuman turned himself into a cat so that he could creep easily around the city, even wandering into the great Ravana's bed-chamber to give messages to Sita.

Hanuman became of great service during the many battles with Ravana. Perhaps his greatest feat was to fly to the Himalayas in search of special healing herbs to cure Rama of his wounds. The demons and evil spirits set many traps to try to prevent Hanuman from reaching the mountains. The first was Kalanemi, a great ogre, who had been offered half the kingdom if he could kill Hanuman. Kalanemi flew ahead to the Himalayas and invited Hanuman to dine with him on his arrival. But Hanuman had already been warned. Seizing the evil demon by the leg, he hurled him all the way back to Lanka, where the ogre fell in a heap at Ravana's feet.

Indra was, however, still angry with Hanuman for trying to eat the sun, and she made it difficult for him to find the curative herbs. Eventually, the monkey deity shrugged his shoulders and simply tore up the whole mountain and flew off back to Lanka with it under his arm. He was given a difficult time on his return. He flew with such speed and force that he created a whirlwind and irritated the great Bharata, who shot him down with an arrow. When Bharata discovered he had shot Hanuman, he picked him up and offered to put him on another arrow and shoot him back to Lanka. Hanuman carried on alone and eventually reached Lanka as the evening was turning to night. As he drew near the city, he saw the moon beginning to rise and knew that moonlight would prevent the herb from working. So he swallowed the moon and safely delivered the magic herbs to Rama.

After the battle of Lanka was won, Rama offered Hanuman anything he chose. Hanuman asked to be allowed to live for as long as Rama's name was spoken by men. Rama's memory never died, and so Hanuman became immortal.

CIRCE, THE WITCH-GODDESS

GREECE, 750BCE

CIRCE (falcon) was the daughter of Helios, the sun-god, and Hecate, the goddess of magic. She was a powerful witch with an insatiable sexual appetite for young mortal men, but her duality made her love-life extreme in all ways. Many of her lovers were doomed to be cast under her more destructive spells. From her mother she had inherited the wickedness and power of black magic, and from her father the beauty and dazzling radiance of the sun. The alchemy of this potent mixture was sure to bring her a passionate but highly destructive love-life.

In one account Circe was attracted by the beauty of the Italian prince Picus, son of Sterces (or Saturn). Picus was a hunter and wore purple robes and carried glinting spears. One day he went out with his usual hunting party near the River Tiber where Circe happened to catch a glint of sunlight from his spear. She assumed that her father, Helios, was giving her a signal, and she transformed herself into a mist and came down to the riverside. As soon as Circe saw Picus she desired him and was determined to have him. From her invisible mist she wove a thread of cloud into a wild boar, which only Picus could see.

As the boar passed him, he galloped after it, following it towards the wilder part of the marshes and away from the rest of the hunting party. Circe immediately transformed herself into her beautiful witch form and stood before him. Picus was confused by her presence. Circe did everything she

235

could to seduce him, reminding him that she was the daughter of a god, just as he was the son of a god. She begged him to leave Venilia, his river-nymph lover, but he angrily refused. In her outrage at being rejected, she turned Picus into a woodpecker and left him clinging to a tree.

Another of Circe's victims was Scylla, a beautiful sea-sprite. Circe had taken a fancy to the great god of the sea, Glaucus, but Glaucus's attention was firmly fixed on the rapturous delights of Scylla. In her jealousy, Circe transformed poor Scylla into a disgusting monster. Her top half was still human, but from her waist sprouted twelve dogs' legs and six horrible snake necks on which were six dogs' heads, which yapped and bared their razor-like teeth. Glaucus was revolted by this sea-monster but equally shocked by Circe's behaviour, and he refused to have her.

Circe eventually married the prince of Colchis, but unwilling to give up her divine power for earthly dullness, she poisoned him and took all his wealth and lands for herself. Her father, Helios, roared his chariot through the skies and carried her away, realizing that she might not survive the anger of the people of Colchis. He gave her an exquisite island all for herself called Aeaea, the Island of Dawn.

On her fabulous island, Circe would sit in her splendid palace waiting for sailors or mortals to land so that she could seduce them. Her palace was surrounded by thick woods, and wild lions, boars and wolves prowled the forest looking for any men who had landed. However, these beasts did not attack those who came to the island – they stood on their hind legs and caressed the visitors who would be put under Circe's spell.

One day Circe sat at her loom spinning and singing the most magical of songs. Out at sea, not far from her palace, Odysseus and his men had anchored their ships to take shelter for the night. It was agreed that Eurylochus should take twenty-two men on shore to reconnoitre the island while the others would stay to guard the ships. Eurylochus and his companions found the lush vegetation and the wonderful animals that roamed without fear, and they became entranced by the magic of the island. They heard Circe singing at her loom and were drawn to the palace gates where Circe appeared with her bewitching smile. She invited them to dine at her table, and all followed her, except Eurylochus, who, suspecting a trap, lingered near the gates until they had all entered. The witch-goddess served up cheeses, honey, barley and wine to the hungry sailors, but the food was drugged, and as soon as they began to fall into a daze, Circe tapped each one on the shoulder with her wand and transformed them into pigs. She led them to the pig sties and shut them in with a few handfuls of acorns, leaving them to wallow in self-pity.

Eurylochus, who had seen what had happened through the window, fled back to Odysseus for help. Odysseus took his sword and ran blindly towards the palace, not knowing how he was to approach this witch-goddess. But as he stopped for breath at the crossroads he met the god Hermes, who offered him an antidote to Circe's magic. It was a scented white flower called moly (wild garlic), a talisman against her powers.

Odysseus was greeted warmly at the gates, and Circe invited him to share her dinner with her. They enjoyed the food and she entertained him in all her most seductive ways until the moment when she tapped him on the shoulder with her wand to turn him into a pig. But Odysseus had taken a deep sniff of the moly flower and he remained himself. Circe was horrified. Odysseus pulled out his sword and threatened to kill her unless she set his men free. Circe knew that he was there with the protection of the gods and that she could do him no more harm. She promised to turn all his men back into human form, and together they enjoyed another feast.

Odysseus stayed on Aeaea with Circe for seven years and she bore him three sons, Agrinus, Latinus and Telegonus. But Odysseus was a wanderer and longed to be travelling again. Circe agreed to let him go but told him he must visit the underworld to see the Trojan heroes and learn his future. Odysseus's men were not keen to leave the beauty of Aeaea for the terrors of the land of Hades, but Circe conjured up a fine sea breeze that took them quickly to the land of Perpetual Dusk and the entrance to the underworld.

Circe it seems eventually married Telemachus, the son of Odysseus and Penelope. Some say that Telemachus accidentally killed Circe and was banished forever, others that Circe and Telemachus travelled south to a country unknown to the Greeks and called it Italy. Circe's son, Latinus, was the first of the Latin people.

HERMES

GREECE, 750BCE

HERMES was the son of Zeus and Maia, a wood-nymph. He was born in a cave in Arcadia on Mount Cyllene, and as soon as he was born he wanted to get up to mischief. His anxiety to find something to do, rather than just lying around in his cot, provoked him to get up and explore the world. At this time, Hermes was probably only a few hours old. As he walked out of the cave into the bright spring air his first encounter was with a tortoise. Gazing at the beautiful shell, Hermes decided that there were far better things he could do with it than just look at it. Killing the poor tortoise, he proceeded to remove the shell, stretched some cow-hide across it and plaited some grass to make the strings. Maia never scolded him for killing the animal because he played the lyre so well.

Eventually Hermes got bored with the lyre, threw it into his cot and went in search of something else to amuse him. By now he was feeling hungry, and he came across a field of cattle belonging to his brother Apollo. The cattle were guarded by two watchdogs, so Hermes drugged the dogs and led the cattle backwards out of the field, so that their footprints were pointing in the opposite direction to the way that he was leading them. He dragged them by their tails all the way to a cave at Pylos, disguising his own footprints by making a pair of grass sandals so that he left no trace behind.

He killed two of the cattle to cook, divided them up into twelve portions to make a sacrifice to each of the gods, and kept a bit for himself. After he had devoured his sacrificial supper, Hermes wandered back, turned into a wisp of cloud and entered his home through the keyhole. He climbed into his cot and cuddled his tortoiseshell lyre under his arm as if it were a soft toy.

But it wasn't long before Apollo found out that Hermes had stolen his cattle. On his way home, in his usual boastful fashion, Hermes had told an old man that he had robbed his brother of his herd. Unfortunately for Hermes, this old man was none other than Battus, the god of gossip. Apollo arrived at the cave and confronted the sleeping Hermes who protested his innocence from the safety of his cradle.

'Do I look like a cattle-thief? I'm only two days old and all I want is sleep and milk. Newborn babies don't steal cows, my feet are too soft to run, and I don't even know what a cow looks like yet'.

But Apollo was not convinced by Hermes's lies. 'You're a deceiver and you speak like a thief. You'd better come with me to see Zeus, our father. It will be for him to decide your fate.'

So Apollo snatched Hermes out of the cot and dragged him kicking and screaming to Zeus. Hermes cursed every cow in the world and behaved like the brat he was. But when Zeus saw them together, he was charmed by Hermes naïvety and couldn't believe that he had stolen anything.

Apollo pleaded his case, but Hermes just carried on telling his lies, until Zeus, who was finding the whole thing highly amusing, ordered the brothers to be friends and to make up. Hermes agreed to take Apollo to where the cattle were hidden, and when they arrived Hermes began to play his magical lyre. Apollo was enchanted by the music of the lyre and asked Hermes if he would share its secret. Hermes agreed only if he were to have a share of Apollo's cattle. So the bargain was struck, and Apollo and Hermes became close friends. It was, in fact, Apollo who taught Hermes how to tell the future by reading the patterns that ripples made on water.

Hermes was not a robber, but a thief. The subtle distinction here was that he became the patron of stealth, rather than of outright burglary or mugging. Zeus would often use him to rescue others, particularly divine children, from danger.

He became the messenger of the gods, flying between heaven, earth and the underworld, the only god who could travel freely between these places. He was the supreme trickster, and because no one could cheat him and get away with it, he was given the job of accompanying the souls of the dead on their way to the underworld. It was he who escorted Persephone, Eurydice and Orpheus back from the underworld.

Hermes's trickery was invaluable when it came to rescuing and saving others, as when he came to the aid of the child, Heracles. Heracles was the son of Zeus and a mortal woman, Alcmena. Because he was not wholly divine, Heracles was in danger from Hera's malicious jealousy. The consequences of Hera ever finding out that her husband Zeus had slept with a mortal who subsequently bore him a child were usually murderous.

Hermes decided to help Heracles. If Heracles were to become divine, Hera could not harm him. The only way he could do so was to suckle the milk of a goddess. This is when Hermes came up with one of his better plans. He lay the baby Heracles on a path in the woods and asked Hera if she would like to go for a walk with him. Hermes was a bit of a flirt and as they talked and walked, he idly commented upon the beauty of Hera's body and breasts. Hera was, of course, flattered by the youthful Hermes and his complimentary words. They came across the crying baby lying on the path. Heracles had been wrapped up well so that Hera couldn't recognize him. If she knew the child to be mortal or one of Zeus's offspring, she would have killed it. Hermes looked down at the poor thing and said: 'This baby seems so hungry, and you, Hera, with your beautiful breasts, you could give this child such wonderful milk.'

Hera, still flattered by the attention from the young god, agreed and proudly took the baby to her breast. She began to feed Heracles, but as he suckled she guessed that this was no divine child. She pulled her breast away from the child and drops of milk spurted out into the sky to form the Milky Way. As for Heracles, thanks to the intervention of Hermes, he had received just enough divine milk to become god-like and to follow his own heroic path.

HEIMDALL

NORTHERN EUROPE, 300CE

HEIMDALL was one of the lesser gods in the Nordic pantheon, but he was often the shape-shifting adviser to many of the other brainless deities. Although Loki had a far superior role as shape-shifter and major trickster, Heimdall, half-giant, half-god, became a useful minor accessory in many of the longer, more elaborate tales. Perhaps Heimdall was more like a 'fool' or court jester to the gods, carrying sound advice to those who had no time for reflection.

Heimdall's birth was a gynaecological mystery. He was apparently born from nine giantesses, the Wave Maidens, who all had sex simultaneously with Odin.

Heimdall was beautiful, wise and benevolent, and he was regarded as Loki's equal as a shape-shifter. He was given the job of guarding the Rainbow Bridge, Bifrost, to stop the giants' invasion of Asgard. He was also endowed with incredible senses. He could remain awake for days on end and had the acute hearing of a bat – he could hear the grass growing in a distant field and the ice melting on a frozen lake.

Like many other shape-shifting deities, Heimdall's other delight was wandering around in the land of the mortals, having sex with anything and fathering many children. In one trip to the mortal world he changed into a man called Riger and visited the oldest mortals, called Ai and Edda. He was invited to stay and dine with them, and as was their custom with strangers, he shared their bed with them for three nights. But each night Heimdall would move into the middle of the bed between the two and have sex with Edda. Ai was probably a very sound sleeper because nine months later Edda gave birth to a son, Thrall. This was Heimdall's son, and although not a very bright character, he was a good worker, and he and his wife, Thir, became the ancestors of every serf born on the earth.

Heimdall, meanwhile, had been roaming the hills of Midgard and come across another couple, Afi and Amma, who invited him to stay in exactly the same circumstances. Again, nine months later a boy Karl was born. When Karl grew up he married Snor, and they became the first of the free labourers.

The last visit he made to Midgard resulted in his son Jarl. This particular mating had been a far more delicate affair, and Jarl grew up to be handsome and refined, and had the power to use the runes. Jarl married Erna, and they became the ancestors of all the ruling classes on earth.

Heimdall's shape-shifting powers came in useful when he came to blows with Loki over Freya and the return of the Brisingamen. Loki first became a fire, and so Heimdall turned into a cloud to rain above him and put him out. Loki turned into a polar bear and was ready to swallow the water, but Heimdall became a bigger bear and attacked him. Both of them changed into seals and fought in the water, until eventually Heimdall won. This underlines the belief that Loki and Heimdall will meet again at Ragnarok and that Loki will be killed by Heimdall, but Heimdall will also lose his life.

LOKI

Loki is probably one of the best known trickster-gods in European mythology, and true to his dual nature he is both the oldest god and the youngest god. He existed as a concept before creation, and also came into physical being by slipping into bodily shape through his own cunning. There are numerous tales about Loki, who is the god of mischief and also the god of lies and deception. The main differences between Loki and the other gods in the Nordic pantheon are that Loki's personality evolves and he has more human traits than any of the other more two-dimensional gods.

Loki, which means 'alluring' or 'fire', was not only mischievous and amoral; he was also highly adept at changing shape to any form he chose. Sometimes he would be a fly or a fish or a tiny grain of sand. He could even be the frown on a giant's face or the heel on a man's shoe. Sometimes he befriended humans who he thought were getting a rough deal.

One dark, stormy night, the giant Skrymsli was pestered by a peasant who was feeling lucky. The peasant asked the giant to play a game of chess. Unfortunately for the peasant, Skrymsli's stakes were high. The giant suggested that if he were to win the peasant must forfeit his own son to the giant, unless, of course, he could hide him so well that the giant could never find him. The peasant foolishly agreed to this bet, complacently confident that it would be a stalemate and they would go their ways in peace. As usual, however, Skrymsli won. The peasant was horrified. Realizing that the giant meant what he had said, he rushed to Odin for help, and the god grudgingly changed the boy into a grain of wheat.

Skrymsli saw right through this ridiculous disguise. He tramped across the fields to where the boy was hidden and ploughed up the wheat until he came to the grain. Odin snatched the grain from his hand at the last moment and gave it back to the terrified parents. But Odin had more important things to do than sort out minor disturbances with man and the giants, and he had become bored with the whole affair.

The peasants next went to Hoenir, Odin's brother, who transformed the boy into a feather, attaching him to the downy chest of a swan. The giant again saw through this pathetic charade and set off to eat the swan, but Hoenir managed to stir up enough wind to ruffle the swan's feathers, and the feather-boy wafted away on the breeze just as the giant's mouth came down on the swan's neck.

Hoenir, too, lost interest in this rather dismal episode of human suffering, and so the peasants eventually turned to Loki for help. Loki quickly transformed the boy into a fish egg, but Skrymsli went fishing as soon as he

241

realized what Loki had done. Thinking Loki rather stupid just to change the boy into a fish egg, he caught the fish and proceeded to pick through all the eggs inside the roe. Skrymsli was close to devouring the right egg when Loki grabbed it out of the fish's gut and ran away. The egg was transformed back into the boy, and Loki told him to run home as fast as he could, taking a detour through the boathouse.

So the boy set off at a pace and the giant began to run after him through the boathouse. Seeing that Loki had set a trap for the giant, the boy jumped over the great metal spike protruding through the ground, but Skrymsli, his eyes fixed only on the boy, tripped on the spike and fell, blood streaming from his foot. Loki quickly chopped off one of his legs, but it began to grow back almost as fast as it had been severed. So Loki whacked off Skrymsli's other leg, and before it could grow back he placed a steel and flint block between the limb and the body to disable the magic. The giant was destroyed and bled to death. For once Loki had helped a human in distress more willingly than even the great Odin.

Loki was not always such a benevolent god, however, and he could be quite ruthless when he wished. Always restless and in search of new experiences, he began to be laughed at by the gods, especially by Odin, who had no respect or time for him whatsoever.

Loki resented this treatment and decided that the ultimate trick would be to do something to the great Odin himself. He had also grown quite jealous of Balder, Odin's son. The most beautiful of all gods and a threat to Loki's hilarious antics, Balder was the god of light and had runes carved on his tongue. He was a great herbal doctor and could see into the future. But his premonitions became terrifying nightmares that foresaw only an awful fate awaiting him. The light left Balder's eyes, and so Odin and Frigga demanded from every object, mortal and creature in the world that nothing or no one would harm their son. The only thing Frigga forgot to tell was the mistletoe, but she was certain it could really do no harm to Balder at all. Balder had suddenly become invincible, he was not only beautiful and clever but now also a great attraction to the other gods.

Loki heard how many gods had been testing Balder's new-found resilience to anything in the world. Groups of deities would journey to Gladsheim just to see if anything could hurt him. They threw rocks at him, fired arrows and hit him with their axes, but nothing had any effect. In fact they all had so much fun that Balder's popularity became widespread, and Loki's mischievous fun began to turn stale and dull in comparison. Balder's increasing fame also stirred Loki's jealousy and anger.

Loki decided that the god of light would soon be the god of darkness. He plotted to kill Balder, which would also be a fine way of hurting Odin. Loki travelled to Gladsheim and changed himself into the form of an elderly woman. He found Frigga spinning in the great hall. He knew that she had given Balder his invulnerability, but he felt certain that there was a way to find a chink in his invisible armour.

With the guile and cunning of a fox, he eventually found out from Frigga, as they sat spinning together, that she had forgotten to enlist the help of the mistletoe. Loki yawned wearily. He told Frigga that he was very tired and his back ached, and he really should go and take some rest. But as soon as he was out of the great hall, Loki turned into his own form and rushed into the woods to find some mistletoe. He removed the berries, stripped the leaves until there was one long straight piece and sharpened one end like a pencil.

Down in the great court the gods were having fun with Balder. Each was taking it in turns to throw rocks or missiles at Balder's head, and each time they roared with laughter as Balder just stood there smiling his radiant smile. Loki watched from the door, livid with envy, until he spotted the blind Hoder who was doing his best to join in the fun. Because Hoder could not see where he was aiming, he kept missing Balder altogether, which made everyone laugh even more. Loki went up to Hoder, disguised again as an old woman, and offered to guide his hand in the right direction if he wanted to chuck something at Balder. After all, why shouldn't he join in the fun? Hoder nodded enthusiastically and Loki gave him the sharp mistletoe stick he'd pulled out from under his sleeve. Hoder agreed to throw the dart. Loki took his hand and aimed the dart straight at Balder's heart. As Hoder let go he heard the stick whiz through the air and only silence when there should have been cheers. The dart had struck Balder's chest and he fell dead to the ground.

The gods were horrified; they guessed it was Loki who had tricked Hoder into throwing the dart, but it was Hoder who would have to pay the price for his brother's death.

Odin and Frigga were heart-broken and attempted to save Balder as he lay in Niflheim. Their only chance was to make sure that the whole world, every god, goddess, animal plant and creature, mourned for Balder and he would then rise again to Asgard. But one giantess, Thok, refused. This giantess was, of course, Loki in disguise.

Loki was subsequently banished from feasts at Asgard, but he always turned up to irritate and inflict pain on gods and mortals alike. His tricks became more and more spiteful and stirred the gods against one another. Uninvited to one banquet, he turned up anyway and began throwing insults at all the gods. No doubt his words conveyed more than a little truth, and the gods decided Loki had to be destroyed.

Loki knew that Odin and the other gods would easily track him down. Odin was all-seeing, so Loki prepared himself for a visit from the gods. First, he made a net. As he was the cleverest of the gods he reckoned that if he couldn't make a net strong enough to catch him, no one else could. But his incredible skill enabled him to make a net capable of snaring even himself.

Horrified at his own incredible creation, he was just about to change his plan, when Odin, Thor and Kvasir came storming towards his house. Panic-struck, Loki jumped into the river, turned into a fish and began to swim away. But the three gods found the strong net and threw it into the water, dragging the flailing fish to the shore.

To make sure that Loki would never plague them or the universe again, they imprisoned him in a deep cave. First, they changed Loki's son, Vali, into a wolf and set him on his brother, Narfi. Vali tore Narfi apart, and the gods used Narfi's entrails to tie Loki to three huge rocks deep in the dark, dank cave. This was the kingdom of Skadi, the giantess. She hated Loki for the various tricks he had played on her in the past, and she was quite happy to hang a serpent above his head so that the venom dripped onto his face until Ragnarok – forever. This was so painful that Loki's wife, Sigyn, who had always been loyal and faithful to him, sat by his side, catching the drips in a cup she held above his head. It is only when she moves away to empty the bowl that the drips fall on Loki's face, causing him such pain and agony that earthquakes shake across the world.

When this cycle of time ends and Ragnarok comes, Loki will escape from the cave and destroy all the gods. Only fire and ice will be left as it was at the beginning of creation.

MERLIN AND NIMUË

CELTIC, 300CE

MERLIN, or Myrrdin, was the famous magician of Arthurian legend. His magic was renowned and some sources suggest he was credited with the powerful supernatural construction of Stonehenge. As a seer and sorcerer, he was best remembered for his wise counsel and spiritual guardianship of Arthur. He was also probably responsible for creating the Round Table and for the layout and design of Camelot.

Merlin's birth was shrouded in mystery. The Britons had been told by a seer that before their sacred place (possibly near or at Stonehenge) could be consecrated, it must be covered with the blood of a child who had no mortal father. The discovery and subsequent sacrifice of a half-human child seemed a highly remote possibility, until it was learned that a beautiful nun had given birth to a child who's father was a demon. This child was Merlin. How Merlin actually avoided being sacrificed is still obscure, but with his inheritance from his demon father and with the assistance of two dragons, it seems that the sacred fortress was made pure, and Merlin's own powers were at once revealed to him.

Merlin was both mortal and yet also a shape-shifter. This force enabled him to both love the mortal world and help those within it, but also revealed his other side, the restless shape-shifter, whose own darker sexual longings may have resulted in his death.

When he took on human form he was the prophet, the wizard and the counsellor. He advised Arthur on numerous occasions. The king implicitly trusted Merlin's guidance and often used him as his messenger, knowing that he could assume any form he desired. Many times Merlin would shape-shift into the form of a seductive young man. He fell easily in love, and there were many women who were clearly destined to return his fateful attraction. But sometimes he left the mortal realms altogether and changed into a cloud, the wind, a storm or the ripples on a pond.

Nimuë was the daughter of a siren – in some accounts she is the same being as the Lady of the Lake – and she was also a shape-shifter. She brought Merlin up when he was young, and she lusted after him every time he changed into a beautiful youth. But Merlin's love was not for Nimuë, and he eventually left her to enjoy himself in the mortal world. Nimuë's love turned to jealousy. She began to hate Merlin's easy seduction of so many women. Her own unrequited love turned to venomous resentment, and all she could think about was destroying him. She tried to outwit him in a contest of shape-shifting, and took on every form imaginable to catch him and trap him for ever. But Merlin's skills were more refined than hers were.

Nimuë would not give up, and remembering that Merlin's one weakness was beautiful women, she turned herself into a mortal and waited for him in the woods, knowing he would be infatuated as he rode by. When Merlin saw her he was blinded by his own desire, unable to see the truth of who she was. For the first time, his insight and prophetic powers let him down because of carnal lust and mortal longings. Merlin made passionate love to her. They fell into an ecstatic embrace and as he entered her, she changed into a drop of amber and engulfed him forever.

Together they are trapped for eternity, for each knows the other's secrets and can never escape. One day, Sir Gawain passed by where Merlin had been trapped by Nimuë's spell and he heard Merlin say: 'I loved another more than I loved myself. I taught my beloved how to bind me to herself, and now no one can set me free.'

HUVEANE AND HLAKANYANA

HUVEANE is well known among the peoples of southern Africa as both the first man and also, in some localities, as the original self-creating trickster-deity. Huveane also appears as Huve in the myths of the Bapedi and Baventa peoples of the Bantu and is found right across southern Africa.

Hlakanyana plays a more conspicuous role in Zulu mythology and legend. There is much uncertainty about his true nature. It seems likely he is associated with the weasel, but some of his adventures are very similar to those of other Bantu tribes, whose epic figure and the ancestor of Uncle Remus's Brer Rabbit are ascribed to the hare.

HUVEANE

One day Huveane had a child. No one knows quite how, or even why, but he did so and that was that. Huveane kept the child in a hollow tree, and he would creep from his parents' house every morning to feed it with milk before he went to work with the goats and the sheep. One day his father noticed there was an awful lot of milk missing and decided to follow Huveane as he left the house. His father saw Huveane with the tiny child in his arms feeding it in the stump of a great tree. He waited until Huveane left, took the baby and gave it to his wife. The wife, unsure what to do with it, hid it among the firewood stacked up in the hut. Both Huveane's parents were suspicious about whose baby it was, so they decided to wait and see how Huveane reacted to the child's disappearance.

Huveane was most distressed when he found that the baby had gone, and he ran to the fireside and began to cry. His parents said: 'What's wrong, Huveane?'

'Nothing, it is only the smoke in my eyes,' he replied miserably.

His mother became irritated by his constant self-pity, and eventually told him to go and fetch some wood for the fire. As he dug around the pile for small pieces to burn quickly, he found the child wrapped in sheepskin and he brought the baby to the table and smiled. Huveane called the infant Sememerwane sa Matedi a Telele (the one who causes so much trouble). But Huveane's parents were more than a little concerned by the child. They could not work out how a baby could have appeared, and rumours began to grow in the village that Huveane had something to do with magic – black magic.

Huveane wasn't bothered by this, and growing more confident about his powers, he began to play more and more tricks on his parents. On one occasion, he kidnapped some of his father's lambs and shut them up in a hollow ant-heap. His mother noticed the ewes wandering around the ant-heap and so Huveane's father went and cleared all the stones and boulders away from the entrance and let out the lambs. Huveane was unimpressed and hit his father with a stick, which really only made matters worse.

Now everyone in the village was sure that Huveane could make magic, and they insisted that his father give him some poison so they could be rid of his evil ways forever. But whatever the villagers tried to do to Huveane he outwitted them. He poured the poisoned drink on the ground because he knew what was in his morning milk. He saw the trap they had set for him as he made his way back from the fields and jumped across the great pit, laughing and cursing them. Everything they did to stop him was useless, and they eventually decided to let him be.

One day Huveane found a dead zebra and sat on the carcass to watch over his flocks of sheep. When he returned home, his parents asked where he had been all day, 'Oh, just by the striped hill over there,' he said cheekily. Of course, everyone was curious about the striped hill, and the next day some of the villagers followed him and found the dead zebra. 'This isn't a hill, this is dead game. Whenever you find a dead animal like this you must cover it with branches and plants to keep the hyenas away, and call us so that we can come and collect the meat.'

Huveane nodded, with a very large smile on his face.

The next day, while he was out tending his goats, he found a dead bird. Piling branches and grass all over it, he ran home to tell everyone what he had found. Most of the villagers followed him, believing he had come across yet more game, and they brought baskets and skins to carry back the meat.

This kind of trick did not go down too well with the elders of the village and one said to him: 'This kind of game should be hung about your neck.' So Huveane did just that and pretended to be a hopeless idiot.

He carried on playing his tricks on everyone in the village until he went to live in the hollow tree that had sheltered his child. As for his child, no one knows what happened to it, but it seems likely that Huveane took it out of the world just as easily as he had brought it there in the first place.

HLAKANYANA

Hlakanyana, a chief's son, was able to shape-shift into a weasel whenever he felt like having fun, and this was usually most of the time. Even before he was born, he could speak and was impatient to get into the world.

Once he had been born he walked straight out into the field where his father and elders were awaiting a feast of meat. The men were terrified by this omen that a child that had just been born could walk, and they ran away. Hlakanyana continued to play his tricks on the villagers and his family until their rather dull mortal responses were not enough to amuse him. He decided to set off on his travels to enjoy better adventures.

After some time, he began to get hungry, and just then he came across some bird-traps. He tried to remove the dead birds for his lunch, but found himself stuck to the ground unable to move. The owner of the traps was an ogre. Irritated by people stealing the birds from his traps, he had laid sticks covered with bird-lime on the ground in front of them. The ogre arrived some hours later, but Hlakanyana was not the least bit alarmed, for he knew he could outwit this ridiculous beast, however dangerous he was.

'Don't beat me yet!' he called out. 'Have you a mother?'

'Yes, I guess I do,' said the ghastly ogre.

'Then take me home and clean off this bird-lime. If you kill me here, my flesh will taste horrible and I'll be ruined. I'll be so bitter you'll only want to spit me out. If you take me back to your mother she can cook and clean me and make me taste yummy, yummy, yummy!'

The simple-brained ogre nodded, took Hlakanyana home and handed him over to his mother for an early evening roasting session. Once the ogre had gone for his pre-prandial stroll, Hlakanyana suggested a game to the old woman.

'It's so boring waiting for your son, let's play at boiling each other.'

The old woman shrugged and put a huge pot of water on the fire to boil. As it began to simmer, he said, 'Let me get in first.' She placed him in the pot and covered him with the lid. After a while he asked to be let out.

'This water really isn't hot enough, we must stoke up the fire.'

As they put more wood on the fire, he reached across to the old woman and began to remove her robe-skin.

'What are you doing?' she demanded.

'It's your turn to be boiled, and it would be shame to ruin your beautiful robe. Anyway, you'll soon be eating me and no one will ever know.' He smiled and put her into the pot and covered her with the lid.

'Let me out, let me out. This is scalding my skin, it's too hot, I shall boil!' she cried.

'If you can scream, it cannot be too hot!' he laughed and held the lid firmly down on the poor old woman. When he could hear her screams no longer he put on her robe-skin and lay down in her sleeping place. It was gloomy there, and there was little light for the ogre to see his disguise.

When the ogre returned, Hlakanyana whispered, 'Go and eat the game, my dear. It tastes good. I am tired now and have already eaten. You can help yourself to the meat.'

So the ogre called to his brother, and together they set themselves a wonderful table, cut themselves the best bits of the meat and placed it on the dishes. While they were gorging themselves on their mother's meat, Hlakanyana tiptoed out of the door, threw off the old woman's clothes and scampered away. After a while he stopped, unable to resist calling back to them, 'You are eating your own mother, you stupid cannibals!'

The two ogres ran after him, but this was where Hlakanyana would always be able to trick a mere mortal. As he reached the swollen river, he turned himself into a piece of wood that looked like a branch that had fallen to the ground. The two ogres, breathless from the run and with indigestion from eating their mother, stopped when they came to the river. They could see footprints leading right up to the river's edge. In desperation they threw the piece of wood across the river, thinking that Hlakanyana was over the other side. The piece of wood, now safe on the far side, turned back into Hlakanyana, the weasel, and laughed and jeered at the two ogres, fuming on the other side of the river.

TALIESIN

CELTIC, 600ce

IN the sixth century CE lived a real Welsh bard called Taliesin, who was buried in the village named after him. Although there are no surviving manuscripts of his work, there is a fourteenth-century collection of poems, The Book of Taliesin, which was written by various authors. It is thought that the following tale was recorded in honour of the real sixth-century Welsh Taliesin.

Taliesin (shining brow) was born as a poor farm-boy called Gwion. Nearby lived a witch called Ceridwen, who had given birth to a very ugly and stupid son, whom she could not bear to see. Ceridwen had resolved to compensate for the child's terrible affliction by making him the wisest and most knowledgeable man in the world. She boiled up a cauldron, filling it with herbs and potions, and vowed to keep it simmering for a year and a day. This would produce a magic liquor that would give her son the power of scientific knowledge, intelligence and inspiration. The ceaseless boiling would eventually reduce to only three drops of liquor to provide the magic potion.

But Ceridwen grew bored stirring the cauldron each day and watching the liquid boil and bubble. So she sent for Gwion from the farm next door. 'Gwion, I have a job for you. I stir this cauldron all day and night, but I need to sleep and I need to have a rest from it. It will be your task to stir the cauldron at night.'

The year had nearly ended, and one night three drops of the magic potion spat out of the cooking pot and landed on Gwion's finger. Overcome by curiosity and wondering what this magic potion he had been stirring for months tasted like, he put his finger in his mouth and licked the beautiful sparkling drops of liquid. Instantly he was graced with supernatural powers and with one-third of all the world's knowledge. Armed also with clairvoyant powers, he sensed that Ceridwen would kill him as soon as she arrived, for what was meant for her ugly son, had now been given to Gwion.

Ceridwen returned to the cauldron and found that Gwion had fled and the pot was empty of all the potion. She ran after Gwion in fury and rage, chasing him across the countryside and determined to kill him. Gwion had also acquired the skill of shape-shifting, and although Ceridwen was equally adept at form-changing, she couldn't keep up with his energetic transformations. Gwion changed into a hare, so she changed into a hound; he became a fish and she an otter; then he was a bird and she a hawk. Lastly, he changed into a grain of corn, dropped onto the floor of the threshing barn, and Ceridwen turned into a hen and swallowed him.

Nine months later she bore a son. Guessing this was Gwion but seeing how beautiful he was, she could not kill him. Instead, she tied him up in a leather bag and threw him into the river.

The currents of the estuary carried the bag far out to sea at first, but it drifted back with the tide. Eventually, the bag fell into a weir beside a salmon leap owned by Prince Elphin. One day Elphin went fishing at the weir, and his line hooking the leather bag onto the shore. When he opened the bag and saw the child inside he was dazzled by the beauty of Gwion's face.

'We shall call him Taliesin – he of the shining brow – and he must return with me to my palace.'

So Elphin took the child Taliesin to be his own, and as he grew up he became Elphin's bard. He wrote praises to Elphin and foresaw great fortune for Elphin in the future. Elphin became richer and more favoured by King Arthur, as did Taliesin's powers as seer and poet. His magic seem to work well for those who lived at Elphin's court.

But Elphin began to sing his own praises a little too loudly. One day, at a grand feast in honour of King Arthur, Elphin boasted that he had a lady more virtuous than any at King Arthur's court and a bard and prophet more powerful than any of Arthur's. He was flung into prison and was told to prove his self-glorification. While he lay chained and ruminating on his misery, an evil fellow named Rhun was sent to try to seduce Elphin's wife to prove that she was no more virtuous than a kitchen maid.

But Taliesin second-guessed what was happening and made his mistress hide. He persuaded one of her kitchen maids to take her place by bribing her with jewellery and beautiful clothes. After dinner, Rhun gave the maid a rich mixture of wine and mead and she promptly fell into a drunken sleep. Rhun cut off the finger that now bore Elphin's signet ring, the one Taliesin had so cunningly offered her as a gift.

Back at Arthur's court, Elphin was brought out of prison to defend his claim of his wife's virtue. On seeing the finger, Elphin shook his head. 'This is not my wife's finger, it may be her ring, but this is not the finger of my wife. First, she could not wear this ring on her middle finger and only ever wore it on her little finger. Second, she always cut her nails, and this nail hasn't been cut for weeks. Third, this finger has been making dough in the past three days, but my wife never kneads dough, for why should she?'

The king, seething with resentment because his plan had failed, ordered Elphin back to prison until he could prove that his bard was as brilliant as he had said. Taliesin knew he must now initiate his second scheme. He travelled to the king's court and on the day when the king's own bards and minstrels were due to play before Arthur, Taliesin appeared in the great hall and sat quietly in one corner. As the musicians passed him by, he pouted his lips and began to play 'blmmm, blmmmmm', with his finger against his lips. Now under Taliesin's spell, the minstrels could play only 'blmmm' on their lips with their fingers.

King Arthur was furious and shouted at them, 'Are you all drunk, or just stupid!'

The head minstrel bowed to Arthur and pleaded, 'My lord, we are not drunk, but under a spell that has been cast over us from the spirit who sits in the corner like a child.'

Arthur demanded that Taliesin come forward. Bowing graciously, he began to sing his story to the king. But his performance brought with it a great storm outside. The castle shook and rain fell in torrents against the walls. Arthur sent for Elphin. He shuffled into the great hall, the chains dragging between his feet. But the music of Taliesin's voice and harp was so powerful a magic, that the chains fell to the ground, snapping apart before the king.

Arthur conceded that Elphin had been right about both his wife and his bard. Taliesin was called many times to Arthur's court to sing and give out his prophecies. He even once led Arthur to the underworld, Annwn, to steal the Cauldron of Plenty.

GLOOSKAP

NORTH AMERICA, 1000ce

GLOOSKAP is both a creator-god and a highly renowned trickster-god among many of the North American peoples, especially among the Algonquian-speaking peoples of the forests and plains of the northwest. Glooskap means 'liar', but in spite of his name, it is not Glooskap who represents evil, as his first conflict with his twin brother Malsum, the wolf, reveals.

Glooskap and his brother, Malsum, were born together. From the body of their dead mother, Glooskap made the sun and moon, the creatures of the world and the human race. But Malsum made terrible things, such as monsters and serpents, or inconvenient things, such as mountains and oceans, just to antagonize and provoke conflict within the human race. But there was no way this co-existence could last forever, especially as each brother had a secret about his own mortality.

One day Malsum asked Glooskap: 'So what is your great secret, dear brother? What is the only way that you can be killed?'

Glooskap felt certain that Malsum would be discreet and honourable, so he confided in him. 'My life can be ended only if an owl's feather touches me.'

Glooskap asked his brother what his secret manner of death was, and Malsum told him that he could die only if the root of a fern pierced his skin.

The cruel Malsum had no remorse. He found an owl's feather and stabbed it into Glooskap's arm, and Glooskap fell dead immediately. But much to Malsum's horror, Glooskap came back to life almost as quickly, jumped up and picked the root of a fern, which he pushed into Malsum's arm. Malsum died instantly and his body was absorbed into the earth, his own mother's being. But his spirit lingered on to haunt the lower world as a vengeful wolf.

So Glooskap fought to prevent the world from falling into more corruption, and he battled against the evil monsters that had infested the world when Malsum had lived. He made people from handfuls of earth and created fairies and dwarfs and other small creatures and supernatural beings. He sought out badness and yet was always fair and gentle in his dealings with mankind. Sometimes he was even humorous and always ingenuous. He outlawed the evil spirits and battled with the giants who ruled the mountains.

One giant sorcerer, named Win-pe, was one of the most evil and powerful of the giants on the earth. He was so tall that his head rose above the highest pine trees. He lived a wretched existence, feasting on both people and animals. He was merciless, and his magic was so powerful that no one dared approach his mountain hideaway – except for Glooskap.

When Glooskap saw the great magic giant, he merely chuckled to confuse the stupid monster and grew his own head until it reached as high as the stars. Then, laughing as if he had made a joke, he leaned forwards and knocked the sorcerer on the head. Win-pe fell down to the ground dead.

But Glooskap had other problems with the human race. The more he conquered and destroyed the evil forces of the world, the more the human race seemed to go its own way and create its own problems. In fact, the people he created seemed to get less wise as time went on. Eventually, they began to exude as much evil as the monsters and the magicians he had fought with for so long.

Glooskap couldn't face this for much longer and resolved to quit the world and let the human race stew. He made a plan that in seven years he would depart and during that time he would grant to anyone who came to him any request that they made. This seemed fair to him. Of course, he made it difficult by living in an inaccessible region, and if he felt that those who reached him came with selfish or manipulative requests they would be suitably punished.

On one occasion four Indians managed to find his secret dwelling. Glooskap asked the first one why he had come. 'My heart is full of evil and I've become a slave to anger. I want to be meek and humble, not driven by rage.'

The second man was poor and wanted to be rich, the third was despised by the people of his tribe and wanted to be respected for himself, and the fourth was vain. This last man was conceited and full of selfish pride. He was taller than the others but had stuffed fur into his moccasins to make him even taller than everybody else. His desire was to be greater than any man and to live longer than anyone else.

So Glooskap pulled out four small boxes from his bag and gave one to each man. He told them that they must not open their boxes until they got home. Each man opened his box alone in his lodge. Inside each of the boxes was richly fragrant oil. The intoxicating perfume was impossible to resist, and they massaged it into their skin.

The angry man became tolerant and gentle, the poor man became wealthy, and the despised man began to gain the respect of his fellow-men. But the conceited man had stopped in the forest clearing on the way back to the camp. He had not listened to Glooskap, because he thought he was always right and could do exactly as he wanted. Opening the box before he got home, he took a sniff of the wonderful ointment and began to rub it into his skin. His wish was granted. However, it was not exactly what he expected. He did grow very tall, taller than everyone in the tribe, because he was changed into a lonely pine tree, the first of the species and the tallest tree that the forest had ever known.

Glooskap often boasted to a certain woman that because he had conquered most of the demons and cunning sorcerers of the night, there was really nothing or no one left to challenge and he was becoming bored, complacent and arrogant about his powers. But the woman laughed and said, 'I think you have forgotten one evil being who remains unconquered, for nothing, no one can overthrow him.'

'Don't tell me there's still an invincible being whom I can trick and with whom I can play games. Tell me who it is?'

'His name is Wasis. But I really do think you should avoid any dealings with him.'

Glooskap instantly wanted to confront this powerful being, but to his surprise found that the great Wasis was only a baby. The child sat on the floor sucking on maple-sugar and gooing and aahhing. Glooskap's knowledge of the world and mortality had made him shrewd and cautious. He thought the only way to approach this being was in as natural a way as possible. He was unused to dealing with babies, but he smiled sweetly at the child and beckoned to Wasis to come to him. The baby smiled back at him but refused to budge. So Glooskap made funny noises and beautiful bird-like whistles to attract his attention. But the baby ignored this and went on sucking his sugar and rocking himself on his bottom, totally oblivious to Glooskap's silly attempts to attract his attention.

Glooskap was dumbfounded. How could a baby be so obstinate? Usually his tricks and antics worked, and now this child was not even responding to his guile. He became angrier and angrier, lashed around in circles and ordered Wasis to crawl over to him at once or he would do terrible things to him. Instead, Wasis burst into a ghastly howling himself, louder even than the god's own ranting and raving. The baby still did not budge.

Glooskap was now brimming with fury and summoned his most magical resources and tricks to his aid. He spoke terrible spells and sang horrifying incantations, burned offerings and smoked out the lodge with strange concoctions, but still the baby sat and gurgled. Even the devil was sent running to the depths of the netherworld at the horrific churnings of Glooskap. And Wasis smiled. He had grown bored with the god's rather silly games. Glooskap rushed out of the lodge, humiliated by the power of the tiny child, while Wasis sat triumphantly on the floor crying 'Goo, goo'.

To this day Indians still believe that when a baby says 'Goo', he is remembering the time he had power over the great Glooskap.

Eventually, the day came when Glooskap had planned to leave the earth. As any trickster-god would do, to celebrate his departure he organized a wonderful feast on the shores of Lake Minas. Every creature of the forest and mountains came, and as the festivities drew to a close, Glooskap paddled past them on his canoe and continued up the streams of water and air until he drifted further than anyone could ever see.

He paddled on east beyond the sunrise, and his enchanted singing grew fainter and fainter until it died away on the wind. And the beasts who had always understood one another became confused and began to speak in different languages so that they became scared and ran away. The creatures feared man, and men went to hunt them because they could not understand one another.

So mankind and the creatures of the earth believe that when Glooskap returns on his canoe, the world will be in harmony again.

BLUE JAY

BLUE Jay is a trickster-god, who changes in and out of human and bird form and appears in many of the myths of the coastal peoples of Oregon and the inland plateau groups. His adventures often resulted in major changes in the natural world and usually show the hero's skill in outwitting his rivals. Blue Jay also appears further south among the Jicarilla Apache of the south-western of North America. Here he is part of lengthy cyclic tales that give him the power to create a way of life for all living things.

'Ioi is always telling lies, Ioi is always telling lies,' was Blue Jay's favourite tease for his sister Ioi.

But Ioi's frustration with Blue Jay's antics soon reached crisis point. Ioi decided that it was time for him to take a wife from among the dead people. A wife would help her with the work in the house and in the fields, but Ioi insisted also on one stipulation: that the woman must be old. Blue Jay liked the idea of a wife, but he totally ignored Ioi's request to take an 'old' dead wife and instead married a chieftain's daughter who had just been buried and had died young from an arrow through her heart.

Ioi scowled when she heard that the wife was young. 'You must take your wife to the Land of the Supernatural. The people will bring your wife back to life.'

So Blue Jay set out with his wife to the Land of the Supernatural. It took him a day to get there, and he was tired and bored with his errand, thinking that Ioi was getting back at him for all the times he had squawked and cajoled her.

The people of the Land of the Supernatural asked: 'How long has your wife been dead?'

'Just a day,' replied Blue Jay.

'We cannot help you,' they shook their heads. 'This town is not for people who have been dead for only one day. You must take her to another place especially for those who have been dead for a day.'

So Blue Jay carried on his journey, following the route that the people had described. Eventually he came to a smaller town and asked the inhabitants if they could restore his dead wife to life.

'How long has she been dead?' they asked.

'Two days,' said Blue Jay.

The people shook their heads. 'Sorry, we can't help you. We restore to life only those who have been dead for one day. But there is another place you can visit where they bring back people who are two days dead.'

So Blue Jay moved from town to town but was always a day late, until after five days he arrived at a town where the people felt sorry for him and restored his wife from the dead anyway. They made Blue Jay their chief and for many moons he lived happily. But Blue Jay became restless in the Land of the Supernatural. There was no fun and no one to tease, so he and his wife set off for his home in the natural world.

On his return, the chief's son heard that Blue Jay had married his sister after she had died, and the boy ran quickly to his father to tell him the news. The chief was outraged that Blue Jay had married his daughter after her death, and demanded that Blue Jay give him all his feathers as a payment for marrying her. The chief sent a messenger to Blue Jay's lodge, but Blue Jay refused to acknowledge the chief. After all, the daughter had died and he owed nothing for a dead woman, did he?

A gathering of the tribe and the chief around Blue Jay's lodge alerted him to their disapproval. Smiling at the fun of it all, Blue Jay turned himself into a bird and flew out of the window. He soared up across the trees of the forest without a word, his wings and feathers fluttering silently. The wife fell to the ground, fainting with fear when she saw him transformed into a bird before her very eyes. There was nothing the chief or any of her family could do – she never recovered, and Blue Jay never returned, no matter how much they called for him to save his wife. She finally journeyed to the Land of the Souls.

Blue Jay had other trouble with wives when the ghost people came one night and took his sister Ioi. Blue Jay found it hard living without her. He needed someone to torment and tease, and after a year of idleness he set out to look for her. But the creatures of the natural world didn't know how to find the country of the ghost people. No matter whom he asked, he always had the same answer: 'How am I to know a place that is supernatural?'

In the end Blue Jay managed to find his way to the country of the ghost people by transforming himself into a 'spirit' who could travel freely between the ghost world and the real world. The ghost people's country was rocky and barren, and he found Ioi surrounded by heaps of skeletons.

'Hello Blue Jay,' she smiled. 'It's good to see you, even though you are such an irritating brother. These skeletons are your in-laws. When there's no one around they rise up and look like people, but loud noises scare them and they turn to bones. If you are quiet you will find them quite pleasant enough.'

So Blue Jay went fishing with his youngest brother-in-law. It was fine for a while, but Blue Jay suddenly started singing a very loud and raucous tune and the boy immediately crumbled into a heap of bones. Blue Jay thought this was an excellent way to pass the time, and began quite callously to sing loudly as often as he could and enjoy watching the crumbling body turning to a heap of bones in the canoe. This was the kind of trick he loved to play, but it didn't get him very far with the rowing.

Every time he thought they had caught a fish, Blue Jay found his net full of leaves and twigs, which he threw them back in the river. Each evening he returned from fishing and told Ioi there were no fish to catch.

Ioi said, 'But those leaves and twigs were really fish. Fancy throwing them away! In the country of the ghost people everything is not as it seems, even you are not what you seem, Blue Jay.'

Blue Jay reminded himself of his favourite line, 'Ioi is always telling lies anyway', which made him feel somehow better about the fishing incidents.

Blue Jay never tired of playing games and pranks or fooling around with the rather dull and uninspiring ghosts. He often swapped the skull of a child with that of a man and made them come alive, so that when they did they looked hilariously funny – to Blue Jay, at any rate.

When Blue Jay returned to the land of the Chinooks a message was sent from the people of the Land of the Supernatural, challenging the Chinooks to a diving competition, the loser to forfeit his life. The Chinooks never refused a challenge and Blue Jay agreed to dive on their behalf. As usual, he had a trick up his sleeve. He placed some bushes in a canoe and before diving with his opponent, he chucked the bushes in the water while the tribe and the people from the Land of the Supernatural were arguing about who should go first. It was agreed that Blue Jay and the woman opponent should dive together and see who could last the longest. But when Blue Jay's breath began to give up he rose to the surface, hid his head under the floating bushes and took another deep breath. He quickly dived down in the water again and called out, 'Where are you?'

The gasping woman replied foolishly, 'Here I am' and, of course, began to lose her breath more quickly than Blue Jay, who repeated this cunning trick four times.

As he dived down for the fifth time he found the woman lying on the bottom of the ocean floor, nearly unconscious. Carrying a club hidden under his pile of bushes, he struck her on the back of her neck with one mighty blow. He rose to the surface and claimed he was the winner.

The people of the Land of the Supernatural marvelled at Blue Jay's success, and they suggested a climbing competition, which he won again by cheating. This time he placed a huge glacier up in the sky. It was so high that it touched the clouds. The supernaturals had chosen a chipmunk to race him to the top, and when they reached a certain height the chipmunk began to tire and close her eyes. They were nearly in the clouds, and the people far below them could hardly see them. The sun shone down, casting sharp light into their eyes from the face of the icy rock. Blue Jay pulled out his club, hit the chipmunk on the neck so that she fell to the ground and flew up to the summit where he again proclaimed himself the winner.

TEZCATLIPOCA

ONE of the great shape-changers of Aztec myth is the highly diverse god Tezcatlipoca (fiery mirror). He carried a mirror shield from which he took his name and in which he could see all the reflections of mankind, its past, its present and its future. He was perhaps one of the most destructive and violent of tricksters. Originally the sun-god, Tezcatlipoca was driven from his position of power by another god, who from then on became his enemy.

Tezcatlipoca became the god of sorcery and magic and of darkness. He was known as Telpochtli (young man), Yoalli Ehecatl (night wind) and Yaotl (warrior). As the night wind he was feared by mankind and was known to bring destruction and chaos as he whirled through the night searching for people to terrify. He would chose lonely people walking along paths and scare them as he hurled his dark wind across their backs. Stone benches were made especially for him to rest on and were placed on main pathways. They were often concealed beneath trees and low bushes so that he had somewhere to lie in wait for his victims at night. If any man could overcome his power he could ask for any wish to be granted from his chosen deity. However, no one dared.

Tezcatlipoca took on other forms than that of the wind. His popularity as a deity grew and his subsequent cult-following was linked to the myth that he was the principal deity of the Aztecs. He overthrew the Toltec peoples who were ruled by the great god Quetzalcoatl. It was against this powerful god, who had vied with him as originator and creator, that most of his anger and vengeance was directed.

The Toltec era had been the golden age, when light, peace and contentment ruled the world. Tezcatlipoca began his ruthless overthrow of this empire by undermining Quetzalcoatl's confidence in himself. He would hold his mirror in front of Quetzalcoatl and remind the great god how old he was, and how he, Tezcatlipoca, could make him beautiful by dressing him in robes of feathers and turquoise masks. He would hold up the mirror again to show the god how young and dashing he now looked, and the desire for youth made Quetzalcoatl more and more distressed that he was getting old.

Then Tezcatlipoca offered the old god wine and earthly delights that lured him from his spiritual practices to the mortal indulgences of man. Wretched with his debauched and immoral acts, Quetzalcoatl became ashamed and full of self-loathing. He began to question his own right to lead the Toltecs but could not yet leave his people. So Tezcatlipoca now turned his attention to the people, and proceeded to torment and enchant the Toltecs until their empire disintegrated and light left the world.

First, he changed into a great performer, and the people wanted only to

258

sing every morning, day and night. As they continued singing and dancing, they began to fall down in exhaustion and die because they could not keep up with the power of Tezcatlipoca's rhythm.

Next, he changed into a great warrior and persuaded thousands of men to join him in battle, then he would change shape and kill all those who had followed him. In his many different guises, he lured people into traps only to destroy them. The Toltec people were eventually wiped out and Quetzalcoatl could do no more and was forced into exile. Quetzalcoatl departed the land. He reached the eastern seashore and put on his feathered cloak and his turquoise mask. He climbed on a raft of serpents and drifted away towards the sun. Tezcatlipoca ruled again as he once did as creator-god.

Other shapes that Tezcatlipoca took on were a black jaguar on earth, and in the sky the great bear constellation. His servants were usually demons and wizards, and he could gaze in all directions and see everything at once without being seen himself. Other forms included that of a nude and beautiful man who set young woman's hearts on fire, seducing them to lust after other male mortals.

But his most favoured trick was to take on the form of a skeleton who would hover in dark woods, waiting for his victims. Beneath his ribs was a throbbing heart and the ribs would open like a trap door to reveal the great beating muscle. The mortal test was to steal his heart, the only way to conquer him. Only the bravest would dare thrust their hand between his ribs to try to tear out this heart. Anyone who succeeded would be offered all the wealth and happiness in the world as long as they put it back again. Of course, he was also a liar.

Because his magical resources were exhaustible, cult rituals included a yearly sacrifice in which a live man's heart was torn out of his body and offered to Tezcatlipoca's altar. But he used the power of his mirror to help those who were good and to punish the wicked. Knowing all human intentions and desires enabled him to help mortals as well as to harm them. His guise as destroyer and trickster was a highly voracious one, but it was perhaps this extremist cult that gave the invading Spaniards their main excuse for exterminating the Aztecs.

ICTINIKE AND THE RABBIT

SIOUX, NORTH AMERICA, 1000CE

ICTINIKE was a highly regarded trickster in the myths of the Sioux people of the plains of North America. He was the son of the sun-god, and there are many tales and myths surrounding his tricks and pranks, most of which involve his main adversary, the rabbit.

After being banished from the sky by his father the sun-god, Ictinike set off across the earth and met the rabbit. Ictinike was, of course, amused at such a creature as the rabbit and in best trickster form pretended he was overjoyed to meet him and called the rabbit 'grandchild', as if he were one of his own. The rabbit was rather pleased that the god had chosen him for some mission, and agreed to help Ictinike in any way he could. Ictinike was his usual artful self and pointed up to the sky at a bird that was circling the heavens above them.

'Shoot that bird down to earth with your bow and arrow, and you will be rewarded,' said Ictinike slyly. So the rabbit shot the bird with his best gleaming arrow and the bird plummeted towards the ground. However, its body landed in the highest branches of a tree.

'You'll have to fetch the bird for me, rabbit. I cannot climb such a high tree.'

The rabbit wasn't particularly keen on climbing the tree himself, but he couldn't really refuse this great god. He took off his own skins to make it easier to push his way through the branches and began the hazardous ascent. But as he climbed higher and higher he realized that he was stuck and couldn't get back down. Ictinike sniggered from the bushes below, and knowing that the rabbit was well and truly stuck, put on his skins and laughed all the way to the nearest village, proud of his new-found attire.

The skins were a great success in the village, for the chief's two daughters were entranced by the virile stranger dressed in beautiful furs. The younger daughter was jealous of her older sister's beauty, and when Ictinike decided to marry the older daughter, she stormed off into the forest to weep and wail. Marching angrily through the deep forest, she suddenly heard a soft voice calling from somewhere above. She looked up into the canopy of trees and there was the rabbit stuck to the sap that was exuding from the tree trunk. She climbed up, cut off the branch and lit a fire, which melted the sticky gum so that the rabbit was free.

'How did you get stuck in that tree?' asked the girl as they shared some berries that the rabbit dug up from the grass.

'Not a pleasant story,' said the rabbit. 'I was tricked by a god who took my best skins so that he could walk on this earth. I have to find him and get them back.'

'He must be the stranger who came to our lodge. He's married my sister, after fooling you and rejecting me.'

The rabbit stood up. 'Take me to your lodge. I am going to get my own back on this trickster-god!'

Together they walked to the village and found Ictinike and his wife. She laughed at the strange skinless being that her sister had brought back. A great eagle appeared in the sky and Ictinike turned his bow and arrow towards it, but missed. The rabbit loosed an arrow, too, and brought the eagle down to the ground with one shot. Every morning one of the eagle's feathers turned into another bird, and each time Ictinike shot and missed, and the rabbit always managed to kill it. This began to wear out Ictinike's skins, until they were falling off him, from wear and tear and sweat and pride.

The rabbit offered Ictinike a brand new blanket of cow-hide, not telling him the rest of the hide had been made into war-drums. Every time the drums were beat, Ictinike's blanket jumped up and down, and jerked and sent Ictinike into a whirl of shaking and juddering through every bone in his body. He eventually jumped up so high that he fell and broke his neck. The rabbit was quite pleased with his own trick and with Ictinike's death.

From that day on, for half of each day, the sun hid his face behind a mask in mourning for his child, Ictinike.

CONIRAYA

INCA-QUITO, SOUTH AMERICA, 1200CE

CONIRAYA was a trickster-spirit who continually maintained that he was the one and only creator. His main skill was deception, and he spent most of his time disguised as a mortal, a poor ragged Indian man.

One day Cavillaca, a beautiful woman, who was greatly admired throughout the region, was weaving beside a fragrant lucma tree. Coniraya was renowned for his seductive powers over women, but Cavillaca was so enchanting that he dared not touch her. Instead he changed himself into a bird of paradise and flew to the top of the tree. Mixing it with some of his own semen, he pounded some of the lucma fruit into a mash and dropped it at the feet of Cavillaca. The girl was about to have her lunch, and picked up the fruit and ate it ravenously.

Some time after this encounter, Cavillaca gave birth to a son. For many years she wondered who had been the father and resolved to find out. As the boy grew older, she became more and more curious to find out the father's identity. She summoned a sacred meeting to which the gods were invited to announce who was the father of the boy. All the local men dressed in their finery, hoping that they would be chosen by the gods to be her husband.

Hearing of the girl's distress, Coniraya disguised himself as a beggar and stood among the impatient suitors. The girl asked the spirits to answer her through their sacred objects, but no one made a sound and no spirit came to her. None of the assembled men dared suggest that they were responsible, for it was for the gods to speak, not they.

But Cavillaca was desperate to find the father, so she sent the child out into the middle of the gathering, knowing he would crawl into the lap of his own parent. The child waddled straight across to Coniraya, gurgled at him and smiled. He sat in the rags of Coniraya's lap, and the men gasped in horror that a beggar could claim to be Cavillaca's husband.

Cavillaca was disgusted at any possible alliance with such a dirty creature. To think that she may have been impregnated by a poor tramp! She fled to the sea-shore near the sacred city of Pachacamac and sat tossing stones into the water, not daring to think of her wickedness. But Coniraya followed her and transformed himself into a magnificent chief. He called to her across the beach and told her to look at him now.

'Look at me, Cavillaca, I am handsome, I am rich. You thought I was a poor beggar, but really I am a proud and worthy chief.' Cavillaca dared not look back at him, remembering only his filthy rags. She ran into the sea to cleanse herself of the carnal encounter she had with such a despicable creature, and she and her child were instantly turned to rock.

Coniraya searched everywhere for her. First, he met a condor and asked him if he had seen a woman. The condor said that he had seen her quite near by, so Coniraya blessed the bird and said that if anyone killed it, that person would be killed also. Next he met a fox, who just shrugged his shoulders and said Coniraya would never find the woman. So Coniraya told him he would always have a terrible smell, and because people would detest him so much he could only ever venture out at night.

Next came a lion, who said Coniraya was getting closer to Cavillaca. So Coniraya told the lion that if anyone killed him, the lion would have the power to punish all murderers and criminals, because his skin would be kept intact and worn at festivals and ceremonies. The lion would always be honoured, even after death. Another fox gave bad news and so did two parrots, who were cursed with having calls so loud that they would be heard from far away and their enemies would always find them.

So Coniraya blessed those who gave him good news and cursed those who gave him bad news. When he came to the sea he discovered that Cavillaca and the child had already been turned to stone.

The great god Pachacamac had two beautiful daughters who guarded a serpent who lived in the caves by the sea. While this serpent slept the daughters would dance, but while he was awake they were to feed him with every fish that came out of the water-goddess's lake. The great Pachacamac would not allow any fish in the ocean, for the serpent was to devour them all. When Coniraya arrived at Pachacamac he found that the deity had turned Cavillaca to stone because she had dared to jump into the sea. Knowing it was too late for Cavillaca, the great trickster decided to take his revenge on the god.

The two daughters danced while the serpent slept, so Coniraya disguised himself as an otter-man and visited their home. He seduced the elder daughter and made love to her, but the younger girl changed into a pigeon and flew away, scared of his power. Coniraya came every day to the older girl as she danced and had sex with her, and each time he came she forgot about the serpent and left the fish in a pool inside the cave. Coniraya visited her for many days, and each time she left the fish in the pool and the serpent went hungry. She was so infatuated with Coniraya that she didn't notice the fish swimming out of the pool down a narrow stream formed by the growing level of the pool water. Coniraya was pleased, for now there would be fish in the ocean, enough for every man. The serpent would not be the only one chosen by Pachacamac to eat fish.

When Pachacamac found out that his daughter had been seduced by an otter-man, who had stolen his fish and given them to the sea, he set a trap for Coniraya. But the god did not know that Coniraya was a trickster and a shape-shifter, and before he had time to churn the seas and fill the underwater caves with foaming water, Coniraya had transformed himself into a fish, slithered down the stream into the open sea and was heading back home. He returned to Huarochiri and resumed his usual form, dressed as a poor Indian, to play more tricks on mankind. After all it was easier, and safer, than clashing with a great god.

MAUI

POLYNESIA, 1600CE

MAUI is a trickster-god who appears in more myths and tales across the vast area of Polynesia than any other god. Maui stories can be found from New Zealand to as far across the Pacific as Hawaii. Like all tricksters, Maui is ingenious and a friend to man, sometimes kind and sometime cruel. He deliberately challenged the authority of the gods to make the world a better place for mankind, but his behaviour, often verging on the ridiculous, was laughed at by mankind, so that the gods began to grow concerned about his meddling. He tried to achieve immortality for man as his last great heroic act and in the process failed and died.

Taranga was a wise woman who had four sons. One day as she walked beside the sea-shore she gave birth prematurely to another child. This child was Maui. But the baby seemed dead and lifeless and as floppy as a jellyfish, so Taranga wrapped Maui up in some of her hair and chucked him into the sea. Maui got caught up in the seaweed, and as the shoals of jellyfish came rolling back to the shore with the tide, Maui was dragged along and gently washed up onto the sand.

On the edge of the beach the seagulls tried to peck him to bits and horrible flies swarmed around him looking for somewhere to lay their eggs. The great god Tama, seeing the deformed creature on the beach, took pity on him.

Tama hung him up from the roof of the sky to dry like a damp sponge. Once Maui had dried out in the warmth of fire, the old sky-god breathed life into him and set him back on the shore.

The sea-nymphs looked after him, but by now Maui was a mischievous boy, and he set off one night to find his real mother. When he reached her house she was in the middle of a great celebration and was about to kiss all her sons as a blessing. So Maui joined the end of the queue and when she bent down to kiss him he spoke, 'Mother, I am your son, too.'

At first she didn't believe him, but he told her the story of his escape from the sea. She was overjoyed and loved him better than any of her other sons. Yet his mother, Taranga, would disappear from the house every day. Every morning, before the children were awake, she would secretly creep out, so young Maui decided to follow her and see exactly what she was up to.

One night he got up and stuffed rags into all the gaps in the house so that no chinks of light could get in at dawn. Taranga overslept and the dawn light did not wake her as usual. When she eventually rose to the brilliant light of the morning sun she rushed out of the house. Maui followed her into the woods. Gathering up a clump of rushes from beside the stream, she seemed to disappear down a tunnel, placing the clump back above her head as she descended.

Maui transformed into a pigeon with the help of his mother's white apron. This turned into the feathers and down. He flew quickly down the tunnel into the darkness below. The tunnel was narrow, but he dived and ducked as rocks and crags tried to tear at his wings. He came to a huge cavern, which opened into a garden filled with trees and plants. Maui flew into one of the trees and perched above his mother and his father, who was Makea, her secret lover, the king of the underworld. Maui chucked some berries on their heads and they looked up in surprise, not able to see him hidden in the branches. So Maui fluttered down to the ground before them and threw off the feather apron. He was now no longer Maui the child, but Maui the fully grown man.

Maui stayed and lived with his parents in the underworld, but he began to use his magical powers to increase his power. He starved his grandmother to death so that he could get hold of her magic jaw-bone and then arranged for the sun to slow down so that people would have more daylight and less night.

Maui wanted to be immortal more than anything, but his father, Makea, suggested to him that it might be more enlightening to take the secret of fire back to the upper world.

Maui enjoyed the challenge of finding out the secret of fire so he got up one night and put out every fire that had been lit in the houses of the villages. The next morning there was no fire and no cooking, so Maui volunteered to go and fetch some from the keeper of fire in the underworld, the goddess Mahu-ika.

Maui's mother warned him how dangerous this mission was. Maui shrugged his shoulders and set off into the darker regions of the underworld to the place that Mahu-ika lived. The ancient goddess rose up like a flame as he approached her dwelling, demanding to know what he wanted.

'I need some fire to do my cooking. We are all just eating raw fish and it's getting boring.'

'Where are you from?' She loomed above him like a great ball of fire.

'My mother is Taranga and my father is Makea.'

'I did not recognize you. If you are my grandson as you say, you can certainly take some fire.'

Mahu-ika plucked out one her fingernails, which contained fire, and gave it to him. He ran off down the path and threw the fingernail on the ground, trampling on it until the fire was extinguished. He returned to Mahu-ika and demanded more fire. 'The fire you gave me went out,' he said. 'Please let me have another.'

So the great fire-goddess pulled another fingernail and gave it to Maui. Enjoying this particular jape, Maui carried on putting out the fires and going back to the fire-goddess nineteen times, until she only had one toenail left. But even Maui's impudence was liable to outrun his luck, and with the request for her last toenail, Mahu-ika became furious and instead of giving it to Maui, she hurled it into the upper world where the earth caught fire.

Like a mighty forest fire, flames raged across the land. Maui transformed himself into an eagle to escape the flames, but his wings were singed as he soared above the inferno. Realizing that the fire might destroy mankind, he knew he had to put out the terrible fire and called on the gods of storm to create a deluge of rain upon the earth. The wind whipped up the flames to rise even higher, but the rains were torrential and heavy enough to dampen the fire. The forest was turned to black sticks and steaming heaps of ash.

Mahu-ika managed to save a few of her fire sparks and tossed them into the trees as she fled back to the underworld. From then on the villagers would be able to make fire by using firesticks, and fire would no longer be the goddess's secret. Maui was, in fact, quite pleased with the way things had gone now that people knew the secret of fire. He resolved to carry on with his good works for mankind.

Maui's other great art was to help ladies in distress, and one day he heard about a woman whose husband was a great eel, a monster of the deep. This eel-monster, Te Tuna, was mostly fish. The woman had became bored with having sex with a fish and wanted to enjoy the pleasures of human flesh. Maui decided to volunteer for this particular deed.

With friendly birds as his companions, Maui's gang danced across the islands as if they were stepping stones. He arrived at the tiny island and spent several days and night enjoying sex with this lonely woman. Unfortunately, Te Tuna was in amorous mood himself. Just as Maui was about to kiss the woman good-bye and creep back home, the sea-monster burst out of the ocean heaving with lust and coiled his great penis around the island. The waves crashed on to the shore, the breeze turned to a wind and the island shook and shuddered as he flailed his ugly way up the beach towards his wife. Maui was not in the least bit scared of the monster. He took the monster's penis and used it to thrash the monster's head until he fell back into the sea, surrounded by blood and his own eel-like slime.

Te Tuna slid back into the great depths of the ocean and was never seen again. As for Maui, he visited the woman on many occasions afterwards, and some say she even became his wife.

Fully aware that Maui was only half a god, Maui's father reminded him that one day he must die. He suggested to Maui that he challenge the great goddess of death and seek immortality for mankind. In addition to being Maui's ancestor, Hine Nui, the goddess of death, was extremely destructive. Makea pointed across the horizon towards a place that flashed with lightning and the land rose steeply to the sky.

'You will find her there. But be careful. Hine Nui's eyes are what makes the sunset so blood-red. Her mouth is like a barracuda, and her teeth are as sharp as slivers of volcanic glass. Her hair is like tangles of seaweed, and her body like that of a man. You may find her indestructible.'

But Maui was not deterred by this extravagantly evil portrait his father had painted. He'd met worse adversaries in his life. So he set off towards the sunset with his friends, the small birds of the forest, and found the great goddess of death sleeping. He whispered to the birds not to make a noise until he made a sign.

'I'm going to creep up between Hine Nui's thighs and get inside death's womb, there I will surely find the answer to immortality. But do not make one sound until you see me reappear between her jaws.'

So Maui slithered between death's thighs and entered her, until only his legs were left sticking out from her vagina. The birds thought this hysterical, but one bird unable to contain his giggles for a moment longer, made a sudden little cheep. Hine Nui woke instantly, and clenching her muscles, she crushed Maui inside her vagina until he was dead.

There is an old Maori saying: 'Men make heirs, but death carries them off.'

OLIFAT

COSMOGENIC myths are rare in most of Micronesia, the area of the South Pacific from the Mariana Islands north of Guam, to the Carolines and the Marshall and Kiribati island groups. Creator-gods or supreme deities are few in this part of the world. It is the tricksters and semi-divine offspring who seem to be favoured in most epic myth cycles and stories. Although the trickster tales are usually filled with humour, there is often an underlying reminder of how difficult it is to live in the naturally hostile environment of sea, storms and vast emptiness.

Olifat was best known as a trickster whose pranks sometimes caused death, but mostly made fools out of mortals. In the Caroline Islands he was also known as Iolofath, Orofat and Yelafath. Like many tricksters, he was the son of a mortal woman and a god, in this case the great god Anulap. Olifat was notorious because his sole concern was to prove how superior he was to mankind, at the same time as amusing himself to avoid the mortal condition of boredom.

His birth was similar to that of many other tricksters in that it was highly unusual. His mother's long ebony hair was twisted up into a knot, held fast by a coconut leaf. One morning, as she pulled the leaf out to release her hair, Olifat fell from the knot. Olifat was highly precocious and matured very quickly. His father, Anulap, had warned his mortal mother that Olifat must never be allowed to drink from a coconut that had a small hole. But Olifat did so, and because he had to tip his head back so far to catch the last of the milk through the tiny hole, he looked up at the blue sky and saw his father in the heavens.

Olifat determined to visit him immediately, and jumping on to a column of smoke that spiralled out of a small fire, he rode up to heaven. Olifat was not popular in heaven. At each stage of his journey, the sky children found he was more likely to sabotage their games than join in with them. He gave the scorpion fish they were playing with real spines on their backs; he gave sharks a menacing set of teeth and the normally docile stingray real stingers on his tail. He plagued many of the gods by upsetting their cooking vessels, keeping them awake when they wanted to sleep and even raping their daughters as he turned from boy to man.

When he arrived at the highest level of heaven, people were busy building a house for the spirits of the dead. Olifat enthusiastically offered to help dig the post-hole. But the men were highly suspicious of the stranger. Olifat was astute as well as being a prankster, and he guessed that the builders were likely to kill him. He hid in a special hollow at the bottom of the post-hole, and as the men rammed the post in, thinking they were crushing Olifat at the bottom, he threw out handfuls of red earth and chewed up green leaves. Seeing the green slime spewing out all over their feet and earth turning to red, they thought Olifat's blood and guts had spurted out of the hole.

Convinced that Olifat had died they plugged up the hole. Olifat asked the termites to help him tunnel through the bottom of the post and up through the wood, until the ants reached the rafters. There Olifat perched on the beams until he saw the men returning to the spirit house. With a piece of taro and a coconut he banged around in the rafters crying 'Soro!' a word that implies a superior being. The men were afraid of this great spirit in the rafters, but his father saw him and ordered him to get down.

After that Olifat would often sit among the beams and rafters of houses. He would send sparks from his fiery fingers to burn out the whole roof of a house. Sometimes he would make holes in the beams until they cracked and the house fell down, then he would call for his friends the termites and the red ants to come and eat their way through the beams.

In fact, Olifat was more aggravating than helpful, and fouled other men's wine, swapped good eggs for bad and came to be the biggest seducer of women of all the gods. It was only through death that mankind could ever escape his ridiculous tricks; yet the dullness of death only made mankind long to return to life and put up with the antics of Olifat.

TJINIMIN

ABORIGINE, AUSTRALIA, recorded 1600CE

IN the myths of the Murinbata peoples of the Northern Territory there is a trickster of the Dream Time called Tjinimin (bat). Like most tricksters he was full of energy and potential for any kind of amoral activity, but Tjinimin's energy was of a particularly lustful kind.

In one version of the myth, Kunmanggur, the rainbow snake, was a powerful sexual fertility deity who was challenged by the lascivious antics of Tjinimin, the bat.

The rainbow snake was consort to the green parrot girls, who were the most beautiful women in the land. One day the parrot girls felt like escaping from the watchful eyes of the great rainbow snake. His rather intense passion and sexual possessiveness made them long for some light-hearted fun. They ran off on the pretence of searching for food, but as soon as they were out of sight of the rainbow snake's eyes, they began to dance naked in the sunlight. Tjinimin had always had a rather lustful eye for the parrot girls, and when he saw them sneaking out of the camp he decided to follow. His excuse for leaving was that he was going to visit the flying fox people. He crept down to the ravine, and seeing the parrot girls naked and alone, jumped on them. The parrot girls were taken by surprise as he forced them down on the rocks and raped them all. The girls were so humiliated that they were determined that he should be punished for his lascivious attack.

The next day they went back down to the same river, knowing that he would chase after them. This time they crossed the dried-up river and climbed up the ravine on the other side, from where they sent hordes of killer bees to sting him and a torrential river to sweep him out to sea.

Tjinimin was carried down the ravine by the sudden force of the swirling waters, but the rocks and boulders were enough for him to cling to and he dragged himself out on to dry land.

He saw the girls above him at the top of the ravine and called to them to help him out, still lusting after them, even now. They laughed to one another and threw him down a rope so that he could climb up. But just as he got to the top they hacked through the rope and he fell to the rocks below, breaking every bone in his body.

Tjinimin was a trickster and, gathering all his magical powers about him, he restored his own bones. He practised on his nose first, by tearing it off his face and putting it back. Now that he had proved to himself that his own magic was as powerful as that of the rainbow snake, he resolved to destroy the rampant snake and take the parrot girls for himself. He created a magical spear, which he pretended was the rainbow snake's, and when he returned to the camp, he hid it.

Next, he organized a great celebration. The diver bird came and warbled songs, and Kunmanggur played his pipe while Tjinimin seduced everyone into dancing. His own sexual antics excited the women into ecstasies of desire, and when they were at the peak of their orgiastic experience, Tjinimin drew out the spear and thrust it into the rainbow snake. At that same moment every one of the dancers turned into flying foxes or birds. Tjinimin ran as fast he could but no one dared to chase him.

The great rainbow snake wriggled across the countryside trying to find some way to stop his blood from flowing. Wherever he rested, water would flow from the rocks creating great rivers and waterholes. Finally, he came to the sea and, writhing among the crashing waves of the ocean, he gathered up all of the fire in the world, placed it on his head as a head-dress and dived to the bottom of the sea. Those who had followed, saw him disappear beneath the waves, the fire extinguished as it touched the water. Now no one knew how to make fire, nor to bring back light or heat. The rainbow snake had kidnapped fire.

But Pilirin, the kestrel, showed the people how to make fire with two sticks. By rubbing them together they could summon the fire-spirits that lived deep within the wood itself.

So the world was saved by the kestrel, and Tjinimin only ever ventured out at night again. From then on, he always slept hanging upside down and kept his eyes on the stars in the sky, so as not be reminded of the fires of sexual desire in the world below.

SEVEN

BEASTS
AND MONSTERS

PERHAPS IT IS THE BEASTS, whether of the imagination or those of the natural world, that have inspired myth-tellers throughout civilization to fabricate the weird and the incredible.

Mythical animals bring us closer to the divine, as well as closer to our own fears, feelings and the projections of those fears from our unconscious world. Monsters and beasts of the mind are as real as the lions and tigers, snakes and eagles that fill myths with a richness that reflects the universe itself. These beasts are another aspect of our search for a meaning in life. In mythology the beasts within us are often manifest as terrible monsters and demons outside of us. Even natural animals take on an identity that appears to symbolize a specific human characteristic. Foxes often represent cunning and snakes sexuality, while giants and ogres depict the fears that haunt us, and spirits, nymphs, sirens and Rakshasas are those unconscious parts of ourselves that we are unable to access directly. This selection of myths reveals not only the common bond of fear and the fertile imagination of the peoples of the world, but also the stark truth that what we chose to alienate in ourselves can often come back to haunt us.

THE EAGLE

CHALDEAN mythology included many monsters and animals, sometimes as symbols of power and sometimes as totemic forms of the gods themselves, including such creatures as the winged bull, goats, the four dogs of Murdak, the pig connected to the sun-god of Nippur and the eagle, which was a symbol of the sun-god of Kis.

The eagle was feeling extraordinarily hungry and decided that nothing would be better than a tasty meal of serpents. The great eagle told his family that he intended to devour the serpent's children, and one of his older, well-educated offspring warned his father that if he ate the serpent's brood he would certainly incur the wrath of the god Shamash. But the eagle wouldn't listen to anyone. He was determined to pluck the young serpents from their nest and eat them in the sky.

Soon after, the eagle did exactly that. Swooping down on the tree where the serpent family had nested, he destroyed the branches and nests that held the tiny serpents in safety and ate each serpent as it fell from the tree through the air.

When the huge serpent returned and found all his children eaten by the eagle he appealed to Shamash for help. Shamash listened carefully to the serpent and told him how to avenge the death of his family.

'You must follow the path that leads into the mountains. There you must hide yourself inside the carcass of a dead ox. Tear open the body and all the birds will come down to feed from its entrails. The eagle will come with the rest and when he does you must circle him quickly and squeeze the life out of him, then bite him with your poisonous fangs. When he is truly dead you must cast him into a pit.'

The serpent agreed, and setting off along the road to the mountains he soon found a body of an ox. He split open the carcass and snaked his way inside between the ribs to hide. A few hours later, in the midday heat, the flies buzzed around him laying their eggs in the flesh and drinking the blood of the ox. Soon he heard the cawing of birds and the flapping of great wings in the air. Hundreds of carrion birds swooped down to eat the flesh, but the eagle was wary and had a suspicion that something was wrong. So he stayed away until the other birds had feasted and he became hungry and desperate for food.

'There is no choice,' he said to his family. 'We must eat the flesh of this ox like everyone else.'

But the same young eagle who had already warned his father against killing the serpents, spoke up. 'Beware father, I am sure that the serpent lies in wait for you. I have a feeling that he hides inside the body and that he may be going to kill you.'

But the eagle laughed. He wasn't scared of a serpent, and anyway, there was hardly any meat left and he was ravenous and greedy. So he swooped down, circled a few times just in case the serpent really was there, and, overcome with hunger for the delectable meat, he took his chance, landing on the ox's belly. As the eagle ripped the flesh from the ox's side the serpent seized him in his jaws and held him so tightly that he could not move. The serpent's body quickly coiled around the eagle until his breath had almost gone. The eagle tried to plead for mercy, but the serpent squeezed even tighter and closed his fangs across the eagle's neck. The dead eagle was thrown into a pit, and from that day on no eagle has ever dared to kill a serpent.

GANESA

INDIA, 900BCE

GANESA, or Ganesh, is the Hindu god who solves problems and generally brings good luck to any enterprise that is begun. He is a pot-bellied man with yellow skin and an elephant's head that has only one tusk, and he has four arms. He holds a shell, a discus, a lotus and a club, and he rides a rat who is the reincarnation of a demon-king. There are several explanations for his appearance and of his parentage, and either Shiva or Parvati is credited with creating him.

One account suggests that Shiva was particularly fond of surprising Parvati as she bathed and demanding to have sex with her in the bath-tub. Parvati became intensely irritated by this lascivious male intrusion into her bathroom, and one day she scraped all the dead skin off her body, mixed it with oil and balms and moulded it into a man's body, then gave it life by sprinkling it with water from the Ganges. She told this creation, Ganesa, to stand outside the bathroom and guard her from anyone who tried to enter. Of course, Ganesa did not know who any of her visitors were and challenged anyone who approached. When Shiva turned up and found his way barred by an irate guard, he cut off Ganesa's head and stormed into the bathroom and demanded to know why Parvati had placed a guard outside. She was overcome with grief when she heard that Shiva had killed her creation, so Shiva quickly sent messengers to find another head for Ganesa. It seemed the first creature they came across was an elephant and it was this head that they placed on Ganesa's shoulders.

Another version of Parvati's claim to Ganesa's parentage is that she prayed to Vishnu for a son. Once the child was born she was so proud of him that that she wanted all the other gods to see how beautiful he was. The gods

came and drooled over his looks, except for Sani, who
at the ground. Cursed by his wife, Sani burned to as
he looked upon with a single gaze. But Parvati, convin
would be immune to such a curse, pressed Sani so m
at the beautiful child. As soon as Sani's eyes looked u
head caught fire. Parvati was filled with rage and turne
son, cursing him with lameness to add to his already

But Brahma came to Parvati's aid. If she found
would be restored to life. So Shiva set off in search
being he came across was an elephant asleep by the Ga
and brought it back for Parvati's son.

Another myth explained Ganesa's strange app
Parvati threw her bath-water into the Ganges. The el
drank some of the Ganges a few moments later and g
phant-headed son. Shiva rescued the deformed and u
rible fate, gave it to Parvati and ensured it had only one

Several myths credit Shiva as Ganesa's cre
approached by the other gods to create a being who c
deeds, so that human success or failure depended o
invoked at the outset of all enterprises. Shiva took s
how he could produce such a creation and turned to g
he did so, a beautiful youth, endowed with his own qu
own face, and all the gods were amazed and enchante
All except Parvati, who was immediately jealous that
duce such a stunning son without her. In her rage, sh
ness, a pot belly and an elephant's head. But Shiva dec
his own son, and that he would be great among the go
worldly affairs. He would be the barometer of huma
was to be propitiated before the commencement o
insignificant or great. His invocation would suggest
would mean failure.

Several reasons are suggested to account for Ga
myth explains that Ganesa was asked by the great sa
the epic poem, Mahabharata, which has about 180,00
is a blend of myth, poetry and philosophical reflecti
Hindu culture. Ganesa cut off one of his own tusks
sure that he understood every word before he wrote it
the Mahabharata's 'editor', and for this feat of endura
the patron god of literature as well as of luck.

A slightly more involved myth relates that one o
was visited by Parasurama (one of Vishnu's incarnati
the entrance to the palace and refused to let Parasura
visitor was not of any great importance and his fath

ng woken. But on repeating his thoughts aloud Ganesa found
rama provoking him into a fight. Before he could stop himself, Ganesa
the man into the air with his trunk, and as Parasurama staggered from
und, he threw his axe at Ganesa. Ganesa instantly recognized the axe
e belonging to his father, for Shiva had given the axe to Vishnu before
been incarnated as Parasurama. Ganesa felt sure that he must honour
her, and he took the full force of the blow of the axe on one of his tusks
split off from his trunk. Parvati was furious when she saw the damage
esa's tusk, but before she could put a curse on Parasurama, Brahma
ned and promised her that Ganesa would be honoured and wor-
d by all the other gods.

anesa and his brother, Karttikeya, were rivals in the pursuit of two
n, Siddhi and Buddhi, who were both only allowed to be married to the
nan. Ganesa and Karttikeya agreed to have a competition to decide who
marry both the women. They would race around the complete circuit
world, and whoever finished first would take both women to be his
Karttikeya set off to travel around the world and for many months he
yed until he returned worn out and dejected. On his arrival home he
Ganesa already married to the two girls. Ganesa had travelled the whole
world in the course of his studies, and had learned about the whole
edge of the world. In this sense he had completed the journey long
his brother, both spiritually and intellectually. His poor brother was
broken, but Ganesa's wisdom had proved him dedicated in heart.

GARUDA, THE BIRD KING

INDIA, 900BCE

RUDA had the body and limbs of a man, and the head, wings, talons and
eak of an eagle. His face was white, his wings were red, and his body was
den and dazzling that he was mistaken for Agni (the fire-god) when he
atched from an egg.

a was the bird-king, who could fly faster than the wind. His mother was
one of Daksha's daughters, and he was born hating everything evil.
w around the world devouring all that was bad, and he particularly
snakes, a sentiment that arose from the tragedy that had befallen his
r, Vinata.

nata had an argument with Kadru, the mother of many serpent chil-
This argument concerned the colour of the horse, Uchchaisravas, who
eated during the churning of the milky ocean. They both agreed that
er was wrong about the horse's colouring would be imprisoned by the

other, and unfortunately for Vinata it was she who chose the wrong colour. Kadru's serpent children imprisoned Vinata in the underworld, so Garuda immediately set off to release his mother from the terrible serpents. The serpents demanded a ransom for her release, refusing to give her up unless Garuda brought them a cup of *amrita*, the god's prized drink of immortality.

Garuda knew he had no choice and set off for the celestial mountains where the *amrita* was kept on the highest peak, surrounded by a ring of flames that leaped high in the sky and a great wheel of fire spiked with deadly knives. But Garuda was not disheartened by this. On his great golden wings he swept down to the world, drank all the water from all the rivers and returned to the wall of flames, dowsing them with water until the fires went out. The revolving wheel of knives was not a problem for him either. Shrinking to the size of tiny fly, he flew quickly between the narrow gaps of the knives.

His next barrier took the form of two fire-spitting snakes, which guarded the *amrita*, so he blew dust into their eyes, and while they were screaming with pain and momentarily blinded, he cut them to pieces. He snatched the *amrita* and flew back with it to the underworld.

But the gods were not pleased that Garuda had stolen their precious amrita, and Indra hurled his mighty thunderbolt at Garuda. But Garuda smashed it to pieces and continued on his way towards his mother and her captors. The serpents freed Vinata, but just as they were about to drink some of the *amrita*, Indra snatched the cup away from them. A few drops of the *amrita* fell to the ground in the struggle, and the gluttonous serpents began to lick up the few tiny drops to become immortal. Yet the powerful *amrita* also divided their tongues, and to this day serpents have forked tongues and renew their skins each year.

Because Garuda had the power to steal the *amrita*, no god now dared challenge him and he was given immortality and a place of honour as Vishnu's steed.

In a different account it is the moon that the serpents requested as ransom to light the underworld. So Garuda set off to capture the moon. Knowing it was a long journey, he stopped to rest near the pole star, the home of his father Kasyapa, the god of time. Garuda was hungry and asked his father for food. Kasyapa pointed towards a lake where an elephant was fighting with a tortoise. The tortoise was seventy miles long and the elephant was twice as high and wide, but Garuda grabbed them in his talons and put them into a tree a thousand miles high because he did not like to see evil in the world. The branches of the tree began to break under the weight, but Garuda remembered that he was hungry so he plucked them out of the tree and ate them instead.

He continued his journey and when he found the moon, he tucked it under his wing and flew off to the underworld. Down in the darkness the gentle light of the moon at once began to bring a pale, ghostlike luminosity to the underworld. The gods were furious. They needed the moon in heaven and snatched the moon back before it could become full. To make sure that Garuda stayed on their side, the gods conspired to free Vinata from the underworld themselves, gave Garuda his immortality and made him Vishnu's charioteer.

THE NAGAS

INDIA, 900BCE

THE Nagas were a race of serpent-gods who were the sons of Kadru and descended from Brahma. In the tale of Garuda's quest to release Vinata from the underworld they were depicted as evil (see page 277), but they could also be like humans and behave ambivalently, whether with altruism or scorn. Although most of the Nagas were demons, a few also obtained immortality by licking the *amrita* that fell to the ground when Garuda rescued Vinata.

These strange snake-gods could also take on any form of human or snake form they wished; sometimes they were half-snake, half-woman, sometimes warriors with snake-like necks. Some of them had five hoods and some seven. They wore superb jewels that lit up the underworld, or they lived in fabulous jewelled palaces in the air or under the sea. The Nagas were the servants of Indra, and the jewels were the water droplets that Indra brought as god of rain.

They often carried the rain on behalf of Indra, and sometimes withheld it if they were feeling indifferent. Those serpents who were connected to the gods were often more virtuous, like Sesha, who was king of the Nagas and the world-serpent upon whom Vishnu sleeps. Sesha lies coiled when the universe is at rest and his seven hoods shade Vishnu from evil. Ananta is also a symbol of the eternal, as he grabs his own tail in his mouth and supports the heavens. Another of the Nagas, Muchalinda, supposedly protected Buddha by coiling round him seven times when he was threatened by a great storm as he sat meditating under the bo tree.

THE RAKSHASAS AND THE DEMON-KING RAVANA

INDIA, 900BCE

THE Rakshasas in Hindu myth represent evil. They do not, however, confine themselves to engaging with the gods; rather, they directly attack mankind.

Ever since they were created by night, the Rakshasas have stealthily crept around the world in different forms, emerging from their mother, night, when all light was gone. They are hideous and grotesque in appearance, but often adopt many different guises to hide their real monstrosity. They range from dwarfs to giants and from multi-limbed grotesque animal horrors to wolves and vultures. Some appear as night demons, with red eyes and lolling tongues, who stalk cemeteries. These are called children of anger, who bring dead bodies back to life and eat the flesh. There are demons who make men insane, and those who attack holy men; there are those who haunt the heads of men and make them do foolish things; and there are Rakshasis, the female equivalent, who can bewitch and enchant men into frenzies of demonic lust. They can slip into and out of body orifices when least expected, and the only thing they fear is fire – and mustard.

The most famous Rakshasa of them all was Ravana, the demon-king. Ravana had originally been a creature of heaven, but he had insulted Brahma and was given the choice of being re-born seven times as Vishnu's friend, or three times as Vishnu's enemy. He took the easier way out, believing that Vishnu would dispose more quickly of his enemies than his friends, and thereby securing himself a place back in heaven sooner. In his first incarnation he was known as Hiranyakashipu and he murdered everyone and anyone who got in his way and was finally destroyed by Vishnu.

As his second incarnation, as Ravana, he was a particularly nasty piece of work. Not only was he a breaker of all laws, but a seducer of other men's wives. He was a horrific monster with ten heads, bulging red eyes, twenty arms, and teeth like the gaping jaws of a dead wolf. He could grow as tall as a mountain and he raged around the world engulfing every being he met. He raped or destroyed in such a foul and cruel manner that even the sun stopped in its course and the oceans were afraid to turn the tides. He could churn up the sea and scatter the tops of mountains around like peas popping out of their pods. He was completely immune to anything the gods themselves could do to destroy him, because only a mortal could in the end destroy him. He had many battles with the gods, and was suitably scarred by Indra's thunderbolt, Vishnu's discus and Airavata's tusks. But it was Rama, one of Vishnu's avatars, who was born on earth specifically to destroy Ravana, who eventually defeated the terrifying and monstrous demon-king.

In his last incarnation, as Sisupala, he was cursed with three eyes and four arms but was more of an irritation to Krishna than the foul, evil murderer of his last incarnation. However, after many conflicts with Krishna, Sisupala finally went too far by insulting and attempting to kill a notable king. Krishna intervened just as Sisupala drew his sword. The discus of the sun fell down and split Sisupala's head in two and carved right through his body down to his legs until he fell into two pieces on the ground. Sisupala's soul left his body in a rushing whirlpool of flames and swirled about Krishna's feet. It became absorbed into the god's own body, and as Ravana became unified with Krishna, he was allowed to return to heaven, forgiven, having paid the chosen price of three lives as Krishna's enemy.

GREEK BEASTS AND MONSTERS

GREECE, 750BCE

GREEK myth is full of demons and beasts, from Medusa to the Sphinx, from the Furies to the giants; these monsters represented the dark unconscious sides of our nature. Some Greek monsters were gentle and guarded a precious treasure, but others caused destruction on land and in the sea. The savage beasts, such as the centaurs and satyrs, who were part-human, part-animal, are more representative of our ancient instinctive wildness.

TYPHON

Typhon clouded the whole of Greece with darkness when he stretched himself out fully. His mother was Gaia, mother-earth, and his father, Tartarus, the bottomless chasm beneath the underworld. His name means 'smoke', and he was formed out of a misty smoke from which grew a hundred dragons' heads. His arms and legs were thousands of snakes, his mouth spat molten rock, and his eyes were like fire.

He was born to avenge the defeat of the earth-giants in the battle for control of the universe. As soon as he was created, he rampaged about the universe and tried to destroy Olympus. The gods were terrified and ran away to Egypt where they disguised themselves as animals.

Zeus was forced by the mocking Athene to return and fight the monster and he made a rather pathetic attempt at killing Typhon with one of his famous thunderbolts. The monster was merely weakened, grabbed Zeus in his serpent-like hands and took him to a cave on Mount Casius. He hacked out Zeus's sinews so that Zeus could not move, but Hermes replaced the sinews in Zeus's arms and legs so that he could chase after Typhon. This time Zeus used his brain, for he knew that Typhon had the strength of a thousand gods. Typhon began to throw rocks and mountains at Zeus, so this time Zeus hurled his thunderbolts at the rocks. The mountainous rocks shattered in mid-air, and enormous splinters and chunks of mountains crashed back at Typhon, tearing at his flesh so that he bled all over the mountains. Eventually Typhon was defeated and some accounts of the myth suggest that Zeus picked up Mount Etna and slammed it down on top of Typhon, who was forced down through the earth's crust and remained in Tartarus forever.

Together, Echidna, the sea-monster, and Typhon created a terrible brood of creatures: Cerberus, the three-headed hound of the underworld; the Hydra, a multi-headed water-snake who lived at Lerna; the Chimaera, a serpent with the legs and body of a goat and a head of a lion; the Sphinx, which tormented Thebes; and the Nemean lion.

THE CHIMAERA

The Chimaera breathed fire from her monstrous lion's head. Her body was half-snake, half-goat, and she was the most hideous creature in existence. For some time she was kept as a pet by the King of Caria, but she escaped and lived on a mountain in Lycia.

King Iobates of Lycia sent for Bellerophon and challenged him to a test of strength, whereby he had to kill the Chimaera. Bellerophon, a mortal, was not totally without fear and so asked the gods for help. He was given a bow, a quiver full of arrows and a spear tipped with lead. The gods also helped him tame Pegasus, the winged horse, and he flew above the Chimaera's cave, shooting arrows at her until she was weakened. He finally hurled his spear between the open jaws of her lion's head. The lead-tipped spear melted to molten lead from the heat of her fiery breath, and she choked to death. Bellerophon tossed her body into a volcano and went back to the king, believing he would set him no further tests. However, for Bellerophon this was merely the first of many tests, which eventually led to his sad downfall.

The Chimaera's name was often used for any monster that was fantastic or improbable like herself.

THE HYDRA

The Hydra was a less romantic monstrosity. She roamed the swamps of Lerna, and her lair was beneath a plane tree at the source of the River Amymone. She had nine snake heads, one of which was immortal and protected her from death. The other heads were mortal, but if one was cut off, another would grow in its place. She had a dog-like body and a dragon's tail that was so powerful it could snap a man in two with one blow. The snake heads were so venomous that even her breath could kill, and her blood was so poisonous that one drop of it could freeze even a god's veins. Just the powerful and foul odour from her urine could end a man's life with one inhalation.

One of Heracles's labours was to destroy the Hydra, and Athene had contemplated for some time the best way to destroy it. Hera had been responsible for rearing the Hydra as a threat to Heracles, and she prepared to aid the Hydra when she knew that Heracles was on his way.

Driven to Lerna in his chariot by Iolaus, Heracles remembered to follow Athene's advice. He forced the Hydra out of her lair by shooting burning arrows until she arose from the terrible murky depths. Heracles held his breath to avoid breathing her terrible vapours and venomous breath, jumped upon her back and began to batter her heads with his clubs. But for every head he managed to crush, another grew in its place. Heracles fell back on to the edge of the bottomless lake at the middle of the swamp. Hera, realizing that now was her chance to intervene, sent a giant crab to scuttle out of the swamp and nip at Heracles's ankles in an attempt to drag him back into the lake. Heracles cried out to the charioteer, Iolaus, for help. The youth stamped and kicked at the crab until he managed to crush it beneath his foot. Iolaus set light to a branch he had pulled from a tree. This time, as Heracles attacked the Hydra's snapping heads for the second time and managed to crush one at a time with his club, Iolaus would rush in with his blazing tree stump and seared the roots of the growing heads with the fiery branch so that they were destroyed.

Finally, only the immortal head was left. Heracles took Iolaus's sword and severed the slimy head, part of which was made of gold. The head hissed and spat from the ground where it fell, and Heracles buried it under a great rock. He disembowelled the still writhing carcass and dipped his arrows in her blood, which then proved fatal to any mortal or god. He threw the bits of her body back into the swamp, which foamed and turned to a terrible sludge.

Hera was furious, but rewarded her ally the crab by setting it in the sky as one of the constellations of the zodiac, Cancer. Heracles's reward was not as great, for Eurystheus, the setter of his labours, decided that killing the Hydra did not count as one of the feats, because Iolaus had given him the blazing branches and Heracles had not destroyed the Hydra alone. He was duly set another task.

THE SPHINX

The Sphinx, or Throttler, was a monstrous woman, with the face and breasts of a female, the wings of an eagle, the body of a lion and the tail of a serpent. Hera had sent her as a curse on the city of Thebes, and it guarded the only pass that led to the city and punished all who entered or exited the city. This was Hera's retribution for Thebes having been the hiding place for one of Zeus's illegitimate sons, Dionysus.

The Sphinx would ask all those who wished to pass by her a riddle. If they failed to give the correct answer she would throttle and devour them on the spot. The riddle was: 'What walks on four legs in the morning, two legs at noon, three legs in the evening and is weakest when it walks on the most?' It seemed that no Thebans could answer this riddle, and many mortals were instantly gobbled up, including children.

Oedipus, however, fresh from unwittingly murdering his own father,

Laius, and remembering the inscription carved across Apollo's temple, 'Remember you are a mortal', shrewdly gave the answer to the riddle. He shouted up to the Sphinx: 'The answer to your riddle is man, for man crawls on all fours as a baby, walks on two legs as a man and leans on a stick in old age, which is three legs, and is of course weakest as a baby.'

The Sphinx, horrified that Oedipus knew the correct answer, threw herself off the cliff and smashed into tiny pieces on the rocks below. As a reward for ridding Thebes of the terrible monster, Oedipus was made king of Thebes and unknowingly married the widowed Jocasta, his own mother.

The Greek Sphinx has nothing to do with the Egyptian Sphinx, a benevolent symbol of royal power and the rising sun.

THE NEMEAN LION

This was the monster killed by Heracles as his first labour. Although most accounts assume it was the offspring of Typhon and Echidna, other versions say that at Hera's instigation Selene, the moon-goddess, moulded the lion from sea-foam and breathed life into it. Whatever its origins, the Nemean lion lived in a cave not far from Nemea and feasted on the people. It was a huge beast with a skin so thick that it could not be penetrated by any weapon, whether of iron, bronze or stone. From its teeth drooled the blood of its victims, and its claws were as sharp as razors.

Heracles arrived in Nemea and took thirty days to find the lair. When he approached the cave he found the lion returning from a day of slaughter, its mouth dripping blood, its legs weary and its belly almost bursting with its contents of human flesh. Heracles knew that this was as good a time as any to attack the lion, while it was sleepy and full from gorging. First, he shot his arrows at the beast, but they merely bounced off the lion's thick skin, and the lion continued to lick his lips and yawn. He tried his sword, but this bent in half as soon as it touched the lion's hide. There was only one place left to try. Heracles raised his club and slammed it right down on the lion's soft muzzle. The lion looked up, and shook its head, dazed not by the blow but by the ringing in its ears, and retreated into its cave to sleep. Heracles ran after it, knowing the only thing he could do was to fight it face to face and attempt to strangle it. Heracles wrestled with the sleepy lion, lost one of his fingers between the lion's razor-like teeth and, with his arms around the beast's mane, he closed his hands on its neck and choked it to death.

The people of Nemea honoured him, and as a reward for himself he skinned the lion by using the lion's own claws (the only things sharp enough to tear through the hide), made the skin into a cloak of invulnerability and used the head as a helmet.

Hera set the lion as a constellation in the sky and made it the sign of the zodiac, Leo.

CERBERUS

Cerberus means 'pit devil', and this monster had anything between three and fifty monstrous dog heads and a hundred serpent-tails. Cerberus guarded the entrance to the underworld and prowled forever at the gates to stop intruders from the upper world. The dead were allowed to pass by as shadows, but the only way the living could get past his terrible fangs was by devious means. Orpheus lulled him to sleep, Aeneas drugged him, and Heracles terrified him.

Heracles's last labour was to bring Cerberus back alive to King Eurystheus. Heracles decided that the only way to gain access to the underworld and to capture the monster was by using his own strength rather than cheating or enchanting his way there. Heracles was guided by Hermes and Athene, for whenever he became exhausted by his labours he would cry out to Zeus, and Athene would come rushing down from Olympus to comfort him. By now, as this was his last labour, he was worn out and exhausted. He was also angrily committed to finishing off his last adversary. His determination in facing the last hurdle was enough to terrify even the old ferryman, Charon, who ferried him quickly across the River Styx.

Even the ghosts fled as Heracles stepped ashore, and his brandishing sword and fierce, warlike glances gave him easy access to Hades's realm. When Heracles demanded Cerberus, who had already run away whining to his master, Hades agreed, as long as Heracles could catch him without resorting to arrows or clubs. So Heracles approached the dog, who had been chained to the gates and caught him by his neck. Heracles was wearing his protective lion-skin cloak and Cerberus's flailing serpent-tail and snarling teeth could not find any way of penetrating the lion's skin and Heracles's grip was so powerful that the monster succumbed. Clamping an iron chain around the dog's neck, he led the docile Cerberus back to the Styx and the passages that lead to the upper world. As the dog emerged into the light, he hid his eyes from the sun and began barking and hissing with all his heads, and the saliva that flew from his mouth across the land gave seed to the poisonous plant, the aconite.

King Euystheus saw the terrible monster Cerberus approaching across the fields, and he ran in fear. So Heracles unchained the dog and let him run back to the underworld, his last labour now complete.

SIRENS

The Sirens (those who bind with a chord) were beautiful sea-nymphs, originally the three daughters of the river-god Achelous and the Muse, Calliope. The daughters had inherited their exquisite singing voices from their mother, and they were loyal and devoted handmaidens to Persephone, the daughter of

Zeus and Demeter. When Hades stole Persephone and took her to the under-world, the Sirens could not hear her calling out to them, and they begged the gods to give them wings so that they could search the world for her. Other accounts suggest that because they failed to help Persephone, her mother, Demeter, turned them into monsters. But most versions agree that they were first bird-like, with women's heads and lions claws, and only later when they became known for their alluring and fatal call to sailors did they gain a repu-tation as fair and beautiful temptresses.

The Sirens lived on a remote and barren island at one of the entrances to the underworld. They sang every time a ship passed by, hoping that Persephone would hear them. Their voices were so hypnotic that no mortal who heard could resist them, and the ship would move closer and closer to the edge of the underworld. Every time sailors came too close, the Sirens would realize that Persephone was not there, and they would tear the sailors' bodies apart with their terrible claws, sending their souls unburied to the underworld. Odysseus was probably the only one who managed to pass by the Sirens without being lured to his death. He told his men to plug their ears with wax, while he tied himself to the ship's mast so that he could not be lured by the Sirens' magical singing and so escaped from their enchantment.

HARPIES

The Harpies (snatchers) were so ghastly that even their own parents were revolted by their appearance, and they were secreted in the deep caverns of the underworld. They were possibly the daughters of Gaia and the Old Man of the Sea. It is not known exactly how many there were, but they had such names as Ocypete (swift), Aellopus (hurricane), Celaeno (dark one) and Podarge (racer). They were also known as goddesses of storms and were feared as snatchers of the weak or the wounded on battlefields, when they car-ried away the injured or children without warning.

Originally they were thought of as beautiful winged goddesses, but they evolved as monstrous beings, half-bird, half-woman. They had bronze talons and they darkened the sky as the flew across the earth in search of bodies to snatch.

Phineus had been blinded by the gods because his prophecies came true too often, and the gods also cursed him with a pair of Harpies as his com-panions. The ghastly, winged creatures would drop their poisonous, slimy droppings all over his table at every meal. They pecked at his eyes and snatched his food away and fouled it so that it not only stank but was inedi-ble.

Jason arrived and wanted Phineus to tell him how to recover the golden fleece. All Phineus could say was: 'First get rid of these Harpies, and then I can help you!' So Phineus laid on a feast for the Argonauts, and the Harpies descended immediately and began to play their disgusting tricks. But two of the Argonauts, the winged sons of the north wind, Calais and Zetes, chased the Harpies across the sea and far away to the edge of the world. Here, they became whirlwinds that spun so fast and in such a tight spin that they tangled each other up. They occasionally stopped spinning when the north wind forgot to keep blowing in their direction, and only then did they prey on unwary mortals again.

CHINESE BEASTS AND MONSTERS

CHINA, 300BCE

WEIRD and wonderful monsters and dragons abound in Chinese mythology. Fragments still remain of a book that may well be over 2000 years old called *Shanhaijing* ('The Book of Mountains and Seas'). This is an extraordinary encyclopedia of the strange and terrifying creatures that the ancient Chinese believed existed on earth, and it was originally recorded as if the writer had first-hand observation and experience of these oddities. Here is a selection of vivid portraits of these monsters and beasts from the *Shanhaijing*, followed by two short Chinese myths that encompass the oriental fondness for dragons and giants.

There are strange people living in Qizhong whose feet point backwards. They walk on their toes because their heels are at the front of their legs, but some people claim they actually walk backwards.

In the southwest there are creatures with foreheads that stick out and chests that rise like great panniers above their heads.

There are birds called Biyi, with only one eye and one wing, and if anyone can ride on the back of one when the bird is flying he or she will live a thousand years.

In the southeast are creatures with small wings and beaks, but they are human in form. They have long white hair and red eyes and their heads are distended like ostrich eggs.

Further south are more creatures who are half-human and half-bird, but they use their wings to support them like legs, waiting beside the seashore to catch large shrimps between their beaks. It is thought they are descended from a man who committed suicide in the South Sea.

A little further to the east are creatures who are like monkeys, but they eat charcoal while it is still burning and carry the embers with them. They are always roasting, and no one can touch them without being singed. Still further to the east there are some strange mutant creatures, who are black from the waist down and hold snakes in each hand. But they also have a green snake hanging from one ear and a red snake hanging from the other. This is the same as the witches who live in the west who travel from Mount Dengbao to the heavens with messages for the spirits. In the same place are strange beasts like pigs but they have a head at each end of their torso.

Further west, in the state of Xuanyuan, are creatures with human heads and snake bodies. They live for thousands of years and some say they are descended from the great Yellow Emperor. Their tails curl up round their necks and the youngest die after 800 years, and because they are so old their tails curl round and round in such a tight grip round their necks that no one can unfurl them even when they are dead.

In the South China Sea lives a band of mermaids and mermen called Jiaoren. These sea-creatures weave at their shuttles all night long and can be heard by those who stand on the beach or go out fishing on still, moonlit nights. The Jiaoren cry like people, but their tears turn into pearls. They have beautiful skin and wild hair that reaches down to the ends of their tails. If they are given wine, their skin turns the colour of peach blossom.

THE GIANT WHO TRIED TO CATCH THE SUN

Youdu was the underworld in the north, where all things were black. In the reign of Ho Tu, Youdu was a great dark city. Here lived black snakes, black wolves, black tigers; and all the plants and trees and mountains were black. Youdu had a gatekeeper, a monstrous and ferocious giant called Tu Bo, but he was glamorous compared to the blackness of everything else. He was endowed with a tiger's head, three eyes and shining silver horns. Tu Bo would hunt out the weak spirits and the ghosts of Youdu in search of blood, for this was his main source of nourishment.

On the edge of the wild mountains further north, well away from the terrible city of Youdu, lived a race of powerful giants who were descended from the King Ho Tu. They looked terrifying, with snakes hanging from their ears and snakes in each hand, but they were dull-witted and gentle. One of the ancestors of these kindly giants was called Kua Fu. Every day Kua Fu would watch the sun set below the horizon, and he would grow increasingly angry with the resulting darkness. He said to the wild mountainside: 'Every day we have to put up with this terrible darkness; I've decided to go and catch the sun and fix it to the sky so that we can have light forever.'

Feeling pleased that he had finally made the decision to do something about it, he hurried off in the direction of the setting sun. He took giant steps over mountains and rivers, striding across lakes and valleys, carefully avoiding crushing anything beneath his feet. Eventually he came to a place called Yugu (deep abyss), where the sun always set. He was exhausted from his long journey and sat down for a moment, bathed in the wonderful warm red glow of the sun. He stretched up his hand to catch the sun but was suddenly taken with an unbearable thirst. He got up and strode across to the Yellow River, lay flat on his belly and drank the whole river in one go. He was still terribly thirsty and so went to the Weishui River and gulped all the water from that, too. But Kua Fu's thirst would not leave him, and, growing hotter and hotter, he decided to travel to the Daze Lake in the north. Surely a thousand miles of water would quench his thirst?

Again his strides took him quickly across the mountains, but as he travelled he grew steadily weaker and weaker, until he fell to the ground, his eyes still gazing on the last ray's of the sunset until his lids closed and he died. Poor Kua Fu's quest for eternal light was now ended.

In the morning as the sun rose in the east, the giant's body could not be seen for he had changed into a mountain. A grove of peach trees had grown quickly from the side of this mountain, and the succulent and delicious fruit would always be there for anyone who passed by instantly to quench that person's thirst.

THE DRAGON-LOVER

In China the dragon has a divine nature, and it was said that the first ruler of the Xia dynasty, Yu, was himself a dragon. Yu had achieved many claims to fame with the help of dragons, as had King Shun, who had dug out hairy dragons from an earth's vein and kept them in a special pen to feed and care for them. The Xia dynasty had a special affinity with dragons, and so did King Ji.

King Ji ruled during the end of the Xia dynasty, but he was very different from many of his predecessors, for Ji believed in fairies and ghosts, was hedonistic in the extreme and had a passion for gold. He was addicted to hunting and had an insatiable appetite for beautiful women, as well as for exotic food and vast quantities of wine.

Ji kept two dragons, a male and a female, but he was becoming more and more obsessed with the sensual delights of the world, rather than caring about dragons. He was not particularly experienced in the art of dragon-keeping and tried to find someone who had specialist knowledge and would be skilled in their welfare. Ji seemed to be fated with good luck, for one day a young man, called Liu Lei, came to his court with ambitions and dragon know-how.

But Liu Lei was not all he seemed. The youth was a descendant of King Yao but his family had been disgraced. Liu Lei desperately needed permanent work, and when he heard that King Ji needed a dragon-keeper, he had rushed off to be an apprentice to a highly skilled dragon-tamer, learning only a few basic skills. Believing himself now to be a fully qualified dragon-keeper, Liu Lei travelled to King Ji's court with an air of self-confidence and was immediately offered the job. King Ji called him the Imperial Dragon Tender, and Liu Lei was overjoyed at being in the king's court.

But Liu Lei's ignorance soon began to show. His professionalism was instantly in doubt as the poor female dragon died for no apparent reason. To prevent the king from discovering his deception, Liu Lei dragged the dragon out of the pool, dismembered it and cooked the meat and offered it to the king as venison killed from one of his very own hunting trips.

The rather foolish king ate the meat and, thinking it was the best venison he had ever tasted, ordered his huntsmen to return to the same forest for more succulent game.

A few days later the king wanted to see his dragons perform. Liu Lei made a few excuses about the female dragon, so the male dragon put on a show for him alone. The king finally demanded to see the female dragon, and this time Liu Lei knew he had no choice but to leave. He packed his things in a bundle and fled from the court never to be seen again.

The king still needed a dragon-keeper. This time his choice was more astute, but his enthusiasm was his downfall. Shi Men was an old master of dragon-keeping. He also had magical powers, ate plum and peach flowers and could turn himself into a flame or climb up to heaven. Shi Men knew everything there was to know about dragons, and he proudly nurtured the male dragon and had him performing the most startling tricks and dances, leaping through the sky and spiralling around the mountains. King Ji was delighted with his dragon and became more and more obsessed with showing it off and training it to do more complex performances. But for all his wisdom, Shi Men was also arrogant, and instead of flattering the king he sneered at him and mocked and laughed at his ignorance behind his back.

One day the king wanted to tie some beautiful streamers to the dragon's tail, but Shi Men refused to do it, saying it would demean the creature. But kings are more likely to do something impulsive than wise, and King Ji ordered Shi Men's head to be cut off at the palace gates.

Shi Men just laughed and said, 'Even if you cut off my head, you will still be defeated.'

A few hours later Shi Men's head was brought to the king, but fearing that the dragon-keeper's spirit would haunt the palace, he told his men to bury it and the body deep in the forest. The men dug a grave in the forest, but no sooner had the last shovel of earth been thrown into the pit than a storm began to shake the trees and lightning flashed down to earth and set fire to the ground. The fire leaped into huge flames and began to roar through the forest. The wind blew stronger and gusted the flames towards the palace gates. King Ji watched horrified from his palace tower, believing the dragon-keeper's ghost had the power to start this terrible inferno. He sent for his sedan and ordered to be taken to the grave to pray to the spirit to save the palace from the flames.

For many hours King Ji prayed at the graveside until the fire had burned itself out and he was surrounded by white ash. He relaxed and thanked the dragon-keeper's spirit, climbed back into the sedan and motioned to be taken back to the palace.

No one knows exactly what happened between the grave and the palace gates, for when the men opened the sedan door they found the king quite dead inside. But the dragon knew, for as the sedan passed by where he lay sleeping in the cool of the evening shade, he twirled the white streamers between his claws, danced high in the air and rose into the sky towards the white clouds above the palace. The dragon curled its way across the heavens and on past the mountains, free from King Ji at last.

HYMIR THE GIANT

NORTHERN EUROPE, 100CE

I T is hardly surprising that the myths of Scandinavia and the north are filled with giants, monsters and strange beasts. This land of ice, darkness, storms, seething springs and snow-capped mountains was a place where terror lurked in every gorge, forest or frozen waste. Giants were the most popular mutant humans, and it was the gods rather than mere mortals who had to contend with either their insolence or their strength.

The gods of Asgard had run out of their favourite brew, a fine mead that only certain gods were able to produce. Thor, the god of thunder, and his friend, Tyr, decided to visit Ægir, the god of the sea, who was usually able to provide the rest of the gods with copious amounts of any fluid they requested. Thor rushed into Ægir's hall and demanded that Ægir should start brewing some mead immediately, but Ægir tactfully pointed out that his own cauldron was rather small and would not really produce enough alcohol for them to become inebriated in the time allocated. Thor was furious, but Tyr remembered that the giant Hymir owned an extremely large cauldron, which would be big enough for all the ale in the world.

So Thor and Tyr grumpily left Ægir's hall and set out to find the giant. At Hymir's hall they were confronted not by Hymir but by two women. One was Tyr's grandmother, now an ancient hag with 900 heads, and the other his mother, who was quite beautiful. Tyr's mother gave the two gods some ale and wisely advised them to hide themselves beneath Hymir's cauldrons before his return. Hymir was not a particularly welcoming giant, especially to strangers, and she warned them that one glance of his penetrating eyes could kill them.

Soon after the two gods had hidden beneath the cauldrons, Hymir returned to his hall. His suspicions were aroused when he saw two half-finished mugs of ale on the wooden table. He banged his fist down on the wood and searched the hall with his piercing eyes, splitting the beams and most of the rafters apart in the process. As tons of wood began to fall to the ground and his roving eye seared through the eaves, the beam that held up the cauldrons collapsed. The two gods screamed with agony as the joist crashed down on their heads, bouncing off their skulls as if they were made of iron.

'Who are you, and why have you come?' he boomed at the gods as they crept out of their hiding place.

'I am Thor, and this is Tyr, your son. We have come in peace Hymir. We need your biggest cauldron, so that we can make enough mead for the gods of Æsir.'

Hymir was reluctant to part with his favourite cauldron, but he deigned to welcome the gods all the same and offered them three oxen he killed in their honour. He was, however, indignant and resentful when Thor devoured two of the oxen in one go so that there was hardly any left for himself and Tyr. Hymir knew that it was not in his interests to challenge Thor and so the following morning he suggested that they go fishing.

'I hope you will be able to provide the bait?' asked Hymir carefully.

Thor merely shrugged his shoulders and killed Hymir's biggest bull, so that he could use the head on his hook. Again Hymir was disgruntled, but carried on with the fishing expedition. The giant and the god rowed out to the deepest part of the ocean. Much to Hymir's horror, Thor insisted that he wanted to try his hand at catching the world serpent, Jörmungand. Thor kept dipping his fingers into the sea to search for the snake, until at long last he felt something slither across his hand. Hymir, meanwhile, had caught two whales and was quite satisfied with the catch. But when he saw Thor trying to pull in the gigantic serpent, he panicked and cut Thor's line so that the serpent writhed and slithered back into the depths of the ocean.

'You maniac! You maniac!' cursed Thor, 'Now I have lost the greatest catch in the sea!' Thor lashed out with his hammer and thrashed Hymir on the head. Luckily, the giant had one of the hardest skulls in the world and was unharmed, but the boat capsized and they had to wade ashore, Thor carrying the boat on his head and Hymir humping the two whales on his back.

Back on dry land Thor began to get the usual stirrings of hunger pangs in his stomach, so they breakfasted on the two whales. But still angry that he had lost the world serpent, Thor vowed to show off his true strength. He picked up his pewter beaker and began to throw it at everything in sight, in an attempt to smash it to bits. But the only thing that was stronger than the pewter beaker was Hymir's head, so Thor threw it against his forehead, and it shattered to bits and Hymir was again unharmed.

Hymir's giantly humour was touched and impressed by this rather gallant show of strength, but he also was quite keen to be rid of Thor and get back to his old ways. So he agreed that Thor should take the cauldron. Tyr was unable to lift it, and even with Thor's help they staggered out of the hall with their backs nearly breaking and the sweat flowing from their faces. Hymir was amused by the struggling gods and invited the other frost-giants to watch the spectacle. But foolish giants are usually avenged by angry gods, and Thor's resentment was now at boiling point. He dropped the cauldron, which fell on Tyr's feet so that he howled and cursed in pain. Momentarily diverted, the giants were confused, and Thor raised his hammer, killing them all when they were least expecting it. The two gods triumphantly left the hall and returned to Æsir with the cauldron perched precariously across their shoulders.

FENRIR, THE WOLF

NORTHERN EUROPE, 300CE

THERE are many giants, dwarfs and unusual creatures in Norse mythology, but perhaps the most feared and yet perhaps the most misunderstood was Fenrir, the wolf. He was fated to be the beast of Ragnorak, the bringer of doom to the gods at the end of time. He was known as 'an axe-age, a sword-age, a wind-age, a wolf-age before the wrecking of the world'.

Fenrir's parents were the trickster-god Loki and a frost-giantess called Angrboda. He was brought to Asgard by Odin and the other gods so that they could keep an eye on him, fearing his rapid growth might threaten the whole world. Odin decided to try to tame the wolf and perhaps cure him of his terrible, savage ways. All the gods were scared of the beast, except for the god of courage, Tyr, who was given the job of feeding and caring for him. But Fenrir continued to grow both in strength and in ferocity. Tyr tried to feed him only small amounts of vegetables and herbs to quieten his nature, but it was no use.

Odin had also heard from the Norns, the goddesses of destiny, that his own fate was inextricably linked with Fenrir. He decided that Fenrir must be tied up so that he could never threaten him or the other gods. They first used a strong chain called the Laeding, but Fenrir just grinned his sharp teeth at them and when they had finished restraining him, the wolf snapped the chain into thousands of pieces. They tried again with an even stronger chain, but again Fenrir proved too strong, and the gods became anxious that they would never be able to stop Fenrir from a ferocious attack.

The last resort was to ask the dwarfs to make a magical fetter, so strong that even Fenrir could not break it. They used strange materials, like the sound of a cat's paw on the ground, the spittle of a bird and the voice of a fish. The tether seemed like a silken strand and when they showed it to Fenrir he became suspicious of its magical powers. The gods promised that it was just another test of his strength. But with his suspicions aroused, Fenrir insisted that one of the gods put his hand between his jaws as a pledge that no magic was involved. Tyr was the only god willing to do such a deed. Of course, he lost his hand when the fetter was place around Fenrir's neck and the wolf realized that he would never escape.

Still unhappy with Fenrir's great strength, the gods bound him to a rock. They placed a sword vertically in his mouth so that he couldn't bite anyone, and the blood that gushed out of his upper palate formed a river. His vast mouth gaped so that the lower jaw touched the ground and the upper one touched the sky.

At Ragnarok Odin will be slain by Fenrir and he can at last take revenge upon all the gods.

THE GREAT MACAW

MAYA, CENTRAL AMERICA, 300CE

THE mythology of the Mayan peoples is obscure and sparse, apart from the stories from the Popol Vuh, which was rewritten, translated and Christianized in the seventeenth century. However, many of the Popol Vuh's concepts and ideas seem to pre-date the Christian influence and correspond to other works of much earlier mythology in other cultures. Popol Vuh is a highly traditional compilation of mythology intertwined with snippets of real history.

There was a great god, loathsome and proud, called Vukub-Cakix. He had once been both sun- and moon-god, and because of this high ranking he boasted daily about his power, lurched around the heavens doing whatever he wanted to do and generally irritated the other gods.

Vukub-Cakix (seven times the colour of fire – the Mayan name for the macaw) had teeth made of emeralds, and he shone as if he were made of gold or silver. Vukub had two sons who were equally despicable, but they were earthquake-giants who arrogantly roamed the lands and caused the earth to shake and rumble when they were feeling in the mood to cause chaos.

The gods in heaven decided it was time to dispose of this rather unruly threesome and so sent the twins Hun-Apu and Xbalanque down to earth.

Vukub was particularly fond of the fruit from a wonderful tree, which he decided he owned. Every morning he would set off in his gold and silver finery and pick the highly aromatic and lush yellow fruit. He would spend the best part of the morning breakfasting upon this, until his emerald teeth turned yellow and his breath smelt like nectar.

One morning he climbed to the summit of the highest tree to look for the ripest fruits. To his horror two strangers were stripping the trees below of all the ripe fruit and stashing the delicacies in huge baskets. Vukub was furious, and in his usual arrogant fashion decided to confront these outsiders and claim his fruit. Besides it would mean he wouldn't have to make any effort to pick his own, and breakfast would be a treat out of someone else's hard work.

But Hun-Apu had seen Vukub climbing down the tree. Raising a blow-pipe to his mouth, he hit the ghastly god between the lips, and Vukub immediately crashed from the top of the tree to the ground. Hun-Apu threw himself upon Vukub and they wrestled on the earth, squashing the fruit to a pulp under their huge bodies. Vukub, in a terrible rage, wrenched Hun-Apu's arm from its socket and roared off with it back to his home, still in pain from the poisoned dart.

Vukub moaned to his wife about his injuries, and in his anger hung Hun-Apu's arm to roast over the blazing fire, satisfied that at least he'd avenged his own suffering. The pain in his teeth and mouth became worse, for the dart's poison worked slowly.

While Hun-Apu's arm was basting over the fire, the ugly giant-god indignantly mulled over the recent invasion of his paradise. If he ever met the two villains again he would tear them to pieces and eat them for supper.

But Hun-Apu and Xbalanque were now willing to risk themselves in their quest to retrieve Hun-Apu's arm. The gods agreed that they needed help, and arranged to meet two great and wise shamans, Xmucane and Xyipacoc. The shamans disguised themselves as healers, and the two young gods as their sons. At Vukub's earthworks they could hear his moans and self-indulgent groans from over a mile away. They smelt the cooking of meat and knew at once that Hun-Apu's arm was being roasted. They must get to Vukub before it was too late. At Vukub's door, insisting they had heard him crying in pain, they said they were healers come to cure him. Vukub was satisfied with the two magicians' credentials, but highly suspicious of the two young men.

'Who are they?' he demanded.

'Just our sons. They are learning to be healers.'

Vukub, as stupid as only a giant can be, let them in. 'So, let the curing commence. The demons who shot me with a poisonous arrow are the cause of all this suffering of mine. If you can remove the pain I will reward you handsomely.'

One of the wise shamans said: 'Your mouth and eyes seem to have received the worst wounding. Your teeth seem to have turned a terrible yellow, and your eyes are so full of blood that they will fall out soon.'

Vukub was terrified when he heard the state of his emerald teeth and his golden eyes, for he was not only a boastful giant but a narcissistic one too.

'What can you do?'

'There is only one cure. We shall have to remove your yellow teeth and your bleeding eyes. We will replace your teeth with grains of maize and the balls of your eyes with fruit from the tree you love so much.'

The foolish giant agreed to their suggestion, and quickly the two shamans removed the giant's emerald teeth and golden eyes. But a change came over the giant god, and his dazzling colours and shining aura began to fade as each emerald was removed. By the time his two eyes were dug out of their sockets, he had faded away and died. Hun-Apu snatched his own arm from the turning spit and the shamans restored the arm to his shoulder.

They left the dead giant and, taking the emeralds with them, they returned to the heavens. They forgot the golden eyes which turned into golden eagles. These golden eagles soared the heavens forever after looking for the gods who had once stolen their precious fruit.

THE DEATH-STONE

JAPAN, 700CE

THE fox is a well-documented shape-shifting spirit in Chinese and Japanese mythology. In China the power to turn into a fox means you are also able to acquire immortality. Legends abound concerning the supernatural powers of the fox. They have the power of infinite vision and all-encompassing knowledge, which they acquire by dabbling in the classics of all civilizations. Their great wisdom enables them to shape-shift from fox to man, from man to fox. They can transmute and they can delude. They will often take the form of a beautiful woman to extract a man's semen during sexual intercourse, thus adding to their own potency and energy, which can lead to immortality. The more men a fox-woman can seduce, and the more men who reach orgasm, the greater will be her life essence, but the men will lose all of theirs. The only way you can know if you are in the company of a fox-woman is to watch out for her shadow on water. A fox spirit's shadow will be cast as the outline of a fox.

This story illustrates the shape-shifting power of the fox-woman.

A very long time ago there was a Buddhist priest called Genno. After many days of travelling, exhaustion overcame him and he went to rest under the shadow of a great stone on the moor of Nasu. He was just about to lie down and place his head against the soft sand at the base of the stone when a cloud-spirit suddenly swirled into a formless being before him. 'You must not rest under this stone, dear priest, for this is the death-stone. Every man, beast or bird that has touched it has instantly died!'

The priest immediately sat up, convinced that the spirit's warning was genuine. His curiosity was now aroused, and just as the spirit was about to disappear he urged the being to tell him more about the death-stone. 'Please, do me the honour of telling me how this terrible stone came to be so. I am in need of company, and a drink from the pool before I continue on my way.'

So the spirit began: 'Many full moons ago there was a beautiful girl who lived at the court of Japan. She was so exquisite – eyes as green as jade, hair the colour of a million ravens – she was called the Jewel Maiden. Her wisdom was as incredible as her beauty. She was educated in Confucian classics, and in all the poetry and sciences of China as well as Japan. Because no other woman displayed such wonderful qualities and could not rival her for looks or skills, she had soon enchanted the Mikado's heart.

'The Mikado lusted after the Jewel Maiden and arranged a great feast at the Summer Palace, where he could finally tell her of his desire for her. He invited all the wisest, wealthiest, wittiest and most important people in the land, including the Jewel Maiden herself. The court was filled with music, with food and drink, with laughing and brilliant minds. The feast included the best delicacies, and the music was the sweetest ever heard. But as the evening turned to night, dark clouds gathered across the court. The sky became dark, blackened by fast-moving shadows that scudded across the stars, until there were none left to see. The night became pitch black. Suddenly a strange wind whistled through the court and many of the guests sat rigid with fear. Others ran out of the court, only to find they were in complete blackness. Amid the chaos and the confusion one guest cried out, "I see a light! Look, a light!"

'The gathered revellers stared at a mysterious spark, darting and sparkling into a flame from the centre of the Jewel Maiden's body. The light seemed to emanate from within the Jewel Maiden and gradually to glow throughout her whole being. The Mikado felt that he had to go to her as if he had been hypnotized – he was unable to resist her dazzling gaze. The light pierced every corner of the palace, and the brilliant glow forced everyone else to turn their eyes away. Some looked down to the floor, others covered their eyes with their hands, and others fell into a heap on the floor. After some minutes the light began to die down, it grew smaller, losing its luminous power until the sparkling flames disappeared back inside the Jewel Maiden's heart. The Mikado was dazed, for somehow he knew he had been enchanted. For while the glorious light had shone throughout the court he had made love with the Jewel Maiden, entranced by the power of her sexual desire.

'Within hours the Mikado became very ill. He developed a fever and lay thrashing on his bed until the court magician arrived. The magician frowned as the Mikado refused to eat or drink. Finally he spoke to the gathered courtiers: "This is the doing of the wicked Jewel Maiden. She has captured his life essence. The light that came to you at the feast has drawn the Mikado's own inner potency from him."

'The Mikado tossed and turned in despair, for not only did he still long for the Jewel Maiden but now knew she had drained all his sexual potency from him. He would never be able to enjoy such pleasure again. Floundering in his impotency, he vowed never to speak to any woman again, especially the Jewel Maiden.

'Once the Jewel Maiden realized that her love had been rejected by the Mikado, she turned herself into her original form, and ran as fast as she could away from the palace. The fox-woman ran and ran until she reached Nasu Moor, and here she came to rest at this very stone.'

The priest frowned suspiciously. 'It's you, isn't it?'

The spirit nodded. 'Yes, I am the demon-spirit that once dwelt in the soul of the Jewel Maiden, and now I live in the death-stone for ever!'

The priest was shocked and slightly fearful now that the spirit had so blatantly revealed itself, but he knew as a priest he had no right to judge.

'You have found great wickedness in your spirit, but you can also find great virtue. Take this begging bowl and priestly robe and reveal your true fox form to me.'

But the spirit wailed pitifully that it could not do so, and immediately vanished into thin air. Genno was not put off by the weakness of the spirit, and so that it might attain Nirvana he burned incense and offered flowers and recited the Buddhist scriptures before the stone. He bowed his head and spoke: 'Now spirit of the death-stone, come to me and tell me how you came to be this demon.'

Suddenly the stone burst open and the spirit appeared. Shimmering from the centre of the rock, the air turned a lurid green and the light swirled like a green luminous mist around Genno, until it was transformed into the fox. But the fox changed again into a beautiful girl and was able to speak. 'In this form I have caused much unhappiness and tried to destroy the imperial line. Many emperors have I slept with to drink their life's essence, to end their potency. I went to the court of the great Mikado where I wanted to seduce him, too. But the court magician had great power, and I was driven from the palace and came to this moor where I have stayed ever since, haunting those who come by. But now the Lord Buddha has come to give me a chance to make peace with myself, but I can do so only if I return forever to this stone.'

It was too late for Genno to stop her, and as quickly as she had come to him in this world, she left it. The cloud of swirling colours and the beautiful maiden before him changed back into a fox, and finally into a formless demon, a wisp of black smoke that struggled as the death-stone sucked the spirit back into the solid rock for ever.

THE KINDLY SKELETON

IROQUOIS, NORTH AMERICA, 1000CE

THERE was a young child called Little Arrow who lived in the dark woods. His uncle had cared for him since the untimely murder of his parents by the ogres. Little Arrow's sister had also been kidnapped by one of the cruel ogres when she went to play in the Eastern Woods, and had not been seen again. Ever since her abduction, his uncle warned Little Arrow never to go towards the east but always to stay by the lodge or to walk only to the western end of the wood. But as Little Arrow grew older he became more and more curious to see exactly what horrors lay to the east.

Several moons passed, and one day his uncle was out on a day's hunting expedition. Little Arrow seized the chance to set off to the east for the adventure of a lifetime.

The eastern end of the forest seemed no different from the western end, but the path was easier and the light was so clear and the sky so brilliantly blue that the moon was visible. Little Arrow reached a lake and stopped to rest. He gazed at the beauty of the landscape around him and lay back on a rock to doze. Squinting through the glare of the morning sun, he saw a figure walking towards him, but before he could run away, the strange man suddenly tapped him on the shoulder.

'Who are you? What are you doing in my land?' asked the man.

'My name is Little Arrow. I came to explore this part of the world. I have never been east before.'

The man nodded briefly then challenged him to a shooting match with his bow and arrows. 'Let's see who can shoot the highest,' he said.

So they stood side by side, and the dark stranger and Little Arrow pulled back their bows together. Little Arrow was sure that this man would have more strength and more control than he, and yet it was the boy's arrow that rose higher in the sky.

Next the man suggested a swimming competition. 'Let's see who can swim the furthest underwater,' said the stranger.

Little Arrow could hardly refuse, for he wasn't sure what the stranger wanted from him. So they dived into the lake together and it was Little Arrow who held his breath longer and swam further and further out into the deep water.

The stranger smiled and pointed to a canoe tied to an old log on the shore. 'Come with me on my canoe to the island out there in the middle of the lake. There you will see the most beautiful birds of all these lands.'

Little Arrow again could hardly refuse, so they clambered into the canoe, which was pulled across the lake by three white swans. As they drifted slowly towards the island the stranger began to sing an unusual song, and the swans paddled faster across the blue water. At the island shore Little Arrow jumped off the canoe expecting to see the beautiful birds promised him by the stranger. But there were none. He turned to the man, a confused frown on his face, and realized that the stranger had tricked him.

It was too late to stop the man from abandoning him. The stranger had already turned the canoe around, and the swans were pulling him further and further away across the lake. The boy was furious. He had been marooned on the island and was all alone.

As night fell his anger turned to fear. He was terrified by the strange noises and the different darkness of the sky above. It was not like the sky in the west; here in the east there were no stars, and the moon he had seen in the daylight did not shine at night. He sat cold and alone beneath a tree and dared not sleep for fear of monsters and beasts that might attack him.

Just as he was about to doze off he heard a deep growling voice behind him and, looking round, saw a skeleton lying on the ground.

'You're in trouble aren't you?' said the skeleton, 'It's all right, I'm a friend and I may be able to help you. But first you must find my tobacco pouch and my pipe and flint. They're hidden in the earth beneath that tree.'

The boy nodded and dug around in the earth until he found the pouch and the pipe. He filled the pipe with tobacco, lit it and placed it between the skeleton's jaws. The skeleton's skull was full of baby mice, which darted in and out as the smoke blew through the eye sockets, and rats ran between his ribs and out through his pelvis as the smoke began to swirl around his bones. Once all the creatures were smoked out of his carcass, the skeleton sat up.

'You must hide tonight, Little Arrow, for a stranger will come with three dogs to find you. You must make tracks everywhere, all over the island, all in different directions to confuse the dogs, then you must hide in the hollow tree.'

So Little Arrow ran around over the island, backwards and forwards – around the beach and down every path until his footprints were everywhere and his scent was everywhere. He hid in the hollow tree and waited until morning, hoping and praying that the hunters would not find him. As the sun rose the next day the boy came out of the hollow tree and the skeleton told him that the man and the dogs had given up looking for him.

'But tonight,' continued the skeleton, 'the stranger who brought you to the island is coming back to drink your blood. You must dig a hole in the ground and hide in it. When the stranger leaves his canoe, you must run down to it and call to the swans "time to go home now". You must not look back. If the man calls out to you, do not turn, do not stop, do not hesitate, just go.' The boy refilled the skeleton's pipe with tobacco, and dug a deep pit in the sand where he could hide.

As night came, everything happened just as the skeleton had told Little Arrow. The stranger's canoe came ashore, and from the safety of his pit Little Arrow saw the man walk into the woods in search of blood. Little Arrow took his chance and ran down to the canoe. 'Time to go home now,' he said quickly to the swans and jumped into the boat. The swans obediently carried the boy across the lake and he dared not look back at the shore for he heard the stranger calling to him.

The swans reached a limestone cave and Little Arrow found food and clothing to warm him. But Little Arrow was determined to go back to the island and thank the skeleton for his help. The following evening he returned and found that the terrifying stranger was dead. The skeleton was pleased the boy had returned, but said there was one more thing he must do.

'I know who has stolen your sister, you must go and rescue her. There is a gruesome ogre who lives on another island not far from here. He makes her cook for him and will never let her go. Only you can save her.'

Little Arrow was heartened to hear the news of his sister and was anxious to trace her. He set off with renewed hope, knowing that even he, Little Arrow, could now challenge a monster such as an ogre.

On the next island he found his sister cooking broth beside a small fire. 'Come sister, we must go. I have a canoe on the shore. Let me take you home.'

'Not now, dear brother. I have been married to a very dangerous ogre who is about to return home from the forest. If he finds you he will kill you. You must hide and we can escape together when he leaves for his afternoon hunt.'

So Little Arrow dug another pit and hid beneath the sand. With his dinner over his shoulder the ogre lurched home and banged his fists down on the table.

'You've had visitors?' the ogre snarled as he gnawed his way through some goat's meat.

'No one has been here,' said the sister carefully.

'Hmmm,' replied the suspicious ogre. His dogs had been sniffing around the camp since his return and he was convinced his wife was lying. After feasting on the raw goat, the ogre set off hunting. Once he was past the clearing he doubled back and waited beside the track to see what his wife would do. Sure enough, a few minutes later he saw the girl and Little Arrow running down the path towards the shore.

The brother and sister jumped into the canoe, but the ogre, sprinting up behind them, threw a hook across the beach, which clamped on to the side of the boat. Little Arrow broke the hook with a rock he had picked up from the beach, and they began to float away into the middle of the lake to safety. Ogres are, however, unrelenting. Hurling rocks into the water, the ogre began to lumber after them screaming for their blood. As a last resort he began to drink the lake, and the canoe started to drift back towards the shore as the water was sucked up into the ghastly orifice of the ogre's mouth. But Little Arrow was courageous, and he grabbed the rock and threw it at the ogre's left eye. As the boulder crashed into the ogre's head he reeled back. The water surged out into the lake, and the ogre fell down dead from the massive blow that had driven the stone right into his head.

When the skeleton heard what Little Arrow had done, he urged him to take his sister home to his uncle's lodge.

'You have done well Little Arrow, and as my last request, return here alone one night, and say to every bone on this island, "Arise" and they will be alive again.'

Little Arrow's uncle was overjoyed to see his nephew and niece again. When the boy told him about the living skeletons, they built a large lodge in the hope that Little Arrow would return with the skeleton people. When the lodge was finished, the boy left for the island. His friend was now just a pile of bones, and heaps of skeletons lay strewn across the island from the terrible activities of the ogre and the dark stranger. So Little Arrow said 'Arise' and all the bones came alive. The skeleton people followed Little Arrow back across the lake and they lived happily as men and women for many years in the lodge in the west.

THE PURSUING HEAD

THERE was once a poor family who could barely scrape together enough food and who lived mostly on berries and wild roots. One night the man had a dream in which he was told by a voice to hang a large spider's web in the forest. This would trap many animals and give him plenty of food. So the following day he hung the spider's web in the forest, and when he returned many rabbits and small deer were trapped like flies in the magical web. The family began to get bigger stomachs and firmer flesh on their bodies now that they were eating meat. The man was happy, and he soon had no difficulty catching plenty of game for his wife and two children.

One day, just as he was leaving on a hunting trip, he noticed his wife was dabbing sweet pine oil on her skin. She had never done this during the day before and never at night when they slept. He instantly suspected that she might have a lover.

The man decided to test her. He told her to go and fetch the remains of a carcass he had buried in the forest, part of a deer that he had been unable to carry all the way home. He wanted to see if she would go there straight away. So the woman set off, wondering now if her husband had some evidence of her infidelity. Feeling a little confused and suspicious herself, she stopped at the top of the hill to see if he was following her, but he was still sitting where she had left him so she carried on up the path.

The man soon tracked her route, and when he came to the top of the hill he saw that she had gone away from where he'd left the deer's carcass. He returned to the camp and asked the children where their mother went to gather firewood, believing that this was probably the place she had her illicit meetings. He found the clump of leafless dried-up tree branches that the children had directed him to and began to search desperately for some evidence of his wife's betrayal. He found a den of rattlesnakes and was about to turn round and go home, feeling now guilt-ridden by his assumptions, when the voice that had come to him in his dream came to him in his head and said: 'It is the rattlesnake that your wife loves.'

In a rage, he set light to the wood and the flames burned down the dead trees and the den of snakes was destroyed.

After his anger had subsided, the man told his children that they should leave the lodge before their mother returned. He was sure she would be in a fit of rage and possibly try to kill them all. He gave the two children three things that might be of use – a stick, a stone and a bunch of moss to throw behind them in case their mother chased after them. The children ran away in fear, and the father hung the magic web across the door to the lodge. Seeing in the distance the terrible fire that her husband had started, the woman returned to the lodge, rushed through the doorway without thinking and was caught in the magic web. The more she struggled the more she was caught in the terrible trap, then as she pushed her head through the other side of the web, her husband raised his axe and chopped off her head. He ran quickly out of the lodge and down the hill, but the woman's body came running after him while her ghastly head rolled along the ground after the children.

The boy turned to see where his father had gone, and realized what was chasing after him. The dreadful head was increasing in speed so the boy quickly threw the stick behind him. It turned into a thick dense wood, which for a while slowed down the revolting head. But the children began to grow tired and the frenzied head soon began to catch up with them again, its eyes almost popping out of its sockets and blood spurting from its ears as it made terrible shrieks that were like tortured demons of the night. The boy threw the stone behind him, and mountains suddenly rose towards the sky, so that the head's path was now completely blocked by the immense peaks of the mountain range. The head realized it could not climb the mountains, so it asked two grazing rams if they would butt their way through the mountain in return for any request being granted. The two rams tried again and again to push their heads against the mountains, but they got nowhere and their horns broke.

The head was getting in a frenzy. It saw a colony of ants and asked them to dig a tunnel through the mountain. If they did so the head would grant them any request. The ants set to work and eventually made a passageway through the base of the mountain. The head rolled down the tunnel and through to the plains on the others side, increasing in speed as it sped downhill behind the two exhausted children.

When the girl saw the head still relentlessly pursuing them she took the last thing that their father had given them. Dipping the moss in a stream so that it was sodden with water, she wrung out the moss on the ground behind them. Instantly the water turned to a huge expanse of sea, separating them from the land. They looked back across the wide strait of water at the terrible head plunging downhill towards the water, unable to stop. Its eyes were terrified, and its teeth were gnashing at the ground to try to bite on to something to stop itself. But it was too late for the head, it rolled remorselessly towards the water, plopped straight in and drowned.

The children returned to their own land by making a raft and sailing across the water. But the body of the mother still chases the father, for she is the moon and he is the sun. If she manages to catch him she will kill him and there will be darkness forever. But while he manages to escape there will always be day, and there will always be night chasing after the day.

THE SNAKE-MEN

SIOUX, NORTH AMERICA, 1000CE

ONE winter's new moon a party of warriors returned homewards, hungry and tired from a battle. With one day's travel still ahead of them, they camped for the night and began to wander off in search of food. One of the twenty braves put his ear to the ground and heard what sounded like buffaloes approaching. He told the chief that ambushing the herd of buffaloes would be a far easier way to catch their dinner than splitting up in search of rabbits or stoats. So the band of warriors gathered together and lay very still, hidden behind the branches of a ghostly white tree trunk that lay across the sand.

The rumble of hooves came nearer and they were sure now that hundreds of buffaloes were charging across the ground. Nearer and nearer came the deafening sound, but as they jumped up to aim at the passing herd the chief froze in horror. For what came hurtling towards them was not buffalo but a snake with blood dripping from its fangs. The snake had a rattle as large as a man's head and it moved as swiftly as the wind. The warriors nearly turned to run, but their fearless nature was enough for them instinctively to draw their bows. They all fired their arrows at once into the serpent, and within minutes it lay thrashing its deadly coils across the ground until it was dead. The men gazed upon it with terror, for even though it was dead such monsters were known to have powerful spirits. For some time they discussed what they should do with the carcass but finally agreed that because they were all so hungry the only thing they could do would be to cook and eat it.

Some of the warriors had been reluctant to eat the meat, but once cooked it smelt delicious. Every man, except one young boy, tucked into the meal and decided the monster snake was as tasty as any buffalo. The young boy still refused to eat any of the snake, and eventually they fell asleep beside the fire.

During the night a strange thing happened. One by one, the men began to turn into snakes. The chief woke up with a shock to find himself on the verge of his own metamorphosis, for he was already half-man, half-snake. When the snake-warriors saw that only the boy had not turned into a snake, they comforted him and gave him all their skins and possessions. To begin with he was terrified that they might harm him, but they told him to lead the group to the top of a high peak and leave them there.

303

The chief spoke: 'When you have left us on the top of that mountain you must return to our lodges and tell our families that we will return in the summer. Make sure that our wives and children are ready to greet us.'

So the boy went back to the village and related the terrible story of the monster snake and how the men had turned into snakes themselves. The families cried, and the village seemed like a village of ghosts.

One day, when the sun was high in the sky, the snake-warriors came and gathered in a circle outside the village. The boy took the friends and families to meet them, but most of the people could not believe that these were the brave men they had lost so many moons ago. The snakes insisted that the families bring out their horses and belongings, their moccasins and skins.

The boy said: 'Don't be afraid of them, you must not run from them or you may come to harm.'

So the people gave them their horses and clothes and watched as the snakes slithered and rattled around their belongings and hissed and formed themselves into sleepy coils. The snake-warriors stayed all summer in the village, but when winter came they vanished and took their horses and possessions and were never seen again.

THE OGRE-KILLERS

MICRONESIA, 1600CE

THROUGHOUT Polynesia and Micronesia the bringers of evil or doom are often ogres who have the characteristics of brute strength and stupid minds. In New Guinea and right across to the Solomon Islands, the theme of an ogre-killing child is prevalent. The actual monster who devours people can come in many forms, such as an unpleasant beast, a demonic spirit and even giant humans, but it is the ogre-killers of these terrors who are fairly consistent. In most parts of Micronesia it is usually either a pair of twins, two children or, as in this particular story, a single heroic boy.

The ogres of one island were a family of ten brothers. The first brother had one head, the second had two heads, the third had three heads and so on. Each of these ogres pestered and terrorized the island to such an extent that even the people's usual methods of driving them away didn't seem to have much effect. They tried blowing on conch-shell trumpets and making a lot of noise to deafen the ogres. They tried hiding in hollow bamboo shoots and luring the ogres in to trap them. In the end they decided that the whole island would have to be abandoned unless someone gave birth to an ogre-slaying child.

The villagers began to pack up their belongings. They had become more and more petrified of the ogres, who had started eating anyone they found alone on the path. The people filled their canoes with possessions and family, until all the boats were full. One woman who had no relatives tried to join each of the boat parties but was pushed away on the shore because there was no room for her. She watched the canoes set off for the next island and stood alone on the beach, sure that the ogre brothers were watching her, the only human left on the island.

That night she dug a hole beneath a tree and hid in the tiny space without moving an inch. During the darkness the ogres roamed the island in search of human flesh, roaring and shrieking as they trampled above where the woman lay hidden.

At the next new moon the woman gave birth to a one-legged boy who grew very fast. Two weeks later, at the full moon, he had grown to the size of a fifteen-year-old youth. He was strong and brave, and he yearned for company because the island was empty of people. His mother had warned him never to play with the ogres if he saw them, especially as his one leg would mean that escape would be impossible. But in his boredom, and with no other youths or girls to amuse him, he went in search of the ogre brothers. If he could trick them and kill them, perhaps the rest of the islanders would return to their homes again.

He hobbled into the densest part of the island forest until he found the ogres' mother cooking some stew in a huge pot. The ogre brothers had gone fishing, so the boy knew that this was a good time to sow the seed of his plan. Now, the mothers of ogres are usually very quiet and helpful people, not at all like their sons. The one-legged boy also knew this and so he upset her pot, ate her food, then hopped away laughing.

The next day one of the ogre brothers stayed with his mother, waiting for the stranger who had upset the food. The boy came back and told the ogre-brother he had better stir the stew in the pot before putting any more ingredients to it. The stupid ogre bent over the pot and the boy simply sliced off the ogre's head with his sharp thumbnail. He placed the head on the beach for the other ogre-brothers to find. They were suitably incensed and so each day another ogre would stay behind to wait for the boy. But each ogre was just as stupid as the last, and the one with two heads lost two heads and so on, until the last brother with ten heads had them all sliced off by the sharp thumbnails of the one-legged boy.

Now all the ogres were dead and the boy and his mother waited on the beach and built a fire so that the other islanders could see them and know it was safe to return. When the canoe parties landed, the one-legged boy was made their chief and a great hero. The villagers made sure that the fifty-five heads of the ogre-brothers were hung from the coconut trees to remind other ogres that a highly skilled ogre-killing boy lived there.

BAT-LIGHT

BEFORE there were any human beings there were only birds and reptiles and a few mammals. Every year, when the spring arrived, the different animal tribes would gather for a festival of dancing, eating and story-telling. One tribe, the bird tribe, were incessant chatterers. They decorated themselves with beautiful flowers and leaves, and they would dance in front of the other tribes, showing off their plumage and displaying how well they had preened their feathers. Because everyone else admired them they became very conceited. The cockatoo, who was a very proud bird, went to the chief of the feathered tribe one day and said: 'Eagle-hawk, isn't our feathered tribe greater than those of the carpet-snakes or the kangaroos or the goannas?'

The eagle-hawk, who was not above the same kind of self-indulgent smugness, replied: 'Of course, of course we are far superior to everyone else.'

But the animals of the other tribes were obviously angry when they heard the self-adulation of the birds, and for some time they all quarrelled and generally accused one another of terrible things. So the feathered tribe eventually challenged the other tribes to prove who, of them all, was superior. The bat tribe decided not to get involved and to remain impartial, refusing to take sides until they were sure that one side was winning. Then, of course, they would join the victors!

The battle began at dawn. Animals and birds threw weapons and spears, and those who were fast and agile gained the upper hand. Seeing how the birds were now in a good position to capture the animals, the chief bat decided to join forces with the feathered tribe. The bats stood with the crows and the magpies and the cockatoos and threw their boomerangs so that they whizzed through the sky.

There was a lull in the fighting, and the chief kangaroo recalled his forces and changed tactics, driving the bird tribe back beyond their defences. The bats were most alarmed to be on the losing side and immediately changed allegiance and joined the animals. So the battle carried on like a pendulum. For one hour the birds would be winning, then the animals were winning, and the bats would keep changing from one side to another.

Finally, the chief kangaroo came face to face with the chief emu and both gazed in despair at each other. The kangaroo, who was a kindly animal, dropped his weapons and said: 'This is pointless, why must we fight? Why must this all end in pain and misery and death?'

The emu nodded and dropped his weapons, and the two chiefs clasped paws to end the battle. When the other animal and bird tribes saw this friendliness, they all did the same. The cockatoos shook hands with the wombats, the crows shook hands with the dingoes, and there was a general feeling of peace among the tribes.

But the bats were unsure what to do and whose hands to shake, for their treachery and betrayal of both parties meant that no one could trust them. So the bat tribe went to live with the wicked owls, who lived alone in the darkness at the other end of the universe.

Seeing the terrible battles between the animals, the sun declared: 'It is so sad how the world has come to such conflict, I cannot bear to look upon you anymore.' He hid his face so the world became dark. Life without sunlight was impossible for most of the tribes, but the owls and the bats didn't give a hoot, for they loved the dark.

One dark day the emu met the kangaroo. 'What are we going to do? We can't find food in the dark, and all our tribes are lost and need light to live by.'

The kangaroo sat in his favourite dried-up river-bed and reflected deeply upon the matter. Then he came up with an idea. He told the emu to gather wood and light bonfires everywhere to keep them warm, which would also provide them with light and somewhere to cook food. So for many months the birds and the animals built fires and took wood until they burned so much wood that fuel became scarce. The kangaroo decided to have a great rally of all the animals and birds to see if anyone could come up with an idea to bring back the sun or find a new source of light or fire. But the only suggestion was from a little lizard, who tentatively pointed out that it was the owl and the bat who actually held the answer to bringing back the sun.

The lizard was duly sent to invite the owl and the bat to their meeting. They were pleased to be invited as guests to the conference.

'So, great owl and bat, welcome,' said the kangaroo. 'We believe you can bring back the sunlight? Will you do this for us?'

The owl shrugged his shoulders. 'I do know how to get the sun back for you, but why should I? I prefer the darkness to the light, and so do my children. I have no reason to help you.'

On hearing this remark, the curlew and the dingo howled loudly for the light and begged the owl to change his mind. But no matter how much the curlew cried and the dingo howled, he would not budge from his decision. So all the animals began to howl and the sounds were so pitiful and the wailing so intense that it reached the ears of the bat in a way that pierced his soul. His conscience was awakened, and he realized that he could now do something to make amends for his past treachery. He shouted, 'I can get the sun back!'

The animals and bird tribes stopped crying, and the bat asked for a boomerang.

'I have one,' said the small lizard and gave it to the bat.

Taking the boomerang, the bat spoke to the gathered tribes: 'My bat family love the eternal darkness, but I know that you must have your light, too. If I do this for you at least I shall be welcome to enjoy my darkness.'

He hurled the boomerang towards the northern sky, and it whizzed through the air and travelled right round the earth and back into his hand. He hurled the boomerang again, this time to the west. It spun off around the world and came back, this time from the east. But just as he was about to hurl it again, the jackal laughed and shouted, 'Hey, we don't want to see how good you are with a boomerang. We want the sunlight back!'

'I know,' said the bat. 'I am dividing the darkness. I am going to give you light and I need some darkness for myself, so I must divide it up fairly.'

So again he threw the boomerang to the west and this time, as the boomerang came hurtling towards them from the other side of the earth, the bat shouted: 'Look, look, can you see the light is coming from the east. Can you see it?'

The bird tribe saw the light coming and began singing and twittering and chattering, which is why they always do so at dawn. As soon as the boomerang touched the bat's fingers the sun rose and the kangaroos leaped around the trees for joy and the dingoes ran fast and the jackals laughed with joy. Every animal was happy, except for the wicked owl, who only comes out at night. If he appears in the day the other birds peck at him and tug at his feathers because he was so selfish and wouldn't let them have the sunlight. So the bat returned to his home in a cave as soon as the sun had set in the west, and when he comes out just before or after sunset to dance in the sky, no bird will ever kill him or bother him. They treat him with respect because he was so keen to make amends for the wrong he did by bringing back the sunlight that brings life to the earth.

Meanwhile, the little lizard sits all day on his rock, staring at the sun, and on his neck he carries the boomerang that he lent to the bat to divide the darkness from the light.

KINIE GER

ABORIGINE, AUSTRALIA, 1600ce

THE Kinie Ger was part-human, part-cat, a grotesque and evil creature who roamed the night in search of animals or birds to kill. He had the head, mouth, ears and body of a cat, and his limbs and feet were like a human's, but his tail twitched as sensitively as a domestic cat's today when it is ready for a kill.

Kinie Ger did not have the power of reason or of feelings, only the habit of a cat that sneaks up on its prey and enjoys the thrill of the chase and the torture of its victim. He had inherited the innate desire of a cat that kills for the thrill of it, not just because it is hungry. Kinie Ger was particularly fond of watching his victims die slowly and painfully, and his happiest moments were those when his victim's eyes would drain of life and the blood would stop flowing from the wounds he inflicted with his claws and teeth.

All in all, Kinie Ger was a loathsome and much-feared creature and his fame for cruelty spread quickly. One of the elder kangaroos gave out warnings to the young men of every tribe to be on guard from Kinie Ger and never to venture out alone, but always to go with another. A bodyguard of trained warriors was sent out with many kangaroos on hunting trips or when messages were being transported. But it did not prevent Kinie Ger from his insatiable blood-thirsty massacres.

One young arrogant and foolish kangaroo was not alarmed by the idea of the prowling cat. 'I'm going west to gather berries, but don't worry about me. I'm so strong and so fast that nothing can stop me from returning at sunset.'

Many of the elder kangaroos warned him about the evil cat, but he merely tossed his tail and rubbed his ears and boasted that no cat could ever bring him down. His huge leaps took him quickly across the plains and he soon disappeared. At sunset he still had not returned, so a party of warriors and hunters set off towards the west. Under the last rays of the sun they found the proud young kangaroo dead. A great gash across his body, like a black stripe of blood, had dried up in the sun. The male kangaroos were alarmed and as they sat round the camp-fire discussing the terrible death, they all knew this was the mark of Kinie Ger.

But Kinie Ger was merciless. He killed far and wide and chose no one in particular. Whatever animal or bird he came across would fall prey to his obsessive lust for cruelty. Birds, lizards, snakes and mammals – all were slowly butchered. The kangaroo, the emu and the carpet-snake met together to try to work out a way to put an end to Kinie Ger and his killings. But it was only the brave emu who finally decided he would go alone and try to kill the cat. He set off with his spear, but by twilight a bird flew down to their camp and told them he had seen the emu die bravely at the hands and spear of Kinie Ger.

This miserable fate had befallen some of the other bird tribes. The owl and the crow had married twin sisters and had lived happy and peaceful lives. But one day, as the two mothers peeped into their nests where their tiny babies chirped and tweeted, they found only blood and death. Each baby bird's heart had been torn from its chest, and a gaping wound filled with blood was all that was left of their children.

The owl and crow families were heart-broken and vowed to find the Kinie Ger and destroy it. They sent smoke-signals to the north and south, asking that the two water-holes within two days' journey be strictly guarded. The water-hole that was only half a day's journey towards the rising sun was to be left unguarded. No one was allowed to camp there or hunt or walk about it. It must remain forbidden territory.

Many birds, animals and lizards came to the home of the owl and crow to express their sympathy and their grief. The owl made a passionate speech, imploring all to avenge the sad deaths of the children by destroying Kinie Ger, and the birds and animals began to dance an old war-dance of revenge.

The owl and the crow, their anger aroused, set off to the well, seeking revenge. Together they communicated only by signs and gestures. They walked to a bush about forty paces from the well, dug a deep hole and stood in it up to their waists. For many hours they waited in this hole. The day was hot and the wind blew dry and dusty from the north, choking their throats. A dust storm blew up, forcing the animals and birds to go to water-holes to drink. But the owl and the crow remained rigid in their hole, knowing that at any moment Kinie Ger would appear in search of water himself.

As the sun fell half-way down the western sky, the huge cat-like monster slunk across to the well. It was the only one unguarded by warriors, and he knew he could drink peacefully here. He carried his spear and his wommera in case of attack, but the dust and the heat had driven him to seek water. Kinie Ger knelt down at the well to drink. This was the moment for which the owl and crow had been waiting. As he bent his head forwards, the two birds threw their spears at Kinie Ger. One penetrated his heart, and the other his head, killing him instantly. The owl and the crow ran forwards, pulled out their spears and stuck them again and again into the lifeless body until Kinie Ger's blood flowed across the ground and soaked the dust red.

As the sun set in the west, they lit a fire and placed the monster's body on the flames. Kinie Ger burned slowly. One spark larger than all the others flickered from his body and rose into the sky. They watched it rise higher and higher into the night sky to take its place in the Milky Way as a star.

The following day the other birds, the lizards, the kangaroos and the snakes came to see where the mighty Kinie Ger had died. They saw the huge bloodstain on the ground and the heap of ashes. The dingo discovered some footprints of a strange and tiny being that led away from the blood of Kinie Ger. For some days the animals followed these tracks until they found in a tree a small cat, quite harmless and purring softly, a shy creature that wanted only to sleep all day.

FURTHER READING

Abrahams, Roger D., *African Folktales*, Pantheon Books, New York, 1983

Alpers, Antony, *Maori Myths and Tribal Legends*, Longman Paul, Auckland, 1982

Bedier, Joseph, *The Romance of Tristan* (trans. by Hilaire Belloc and Paul Rosenfeld), Pantheon Books, New York, 1945

Branston, Brian, *Gods of the North*, Thames and Hudson, London, 1980

Bullfinch, Thomas, *The Golden Age of Myth and Legend*, George Harrap & Co., London, 1917

Burland, C., and Wood, Marion, *North American Indian Mythology*, Hamlyn, Feltham, Middlesex, 1965

Byock, Jesse L. (trans.), *The Saga of the Volsungs: The Norse Epic of Sigurd the Dragon Slayer*, University of California Press, Berkeley, 1990

Christie, Anthony, *Chinese Mythology*, Hamlyn, London, 1983

Cotterell, Arthur, *Encyclopedia of Mythology*, Lorenz Books, London, 1996

Cowan, James G., *The Elements of the Aborigine Tradition*, Element Books, Shaftesbury, Dorset, 1992

Davidson, H.R. Ellis, *Scandinavian Mythology*, Hamlyn, London, 1982

Eliot, Alexander, *The Universal Myths*, Meridian, New York, 1990

Graves, Robert, *The Greek Myths* (2 volumes), Penguin Books, Harmondsworth, Middlesex, 1955

Grey, George, *Polynesian Mythology*, Whitcombe & Tombs, London and Christchurch, 1965

Hadland Davis, F., *Myths and Legends of Japan*, Harrap, London, 1913

Hart, George, *A Dictionary of Egyptian Gods and Goddesses*, Routledge & Kegan Paul, London, 1986

Hesiod, *Theogony, Works and Days* (trans. by M.L. West), Oxford University Press, Oxford, 1988

Homer, *The Odyssey* (trans. by E.V. Rieu), Penguin Books, Harmondsworth, Middlesex, 1946

Homer, *The Iliad* (trans. by E.V. Rieu), Penguin Books, Harmondsworth, Middlesex, 1950

Hooke, S.H., *Middle Eastern Mythology*, Penguin Books, Harmondsworth, Middlesex, 1985

Hope Moncrieff, A.R., *Classic Myth and Legend*, Senate, London, 1993

Ions, Veronica, *Indian Mythology*, Hamlyn, Feltham, Middlesex, 1967

Kennedy, Charles W. (trans.), *Beowulf, the Oldest English Epic*, Oxford University Press, Oxford, 1977

Lang, Jean, *Myths from Around the World*, Bracken, London, 1996

Larousse Encyclopedia of Mythology, Hamlyn, London, 1959

Leeming, D.A., *The World of Myth*, Oxford University Press, Oxford, 1990

Leland, Charles Godfrey, *The Algonquian Legends of New England*, Collier Books, New York, 1884

McCulloch, J.A. *Celtic Mythology*, Dorset, New York, 1992

MacKenzie, Donald, *China and Japan – Myths and Legends*, Senate, London, 1994 (reprint)

MacKenzie, Donald A., *Myths of Babylonia and Assyria*, Harrap, London, 1913

Marriott, Alice, and Rachlin, C.K., *American Indian Mythology*, Thomas Y. Crowell, New York, 1968

Morris, William (trans.), *Volsunga Saga, The Story of the Volsungs and Niblungs*, Collier Books, New York, 1971

Nicholson, Irene, *Mexican and Central American Mythology*, Bedrick, New York, 1983

Nivedita, Sister, and Coomaraswamy, Ananda K., *Hindus and Buddhists – Myths and Legends*, Senate, London, 1994

Norman, Howard (ed.), *Northern Tales: Traditional Stories of Eskimo and Indian Peoples*, Pantheon Books, New York, 1990

Osborn, Harold, *South American Mythology*, Bedrick, New York, 1986

Parrinder, Geoffrey, *African Mythology*, Bedrick, New York, 1991

Reed, A.W. *Aboriginal Myths*, Reed Books, New South Wales, 1992

Rolleston, T.W., *Myths and Legends of the Celtic Race*, Harrap, London, 1911 (reprinted Senate, London, 1994)

Rolleston, T.W., *The Illustrated Guide to Celtic Mythology*, Harrap, London, 1912 (reprinted Senate, London, 1994)

Rundle Clark, R.T., *Myth and Symbol in Ancient Egypt*, Thames and Hudson, London, 1978

Sandars, N.K. (trans.), *The Epic of Gilgamesh*, Penguin Books, Harmondsworth, Middlesex, 1960

Shorter, Alan W., *The Egyptian Gods: A Handbook*, Routledge & Kegan Paul, London, 1937 (reprinted 1979)

Sproul, Barbara C., *Primal Myths*, HarperCollins, San Francisco, 1979

Werner, Alice, *Bantu Myths and Legends*, George Harrap, London, 1932

INDEX

Aapep 52
Aborigines
  beasts and monsters 306–10
  creation myths 46–7
  sun, moon, heaven and earth myths
    89–90
  tricksters 268–70
Achilles 58
Acrisius 140, 142
Adonis 196
Africa
  creation myths 19–20, 26–8, 47–8
  death, re-birth and the underworld
    110–13, 126–8
  heroes and warriors 149–51
  sun, moon, heaven and earth myths
    70–1
  tricksters 246–9
Ag-Ag 86–7
Agni 54, 55, 100, 139, 276
Ahaiyuta 173–5
Ailill 209–11
Algonquian
  beasts and monsters 301–3
  legendary lovers 224–6
  sun, moon, heaven and earth myths
    81–3
  tricksters 251
Altair 215–17
Amana 44–5
Amaterasu 71–4
Ameta 21–3
Amphitrite 60
Anapou 192–5
Andromeda 141–2
Anglo-Saxons, heroes and warriors 176–9

Anguta 121–2
animals 271–310
Anubis 95–6, 97, 99
Anulap 267
Aphrodite 189, 195–7, 198, 200
Apollo 56–7, 58, 198, 206, 238
archetypes 8
Argonauts 285–6
Arjuna 130
Artemis 57
Arthur, King 218, 244, 245, 250–1
Aryans 18, 52, 54
Asagao 221–4
Asante, death, re-birth and the under-
  world 126–8
Asclepius 58
Aset 231
Asgard 69–70, 107, 243, 290
Ashtart 189
Ashtoreth 189
Ashurbanipal, King 15, 131
Astarte 98, 189
Aswins 55
Athene 198, 281, 284
Atum 14–15, 51
Australia see Aborigines
Aztecs 45
  heroes and warriors 179–80
  tricksters 258–9

ba 95
Babylon
  beasts and monsters 273–4
  creation myths 15–16
  legendary lovers 189–90
Balder 107–8, 242–3

Banks Islands 33
Bantu
  creation myths 26–7
  death, re-birth and the underworld
    110–13
  tricksters 246–9
Bao Chu 62–4
Bapedi peoples 246
Barotse, creation myths 27–8
'Bat-light' 306–8
Baventa peoples 246
beasts and monsters 271–310
Bellerophon 281
Beowulf 176–9
Bharata 137
Bitiou 192–5
Blackfeet, sun, moon, heaven and earth
  myths 77–9
Blue Jay 255–7
Bolivia, death, re-birth and the under-
  world 125–6
Bomong 17–18
Bong 17–18
'The Book of the Dead' 96
Borneo
  heroes and warriors 183–6
  legendary lovers 226–8
Brahma 99–100, 275, 278
Brer Rabbit 246
Brighu 54
Brisingamen 212, 213–14, 240
Brittany 218
Brynhild 107, 163–5
Bumba 26–7
Bushongo kingdom 26
Byblos 98

Calina, creation myths 44–5
Callisto 199
Calypso 147
Caroline Islands 267
Cassiope 141–2
Cavillaca 261–2
Celts
  heroes and warriors 154–61
  legendary lovers 208–12, 218–21
  tricksters 244–5, 249–51
centaurs 58

Central America
  beasts and monsters 293–5
  heroes and warriors 179–80
Cepheus 141–2
Cerberus 103, 205, 281, 284
Ceridwen 249–50
Chacopee 180–3
Chaldean myths 273–4
Charon 103, 205, 284
Cherokee, creation myths 45–6
'The Children of the Sun' 83–4
Chimaera 281
China
  beasts and monsters 286–90
  creation myths 28–9
  heroes and warriors 151–4
  legendary lovers 215–17
  sun, moon, heaven and earth myths
    61–7
Chinook, tricksters 255–7
Chiron 58–9
Chuckchi Inuit, creation myths 42–3
Circe 146–7, 148, 235–7
Coatlicue 180
'The Cold Weather Lord' 77–9
Conaire Mór 159–61
Coniraya 261–3
'The Convolvulus Fan' 221–4
Cook, Captain James 33
Coyote 36–8
creation myths 8, 11–48
Cù Chulainn 154–9
Cyclops 146

Daksha 55–6
Danae 140, 199–200
death 91–128
'The Death-stone' 295–7
Delphinus 60
Demeter 104–5, 231, 285
Di Jun 64–5
Djanggawul 46–7
'The Dragon-lover' 288–90
Dream Time 46, 268
Dubiaku 126–8
Dumuzi 93, 94

eagles 69, 273–4
'The Earth-Born Giants' 143

'Earth-initiate' myths 36–8
Ecuador, sun, moon, heaven and earth myths 85–6
Edda 240
Egypt
  creation myths 13–15
  death, re-birth and the underworld 95–9
  heroes and warriors 135–6
  legendary lovers 192–5
  sun, moon, heaven and earth myths 51–2
  tricksters 231–2
elephants 70–1
Elphin 250–1
Elysium 103
Emer 156
Emma-O 115–16
Enki 94, 232–3
Enkidu 131–4
Eochy 208–12
Erebus 103
Ereshkigal 93–4, 189, 190
Eros 196
Eskimo *see* Inuit
Etain 208–12
Etsa 85–6
Europa 199
Europe
  beasts and monsters 290–3
  creation myths 23–5
  death, re-birth and the underworld 106–8
  heroes and warriors 154–69
  legendary lovers 208–15, 218–21
  sun, moon, heaven and earth myths 67–70
  tricksters 239–45, 249–51
Eurydice 102, 204–6, 239
Eurylochus 236
Eurynome 13

fables 9
fans 221–4
Fasa, heroes and warriors 149–51
Fenrir 292–3
Fine Weather Woman 88–9
Finland, heroes and warriors 165–9
fire 74–6

foxes 295–7
France, legendary lovers 218–21
Frey 214–15
Freya 70, 107, 212–14
Frigga 242–3
Furies 143, 280

Gaia 20–1
Ganesa 274–6
Garuda 276–8
'Gassire and the Singing Lute' 149–51
Genno 295–7
Gerda 214–15
Ghana, death, re-birth and the underworld 126–8
ghosts 110–13
'The Giant who tried to catch the Sun' 287–8
Gilgamesh 130, 131–4
'Gitagovinda' 190
Glooskap 81–3, 251–4
gods and goddesses 8, 9, 92
Gorgons 140–1
'The Great Macaw' 293–5
'The Great Yu' 151–4
Greece
  beasts and monsters 280–6
  creation myths 13, 20–1
  death, re-birth and the underworld 102–5
  heroes and warriors 140–8
  legendary lovers 195–201, 204–6
  sun, moon, heaven and earth myths 56–60
  tricksters 235–9
Greenland 79
Grendel 176–8
Guarayu peoples, death, re-birth and the underworld 125–6
Guatemala, creation myths 25–6
Gun 151–2
Gwion 249–50

Hades 59, 93, 102–5, 204, 205, 285
Hainuwele 21–3
Hanuman 138, 233–5
Harpies 285–6
Hawaii, sun, moon, heaven and earth myths 74–7

Hawaiki 116
Hecate 103–4, 235
Heimdall 239–40
Helen of Sparta 144, 197
Helios 56–7, 105, 235, 236
Hen-O 64, 65–7
Hephaestus 195, 196, 198
Hera 57, 198–9, 200, 201, 231, 239, 281, 282
Heracles 58–9, 103, 143, 239, 281–2, 283, 284
'The Herdsman and the Weaver Girl' 215–17
Hermes 237–9, 280, 284
heroes 8, 129–86
Hesiod 20
Hi'aka 74–5
Hinduism
    beasts and monsters 274–6, 278–80
    creation myths 18–19
    death, re-birth and the underworld 99–100
    heroes and warriors 136–9
    legendary lovers 202–3
    sun, moon, heaven and earth myths 55–6
    tricksters 233–5
Hlakanyana 246, 247–9
Hoenir 69
Homer 144
Hopi, creation myths 38–42
Horus 52, 96, 99, 231
Hrothgar 176–8
Hui Nang 61–2
Huitzilopochtli 179–80
Humbaba 132–3
Hun-Apu 108–10, 293–5
Hurakan 25–6
Hutu 117–18
Huveane 246–7
Hydra 281–2
Hymir 290–2

'Ictinike and the Rabbit' 259–61
'Idun and the Golden Apples' 68–70
Ijaw, creation myths 19–20
Iliad 144
immortality 92
Inanna 93–4, 189, 195

Incas
    sun, moon, heaven and earth myths 83–4
    tricksters 261–3
India
    beasts and monsters 274–80
    creation myths 17–19
    death, re-birth and the underworld 99–102
    heroes and warriors 136–9
    legendary lovers 190–2, 202–3
    sun, moon, heaven and earth myths 52–6
    tricksters 233–5
Indonesia, creation myths 21–3
Indra 52–3, 54, 100, 234
Inuit
    creation myths 42–3
    death, re-birth and the underworld 120–2
    sun, moon, heaven and earth myths 79–81
Io 201
Ioi 255–7
Ireland
    heroes and warriors 154–61
    legendary lovers 208–12
Iroquois
    beasts and monsters 297–300
    death, re-birth and the underworld 119–20
Ise 221
Iseult 218–21
Ishtar 93, 133, 189–90, 195
Isis 51, 96–9, 231–2
Itasca, Lake 77
Itciai 43–4
Izanagi 29–31
Izanami 29–31, 115

Japan
    beasts and monsters 295–7
    creation myths 29–31
    death, re-birth and the underworld 113–16
    legendary lovers 221–4
    sun, moon, heaven and earth myths 71–4
Jewel Maiden 295–7

Ji, King 288–90
Jiaoren 287
Jicarilla Apache 255
Jivaro, sun, moon, heaven and earth
  myths 85–6
'The Journey to the Land of the
  Grandfather' 125–6
Jung, C.G. 8, 9

ka 95
Kadru 278
Kalevala 165
Kama 202–3
Kamonu 27–8
Kansa 190
Kenya, sun, moon, heaven and earth
  myths 70–1
Khnum 95, 193
'The Kindly Skeleton' 297–301
Kinie Ger 308–10
Kis 273
Klang 86–7
Kojiki 29
Komagawa 221–4
Krishna 190–2
Kronos 58, 59, 143, 197
Kua Fu 287–8
Kuma 43–4
Kunmanggur 268–70

Lakshmana 136, 137, 139
'The Land of Ghosts' 110–13
Leda 200–1
legends 9
Lemminkainen 168
lions 283
Little Arrow 297–301
Liu Lei 288–9
Livingstone, David 27
Lohiau 74–5
Loki 69–70, 107–8, 163, 213–14, 239,
  241–4, 292
lovers 8, 187–228
Lui Chun 61–2, 64

Ma'at 51, 96
Mahabharata 275
Maidu, creation myths 36–8

Malaysia, sun, moon, heaven and earth
  myths 86–7
Malsum 251–2
Mama 83–4
Manco 83–4
Mani 67–8
Maoris
  creation myths 32–3
  heroes and warriors 169
Marduk 15–16
Markandeya 101
Marwe 111–13
Matuka 169, 171–2
Maui 76–7, 263–6
Maya
  beasts and monsters 293–5
  death, re-birth and the underworld
    108–10
Medusa 60, 140–1, 142, 280
Melanesia, creation myths 33–4
Merlin 244–5
Mesopotamia
  heroes and warriors 131–4
  tricksters 232–3
Metis 197–8
Mexico
  death, re-birth and the underworld
    108–10, 122–4
  tricksters 258–9
Micronesia
  beasts and monsters 304–5
  tricksters 267–8
Midir 208–12
Mikado 296–7
Milky Way 72, 215, 239
Minokichi 113–15
Miyuki 221–4
monsters 8, 271–310
Montezuma 122–4
moon and sun myths 49–90
Mosaku 113–14
Mozambique, creation myths 46–7
'Mulungu and the Chameleon' 47–8
Murdak 273

Nagas 278
Nahua peoples 179
Nantu 85–6
Native American myths see North America

Negrito, sun, moon, heaven and earth
    myths 86–7
Neith 13–14
Nemean lion 281, 283
Nemesis 103, 201
Neptune 59
New Guinea 304
New Mexico, heroes and warriors 173–5
Ni Lang 216–17
Nigeria, creation myths 19–20
Nihongi 29
Nile, River 51, 98
Nimuë 244–5
Ninhursaga 233
Nippur 273
Norse myths
    beasts and monsters 290–3
    creation myths 23–5
    death, re-birth and the underworld
        106–8
    heroes and warriors 161–5
    legendary lovers 212–15
    sun, moon, heaven and earth myths
        67–70
    tricksters 239–45
North America
    beasts and monsters 297–304
    creation myths 36–43, 45–6
    death, re-birth and the underworld
        119–24
    heroes and warriors 173–5, 180–3
    legendary lovers 224–6
    sun, moon, heaven and earth myths
        77–83, 88–9
    tricksters 251–4, 255–61
Nu Chou 64–5
Nu Ji 153
Nut 51
Nyambi 27–8

Odin 67–8, 69–70, 106, 107, 163–4,
    213–14, 240, 241, 242, 243–4, 292
Odysseus 130, 140, 144–8, 236–7, 285
Odyssey 144
Oedipus 282–3
'The Ogre-killers' 304–5
Olifat 267–8
Olympus 143
Omoigane 73

Oregon 255
Orpheus 102, 204–6, 239, 284
Osiris 95–9, 231
Ouranos 20–1

Pachacamac 262–3
Palamedes 144–5
'P'an Ku and the Cosmic Egg' 28–9
Papa 32–3
Papan 122–4
Pare 117–18
Paris 196–7
Parvati 202–3, 274–5
Pegasus 60, 141, 142, 281
Pele 74–6
Penelope 144, 147, 148
Persephone 93, 102–3, 104–5, 196, 205,
    239, 284–5
Perseus 140–2, 200
Phaethon 57
Phineus 285–6
phoenix 63–4
Picus 235–6
Plutarch 14, 51
Po 116
Polotu 116
Polynesia
    beasts and monsters 304
    creation myths 32–3
    death, re-birth and the underworld
        116–18
    heroes and warriors 169–73
    sun, moon, heaven and earth myths
        76–7
    tricksters 263–6
Polyphemus 146
Pomona 206–8
Popol Vuh 25, 108, 293
Poseidon 9, 59–60, 141–2, 145, 148, 198,
    200
Poua 171
Pradyumna 203
Prometheus 58–9, 198
Psyche 196
Ptah 135
Puana 43–4
Puloma 54
'The Pursuing Head' 301–3
Purusha 18–19, 202

Qat 33–4
Qizhong 286
'The Quest for the Sun' 61–4
quests 129–86
Quetzalcoatl 258–9
Quiche, creation myths 25–6

Ra 14–15, 51–2, 97, 99, 135, 192, 231–2
Radha 190–1
Ragnarok 107–8, 161, 292, 293
'Rakian and the bees' 226–8
Rakshasas 278–80
Rama 136–9, 234, 235
Ramayana 136, 233
Rameses the Great, Pharaoh 192
Rangi 32–3
Rata 169–73
Rati 202–3
Ratri 55
Ravana 136, 137–9, 234, 278–80
Raven 42–3, 79–81
rebirth 91–128
Remus, Uncle 246
'The Resurrection of Papan' 122–4
Rig-Veda 18
Romans, legendary lovers 206–8

Sacred Otter 78–9
Sarawak, heroes and warriors 183–6
Sawoye 112–13
Sayadio 119–20
Scar-face 224–6
Scáthach 156, 158
Scylla 236
Sea-Dyaks, heroes and warriors 183–6
Sedna 120–2
Sekhmet 135–6
Selene 104, 231, 283
Semele 200
Setanta 155
Seth 97–8, 99, 231
Shamash 273
Shanhaijing 286
Shi Men 289
Shinto 71
Shiva 101–2, 202–3, 274–6
Siberia 79
Siggeir 161–2

Sigmund 161–3
Signy 161–2
Sigurd 107, 161, 163–5
Simpang Impang 183–6
Sin 88–9
Sioux
    beasts and monsters 303–4
    heroes and warriors 180–3
    tricksters 259–61
Sirens 147, 284–5
Sirius 51
Sita 136–9
skeletons 297–301
Skirnir 214–15
Skrymsli 241–2
Sky-Spirit 126
'The Snake-men' 303–4
'The Snow Spirit' 113–15
Sol 67–8
Solomon Islands 304
Soma 55–6
Sothis 51
Soto, Hernando de 45
Sotuknang 38–42
South America
    creation myths 43–5
    death, re-birth and the underworld 125–6
    sun, moon, heaven and earth myths 83–6
    tricksters 261–3
Sphinx 280, 281, 282–3
Spider Woman 38–42
Stonehenge 244
Styx, River 103, 205, 284
Sumeria, death, re-birth and the underworld 93–4
sun and moon myths 49–90
'The Sun Tamer' 76–7
Surya 55
Susano 71–4

'Ta'aroa and the Egg' 34–5
Tahiti, creation myths 34–5
Taiowa 38–42
Taliesin 249–51
Tammuz 93, 189–90
Taoism 21
Taranga 263–5

Tartarus 103–4, 280
Tawhaki cycle 169
Telemachus 237
Tezcatlipoca 258–9
Theseus 103
Thiassi 69–70
Thor 290–1
Thoth 52, 96, 97
'Thunder and the Elephant' 70–1
Tiamat 15–16
time chart 9–10
Titans 59, 102, 143, 197
Tjinimin 268–70
Tnong 87
tricksters 8, 229–70
Tripitaka 233
Tristan 218–21
Troy 145, 196–7
Tsukuyomi 72, 73–4
Tu Bo 287
Tuatha Dé Danann 208
Tutankhamun, Pharaoh 13
Tvashtri 53
Typhon 280–1

underworld 91–128
Uruk 131–4
Ushas 55
Utnapishtum 131, 133–4

Vainomoinen 165–9
Valhalla 106–7, 108
Valkyries 106–7
Vanuatu 33
Varuna 100
Vedas 52–4, 55, 190–2, 202
Vega 215–17
Venezuela, creation myths 43–4
Venus 189
Vertumnus 206–8
Vikings 176
    see also Norse myths

Vinata 276–8
Vishnu 136, 190
volcanoes 74–6
Volsunga Saga 161
Vritra 53
Vukub-Cakix 293–5

Wagner, Richard 161
Walumba, creation myths 46–7
warriors 129–86
'Water Beetle and the Great Buzzard'
    45–6
West Ceram, creation myths 21–3
West Lake region, China 61
wolves 292–3
Woyengi 19–20

Xbalanque 108–10, 293–5
Xi Wang 65–6
Xia dynasty 151, 288
Xibalba 108–10
Xquiq 109

Yama 99–102
Yao, creation myths 47–8
Yao, King 64–5, 151–2
Yaruro, creation myths 43–4
Yellow Emperor 151–2, 287
Yggdrasil 108
'Yi and the Ten Suns' 64–7
Ymir 23–5, 67
Yomi 115–16
Youdu 287
Yu 151–4, 288
Yuki-Onna 113–15

Zaire, creation myths 26–7
Zambia, creation myths 27–8
Zeus 9, 57, 58–9, 102, 104, 105, 140, 143,
    197–201, 238, 239, 280
Zulus 246
Zuni, heroes and warriors 173–5